Loving Warriors

Loving Warriors

SELECTED LETTERS OF

Lucy Stone

AND

Henry B. Blackwell,
1853 TO 1893

EDITED AND INTRODUCED BY

LESLIE WHEELER

THE DIAL PRESS NEW YORK

To my husband, Philip Lief,
for his own "abundant and unselfish"
support and encouragement

Published by
The Dial Press
1 Dag Hammarskjold Plaza
New York, New York 10017

Manufactured in the United States of America
First printing
Design by Francesca Belanger

Library of Congress Cataloging in Publication Data

Stone, Lucy, 1818–1893.
Loving warriors.

Includes bibliographical references and index.
1. Feminists—United States—Correspondence.
2. Stone, Lucy, 1818–1893. 3. Blackwell, Henry
Browne, 1853–1909. I. Blackwell, Henry Browne,
1825–1909. II. Wheeler, Leslie, 1945- .
III. Title.
HQ1413.S73A4   1981   305.4'2'0922   81-957
ISBN 0-8037-9469-X   AACR2

EDITOR'S NOTE *and* ACKNOWLEDGMENTS

At the very outset of their correspondence, Henry Blackwell wrote to Lucy Stone regarding his letters: "you can burn them if you dont have time to read them & either answer them or not as you feel inclined & have liesure." Fortunately, she not only read his letters, but felt inclined to answer them. And for this, we can only be grateful to her, because their correspondence, thus established and preserved, provides an intimate portrait of a feminist marriage in Victorian America.

The 221 letters in this volume represent a selection of the several hundred surviving letters that Lucy Stone and Henry Blackwell wrote to each other over a forty-year period from 1853, when he first began to court her, to 1893, when she died. Because of the extent and quality of their correspondence, deciding which letters to include and which to omit was not an easy task. But I have tried to select those letters which best illuminate the various facets of the two correspondents' personalities, their relationship with each other, and the times in which they lived; and I have used the same criteria in editing individual letters. Since Lucy Stone's activities in later life—particularly in connection with the woman suffrage movement—are not always well documented in the letters she wrote to her husband, I have supplemented these with a number of her letters to Susan B. Anthony and other suffragists.

Excerpts of some of Lucy Stone's and Henry Blackwell's letters have appeared in the two existing biographies of Lucy Stone, Alice Stone Blackwell's *Lucy Stone, Pioneer Woman Suffragist* and Elinor Rice Hays's *Morning Star: A Biography of Lucy Stone;* in Elinor Rice Hays's collective biography of the Blackwell family, *Those Extraordinary Blackwells;* and in a few other books dealing with the nineteenth-century feminists. However, most of the letters in this volume have never before been published. With three exceptions, they all come from the Blackwell Family Papers at the Manuscript Division of the Library of Congress. The exceptions are the following: Henry Blackwell's letter to Lucy Stone of February 22, 1877, the original of which is in the Blackwell Family Papers at the Arthur and Elizabeth Schlesinger Library on the History of Women in America, Radcliffe College, and which John Blackwell kindly gave me his permission to quote from; and Henry Blackwell's and Lucy Stone's letters to Elizabeth Cady Stanton and Susan B. Anthony of April 21, 1867, and May 1, 1867, respectively, which are quoted from the *History of Woman Suffrage*, Volume II, c. 1881 by Susan B. Anthony, Elizabeth Cady Stanton, and Matilda Joselyn Gage.

Most of the letters in this book have been transcribed directly from the originals or from Xerox or microfilm copies of the originals, although in a few cases where the originals were no longer available, I have had to rely on copies made by others of the originals. In the transcription from the originals, Lucy Stone's letters presented more of a problem than Henry Blackwell's. For while he wrote a good and legible hand, she did not, and her tiny, irregular script was often difficult to decipher. Not only are her individual words hard to make out, but her periods are often indistinguishable from her commas, and her capitals from her lower case letters. Thus I frequently had to make educated guesses as to her punctuation and choice of words. In cases where I have been unsure of a particular word, I have inserted a question mark enclosed in brackets, and where words could reasonably be assumed to be missing, I have added them in brackets.

Out of consideration for the modern reader, I have made a few changes in these letters. Especially in the beginning of their correspondence, Henry Blackwell had a habit of writing his letters all in one paragraph, and thus I have taken the liberty of inserting paragraphs where logical breaks occur. He also had a tendency to use dashes in place of full stops, and to avoid giving the printed page an excessively broken-up appearance, I have replaced many of these with periods, although I have retained dashes where they occur within sentences.

Otherwise I have tried to retain as much of the unique flavor of their letters as possible by adhering to the original spelling and punctuation—including the many commas that Lucy Stone sprinkled throughout her letters, and the ampersands that both were fond of using. Neither Henry Blackwell's nor Lucy Stone's orthography deviated very sharply from the norm, but they both had a few idiosyncracies, which are worth noting here. While they tended to omit the apostrophe from contractions (*cant, dont*), they did sometimes use it in possessive pronouns such as *your's* and *their's*. Words containing the joined vowels *i* and *e* are frequently misspelled (concieve, recieve, liesure); *independence* is sometimes spelled *independance;* *connection* is given the British spelling of *connexion; development* is spelled with an additional *e;* and in certain words, an extra consonant has been added (*carreer, ballott, parrallel, symmettrical, sufferred*). Henry Blackwell had a habit of omitting periods after abbreviations such as *Mr* and *Mrs, PM* and *AM,* while Lucy Stone occasionally used the verb *dont* where *doesnt* would have been the correct form. However, like most people, they weren't consistent about their spelling, punctuation, or capitalization. Thus a word may be spelled two different ways in the same letter, or may appear capitalized in one place and lower cased in another. Where proper names are misspelled in their letters, the correct spelling is given in the notes. The italics represent the many underlinings they both used for emphasis; the words in capital letters, the double and triple underlinings they occasionally employed for extra emphasis. Where a letter appears unsigned, the reader can assume that it is thus in the original.

Both Lucy Stone and Henry Blackwell were fairly scrupulous about dating their letters, but in instances where dates are missing, I have usually been able to place the letters within an approximate time-frame by relying on internal references. I have also made use of such references to establish the locations from which various letters were written, in cases where this information does not appear in the headings of the originals.

The introduction, the narrative passages interspersed among the letters, and the notes are designed to make Lucy Stone's and Henry Blackwell's correspondence accessible to the general reader who may not be familiar with either them or the period. To avoid cluttering the letters with additional markings, the notes are designated by letter and by phrase, and can be found at the back of the book. The interpretations made in the introduction and in the narrative passages are my own, and are based chiefly on my study of the letters themselves and other biographical material contained in the Blackwell Family Papers. However, I wish to acknowledge my indebtedness to such recent feminist scholars as Nancy F. Cott, Ellen Carol DuBois, Aileen Kraditor, and Gerda Lerner, whose work provided me with important insights into the nature of nineteenth-century feminism.

Finally, I would like to express my thanks to Paul Heffron and the staff of the Manuscript Division of the Library of Congress; to John Kelley of that library's Photoduplication Service; to Kathy Kraft, archivist, and Robin McElheny, photograph cataloguer at the Arthur and Elizabeth Schlesinger Library, Radcliffe College; and to Susan Boone, photograph librarian at the Sophia Smith Collection (Women's History Archive, Smith College) for their invaluable assistance while I was gathering the letters and photographs that appear in this book. For their help in locating biographical information about various individuals who are mentioned in the Stone-Blackwell correspondence, I would also like to thank David Dearborn of the New England Genealogical Society; Peter Drummey of the Massachusetts Historical Society; Catherine T. Engel of the Colorado Historical Society; Bonnie Gardner of the South Dakota Historical Society; Jim Hansen of the Wisconsin Historical Society; Dr. Carl Lane of the New Jersey Historical Society; Judy Metzger of the Long Island Historical Society; Nancy Pryor of the Washington State Historical Society; Nancy Speers of the Friends Historical Library, Swarthmore College; Robert M. Warren of the Bentley Historical Library, Michigan State University; Conrad Weitzel of the Ohio Historical Society; and Diane Wilhelm of the Illinois Historical Society. Additional thanks go to the New York Public Library, the Berkshire Athenaeum, the Great Barrington and Lenox libraries, and the library of Simon's Rock of Bard College for the use of their facilities. I am also very grateful to my agent, Meredith Bernstein, for her enthusiasm about the project; to my editor, Nancy van Itallie, for her helpful comments on the manuscript; to David Falk for his careful copyediting; to my parents, John Wheeler and Helene Albright Wheeler, for believing in me and my work and for providing a good working environment during numerous visits to Washington, D.C.; and to my husband, for his sensitivity, patience, and involvement in the process of creating this book.

L.A.W.

CONTENTS

❧

Photographs appear following page 214

Loving Warriors

INTRODUCTION

How soon the character of the race would change if
pure, and equal, real marriages could take the place of
the horrible relations that now bear that sacred name!
Lucy Stone to Henry Blackwell, July 27, 1853

The letters of Lucy Stone and Henry B. Blackwell tell the
story of a marriage that would have been considered remarkable by the standards of any era, but was all the more
so given the fact that it occurred in nineteenth-century
America.

At a time when most marriages were cast in the mold of male
dominance and female submission and any deviation from this norm
was regarded as a shocking violation of human and divine law, Lucy
Stone and Henry Blackwell entered into a marriage of equals. On
their wedding day in 1855 they stood together and read a protest
against "such of the present laws of marriage, as refuse to recognize
the wife as an independent, rational being, while they confer upon
the husband an injurious and unnatural superiority, investing him
with legal powers which no honorable man would exercise, and which
no man should possess."

Lucy Stone also insisted on retaining the use of her maiden
name, and as the first woman ever known to do so, she launched a
long tradition of "Lucy Stoners" that has survived to the present day.
In her own lifetime, however, her action created difficulties: The only
way she could sign many legal documents was as "Lucy Stone, wife
of Henry Blackwell," and when they traveled together, she used this
form in signing hotel registers. Otherwise, people might accuse them
of belonging to the small band of sexual radicals known as free-lovers—which, in fact, their political opponents sometimes did anyway.

Underlying Lucy Stone's use of her maiden name was a determination not to lose her separate identity. Her critics had looked

forward to the time when a "wedding kiss" would "shut up the mouth of Lucy Stone," assuming that like many other famous women, she would give up her career rather than challenge her husband's innate sense of superiority. But in the first years of her married life, they were sadly disappointed. Before her marriage Lucy Stone had earned a reputation as one of the most gifted orators of the antislavery and woman's rights movements, and in the beginning at least, marriage did not bring an abandonment of her successful career as an itinerant agitator.

However, with the birth of a daughter in 1857, she withdrew from public life for almost a decade. Her decision to do so did not come easily; indeed, it was one of the most difficult choices she ever had to make. Pressured by other feminists like Susan B. Anthony to remain active, and goaded by her own compulsive sense of duty to the cause, she nevertheless turned her back on it to devote herself to the rearing of her daughter. For like most of her contemporaries, feminist and nonfeminist, Lucy Stone believed that a woman's primary responsibility was to her home and family even as she pressed for woman's right to work outside of the home. Moreover, she demanded nothing less than perfection of herself in her role as wife and mother."I *am* trying to be a good wife and mother," she wrote her absent husband. "I have wanted to tell you how hard I am trying, but I *have* tried before and my miserable failures hitherto, make me silent now. But if I have conquered myself, or gained anything in all these weary weeks you will find it in my actions. . . . We will be patient with each other."

She might have been any discouraged wife, but the fact that she was Lucy Stone, the "morning star" of the woman's movement, lent especial poignancy to her words. Her inner struggles led to migraine headaches and periods of extreme depression. Yet she didn't sink into total invalidism like so many other frustrated women who had failed to find an appropriate outlet for their energy and ability. That she did not was a tribute to the force of her personality, but also to her husband's unusual degree of supportiveness.

Henry Blackwell's firm belief in the equality of the sexes distinguished him from most of his contemporaries. His wife's fame wasn't a threat to his ego; instead he admired her for having a career, and encouraged her in it. When she withdrew from public life, he came to realize that it was a waste of her considerable talents for her to remain mired in domesticity. He urged her to return to the lecture platform, and because she felt unsure of herself after so many years' absence, he offered to accompany her. In 1867 the Stone-Blackwells stumped the state of Kansas in behalf of woman suffrage, and in later years they traveled around the country, lecturing and participating in suffrage meetings and conventions. In 1869 they were instrumental in the formation of the American Woman Suffrage Association, remaining active in this organization throughout their lives. They also collaborated on *The Woman's Journal*, the longest-lived of all the suffrage papers. Established in 1870, the *Journal* was published until 1917, first under their editorship and then under that of their daughter, Alice Stone Blackwell.

In the annals of the suffrage movement Lucy Stone and Henry Blackwell were as much a team as Elizabeth Cady Stanton and Susan B. Anthony. At one point Lucy Stone even compared them to a team of horses pulling a wagon; "How long we have jogged on, pulling together," she wrote; and the metaphor, if homely, was apt. For theirs was a rare partnership; after nearly forty years of married life they had become the "gray-haired champions" of feminism.

Had she not married, Lucy Stone would probably have followed Susan B. Anthony's pattern of channeling all her energies into the woman's movement and meeting all her emotional needs through sisterhood. But because she married and had a child, her life took a very different turn. Unquestionably, marriage and motherhood complicated her mission with additional cares and responsibilities that made much of her life a constant juggling act. But at the same time it can also be argued that the quality of her work was enhanced by her marriage, just as her marriage was made better by her work. Her private efforts to implement in her own marriage the reforms she preached in public gave her life a coherence it would otherwise have lacked, and established her influence as an exemplar of the ideals of nineteenth-century feminism as well as one of the movement's most prominent leaders. For combining as she did marriage and motherhood with a career outside of the home, she helped to establish a significant precedent for future generations of women.

Their marriage had a profound impact on Henry Blackwell as well. If he hadn't succeeded in convincing Lucy Stone to marry him, he might have lived out his life as the devoted bachelor brother of his five spinster sisters. But given his belief in the "imperious necessity" of marriage, it is more likely that he would have found someone else to marry, and then with his shrewd instincts as a businessman, he might well have become another American millionaire, salving his conscience with occasional bursts of philanthropy. In this role he might have been more comfortable, but by the same token he would have lost much of the fascination he holds for us. For, as with Lucy Stone, their marriage created conflicts which made his life more difficult but also richer and more complex.

Along with more than a few men of his era, Henry Blackwell was torn between a desire to better the world and an interest in pursuing the Almighty Dollar. It was his personal tragedy not to achieve—at least in his own eyes—distinction in either arena; he didn't become a millionaire, and considered himself at best a mediocre reformer. Throughout their life together and for years after his wife's death, he was dogged by a sense of unworthiness; in a characteristic vein, he wrote to her in 1878: "I know I have tried you in a thousand ways,—but most of all, by not being able to show you the sincere good will I have had. If it had been necessary I would have *died* for you at any time, but it is far harder to live so as not to wound and grieve the heart that loves one."

Henry Blackwell's and Lucy Stone's letters to each other bear eloquent testimony to their struggles to realize their own high ideals of marriage. Of the two, he was the more fluent writer. Indeed, his main problem was that his thoughts often overflowed his writing paper supply, with the result that he had to turn the paper around and write across what he had already written. His habit of cross-writing gave his letters a peculiar latticework appearance, and at one point, prompted his wife to write, "I want to send you some money to buy paper with, so that you need not *cross write* all your letters!!!" But cross-writing or not, his letters are a genuine pleasure to read. He possessed a sharp eye for detail, and an ability to convey his impressions of people and places with humor and grace.

Although Lucy Stone wasn't a natural-born writer like her husband, she tended to exaggerate the defects of her "literary culture," apologizing for her illegible handwriting, and referring disparagingly to her letters as "mere scraps." Her handwriting was tiny and crabbed, but her letters were hardly scraps. Studded with quotations from the Bible, from the classics, and from her reading of current poetry and fiction, they bore witness to the gift of self-expression that made her such a compelling speaker, and like her speeches, contained much heartfelt philosophy. Writing may not have come as easily to her as it did to her husband, but she pursued it with characteristic determination. As she grew older, her stiff, rheumatic joints made it difficult for her to control her pen, and her handwriting took on a jagged appearance. Nevertheless, she refused her husband's suggestion to engage an amanuensis and dictate her letters.

The content as well as the appearance of Lucy Stone's letters changed over the years. Her later letters are less philosophical and less purely literary than her earlier ones; domestic details often take precedence over ideology, and lofty flights of prose frequently give way to the plain-spoken language of her rural childhood. Especially when she was angry, she could be remarkably direct: On one occasion she wrote, "I suppose the wretched people there, are eating our cherries (May they choke them!)"; and on another, said of a man who had given his wife a particularly difficult time, "May the buzzards get him!"

Such outbursts contrasted sharply with the gentle, motherly image Lucy Stone presented to the outside world. Yet a certain harshness was as much a part of her personality as was the gentleness and motherliness. Toward the end of her life Lucy Stone remarked to her daughter Alice how surprising it was that "Papa should have married so grim a person as myself." And in fact, when they first met, she was a confirmed spinster with a legacy of resentment and distrust of the opposite sex stemming from her earliest years.

She was born on August 13, 1818, the eighth of Francis and Hannah Stone's nine children—seven of whom survived into adulthood. Her father's people were long-established New Englanders: Her ancestor, Gregory Stone, had emigrated from England to Massachusetts in 1635 in search of religious freedom; her great-grandfather, Jonathan Stone, had fought in the French and Indian War; and her grandfather, Francis Stone, had served as a captain in the American Revolution, and later, as one of the leaders of Shays's Rebellion. Her father was a former schoolteacher who became a tanner and then a successful farmer. Two years before Lucy's birth the family moved to a 145-acre farm on Coy's Hill near West Brookfield, Massachusetts, and here she spent her childhood and early womanhood.

These were years of hard work mingled with simple pleasures, and they bred in her a self-reliance that had been characteristic of American women in Colonial times. Along with her three sisters—two older and one younger—she helped her mother with the housework and sewed rough shoes to be sold at the local store. She also shared with her three brothers such outdoor chores as driving the cows to pasture and filling the woodbox. But, though she performed many of the same tasks as her brothers, and performed them as well, if not better, she was regarded as inferior. This knowledge, combined with a growing awareness of the economic and sexual nature of woman's bondage, caused her to rebel.

Her mother's life exemplified both roots of bondage. Although Francis Stone prospered as a farmer, Lucy remembered that he was "ugly" to her mother about money. There came a time when Hannah Stone stopped asking for it; instead she pilfered small amounts—six and a half cents at a time—from his pocketbook, and every now and then when she needed extra cash, she sold a cheese on the sly. Sparing of money, Francis Stone did give his wife one thing—too many children. By the time Lucy was born, her mother at thirty-nine was already an old woman, worn out by years of excessive toil, the births of nine children, and the rearing of those who survived. The night before Lucy was born she had to milk eight cows because the menfolk had rushed off to save the hay from a sudden rainstorm. So it was little wonder that when she learned the sex of her new baby, Hannah Stone is said to have exclaimed: "Oh dear! I am sorry it is a girl. A woman's lot is so hard."

Lucy blamed her father for her mother's difficult life, and her resentment of him was intensified by his own treatment of her. Francis Stone was as stingy with affection as he was with money, and what little of either he could bring himself to dole out went first to his sons, and then to Lucy's sister Sarah, a pretty child and the baby of the family. While Lucy watched enviously, her father sang to Sarah and "trotted" her on his knee. Not surprisingly, Sarah didn't grow up with a strong sense of woman's oppression, nor did she think her father had been especially harsh toward his family. Lucy's recollections of him, on the other hand, were darkened with instances of cruelty: her father beating her with all his strength; her father unjustly accusing her of lying; her father telling her that her face was like a blacksmith's apron, because "it keeps off the sparks." Indeed, one of her earliest memories concerned a time when, waking to find her mother gone, she got out of bed and went to sob by the hearth. Her father found her there, and scolded her so severely—threatening "to lay on the slaps"—that she returned to bed and cried herself silently to sleep. The incident is revealing not only of her father's attitude toward her, but also of the tension between remaining silent and crying or speaking out, between self-abnegation and self-assertion, that was to become central to her character.

Her self-denying mother represented one of these two polarities, her domineering father, the other. Lucy would incorporate both elements into her adult personality, combining gentleness with power. Like her mother she was already beginning to display a selflessness verging on martyrdom. Thus at the age of twelve she took on the burden of the family laundry and kept at it even though the extra effort made her pale and faint. In later life she would devote herself first to her daughter and domesticity, and then to *The Woman's Journal* and her suffrage work with a relentlessness that brought her close to mental breakdown in the first case, and severely taxed her health and stamina in the second. She also, at an early age, tried to emulate her mother by placing strong curbs on her own passionate nature. In time her emotionality would find an outlet in brilliant oratory, but as a child she was determined to control her fiery temper, resolving never to speak when she was really angry.

Still, she found it difficult to be the meek and submissive woman her mother was. When she came across the phrase in the Bible, "Thy desire shall be to thy husband and he shall rule over thee," she ran straight to her mother and demanded to know what she could take to kill herself. Learning the cause of her daughter's despair, Hannah Stone, a pious woman who accepted the Bible quite literally, explained that woman's subservient role was part of the curse laid on all daughters of Eve. However, this explanation was unacceptable to Lucy; she wasn't ready to dismiss the Bible, but she could question the accuracy of the translation from the original Hebrew, which, after all, had been made by men. From this questioning arose a desire to go to college and learn Hebrew and Greek in order to read the Bible in its original form and see for herself what it said about women.

Lucy probably didn't arrive at this conclusion right away, but faced with the choice between the passive resignation traditionally expected of women, and the aggressive seeking out of knowledge associated with men, she opted significantly for the latter. In her desire to acquire an education she was encouraged by her older sister Rhoda, herself "an efficient teacher and brilliant scholar," and by a chance meeting with the educator Mary Lyon. While trying to raise money for the founding of Mount Holyoke Seminary for girls, Mary Lyon came to speak before a church sewing circle of which Lucy was a member. Her talk about the need to educate women as well as men struck a responsive chord: Lucy put down the shirt she was sewing to help pay for the education of a needy theological student and never picked it up again. Henceforth her efforts would be directed toward getting an education herself.

It was a long uphill struggle. Her father was perfectly willing to finance the higher education of her two oldest brothers, Frank and Bowman, but he saw no point in providing the same opportunities for his daughters. Even as a small child, Lucy had to gather nuts and berries in the woods and sell them to pay for the new schoolbooks her father refused to buy her, and by the time she had reached her early teens, he announced that she must leave school altogether. Only when she pointed out that by continuing her education she would be able to teach and earn her own living, did he grudgingly come forth with the money she needed—in the form of a loan, for which she had to sign an IOU.

Fortunately for her, she was not forced to depend entirely on her father as a source of support. The expansion of the district school system in New England beginning in the 1830s had brought with it greater opportunities for women teachers, although their salaries were considerably lower than those paid their male counterparts.

Thus, at the age of sixteen, Lucy started teaching at the district school at the salary of one dollar a week plus board. For the next nine years she alternated between periods of teaching and periods of study at one of the several secondary institutions which admitted women. When she had saved enough money from teaching, she would go back to school, and when her money ran out, she would return to teaching.

During this period she was already demonstrating the ability to make effective use of her mother's gentleness as a means of disarming her opponents. Engaged to teach in a school which for two successive years had been disrupted by a group of rowdy older boys, she brought the school to order within a few days by taking each of the more difficult students aside and showing him a special kindness. At the same time that she was developing techniques for dealing with difficult situations, she was becoming increasingly involved in controversy through the antislavery movement.

Antislavery gave Lucy a moral crusade with which she, as a woman already sensitive to the injustices she suffered because of her sex, could readily identify; and it also provided her with models of assertive womanhood. During the years of her struggle to get an education, the female antislavery agents, Sarah and Angelina Grimké, became the first American women to speak in public before mixed or "promiscuous" audiences. They were widely censured for doing so, and the Massachusetts clergy joined in the attack with a "Pastoral Letter of the General Association of Massachusetts to the Congregational Churches Under Their Care." Present in church when this letter denouncing the Grimké sisters was read from the pulpit, Lucy never forgot the indignation that "blazed" within her. She turned to her cousin sitting next to her, and boldly announced that "if I ever had anything to say in public, I should say it, and all the more because of the Pastoral Letter." She never had the opportunity to hear the Grimké sisters, but she did hear another female abolitionist, Abby Kelley, when she came to speak at the church in West Brookfield. The fiery former schoolteacher made a strong impression on her, and later encouraged Lucy to become an antislavery lecturer herself.

She wasn't yet ready to plunge into public speaking, but she found other ways of expressing her abolitionist convictions. Earlier, when an antislavery deacon was about to be expelled from her own church in West Brookfield, she had attempted to vote in the deacon's favor. She raised her hand six times in the course of the meeting, but each time it was ignored, because as a woman she wasn't considered a voting member of the congregation.

She also clashed with her former mentor, Mary Lyon, over the question of slavery. By 1839 Lucy had saved enough money to attend Mary Lyon's school in South Hadley, Massachusetts. Founded two years before, Mount Holyoke hadn't yet achieved collegiate status, but as a secondary school it was the best an ambitious young woman like Lucy could hope for. Nevertheless, the school fell short of her expectations. This was because Mary Lyon was unable to conceive of education for women as an end in itself; instead, according to Lucy, her aim was to better equip young women to become wives of missionaries. The strong religious orientation of the school was evident in the mite boxes that teachers and students were supposed to keep for the support of foreign missions. Lucy, however, kept her mite box for the support of the American Anti-Slavery Society, and deliberately left copies of the antislavery paper, *The Liberator*, in the school library after she had finished with them. Realizing who was responsible, Mary Lyon called Lucy into her office and reminded her that the slavery question was a very grave one, "upon which the best people are divided." No further rebuke was necessary, because three months after her arrival at Mount Holyoke, Lucy was called home by a family tragedy—the death of her sister Rhoda.

The tragedy was compounded by the fact that just a year before her oldest sister, Eliza, had also died. Kind and good but apparently not as smart as the other Stone children, Eliza had married a neighbor, Ira Barlow, and had two children by him. After her death Lucy wrote her oldest brother Frank: "Ira has got a white gravestone— rather small, though perhaps as large as any in that yard. Elizabeth wife of Ira Barlow died March 7 1838 is all there is on it." She brooded over these words on her sister's tombstone until finally at a woman's rights meeting a number of years later, she was able to verbalize her feelings. Then she said, "All that is left of a married woman to be marked on her gravestone is that she was the wife of somebody who had owned her."

Rhoda was different: Possessed of the intelligence her older sister lacked, she had excelled in school, and gone on to become a teacher. It was she who encouraged Lucy to get an education, and who gave her her first novel to read—after first determining there was nothing sinful or immoral in it. Although Rhoda hadn't lived long enough to fulfill much of her early promise, in death at least she had maintained her individuality. She hadn't like her sister become just another man's wife, and as Lucy mulled over the contrast in her sisters' brief lives, her own course was all the more clear to her.

She was twenty-one when Rhoda died, and she would be twenty-five before she had paid off her debt to her father, and scraped together the seventy dollars it cost for a single term at Oberlin Collegiate Institute in Ohio. Established in 1833, Oberlin was closely identified with the various reform movements of the day. The college was a station on the Underground Railroad, and was also the first institution in the country to open its doors to both women and blacks. Nevertheless, Lucy was afraid to apply to Oberlin directly; instead she asked her brother Bowman, now a Congregational minister, to make the application in her behalf. It was accepted, and in late August of 1843, she set off for Ohio.

Her first years at Oberlin were especially trying because of money problems. Board at the college was only a dollar a week, but even this was too expensive for Lucy. She managed to cut the cost in half by doing her own cooking in her tiny room, and met her other expenses by doing housework in the Ladies Hall at three cents an hour—positioning her Greek book on a ledge over the basin so she could study while she washed dishes. In the second year both Bowman and Sarah, who was now teaching school, lent her money, and she was also allowed to teach in the college's preparatory school at twelve and a half cents an hour. Her students at the preparatory school were adult blacks, many of whom could barely read or write, and so were unable to qualify for regular admission to the college. But instead of welcoming the remedial classes Lucy was prepared to teach, the black men objected strongly to receiving instruction from a woman. Although some of them were former slaves, they were still men, and considered themselves superior to any woman, slave or nonslave. Before she could win their cooperation, Lucy had to convince them that getting an education was more important than the sex of the teacher.

It was a lonely time for her: She lacked the money to return home, and so for the four years she spent at Oberlin, she had to remain at the college, working to finance her education during the winter and summer vacations. Her letters to various family members during this period indicated the extent to which she missed them, and also the sense of loss she experienced as, one by one, her three brothers and remaining sister married and began to establish families of their own. Before her sister Sarah's marriage to Henry Lawrence in the spring of 1845, she wrote of "the bitter tears that come brimming to my eyes, as I think that the last one of all our family, who was left *entire* to me, must go away."

Her advice to Sarah before her wedding showed that for all her rebelliousness, she continued to place a high premium on domesticity. She did urge "perfect open-heartedness" between Sarah and her husband, and on the subject of money—a source of bitterness in her parents' marriage—said that she believed "wives have a *right* in common with their husbands to the 'purse.' " Yet at the same time, she maintained that a "neglect of domestic duties" was the major source of marital discord, and exhorted her sister not to fall behind in this area: "You know that you love to read a great deal, but Sarah make it a matter of conscience, *never* to *read* until your domestic duties are *all done*, for if you wish to retain your husband's love, and make your home a happy one, you *must make it a well ordered* one."

Lucy's last two years at Oberlin were made easier because her father relented and agreed to help her out financially, though again the assistance came in the form of a loan, which she was expected to pay back, and which she eventually did. She continued to work, but as the pressure to support herself wasn't as great as before, she could afford to devote more time to her studies.

When Oberlin first opened, its women students were only permitted to follow a simplified course of study which wouldn't put too great a strain on their supposedly weaker intellects. But by the time Lucy enrolled, the college had changed its policy, allowing women to take part in the full course of study. However, as she soon discovered, there were limits to the college's liberal attitude toward her sex.

Lucy's first clash with the Oberlin authorities came when she removed her bonnet during chapel to ease the pain of a particularly severe headache. References in her letters show that headaches had been a problem before she came to the college, but there were circumstances peculiar to Oberlin and its chapel which conspired to bring on a new attack. In chapel she had to sit and listen respectfully while the Reverend Charles Grandison Finney, a spellbinding evangelist yet to Lucy "the crossest looking man" she had ever seen, preached one of his searing hell-fire and damnation sermons. By giving her a strong sense of life as a battle against evil, religious revivalism undoubtedly influenced her decision to become a reformer. Yet at the same time she recoiled from the evangelical emphasis on sin and damnation. To her sister she wrote: "Oberlin is, of all things, the place to harden *sinners*. There is so much truth preached, which the students are *obliged* to hear, that they do not yield to it." Unable herself to yield to some of the harsher "truths" of evangelism, she ultimately abandoned it in favor of the calm reasonableness of Unitarianism with its stress on human perfectibility. In the meantime, there was the pain in her head, and the displeasure she aroused by removing her bonnet in chapel. To the college authorities her action was a shocking violation of the Biblical injunction that women must keep their heads covered in church. She was called before the Ladies Board, a conservative group of professors' wives, and asked to explain herself. Lucy cleverly parried their criticism by pointing out that if she had a bad headache, she wouldn't be able to accomplish anything for the rest of the day, and then, "What account shall I give to God of my wasted Sunday afternoons?" Finally, a compromise was reached: She might remove her bonnet when the pain became unbearable, but she must sit in the last row of the chapel.

Her politics as well as her religion set her on a collision course with the Oberlin authorities. In 1840 the antislavery movement had split into two factions; the more radical, led by William Lloyd Garrison, looked to moral suasion as the means of ending slavery and also supported women's claim to an active public role in the movement, while the more moderate group favored political action and wanted women excluded. Lucy sided with the Garrisonians; the leading lights of Oberlin with the moderate group. Thus she complained to her parents: "They hate Garrison and woman's rights. I love them both, and often find myself at swords' points with them."

Another source of friction was her outspokenness on the subject of sex. Having witnessed the physical and emotional toll which too many pregnancies had taken on her own mother, Lucy argued that married couples should limit the size of their families, and in the absence of any other effective means of birth control, urged masculine self-restraint. When the Ladies Board heard about what she was telling the other young women at the college, they called her in for another reprimand, warning her not to meddle in matters about which she knew nothing. But meddle she did: Besides discussing the question with her classmates, she also raised it in letters to her married siblings. Each of her three brothers responded differently: Bowman agreed that whatever was harmful to the mother's health was wrong, but added that husbands and wives were meant to sleep together; Luther was opposed to "indulgence in the Beast-like use" of the generative organs, but also said, "Lucy I think It As Great A Sin To Not Suffer These Organs To Be Used At All As To Use Them Too Much"; and Frank took the Biblical command to multiply and replenish the earth quite literally.

Lucy's radicalism on this and other questions set her apart from many of the other students at Oberlin. But not everyone was intimidated by her; among the men students, she found brothers, and among the women, one true "sister of the heart."

Seven years Lucy's junior, Antoinette Brown had been a religious prodigy as a child, and it was assumed that when she grew up, she would marry a minister or a missionary. Antoinette, however, was determined to be ordained herself, and she did eventually become the first Protestant woman minister. She was also to become Lucy's closest friend and later her sister-in-law. Yet as she traveled to Oberlin by stagecoach in 1845, she was warned by one of the trustees of the college, who was also a family friend, to steer clear of Lucy Stone—"a young woman of strange and dangerous opinions."

Antoinette immediately sought out Lucy, and the two young women formed the type of close attachment that was common among nineteenth-century women, and was the result of the age's segregation of the sexes into different spheres of activity and aspiration. As Antoinette later recalled, "That was the time when I used to slip over and sleep with Lucy and talk almost all night, of everything, present, future, and more or less of the past." They had their differences. While Lucy was an ardent Garrisonian, Antoinette disliked Garrison's brand of antislavery because of his repeated attacks on the clergy. Lucy didn't completely approve of these attacks either, yet she had moved far enough away from the Congregational faith of her youth to protest the idea of Antoinette becoming a Congregational minister. "I wonder if you know how dreadfully I feel about your studying the old musty theology," she wrote Antoinette at one point. Finally, there was the matter of personal adornment: Lucy dressed with Quaker plainness and was so upset by the sight of her friend in a flowered hat that she burst into tears when Antoinette refused to remove the offending headgear.

However, they both decided that it was time to challenge the college authorities on the issue of women speaking in public. They were taking a class in rhetoric, but had no opportunity to practice what they were learning, since female students weren't allowed to take part in the class's weekly debates. When Lucy and Antoinette protested this state of affairs to their professor, he agreed to let them debate each other. A huge crowd gathered to witness the debate between Lucy Stone and Antoinette Brown, yet when it was over, the outraged college officials announced a ban on public debates for women. In order to gain additional practice, the two had to form a secret debating society, which met at first in the woods, and later on at the home of a sympathetic black woman.

A yearly celebration within Oberlin's black community gave Lucy the opportunity to make her first speech in public. At this event, held in commemoration of the freeing of the slaves in the British West Indies in 1833, she read an essay entitled "Why Do We Rejoice Today?" Not surprisingly, the speech drew censure from the Ladies Board; hadn't she felt "embarrassed and frightened" to find herself on the platform with so many men, they asked.

Her final showdown with the Oberlin authorities came at the time of her graduation. It was customary for each year's graduating class to select its outstanding members to prepare and read essays at the commencement exercises, and Lucy was among those chosen by the class of 1847. But because women students weren't permitted to read their own essays, she refused to prepare one. Students, faculty, and administration quickly took sides on the issue. Although Oberlin's president thought she should be able to read her essay, most of the faculty disagreed, some even arguing that she shouldn't be allowed to graduate unless she wrote an essay and let one of the male professors read it. The other students, however, backed her up: All except one of the women selected refused to prepare essays, and so did two of the men, and the substitutes chosen to replace the protesting students.

In the end, Lucy didn't prepare an essay, but she was permitted to graduate, thus becoming the first Massachusetts woman to receive the A.B. degree. At the commencement exercises she finally met her

hero Garrison—in the area for antislavery meetings—and impressed
him with her freedom of spirit and her determination "to go forth as
a lecturer, particularly in the vindication of the rights of women."

Her family, however, was aghast at this plan. Her mother
wanted her to teach instead, or if she must lecture, hoped she would
do so more discreetly by going from door to door. Her father agreed
with her mother, although by this time he was well aware that "you
will do that way which seems right in your own eyes I suppose."
Sarah, too, thought that Lucy should teach instead of lecture, adding
that as far as she was concerned, women weren't really oppressed.
The only members of her family who supported Lucy were her brothers Frank and Bowman, and neither was especially enthusiastic about
her speaking on woman's rights. Frank found it a rather "lean" subject, and Bowman wrote: "I think that those who are sighing for de-
liverance from bondage have a stronger claim upon our efforts than
those who hug their chains."

Her mother and sister's disapproval was hard to bear, but as she
explained to Sarah, her own "approving conscience" was her guide
now. She spent the winter of 1847 teaching in North Brookfield to
pay off her debt to her father, and also at this time delivered her first
public address outside of Oberlin at her brother Bowman's church in
Gardner, Massachusetts. Her subject was woman's rights, and the
speech was an important one because it represented the first time a
woman had devoted an entire speech to this topic. Moreover, Lucy's
speech was made almost a full year before the alleged beginning of
the woman's movement was officially launched at the convention in
Seneca Falls in September of 1848.

Later when she lectured in West Brookfield, her father was in
the audience—at first so ashamed that he hid his head in his hands.
Yet as his daughter spoke on, winning her audience's respectful attention, he sat up and listened himself. She had finally earned the
recognition denied her throughout her childhood, though it came too
late to make up for all the years of her father's indifference.

In the spring of 1848 Lucy became a salaried lecturer for the
Massachusetts Anti-Slavery Society. She was expected to speak only
on abolition, but she found it difficult to keep silent about woman's
rights. While lecturing in Boston, she went early one morning to see
Hiram Powers's statue, "The Greek Slave," and this nude statue of a

beautiful Greek Christian woman, being sold into slavery by her Turkish captors during the Greek war for independence, brought the "hot tears" to her eyes "at the thought of the millions of women who must be freed." That evening she "poured out her heart" on the subject of woman's oppression, prompting a kindly rebuke from the Reverend Samuel J. May, the agent of the Anti-Slavery Society who had originally hired her. She answered his objection with the words, "I was a woman before I was an abolitionist." It was agreed that thereafter she would speak for women at her own expense during the week, and for the Anti-Slavery Society on weekends.

She received four dollars a week for her time on weekends, and in the beginning financed her lectures during the week by taking up collections. However, after joining forces for an evening with the Hutchinson family, a group of antislavery singers whose practice was to charge admission, she decided to do the same herself. She charged only a nominal amount per person, but as her lectures usually drew large crowds, she was able, in three years, to amass a total of seven thousand dollars—a considerable sum for those times.

She was a highly effective speaker, capable in her own words of swaying her audiences "as the wind the grain." She did not write out her speeches, but rather spoke extemporaneously, letting her own strong convictions guide what she said. Her ideas were not strikingly original; she had virtually no sense of humor and could on occasion be dogmatic and rigid; yet her voice—soft and musical "like a silver bell"—and her simple, unpretentious manner captivated audiences. Also, perhaps more than any other woman speaker of the period, she understood the importance of cultivating the goodwill of her audiences and was especially adept at doing so. Thus, in one of her woman's rights speeches, she did not attack man as the oppressor as had the women at the Seneca Falls convention, but instead expressed thanks for the help of "those noble men who are with us today," and even admitted that "it is not without reason that men complain of the wives and mothers of today."

Despite all her efforts to pour oil on troubled waters, as a lecturer on unpopular subjects and a woman besides, she was bound to arouse a great deal of hostility. People tore down the posters advertising her lectures, burned pepper in the auditoriums where she spoke, hurled prayer books and other missiles at her, and once in the dead of winter drenched her with water from a hose. She was expelled by her own church for conduct "inconsistent with her covenant engagements," and widely denounced from the pulpit and by the press.

Typically, her critics pictured her as a big woman with a bellowing voice, who tramped around in boots, puffing on a cigar and swearing profusely. However, Lucy's actual appearance and demure, ladylike manner belied this caricature of the "masculine" woman. She was small and nicely proportioned, and while no ravishing beauty, wasn't unattractive either with a slightly turned-up nose, round ruddy cheeks, and gray eyes that were particularly expressive when she was animated. She wore her brown hair cut short at the neck and dressed plainly in dark-colored gowns with neat white collars. Although she took no special pains to attract the opposite sex, she had her share of suitors. While still living at home, she had aroused the interest of a young divinity student, who told her she would make a fine missionary's wife driving a team of horses over the Rockies; and there were other admirers later on.

Yet if she wanted to remain her own person, Lucy seemed destined to a life of celibacy, and to a certain extent she had reconciled herself to this denial of her femininity. Independent and self-supporting, she could look back proudly on all she had achieved. True, her life was difficult and often lonely, but she was doing work she believed in. Her family's initial objections had given way to approval of her course, and she could turn to a small circle of friends within the antislavery and woman's rights movements for support and encouragement. Nevertheless, she was keenly aware of the high price society exacted for her self-reliance. "It is horrid to live without intimate companionship and gentle loving influences which are the constant attendant of a true love marriage," she wrote Antoinette Brown in 1853. "It is a wretchedly unnatural way of living. . . . We could do so much more good in a natural than in an unnatural position." Although she yearned for love and marriage, she was quick to add in the same letter: "I shall not be married ever. I have not yet seen the person whom I have the slightest wish to marry, and if I had, it will take longer than my lifetime for the obstacles to be removed which are in the way of a married woman having any being of her own."

When Lucy Stone wrote these words, she had met Henry Blackwell only once and then too briefly to form much of an opinion of him. But she was soon to meet him again, and to learn that here indeed was a man whom she could love and marry without sacrificing her individuality.

Harriet Beecher Stowe remembered him as a "wild boy," and when he was well into middle age, his own daughter said that he was "as sinful as ever." Of his three brothers, he was the most fun-loving and irreverent. Yet at the same time, he was the one most tormented by self-doubt and self-reproach; and while his brothers concerned themselves solely with business, he alone combined the two careers of businessman and reformer.

Henry Browne Blackwell was born on May 4, 1825 in Bristol, England, the fifth of nine surviving children. He grew up surrounded by women—a circumstance that helps to explain the remarkable degree of empathy he developed for members of the opposite sex. Besides his mother, there were five sisters, three older and two younger, who all benefited from their father's belief that girls should be educated equally with boys. There were also four maiden Blackwell aunts, one of whom served for a time as the children's governess. Stern and tyrannical with Henry's brothers and sisters, Aunt "Bar" adored him, and especially delighted in curling his wavy hair, causing passersby to stop and remark on his beauty.

Also present in Henry's early background were the two strands of business and reform activity that were to figure prominently in his adult life. Both his parents belonged to the rising English middle class. His mother's grandfather had been a bookseller, and her father, a watchmaker and jeweler until he was convicted of forgery and sent to Australia. Hannah Lane Blackwell never forgot this disgrace, and it probably affected her attitude toward her own children, as she spent a great deal of time fretting about their spiritual development. Henry's father also came from a family of shopkeepers, but he and an older brother entered into manufacturing—Samuel Blackwell into the sugar refining business, then one of Bristol's main industries, and his brother into ironsmelting. As a successful sugar refiner, Samuel Blackwell was able to provide a comfortable living for his growing family; however, the nature of his business conflicted with his abolitionist beliefs, for sugar was a slave product. He sought a way out of this dilemma by experimenting with methods of extracting sugar from beets—an enterprise his son Henry would also pursue.

Samuel Blackwell's sense of morality stemmed from his religion.

Dissenters rather than members of the Church of England, the Blackwells espoused a strict form of Calvinism emphasizing human depravity and predestination. On Sundays the family attended both morning and afternoon services at a nearby chapel, and on weekday mornings, gathered for a "loud" reading of chapters from the Bible followed by a lengthy prayer session. The children also had to listen to religious stories "of a highly sentimental and devout character, and dealing largely with pain and bereavement and misfortune, death, judgment, and eternity." Certain of these stories so terrified Henry's oldest sister, Anna, that she would wake up screaming in the middle of the night. In his own case, the grim moral instruction of his youth engendered strong feelings of guilt that were to plague him long after he had lost his religious belief.

However, Henry's childhood wasn't entirely spent under a cloud of Calvinist gloom. There were visits from his Uncle Charles Lane, his mother's youngest brother and a dashing army officer, whom Henry described as "gay, lively, full of fun and constantly playing some delightful trick on the children." Since this description would easily apply to Henry himself in later life, his Uncle Charlie was clearly one of his early models. There were also daily outings with pretty Eliza Majors, the governess who succeeded Aunt Bar, and summers spent in rented cottages at various seaside resorts. But in 1832, when Henry was seven, the English part of his childhood came to an abrupt end with his father's decision to emigrate to America. Samuel Blackwell's reasons were ideological as well as financial. He had lost a considerable sum of money with the failure of two major sugar importers, and hoped to make a fresh start in America. Moreover, he had a great admiration for American democratic institutions, and wanted his children to grow up in the freer atmosphere of the New World. As far as Henry was concerned, this and subsequent moves within the United States, may well have contributed to a certain restlessness that was to keep him on the go throughout much of his adult life. Indeed, like his father, he was never so happy as when he was on his way to a new place in pursuit of a new possibility.

The family settled first in New York, where Samuel Blackwell opened up a sugar refinery, but in America as in England, he continued to be troubled by the connection between his business and an institution he considered to be immoral. According to Henry, his father was "greatly disappointed in his experience of the New York businessmen in their complicity with the system of slavery. The Cuban planters from whom he bought sugar said frankly that they made no effort to raise the slaves." Perhaps as a means of salving his own conscience, Samuel Blackwell threw himself into antislavery agitation, attending meetings in New York and contributing to an antislavery newspaper. In the course of his involvement he became acquainted with a number of the American movement's leaders, such as Garrison, the Reverend Samuel May, and Theodore Dwight Weld. These men and others were frequent visitors at the Long Island home to which the Blackwells eventually moved. The house also served as a refuge for two abolitionist brothers fleeing an angry mob in New York, and for an escaped slave on his way to Canada.

Like their father, the Blackwell children were caught up in the ferment of abolitionist protest. Henry recalled attending a stormy meeting in New York, at which the English abolitionist, George Thompson, spoke; and in a lighter vein, remembered writing mottoes for sugar kisses to be sold at an antislavery fair. While the family was living on Long Island, his sisters opened up a school for some black children living in shanties by Northern Creek, and named one of their horses, a mare, after Prudence Crandall, whose own school for black children in Connecticut had been attacked by a mob of her fellow townspeople.

The family remained on Long Island for more than a year, and as Henry recalled, "Those were pleasant days to the children who had the freedom of orchards, field, and outbuildings after study hours were over." But it was also during this period that his father contracted malaria from the mosquitoes that bred in the marsh beyond the garden of their home. He never completely recovered from this illness. The family moved again, this time to Jersey City, and then in 1838 Samuel Blackwell decided to quit the New York area entirely. The depression of 1837 had hurt his business, and further disheartened by the loss of one of his sugar houses through fire, he set his sights on Cincinnati, where he planned to open the first sugar refinery west of the Alleghenies. His oldest children begged him to return to England instead, but Samuel Blackwell was determined to go west.

With the move to Cincinnati, Henry was exposed to a very different part of America than he had known in New York City. A big, raw, sprawling land, the West impressed him with its greater freedom and tremendous potential. Although he was later to settle permanently in the East, he never lost his fascination with the West and traveled there frequently throughout his life.

However, the first few months in Cincinnati were marred by tragedy. Upon the family's arrival, Samuel Blackwell started a sugar house, but within a short time was stricken with a recurrence of malaria, and died, leaving his family with a scant twenty dollars after funeral expenses had been taken care of.

His father's death marked the first real crisis in Henry's life. Understandably, Samuel Blackwell had occupied a central position in his son's childhood. With his "stern, puritan ideas," he was a figure of authority and discipline, but he did allow himself to bend occasionally, and could be warm and affectionate, especially with the younger children. He was also, according to Henry, "a man of fine intelligence," who had belonged to a book club in England, wrote poetry, and with his beautiful speaking voice, was in demand as a lay preacher. Later, Henry would write of the "strange & dignified fascination" his father had exercised over him. Although Samuel Blackwell had uprooted his family, moving them first to New York and then to Cincinnati where he left them in very difficult straits, Henry seems never to have thought of blaming him. Instead, in death, he invested his father with almost godlike proportions, and himself assumed the burden of his father's final failure. He was dogged not only by guilt but by deep-seated feelings of inadequacy. Henry wasn't the oldest son, but since there was only a year and a half's difference between him and his brother Sam, both boys were expected to take their places at the head of the family. Thrust at thirteen into a position of responsibility before he was ready for it, Henry found himself sadly lacking. Early in their correspondence, he confessed to Lucy Stone that his father's old abolitionist friend, Theodore Weld, had touched him "on a weak point" by recognizing his father's face in his, and later on she undoubtedly prodded the same raw nerve when she expressed the hope "that your future will be worthy your father's son." Henry was never to feel worthy of his father, and he was to spend the rest of his life apologizing for his shortcomings.

Yet in the summer of 1838, just after his father's death, sheer economic survival had to be foremost in Henry's mind. He and his brother Sam took clerking jobs at two dollars a week, while his mother and three older sisters—Anna, Marian, and Elizabeth—opened up a school in their home. Two years later the family had managed to save enough money to send Henry to Kemper College in St. Louis, where he planned to study law. They had high hopes for his success, but also certain misgivings, which Henry's behavior on the eve of his departure did little to allay. Deaf to their protests that he would ruin it on the steamboat voyage, Henry insisted on wearing his new suit of clothes; and what was even worse, scandalized his mother when, in answer to her question as to when she would see him again, he replied flippantly, "In the Judgment Day! and on the left hand side of the cross!"

Although Henry did apply himself during the year he spent at college, he feared he would never make a first-rate lawyer because of the difficulty he experienced in making a good "off-hand" speech. He complained that he had "enough ideas to fill a book," but that when he got up to speak in the college debating society, all he could do was stammer out a few sentences before sitting down. It was a disability he obviously overcame in later life; however, at the time, it loomed as a major obstacle to his becoming a lawyer. He wrote his family that he was thinking of civil engineering as a possible profession, but his days of formal education were about to come to an end.

When the Blackwells had first moved to Cincinnati, Hannah Blackwell had become a member of the Orthodox Congregational Church, while her three oldest daughters had veered away from the dissenting religion of their youth to join the Episcopal Church, later switching to Unitarianism, when the young and dynamic minister, William Henry Channing, became pastor of the Unitarian congregation in Cincinnati. According to Henry, their final shift in religious affiliation "gave great offense to the fashionable and conservative society of the city, Unitarianism being regarded as infidelity & very unpopular," and as a result, enrollment in the Blackwell school dropped sharply. Henry was now needed at home to contribute to the family's dwindling income, and so home he came. For the next six years he worked at his former clerking job, and then around 1845 he became a partner in a flour mill business. His partners were two illiterate men who "relied wholly" on him, and as he was in charge of three mills, buying wheat and corn and flaxseed, and selling flour and meal and oil in great quantities, it was—in his own words—"a pretty responsible position for a young man not yet twenty-one." In just one year he succeeded in making a sizable profit, and with the money bought in his mother's name a small brick house with a lot adjoining Lane Theological Seminary in the Cincinnati suburb of Walnut Hills. The house, which had formerly belonged to Harriet Beecher Stowe and her husband, became the Blackwell family residence for the remainder of the time they lived in Cincinnati.

However, as a young man not yet twenty-one, Henry wasn't totally preoccupied with business matters; a journal he kept at this time provides a revealing glimpse into his emotional life. The journal begins in April of 1845 and spans two romances—first with a young woman named Appoline Guilford, who was possessed of "one of the loveliest faces and noblest minds that God almighty ever put on this glorious earth," and then with another young woman named Kate Vail, described with similar romantic hyperbole. The latter romance coincided with a second crisis in Henry's life, which was associated with religion. For several years Henry had been an agnostic—much to the dismay of his extremely devout mother—but now influenced by the pious example of Kate Vail, he decided to try to recover his belief. He went to hear the eminent Congregational minister, Lyman Beecher, preach a sermon on faith, and "perhaps from nervousness or perhaps from a higher cause" was greatly affected. Retiring to his room, he knelt down, and began to pray when Kate Vail burst into the room in tears and pleaded with him to be a Christian. He promised he would try, and spent the next several months reading the Bible, praying, and discussing "the blinding power of sin" with friends. Yet just when he was ready to make good his promise, he discovered that Kate Vail had decided to marry a seminary student, whose unwavering faith made him more attractive to her than Henry with his "honest doubts." Later, during his courtship of Lucy Stone, he would undergo another period of questioning and intense self-examination—this time in connection with his abolitionist beliefs—followed by an affirmation of faith in the form of direct action. But for the moment, he remained unattached. As he confided to his journal, "What between Ap. [Appoline Guilford] Kate & my own dear Sisters Marian and Elizabeth—my standard of female excellence is so high & definite that I shall not easily get caught."

Henry's choice of his older sisters as models for his ideal woman was significant, because all his sisters were strong-minded, unconventional women. Instead of following the traditional route of marriage and motherhood, they remained single and adopted children. Moreover, with the exception of Marian, who sank into invalidism, each of the Blackwell women distinguished herself in some way: Anna as a newspaper correspondent in Paris, Emily as a doctor, and Ellen as an artist and writer. Henry's favorite sister, Elizabeth, became best known as the first woman in the country to qualify as an M.D. She was to establish the New York Infirmary for Women and Children, whose all-female staff included her sister Emily, a nurses' training school, and ultimately the Women's Infirmary Medical School, which was later incorporated into the Cornell University Medical College when that institution finally opened its doors to women at the turn of the century.

But in the summer of 1846 when Henry closed his journal, Elizabeth was just beginning her long uphill struggle to acquire a medical education, and her adoring brother could only applaud her "high purpose," and reproach himself for his inability to do more to help her and his other sisters. Not long after the disastrous end of his romance with Kate Vail, Henry went to New York to learn the sugar refining business from one of his father's former employees, Dennis Harris. The Blackwells had originally met Harris on the boat coming over to America. He was a bricklayer from Bath and a lay Methodist preacher whose "resolute aggressive Methodism as it asserted itself among godless passengers," pleased Henry's father so much that when Harris was unable to find work in New York, Samuel Blackwell employed him as a foreman at his sugar refinery. After Samuel Blackwell's departure for Cincinnati, Harris had stayed on, weathered the depression, and become successful. Now he welcomed the opportunity to help his former benefactor's son learn the business, but Henry soon found that he disliked Harris for the same reason that his father had approved so heartily of him: The man's "narrow" Methodism clashed with his own avant-garde philosophy. For Henry, like his older sisters Anna and Marian, had by this time come under the influence of the French philosopher, Charles Fourier, whose vision of a social utopia organized into units or phalanxes of 1,620 people each had led to the establishment of a number of idealistic communities in the United

States. Disenchanted with Harris, Henry bought some old machinery from him, and returned to Cincinnati, determined to start his own sugar refinery. Unfortunately, he was unable to produce a good enough quality of sugar with the equipment he had, and the business was already teetering on the brink of failure when the sugar house caught fire and burned to the ground.

The summer of 1848 found Henry back in New York working for Dennis Harris as a bookkeeper, and discontented as ever. He even considered joining his sister at medical school, for Elizabeth had finally found a school that would accept her, and was studying at the Medical Institution of Geneva College (later Hobart College) in Seneca Lake, New York. Although he decided against this plan, he was the only family member present to witness her triumph when on January 23, 1849, his beloved older sister was awarded her medical degree.

In the meantime, Henry had fallen victim to the "yellow fever" that was sweeping the country. One of his fellow boarders in New York had persuaded him to invest all his capital—a few hundred dollars—in the manufacture of patent cradles or rockers to separate grains of gold from gravel; and much to his family's consternation, he was about to join the gold rush in California. Kenyon Blackwell, a cousin then visiting from England, was sent to New York with the specific purpose of bringing Henry back to his senses. He finally succeeded in doing so by lending Henry and his brother Sam $5,000 so that, together with two other young men, they could buy out a wholesale hardware business in Cincinnati. According to Henry, they "found [themselves] owners of a large stock of hardware—much of it no longer salable." He became the firm's traveling partner and salesman, and once again rejoined his family in Cincinnati.

Although he had returned to the life of a "mere country merchant," there were compensations. The Blackwells belonged to a cultivated circle which included the Reverend Lyman Beecher, his daughter Harriet, and her husband Calvin Stowe. Earlier, Henry and Sam had organized a debating club with some of the students at the Lane Theological Seminary, and now, together with Henry's scholarly friend, Ainsworth Spofford, later chief librarian of the Library of Congress, they formed a literary society, the Cincinnati Club, whose members met regularly to discuss a variety of subjects ranging from literature to politics, science, music, philosophy, and travel. Long a fixture of Cincinnati's cultural life, the club's membership included two presidents: Rutherford B. Hayes and later William Howard Taft.

The Blackwell brothers also enjoyed an active social life of parties, country outings, and evening singing with other young people. Henry was an attractive young man. Like the other Blackwells, he was quite short, but he had the wavy black hair that had delighted his maiden aunt when he was a boy, blue eyes, and teeth so white they earned him the nickname of Carker when Dickens's novel *Dombey and Son* became popular reading in the 1850s. He was also witty, charming, and energetic. Yet despite these appealing qualities and his own susceptibility to the opposite sex, he remained single. While living in New York, he had written a friend that if he simply wanted a "pleasant comfortable jog-trot life," he would stay in the West, marry someone or other, and take it easy. But he could not envision this sort of life for himself because "life is to all a solemn & earnest thing if viewed aught—but to those who have been favored by God with a knowledge of sublime truths and a key unlocking the enigma of *evil* & solving the problem of Human Destiny, it becomes fearfully responsible." He felt the need of some noble purpose that would give his life direction and meaning, and he was to find it in the person of "a young middle-aged woman" who quietly entered his hardware store one fall morning.

ONE

Courtship

1853 - 1855

If both parties cannot study more, think more, feel more, talk more, & work more than they could alone, I will remain an old bachelor & adopt a Newfoundland dog or a terrier as an object of affection.

Henry Blackwell to Lucy Stone, July 2, 1853

Millions of slaves sighing for freedom; the great soul of Womanhood crushed and degraded; outcast children and drunken parents, should not be left to suffer on because the developement of a few weighed more than that of all of these.

Lucy Stone to Henry Blackwell, June 21, 1853

When Lucy Stone and Henry Blackwell first met in the fall of 1850, she was thirty-two and he was twenty-five. That summer she had traveled to Hutsonville, Illinois, where her brother Luther was established as a country merchant. The visit ended tragically with Luther's death from cholera, and shortly after the funeral Lucy and her brother's pregnant widow started east. Both women soon became ill themselves: Luther's widow lost her baby, and Lucy was stricken with typhoid fever. After a harrowing eighteen-day siege, she recovered sufficiently to continue on her journey. She was anxious to get back to Massachusetts for the National Woman's Rights Convention—the first of its kind—which was to be held in Worcester in October. In need of funds for the remainder of the trip, she stopped off in Cincinnati to cash a draft drawn up by the treasurer of the Ohio Anti-Slavery Society. The draft was on the previous owner of Henry Blackwell's hardware store; however, as an abolitionist himself, Henry was sympathetic to her situation. He was also "strangely attracted" by her "sweet voice, bright smile, pleasant manner and simplicity of dress and character." But since he was several years her junior, he decided she would be a better match for his older brother Sam, and so the next day Sam was sent with the money for Lucy. Yet nothing came of the meeting, because after paying her the money, Sam immediately departed.

Henry's sisters, Marian and Ellen, were the next members of the Blackwell family to meet Lucy Stone. While visiting in the East that fall, they attended the woman's rights convention at Worcester, and there heard Lucy Stone speak and made her acquaintance. According to Henry, they "were greatly pleased and interested in her and wrote about her in their letters, thus keeping her in memory." Moreover, Lucy Stone's name appeared frequently in *The Liberator*, the *National Anti-Slavery Standard*, and another abolitionist paper, *The North Star*—all of which constituted the Blackwells' Sunday reading.

Henry didn't see Lucy again until the spring of 1853 when he went east to try to find a publisher for a book of poems he had written, and also to attend antislavery meetings in Boston and New York. He was present at the New York meeting where Lucy moved her audience to tears with the story of a slave woman who was fleeing with her baby when a bullet from the gun of one of her pursuers struck the baby's head and killed it. He also saw her at the Boston convention, where he delivered a lecture on the Constitution as an antislavery document; and met her at the Anti-Slavery offices in that city. He was totally smitten by her. He later recalled that "the beauty, charm, and eloquence of Miss Stone captured her hearers & greatly impressed me." He had been interested in an attractive young widow named Nancy Clark, who was studying medicine, but as he put it, "Lucy's larger mental and moral and affectional nature put an end to that affair." To his brother Sam he wrote: "I shall endeavor to see more of [Lucy] before I come West if practicable, as I decidedly prefer her to any lady I have ever met, always excepting the Bloomer dress which I *dont* like practically, tho theoretically I believe in it with my whole soul—It is quite doubtful whether I shall be able to succeed in again meeting her, as she is travelling around—having been born locomotive I believe."

The bloomer costume to which Henry referred consisted of a short dress with a comfortably loose waist, which was worn over a pair of long Turkish-style pantaloons. Elizabeth Smith Miller, daughter of the reformer Gerrit Smith, was the first to wear the new outfit, but the name came from the costume's popularizer, Amelia Bloomer, editor of the temperance and woman's rights paper, *The Lily*. Although the bloomer dress provided a more practical and healthy alternative to the usual mountains of petticoats and tightly laced stays which made movement difficult and breathing near impossible, it generated a great deal of controversy. Newspapers ridiculed the costume, and bloomer-clad women were often harassed by hordes of jeering, egg-throwing men and boys.

Nevertheless, Henry Blackwell wasn't about to let a few unpleasant externals interfere with his appreciation of Lucy Stone's inner qualities. He arranged for a formal letter of introduction from William Lloyd Garrison; and undaunted by Garrison's warning that Lucy Stone was determined never to marry and had already turned down several suitors, he set out for West Brookfield "on a beautiful June morning." He called first on Deacon Henshaw, the same antislavery minister in whose defense Lucy had raised her hand in church years before. With "a twinkle in his eye," perhaps because he suspected Henry's purpose, the deacon told him that Lucy was away, but was expected to return later in the day. After dining with the Henshaws, Henry amused himself by reading Emerson's essays on the banks of Quaboag Pond. Then in the afternoon he walked to the Stone family farm on Coy's Hill. When no one answered the front door, he went around to the back, and there found Lucy, dressed in bloomers, standing on a table and whitewashing the kitchen ceiling. She refused his offer of assistance, but did allow him to help her peel potatoes for dinner. Afterward, the pair walked to the summit of the hill which commanded "a superb view through the rocky pastures to the 'Rock House'—a mass of castellated crags with trees growing in and around it," and Henry wasted no time getting to the point of his visit. Caught off balance in "that strange hour" by the sudden eloquence of his proposal, Lucy accused him of trying to mesmerize her. She was attracted to him more than she cared to admit. But as this attraction depended on his actual presence, he couldn't make much use of it in courting her: His home and business were in Cincinnati, while she, as a "born locomotive," spent most of the year traveling around the country lecturing and attending conventions. The only way he could hope to reach her was by mail, and so, shortly after his visit to her home, he sent her a long letter and a volume of Plato.

The gift set the tone of their first letters. Calmly and philosophically, as friends and nothing more, they entered into a dialogue on the important questions of the day—antislavery, woman's rights, and specifically, marriage—each secretly hoping like "the wise old pagan" Plato to use "the arguments of the [other] to confute them."

❧

New York June 13. 1853

Dear Miss Lucy

I shall leave here for Cincinnati the day after tomorrow to remain a week or two before setting out on a six weeks tour through the Wabash valley. You told me you were going to remain at home and study this summer. Please oblige me by accepting the enclosed translation of Plato. It is the best one ever made and I suppose, to anyone but a *first rate* Greek scholar in the habit of reading the original, is the best form for study. Do not refuse my little gift. It will be such a luxury to me this summer amid the hot & fetid air of Illinois, to imagine you amongst the cool green granite hills of Massachusetts, comfortably chatting with Socrates & his old Greeks, that I shall find the idea a better tonic than quinine & my old enemy the "skunk cabbage." I told Elizabeth that you had not yet seen her book and she desired me to present you with a copy from her. I think you will like her lectures very much. If my partiality for her does not mislead me they are full of sound good sense & animated [by] a very noble idea. As for Plato, I am curious to know how you will like him. I think a good deal is quite prosy and dull, but still he is full of great suggestions & the very finest intuitions.

The evening I left you I came straight to New York to wind up my Eastern visit. Yesterday (Sunday) I spent very pleasantly with Mr. and Mrs. Weld & Miss Sarah Grimke (Aunt Sarah as they call her). They live at Bellville N. Jersey some 3½ miles north of Newark on the Passaic river—a beautiful place shaded by trees & overlooking the water. On going up to the house with my friend Dr. Dorrance we first met the two ladies draped in the Bloomer costume which I have learned to like of late. They were surrounded by a dozen children, three of them their own, comfortably seated on the piazza reading & enjoying themselves as though Sunday was actually made to be happy in. Mrs Weld is a sensible, earnest & very intelligent woman—wide awake and well up to the times. She has evidently been living not vegetating during her married life. We found Mr. Weld working in the garden—a middle aged man with a noble forehead a little bald, clear complexion, a mouth compressed with an expression of firmness & energy and brilliant, piercing eyes full of intellect & fire. He welcomed me very warmly touching me on a weak point by recognizing my father's face in mine though twenty years had passed, since he had known him.

After dinner we all adjourned to a sort of parlor built in the branches of a pine tree, and I tried to draw Mr. Weld out on the reasons why he withdrew from the active advocacy of Reforms. He says the immediate cause was a narrow escape from drowning which destroyed his voice entirely—stopping his public speaking short.

This, he says for the first time for years, gave him time to *reflect*. He found he himself needed reforming. He was all wrong. He had been laboring to destroy evil in the same spirit as his antagonists. He suddenly felt that fighting was not the best way to annihilate error & that he could no longer act as he had been doing. All his old opinions & principles began to loosen & scale off. He threw aside books, newspapers, everything & *for ten years found there was nothing on earth for him to do but to dig ditches & work upon his farm*. And so he did so. I tried to attack his position, but he says it was all right. *That for him*, it was no longer possible nor proper to continue combating. He had done so manfully & when his work in that way was ended he was obliged to resign it to others while he himself entered into a higher sphere of experience. So since then he has thought & worked and taught his children & occasionally lectured and helped all whom he has met who needed help and in short endeavored to live a true manly life.

This all seemed very strange to me. I tried to argue the duty of fighting error so long as it existed, but both he & his wife simply say—"There is a fighting era in every one's life. While you feel so, fight on, it is your duty & the best thing you can possibly do. But when your work in that line is done, you will reach another and a higher view." But though I cant understand the position of the Welds, I see plainly that in *their case* they have acted rightly. I dont think it was *marriage* which is to blame for their withdrawal from public life as so many suppose, but that it arose from a combination of physical, intellectual & moral causes quite independent of it. I wish I had more time to comprehend it. Certainly I dare not criticize too harshly two people so noble & so earnest. If there ever was a true marriage it is their's. Both preserve their separate individuality *perfectly* & on many points differ heartily with the utmost good will. I do hope you will some day meet them Miss Lucy! You will certainly mark them down on your list as No. 3.

For myself, my battle has yet to be fought & God helping me, I will fight it, as I can. Yet it may be that the Weld's are right. These twenty or thirty brave strong earnest children whom they have educated to work in the Future may make a deeper mark than we can imagine. Theodore's "Thousand Witnesses" produced "Uncle Tom," so says Mrs. Stowe—perhaps his ten year's conscientious ditch-digging may eventuate in still more. And I believe that another active era will yet dawn for Mr & Mrs Weld. I hope the great problem of problems "the associative life" will meet their assistance in its solution. Feeling the necessity of a more perfect education for their children, they are about to join the "Raritan Bay Union" and endeavor to realize a life which will be itself an education *to all*. What a great thing it is *to live*!

When I began this note I intended to write six lines & then stop. But talking to you is like talking to myself & I find five thousand things that I should like to say, but will not. Only this much—You & I have talked frankly together & understand each other. Let me be *your friend* & write to you occasionally. If, as I believe, your views on certain subjects change, prove your consistency to Truth, by changing with them. If not stay—where you are. In any case, I shall esteem it a good fortune to have known & still to know you. If I know myself my object is not happiness in itself but to live a manly life and to aid everyone else to do so. Meantime try actual marriages not by your own standard, but by that of those who are parties to them. You will greatly modify your estimate of it. I believe it is as imperfect as the people themselves no more so. I believe some day you ought to & will marry somebody—perhaps not me, if not—a better person. Believe me, the mass of men are not *intentionally* unjust to women, nor the mass of women consciously oppressed. And just as soon and as fast as you can inspire women to step forward and take higher social positions, you will find Society after a period of probation, acquiesce as a matter of course. Positive action *proves itself* and always commands respect.

The difficulty our new theory meets with is, that people generally, wanting our ideal, criticize our position by their low standards of desire & possibility. I do hope & believe you are gradually awakening their minds & elevating their conceptions. But the great mass of people will only be convinced by *constructive* action on the part of women, practically achieving their claims. Let a woman prove that she can speak, write, preach, edit newspapers, practice medicine, law & surgery—carry on business & do every other human thing. And if possible let her prove too that she can do each & all of these & be a true woman in other relations also. If it be true that a woman *cannot be* a wife & mother consistently with the exercise of a profession, it justifies to a great extent the argument of our antagonists who say that very thing. For myself I protest against this doctrine. The more high our ideal of life, the more careful we should be against improper ties—the more dangerous is our experiment in marrying, but still the possibility & propriety of a connection with *an equal to ourselves* remains unaltered. I think if the pursuit of any human profession disqualified me for marriage or any other relation necessary to the highest developement of the soul, I, as a man, should spurn the profession and prefer eternal exile from the paths of men, to falsehood to Nature & Destiny. But herein I think is the legitimate function of Reason, to so organize and construct our circumstances that we may reconcile the conflict of circumstances & duties and be true to our *whole nature* & live a symmetrical, rational life true to all our faculties.

I hope you will forgive me for this very unintentional digression. I shall try to steer clear of discussion hereafter and trust to Nature to back my opinions on this, or any other topic. Knowing as I do, how fully your time is occupied, I neither hope nor expect that you will feel able to reply. If you do, you may make your letter just as short as you please. I shall consider three words & your signature as more than an equivalent. Good bye & believe me

Your friend Henry B. Blackwell

P.S. I see by the Tribune that a Miss Olive Rose of Maine has just been elected "Register of Deeds" by a handsome majority over a gentleman, her opponent. Also that on appeal to the Supreme Court, the Judge has given Jane Trainer to her father, a just decision, but containing the rascally statement that whereas an illegitimate child belongs to its mother, a legitimate one belongs to *the father* in preference, because *he has to support it!* What a farce this *Justice* is!

H. B. B.

Boston, June 21, 1853

My dear Friend

I came home last evening and found at the Anti Slavery office, your valuable and valued gift and letter. Thank you for both. As I have the opportunity this summer, I shall be happy to walk in the centuries that are gone with "the solemn-thoughted Plato," and to owe the luxury to you.

I was much interested in your accounts of the Welds. I have ever felt that they were noble and true to their own standard. That from their standpoint they acted in harmony with their highest convictions, though I never could understand it, and do not now. To me, it is entirely unaccountable how one who is struggling in the waves to rescue a drowning child, can leave it to contend alone, and feebly, with the devouring elements, quietly saying, "There is a higher life for me than this." They could do it and turn to other and noble duties, and for them I have no doubt it was right. The world may be more benefited by the good, brave children they stopped to rear, than it could have been had they continued in the field. None but "He who sees the end from the beginning," can know. So each individual, according to the best of his ability must decide for himself. I hope as you suggest, that they will yet actively aid in settling the question of "associative life." He who finds what our true social relations are, will be one of the world's greatest benefactors. While I acquiesce in this withdrawal from active life, for myself I see no choice but constant conflict—all unnatural—made necessary by the horrid wrongs of society, by circumstances which it will be impossible to change until long after the "grave has laid its cold honors" over all those who now live. I submit to it as a sad necessity from which multitudes may be saved in "the good time which we should aid in bringing if some now yield to it."

I am willing and happy to do it, and to suffer the loss which must result to my personal, harmonious developement. Millions of slaves sighing for freedom; the great soul of Womanhood crushed and degraded; outcast children and drunken parents, should not be left to suffer on because the developement of a few weighed more than that of all of these.

But I have a bright ideal for the Future when wrong will be subdued, that each man and each woman may give to his own intellectual, moral, and physical nature the fullest, developement. Then the song of mortals may blend with that of the "morning stars" and be indeed "only a little lower than the angels."

I am much obliged to you for the suggestion to "measure actual marriages by the standard of those who are parties to them," rather than by my own. It is a relief to me. They are not so bad, and do not suffer, being what they are, as I should in their place. The character of the parties, no doubt, has much to do with that of the rest of the relation, but the idea of marriage as held by the mass of people is a false one. So they do not rise higher than their own idea. What you say relative to woman sustaining all natural relations, and business relations at the same time, suggests so much that I must leave it, either for another letter, or for conversation.

The rascally statement that a legitimate child belongs to the father in preference to its mother, is a simple fact of law to which a legal marriage degrades every such mother. Perhaps the "mass of men are not intentionally unjust to women." We shall see when we come to claim and use our equal rights. If the mass of women are not consciously oppressed, multitudes are. Your idea of a remedy of the action of society, is true I think.

If my "views change on certain subjects, change with them." I have been able to do so hitherto, and hope to in the future, but on certain subjects, I see no possibility of change however much I might desire it.

"May you be my friend and write me occasionally?" The traits of character you have shown me make me glad to welcome you to the rank of a friend, and since words from those who mean to live true and good, to impart and receive, I shall be glad too, to have you write me at any time when you are so disposed. After our very frank conversation, you will not misunderstand me here, nor give to this ready welcome of your friendship, and your letters, any other than their true value. I am sorry that the interests of trade take you into those sickly regions. May you be spared their infection. Ever may you find a love of truth and its Author, more to you than human endearments.

Sincerely your friend
Lucy Stone

Walnut Hills, Cincinnati
July 2. 1853

Dear Miss Lucy

Thank you for your good, kind letter. I received it on the 24th, three days after it was written and have been reading it over at intervals ever since. Since I returned from the East I have been quite busy preparing for my journey & attending to business matters which have accumulated in my absence. At first it seemed quite strange to me, to find myself again in Ohio. The large familiar woods with the beech trees spreading out their branches almost to the ground & the sugar maples with their green symmetrical tops look more beautiful than ever in contrast with the brushy tangled stunted evergreen growth of the East. After all, "there is no place like home." The country is fairly parched with drought. For six weeks there has not been a single shower and during three days & nights past the thermometer has been ranging from 85 to 98 in the shade all the time. But when I get out of the dust & noise of the City into our quiet, unpretending, free & easy homestead with its doors & windows all open, surrounded by shade trees, with nobody about but Mother my two brothers & my books, my seven weeks in N. York & New England seem like a dream & it requires a few little tangible entities like your letter to convince me that I really have been absent.

And so, you are probably at this very time, busy with the meagre records of Anne Hutchinson's earnest, enthusiastic, dreary life. I know at present but little more of her than I have learned from Bancroft & my school history. My impression of her is that she was a noble, persecuted woman of the true martyr spirit, but too much the victim of delusion & religious monomania to be altogether a heroine. I have supposed her to be wanting in intellectual coherence, real wisdom & *balance* of character. But I hope I have underestimated her & that I shall some day, through you, learn to place her amongst my august images of Saints & Exemplars.

Do you know I quite envy you your position as lecturer, engaged in the advocacy of great though unpopular ideas. With all its privations & sacrifices, it is an intellectual life & one identified with principles & elevated by them. Above all, it is a useful one, preparing the way for the *good time* in which you have so devout & beautiful a faith. The very *isolation*, which your opinions, your occupation, above all your dress necessarily incur, has something to me strangely attractive. In thought as in Nature there is something bracing in the air of solitude. I am myself naturally social in all my tastes and habits. I love even too well the sympathy and approbation of my fellow creatures. And therefore I love & reverence the more the motives which lead you to devote yourself to the highest Truth you can attain & to *live your own life* regardless of all the losses which consistency may entail upon you.

Well—perhaps you will ask me—How can *you* reconcile it to your views—instead of going & doing likewise & spending your few & fleeting years as a preacher of the great church of Humanity—to see month follow month & the irrevocable years go by—& you still engaged, like everyone else, in the selfish struggle for material riches? If you do not ask me that question I am sure that I often ask it of myself very seriously. And I sometimes hesitate as to the correctness of my own intention still for at least a year, or two longer to refrain from *active* devotion to only things worth living for. My own feeling in the matter is this—I am not yet thirty—Unless some accident shorten my life I may hope to live thirty years more. My general opinions are I presume in great measure matured. Yet I have reason every day to feel that I want wisdom. I find in every question even in this of slavery—wheels within wheels—difficulty beneath difficulty. The more I consider it the more complex it becomes. It is easy to say it is wrong, foolish, inhuman, inexcusable. Of course, it is & we must & will say so. But how to take the system as it is & do it away?

Here is the problem. The American Antislavery Society has used the sternest denunciations for 20 years. I honor them for it. The hard names are all deserved. It has done them good to say them. But I have seen & known enough of Southern men to feel that this mode of talking does a great deal of real harm as well as good. It does not meet the point. The prejudices of ignorant & excitable people born & brought up in contact with the institution are embittered not softened. They feel keenly that the negro, *as he is*, is not their equal, is not likely to make a judicious use of freedom—they know that practically (human nature being better than the statute book) there is a great deal of happiness amongst many of their "servants" as they prefer to call them—their interests, habits, tastes, modes of living are all involved, & they *cannot* receive as just, or friendly the severe censures of abolitionists. The Absolute truth of these censures gives them point & sting, but does not carry conviction. When they come North too, they see, as strangers, the worst features of our society. They see in all our towns & cities the working classes, the actual producers, in a state of very complete & real servitude & degradation. Bad as is their condition, they exaggerate its evils & honestly though *very* illogically exclaim—"It is only a choice of evils after all." Now dont think I am going to turn apologist for slavery. I hate it as the worst form in which the devil has ever incarnated himself in society—I feel bound to loathe it. But still, to do so effectively & justly—we must adapt ourselves to it as it *really* is & not as it abstractly appears. We should avoid *unnecessarily* awakening the prejudices which unavoidably exist & endeavor to produce *conviction* in the minds of people whose very life is so different from our own. Am I prepared as yet to grapple with so vast a problem. And it is not only so with slavery, but with intemperance, above all with the Woman question greater than all & more difficult therefore than all. It is easy to take sides & fight against, or even for, them—in the spirit of a partisan. But how difficult it is to meet them in that of a philosopher!

Now all this feeling of diffidence on my part is to some extent a damper on my desire to go right to speaking & lecturing as a profession. It makes me feel very strongly that when I do—I must take a position altogether independant. I must be free to speak just where when & what I think best. To do so & to study as one ought, so as to think first & speak afterwards, requires the command of ones own time & action—in other words *pecuniary independance*, the basis of that. Now, after a good many years of hard work, (for my father died a stranger in a strange city, leaving a widow & nine children accustomed to comparative luxury & *entirely* destitute), I have attained a position in business, where, in every human probability, in three years more I can realize such a position & meanwhile fulfill my private duties to relatives & friends whose comfort & position are linked with mine.

Am I right, or am I not, when I decide to continue these three years as I am, in opposition to my wishes, to my character, to my ambition? I wish you could tell me Miss Lucy—for I declare I sometimes get a little puzzled myself. This is why, amongst other reasons, I told you when you gave me your reasons against marrying—that I had at present *nothing to say—nothing to ask*. When I have settled my own course of life, it will be time enough to invite one who, in her own case, has already done so, to share it. Before that time it would be premature, if not worse. For I quite agree with you, that a connection which would be inconsistent with the most efficient prosecution of our highest aims ought never to be formed. However in other respects desirable, it would be on the whole degrading & could never confer real & permanent satisfaction.

I hope you will believe me when I say, that I should consider it a *crime* on my part & a *misfortune* on your's, if I could undertake & succeed in *mesmerising* you, (as you charged me with, once) into any such an attachment. Such is not the marriage I would form. My idea of the relation involves no sacrifice of individuality but its perfection—no limitation of the carreer of one, or both but its extension. I would not have my wife drudge, as Mrs. Weld has had to do in the house, while I found nothing on earth to do but dig ditches. I would not even consent that my wife should stay at home to rock the baby when she ought to be off addressing a meeting, or organizing a Society. Perfect *equality* in this relationship (as in every other one where human beings are concerned) I would have—but it should be the equality of Progress, of Developement, not of Decay. If both parties cannot study more, think more, feel more, talk more & work more than they could alone, I will remain an old bachelor & adopt a Newfoundland dog or a terrier as an object of affection.

Perhaps you will say that in the present state of Society such an Union is impracticable. This is where I think you err. Remember that neither you, nor anybody else ever can nor did lecture five times a week, ten months in the year & spend the other two in compiling fresh ones *always*. This is one chapter in your book of Life. It has already lasted some years. It may last a good many more, but like all other chapters, even the longest, it will come to an end. I do not mean to say you will ever cease to speak in public, at least till you grow old; I hope you will not. But such excessive & continuous labor of one kind will give place to a more varied & different sphere of duty. Perhaps you may write more & speak less. Besides your voice may fail, you may no longer feel the same impulse to speak—many contingencies may happen. I say all this, not to renew a subject which may perhaps be unpleasant to you, but simply to explain my position & my feelings when I say I am perfectly willing to see you pursue just what course you deem proper & fitting on this as well as every other subject—only requesting you to keep clear of the laws of the old Medes & Persians & give me a fair chance in the long run.

I spent an evening a few days since at Mrs *Ernst's*—the lady who may be called the Alpha and Omega of Cincinnati antislavery. She has left for the East & I hope will meet you. I told her that I had made your acquaintance & was very desirous that you should come to Cin^{ti} & lecture this Fall. . . . Should you come to the West, Mother & Sisters, two of whom will probably be here, will hope to have you make our house your home while here.

I took the occasion this morning while conversing with an intimate friend of mine here, Judge Matthews a free soil man & one of our most talented young lawyers to enquire of him the probability of a woman's being admitted to the Bar here if she applied & was properly qualified & of her being able to obtain practice afterwards. He says that he thinks there would be *no difficulty* in getting admission. That while on the Bench a year or two since a woman applied & presented a certificate from Gholson & Miner, very respectable lawyers of this City that she had studied at their office & was duly qualified. He said he was himself consulted & he gave his opinion that she had a perfect right to an examination as the law contained no reservation nor description of sex & she was of course a citizen. As to the other point—i.e. getting practice—he said he saw no *insurmountable* obstacles—none indeed but the general prejudice of community. This however he thought would be exceedingly strong—much more so indeed than in the case of women physicians—there being in that profession an *especial* adaptedness to woman which the law does not seem as a general rule to offer. He thought & I think with reason, that very few *women* would consult a female lawyer—owing to an absurd confidence which they generally not unnaturally feel in the superior ability and formation of men. That this would be so I have no doubt, for Elizabeth finds in this prejudice amongst women themselves, the main difficulty she has first to overcome. Altogether his opinion was that the *study* of law would be a most admirable & desirable one for women—the admission to the Bar a feasible thing & the *practice* of law a *possible* one, but offering many great difficulties & very slight inducements to its *practice*. The lady, I spoke of above, did not press her admission, has since married & the matter therefore, in her case, was not brought to a decision. . . . I think his opinion is entitled to a great deal of weight & if you, or Mrs. Stanton, or any other capable woman ever wish to study, I think we might find here respectable lawyers with whom to read & a liberal set of people to admit afterwards. . . .

I find that here in Ohio our laws with regard to married women though in the main founded on the same unjust basis as elsewhere are in some respects more liberal. The right of a husband to use personal coercion is I believe disallowed. Divorces are granted not only in adultery & bigamy, but also for fraudulent contract, wilful absence of 3 years, cruelty, gross neglect of duty, 3 years habitual drunkenness & for imprisonment for crime. All such divorces are total & the wife where the husband is to blame retains alimony & I believe power. Generally too in cases of Divorce the Courts award the children to the party *not in fault*—though the general principle prevails that unless such an award is made the father's claim is paramount. I see too in Mansfield's "Rights of Woman" a Connecticut Court has decided against the husband's right to the custody of his wife & that it has been finally decided in New York that a husband could not take away his minor daughter from his wife where the divorce rested on the own wife's refusal to accompany him to Nova Scotia to live. I hope you will forgive me for this long letter. On the 5th July I set out into Indiana & Illinois to be gone seven weeks. If the Spirit move me I shall write you again after awhile—& as I shall pay the postage, you can burn them if you dont have the time to read them & either answer them or not as you feel inclined & have liesure. I have just finished reading Plato's Republic. In his 5th & other Books you will find his ideas of women, which are a queer mixture of good sense & folly. Hoping this hot summer is not quite so oppressive to you in Massachusetts as here & that you may find time to do a great deal of study. I remain dear Miss Lucy—

Your friend Henry B Blackwell

P.S. I find that here in the West, as everywhere else, Mr. Garrison's connection with the "anti-Bible Convention," as it is called, in offering those resolutions is bitterly commented upon. Unless such conventions in future can be so got up or managed as to take more positive & distinct ground, I think, as the result of sober thought, after attending the last, that they will do more harm than good—I think Mr. Garrison's resolutions are *true*, yet I confess they were & are a source of regret to me. Nothing is gained by these sweeping attacks upon the Clergy nor on the Bible—No principle is invoked & I think they do harm—don't you?

West Brookfield July 27, 1853

Dear Mr. Blackwell

I was glad to learn, from your welcome letter, that you were safely sheltered, at Walnut Hills—and can well imagine how heartily you exclaimed, "there is no place like home," after the changes and chances, & weariness, of seven weeks travel, and how doubly grateful, in such circumstances, the quiet of your own home. Your forests seemed more majestic than ever, in contrast with our little woody growth. Your trees *are* grander, and more beautiful, than ours, but as I always take the side of the weak, especially, if they cannot *speak* for themselves, I am bound to defend our "brushy, tangled, stunted" trees, and to affirm, what cant be denied, that they *are* a beauty and a blessing, and that with our wild hills, and rocks, and health-giving air, and soft pure water, every child of N. England feels that there is no place like his home. You are now, I suppose in the Wabash Valley, breathing infection, scorched by day, and devoured by mosquitoes at night. I surely do not envy you.

Will the associative idea,—the unitary interest of the race, ever enable us to find all human good, so near our own vine, that we shall not need to go elsewhere, to secure it? I hope so. But a long, weary road, lies between this time, and that. Still let us *hope* for it. You speak, of the good, that comes in a life like mine, notwithstanding its privations, and its isolation. The privations I have learned to endure, and the isolation, I scarcely regret; while the certainty that I am *living usefully*, brings a deep, and *abiding* happiness, which the thorns by the wayside, are not able to destroy. The going to College, (an unwomanly thing) robbed me of many early friends who have never returned; Garrisonian anti slavery lecturing, made the number still smaller, and my dress, diminished the remnant, wonderfully. But they who remain, through the unpopularity & ultraism, and the consequent hatred, are the truest of the true. What I have lost in the *number* of my friends, I have more than made up, in the *superior quality*, of the few who are left. It is better far, to be *alone, and be true*, than to procure companionship by being false; and one can well afford to purchase isolation, if the price, is a life rendered full, and *intense*, by a *worthy purpose*. The consciousness of rectitude, is "its exceeding great reward."

You ask what you ought to do, in the circumstances. I think no one can aid you, to decide. I surely should not dare advise, if I thought you would be influenced by it. Questions of duty, should always be settled, by ones own convictions, since no one else, *can* know so well, all the circumstances, external, and internal. You have, evidently, resolved the question thoroughly, in your own mind, & a real desire to make your life a true one, will I have no doubt, enable you to come to the right conclusion. Allow me however, to say that I regard *moral* independence, as far more needful, than pecuniary independence, though the latter, is certainly desirable. Then too, one should be careful, lest in the wild struggle for material wealth, he lose the *disposition*, to aid his fellow, to the gold that does not perish with the using. We do indeed need time to think, before we speak, but if we wait until all the difficulties connected with any important movement, are solved, we "shall die & leave our errand unfulfilled."

Wendell Phillips said, at the first National Woman's Rights Convention, "The ultimate consequences of any great social change, the broadest, and most farsighted intellect is utterly unable to foresee. Ask yourself on all such occasions, if there be any element of right and wrong in the question, any principle of clear natural justice that turns the scale. If so, take your part, with the perfect and abstract right, and trust God to see, that it shall prove the expedient." As no one can see *all* the consequences, so neither can he see the *whole details* to arrive at those consequences; but he need never be left long in the dark, relative, to the step necessary to be taken next.

The Anti Slavery and Woman's Rights Revolutions do not differ, in their philosophy from that of all other Revolutions. *They* have ever been made successful, simply by a *change* in the *ideas*, and *feelings*, of those who are the object, and the cause, of the revolution. And to ensure this change, a *thorough discontent*, with the existing wrong, must be created, and this is done, by depicting it, in all its naked deformity,—calling every crime and every criminal, by the right name, and if anger most intense swell the bosom of the wrong doer, it is proof the Truth's barbed arrow is fast in the right place. And his anger is far more desirable, than a quiet indifference. Those who *create* this discontent, *must be hated:*—Almost all will deem them too severe and denunciating, while the contest is waging; but *posterity* will marvel, that the *censures* fell *so far behind* the dreadful reality.

When *by their persistent fidelity*, Public Sentiment begins to change, Harriet Beecher Stowe, can take the audience *they* have made for her, and secure their assent, and affection too. And the thoughtless say, "how much better it would have been, if Garrison had done as she has." They do not recognize the fact, that but for the deep and intense interest, *he* had created in the SUBJECT, *she* would have found no readers. The *result* of the course that has been pursued shows that it is the wisest that could have been adopted. . . .

But leaving this subject, upon which, my deep interest made me dwell too long, I fear—Let me thank you, for having given me your beautiful idea of marriage. So far as you have developed it, it seems to me wholly true. I have been often told, by ladies, that no man could ever assent to *such* a marriage. There have been a few I knew, who would. I am glad to add your name to the list. How soon the character of the race would change if pure, and equal, real marriages could take the place of the horrible relations that now bear that sacred name! When you "have settled your own course of life it will be time enough to ask another, to share it with you." Yes, and it will be all too soon until a thorough knowledge of each others character, enables you to know if there is *affinity* between you, which can be the basis of a changeless affection.

Here, I think, is the grave mistake. Parties do not know each other, marry, are disappointed, disgusted, and atone for their rashness by a life filled with sorrows and discords, which affect not them only but their children. On the other hand, when a real marriage is formed by the mutual attraction of two souls, whose "perfect love casts out all fear;"—when thought and feeling and hope and aspirations,—all of joy, and all of grief, and all of life are more than gladly shared,—the character of both, will be ennobled, and being developed more harmoniously, will secure, not only greater happiness to both but will enable each to be more useful. The difficulty or one difficulty is, persons do not find real complement, and so, instead of finding themselves able to "study more, think more, feel more, talk more, & work more," hope is blighted and the whole being dwarfed. When the circumstances, do not allow parties, an opportunity for that thorough acquaintance, by which they can know whether or not, there *is* adaptation between them, it is worse than madness to think of assuming a relation which will put in peril, the happiness, and usefulness, of a whole life, and very probably be destructive of both. Do not think that I regard true marriages, as impracticable. They are so, only as far, as *the true idea, is wanting.* Wherever one exists, there, center, life's blessings. But how rarely they are found!

You ask me "to keep clear of the old Medes & Persians, and give you a fair chance, in the long run." It would be wrong for me to allow you to suppose, that I expect a time will ever come, when I shall feel released, from the obligation, to pursue my present course of life. The objects I seek to accomplish, will not be attained until long after my body has gone to ashes. While so few can, or are willing, to give themselves wholly to the work, the world so imperatively needs, all the more necessary is it, that those who can do so, should not falter. You say that "contingencies may happen" and so they may, but I can concieve of none, except *absolute inability*, which can release me. But a worn-out life is not worth giving, or recieving. I know that by this course, some departments of my nature, will not have their full developement *here.* And if this life, were our only space, for the perfection of character, I should then, have no right to deprive myself of anything, which would secure that developement. But this little life, is to the whole of existence as a pinhole, to the whole of space. I believe too, that every individual, will, somewhere, in the Ages come to the fullest development. So it is only a question of time. And I can wait. "Earth waits long for her harvest time, And the aloe, in the northern clime, Waits an hundred years for its flower. If the aloe wait an hundred years, And God's times are so long indeed, For simple things, as flower and weed, That gather only the light and gloom, For what great treasures of joy and dole, of life and death, perchance, must the soul, Ere it bloom in heavenly peace, find room"?

Pardon that mesmerising word, which escaped me, in that strange hour. I would gladly acquit you of all such intentions. In passing from this subject, allow me to express the hope that the wants of your large, social, and affectional nature, may be fully met, in one who shall be worthy of you, and who will aid you, in realizing your highest idea of a true marriage. I read your sister's book, with a great deal of interest in its style, and matter. It is worthy of the first woman physician. Its practical character, renders it extremely valuable. . . .

As to Plato, the wise old pagan, I have not yet found him prosy or dull. How shrewdly he uses the arguments of others, to confute

them! How deeply philosophic! In many things, he is far in advance
of the present time. His idea of the equality of women, and men, and
their common participation in affairs of State would be scorned by
the wise-acres of our Constitutional Convention. . . . I dont know
but it is wrong to inflict so long a letter, in such an illegible hand
upon a businessman, but pardon me this time, I will not commit the
same offense again.

Walnut Hills August 24, 1853

Dear Miss Lucy
    Your kind letter was the first thing that greeted me on reaching
home early yesterday morning. I had followed the Wabash to its
mouth & taken steamboat at Evansville for Cincinnati which I
reached at daybreak. As the light began to dawn I walked out & upon
entering my room found the little yellow treasure with its familiar
postmark & well known handwriting. I say familiar & well known,
because I had carried your first one with me on my travels as a sort
of talisman & kept it always about me, so that, as you may suppose,
I can testify to your handwriting hereafter if it should ever be necessary. In the course of forty days however my "talisman" began to
show some slight signs of delapidation in spite of my care & I am
very glad to be able to replace it by a new charm of equal potency.
Whether the credit is due to any magical virtues of your first letter,
or not, I can't say, but I certainly enjoyed most excellent health all
the time of my absence & in spite of the great heat returned weighing
some eight or ten pounds more than when I saw you last & indeed in
every way more comfortable than I felt while in the East this
spring. . . .
    About two weeks after I left home I visited that little village of
Bellville, concerning which you entertain so paradisical a recollection.
As soon as I got through with my business, I left two companions
with whom I was travelling, & walked down the National road to
"Uncle Jemmy Egan's." I found the old gentleman outside the house
& asked him if he remembered two ladies who stopped several weeks
at his house three years ago, one of whom was so sick. He welcomed
me very heartily & carried me in to see his wife "Aunt Ann" who no

sooner learned that I had seen you in Mass. this summer, than she made twenty enquiries about Mrs Stone & yourself, particularly to know whether you were either of you married yet, or likely to be so. Both the old folks seemed to have a very kind & pleasant remembrance of you & gave me all the details of your illness—taking great credit of course to themselves for their excellent nursing & attention. Aunt Ann took me into the inner room & showed me the identical bed & bedstead which you occupied & the one Mrs Stone used—I expect everything looked about as it did & I surveyed the whole apartment with a great deal of interest. . . .

How I wish I could be present at your two glorious meetings in New York next month. But I cannot be, so I shall watch the papers with great interest for accounts of proceedings. If I possibly can though, I mean to be at Cleveland on Oct. 4 to attend the woman's convention there & hope I may meet you at that place. But I think it is too bad that you should be in Cleveland without at least visiting Cincinnati & I hope that we shall get you down our way yet. . . .

We just had a very interesting slave case here—the first since 1850 in Cin^{ti}. It was taken before Judge McLean to test the constitutionality of the fugitive law. As might have been expected from a man who has cherished aspirations for the Presidency, he decided that the law was constitutional & remanded the fugitive to bondage. His master however has offered to take somewhat less than the "market value" of the "chattel" & to subscribe $50 himself towards the sum & a subscription has been raised to purchase the man's freedom. I am sorry that our City has been thus degraded. Still more sorry that the devilish law has been thus endorsed. When will an American Judge Mansfield prove equal to his responsibility & win a glorious immortality by a contrary decision. This shows what the antislavery of such men as Judge McLean is worth! . . .

I feel everyday more forcibly how comparatively unimportant are the differences between earnest reformers & how unspeakably more wise it is to agree to differ where we must & to work together where we can. How melancholy—nay, how mean it seems—when two noble, honest earnest anti-slavery men like Phillips & Mann permit a friendly controversy on a question of personal duty (which, as you truly say, "everyone must settle for himself") to degenerate into personal bickerings & innuendoes. As a friend and admirer of *both*, I am sorry to see it—as an anti slavery man I am still more sorry. . . . For myself I have a horror equally of fanaticism & eclecticism. I am not willing to look at the world solely through anti slavery or temperance, or womans-rights, or scientific spectacles. Nor am I willing to shrink from looking straight at it through each & all of these. I think a wise man should be a *many-sided* fanatic. . . .

It seems funny to me to find myself thus, in my letters to you, taking apparently a *semi-conservative* position. I assure you I am in my temperament & impulses singularly devoid of caution. I am looked upon by all my acquaintances as a thorough-bred Radical—& so, thank God, I am! But it is easier to be wise on paper than in life, is it not?

I am glad you sympathize with my theory of *equality* in *marriage*. I knew you would do so of course but still it is satisfactory to hear you express it. But your lady friends were not far out, when they said "no man would ever submit to such a marriage." In practice a minority I think might do so, but *in theory* scarcely any. The *idea* of a loving & protective superiority is *ingrained* in men. They do not thereby suppose any conscious oppression—but regard it as a fixed fact that women do not & cannot desire absolute equality in the active affairs of life.

This summer, I have been travelling in a carriage with two business friends. Every day we discussed anti-slavery & woman's rights. The former to a certain extent they could accept. But the whole womans movement they could not swallow *at all*. My idea of marriage especially struck them as ludicrous & unnatural. Yet both are honest, intelligent & affectionate & will make *excellent husbands*. For women, like men, in that stage of developement, are incapable of appreciating the gospel of *individualism* & the glory of mental & material independence. I believe nineteen women out of twenty would be unhappy with a husband who, like myself, would repudiate supremacy. The proof of my opinion is that the great majority of people, in endeavoring to imagine a contrary state of things, conceive of the woman as the *leader* & the man as the *subservient*. Of course if there is to be a *head* to the family, while women are actually so inferior in developement of mind, no man can think with patience of playing the "hen-pecked husband." Hence the inveterate prejudice you have to contend with. Practically, the superior woman does oftentimes take the lead of the inferior husband & must always do so. But this to my mind is simply just as bad & no worse than, the opposite mismatch. But analyze the opposition to our view—it is based on an apparent *incapability* of understanding *absolute equality* between the sexes on the part of most people. Where there is no subjection on either side there can be, of course, no degradation or conflict of dignities.

I have an intimate friend, a bookseller of this City, a young man of fine mind & wonderful energy of character—a strong antislavery progressive thinker. He married a year ago a lady of most beautiful, amiable character but of an intellect not at all comparable with his own. He seems perfectly satisfied & happy. We often talk on this question of marriage—he differs from me. He thinks it is dangerous for two persons of strong mind to marry—that the great requisite is the possession of opposite qualities for the supply of each other's deficiencies—that while a certain unity of sentiment & sympathy of opinion is desirable—too much resemblance on the whole is very detrimental to the happiness of married people. He laughs at me for my too high ideal. He says I shall never marry in the world, for I shall never find a woman who will come up to my standards.

Now I have felt for years the most imperious necessity for marriage. At times I think I *must* quit dreaming & get a wife. But when it comes to the point, I find that I *cannot* forego my ideal. Equality with me is a passion. I dislike equally to assume, or to endure authority. But the great difficulty in realizing a true marriage after you find the right persons is that all the arrangements of Society are made for the average convenience—& fetter a woman with household cares & ties, while they impose on a man the whole burden of acquiring subsistence. I confess I see no hope of making the future of women *as a sex* what it should be, except by household association. So long as our present system of isolated families is maintained married women will be greatly precluded from public & professional pursuits. And indeed when I consider how degrading & unworthy all human pursuits not strictly scientific or literary are now, I do not feel any great anxiety to see many women undertake them. I feel so thorough a contempt for the whole sphere of business & am so desirous of getting out of it, that I am not able to get up any enthusiasm at the prospect of female merchants, or merchants clerks. I do indeed want to see the scope of women's employment enlarged, so that they may be better able to support themselves, when necessary, but it is only as a choice of evils.

You say in your letter that you never expect to give up lecturing & speaking but from death or old age. I certainly hope you never may, unless for some even wider sphere of action. As a writer if favorably situated, you might perhaps reach even more minds & in connexion with occasional public speaking be even more efficient. Such a position, with the ear of the public, is a grand one but somewhat difficult to attain. I hope to reach it some day through the medium of a widely circulated western newspaper. But surely you never did me the injustice to suppose that I could desire, under any circumstances, that you should withdraw yourself from public effort. Had I been Count Albert of Rudolstadt, I should have desired Consuelo to remain upon the Stage from my love of Art. How much more should I desire that the glorious gift of eloquence which you certainly possess should not be withdrawn from the advocacy of great & unpopular Truths to be wasted upon a few, however dear. It would be like buying some beautiful spot of Nature hitherto the resort of hundreds & fencing it in with "no admittance" & "Spring guns" placarded in true "dog in the manger" fashion.

But for myself I dont see why, in order to do good, you should find it necessary to treat yourself a great deal worse than the Southerners treat their negroes, by depriving yourself of entrance into those personal relations which as you yourself acknowledge are a *want of our nature* & which I regard as a *duty* of our very organization. If this true idea of marriage cannot be realized, what is the use of having it? How can it be so eloquently preached as by *living it out* in practice. You speak of marriage to those in it. They may say to you with reason, as they have said to me—"you never have been married, or you would not so regard it. You know nothing about it." Your idea of the duty of sacrificing the lower to the higher I *fully approve*. But I think you estimate too low the sacred law of the affections, which Theodore Parker places with reason *above* the intellectual faculties—yes—& above even the *moral sense*. I, at first, thought Parker erred in setting the affections above the sense of right & wrong, but on reflection, I agree with him.

I think you are very right in saying that it is absolute madness to enter into marriage until *you know* thoroughly the whole nature of the other party. So I think, too. But if that nature possess the genuine affinity—are circumstances so satanic that marriage involves the withdrawal from public life? I do not see that. A woman unsuitably married like Mrs Stanton may find herself fettered—or in difficult circumstances like Mrs Weld formerly. But a woman who unites herself with a fellow worker with sufficient means & position to prevent the necessity of her drudging—free to be at home when she pleases & to leave it when she thinks it best—with a home of her own to rest & study & with friends to relieve her many responsibilities—is this a position necessarily less influential than your present one? I dont wonder at your resolving never to marry. Situated as women are I think you are wise in omitting the relation altogether from your prospectus of life. But if in the mysterious Providence of God you ever find the right person, you will have to enlarge & vary your theory to greet the unexpected Advent. I do not ask you to assume that I, or anyone else, am that person. I only wish I might prove to be so—that's all.

I am glad you like Plato. I do, too, though his arguments are often far from convincing to me. I like his idea of women in the affairs of state. But I dont agree with him in thinking that the souls of men & women are *alike*—simply because, if I did so, I should on the whole, be compelled to agree with him also in his further statement "that women are in all cases *weaker than men.*" Now I do not believe women are *really* weaker than men except in physical strength for that would be a sort of inferiority—but I think they are *different* It is said "mind has no sex"—I am half inclined to believe that it has sex too. I remember we talked that matter over together & finally came to the rational conclusion that we didnt understand the matter very well. During my travels I read Consuelo a second time with more pleasure & profit than the first time some years ago. I do not believe that a *male mind* could have written that great book. . . .

I think after receiving such an *interminable* letter as this, you may spare yourself any apology for your comparatively brief epistles. I never yet found a friend's letter *too long*—may you not be compelled in this case to say otherwise. Let me know whether you will come to Cincinnati—if so when & how many lectures will you give. Be sure to give me also such directions that I may address you without delay. Good night dear Miss Lucy & believe me

Your friend Henry B. Blackwell

Cincinnati September 9, 1853

Dear Miss Lucy

. . . Do not think that I, out here in the West, am ignorant
altogether of your movements & proceedings. From the Liberator I
have gleaned little items of your Vermont experience with great interest. Last night about 11 oclock . . . I sat down with the "Tribunes" for the week previous & read therein the proceedings of the
Whole World's Temperance Convention, the Sunday meetings of the
Anti slavery Society & the Vegetarian Festival. . . . Thank you for
your fearless & faithful advocacy of the doctrine of Divorce. It is absurd that men who have given up the old idea of *Sacramental* marriage, should claim for the most sublime & responsible contracts a
continuance after all its objects are perished, and its influences incur-
ably vitiated. Better chain a living husband to the dead body of his
wife, or bury the wife in the fiery ashes of her husband's sepulchre
than thus make a violated contract a finality of ruin to the unoffending
party. What right has the mother who suckles her offspring on *milk-
punch* to further duties of maternity? Why should a man legally
compel a woman to become the mother of embryo drunkards? Mr
Greeley's protest against your doctrine seems to have been un-
accompanied by any reasoning whatsoever. Meanwhile Ohio, I rejoice to say, recognizes drunkenness as sufficient ground for divorce.

But, Miss Lucy, I liked best your Sunday evening discourse to
the 3000 people, rowdies included. It was a fine exploit to make them
hear you when Mrs Mott had *given in* & gentlemen were unable to
be heard. I felt to wish I could have collared some of the rascals &
shaken a little of their cheap bully-courage out of them, but I hope
the truths you told them will not be altogether lost. . . .

I am afraid you will think from the *critical* remarks contained in
my last letters that I am only a halfhearted anti-slavery man after all.
Believe me it is not so! I have indeed an inveterate dislike of *parti-
sanship*. I want to see *all sides* of a question & get the absolute truth
of the matter whether it makes for me, or against me. I feel pro-
foundly how we all *trifle* with the truth. To hear some anti-slavery
men felicitate themselves you would think slavery was already abolished. People dont realize that the *blood of souls* flows daily. We few
of us do.

A few evenings since I was looking over my father's papers. He was a man of fine intelligence, had been wealthy by his own energy in business as a sugar refiner in England & New York but having lost heavily by the commercial reverses of /38 emigrated to Cincinnati, to die within a month from a western fever under calomel treatment. In England he had been an Abolitionist & a liberal in politics when to be so was an affair of some heroism. In America from /32, he was one still—was a frequent contributor to the Emancipator and at the time of his death had, amid the cares of extensive & engrossing manufacturing concerns, commenced a series of sketches of his impressions of America. As I sate in the lamp-light looking through long files of forgotten transactions—mingled with occasional hasty utterances of indignant scorn & earnest faith the old boyish days came back. I felt again the strange & dignified fascination which my father always exercised. The old apostolic anti-slavery spirit in which I was born & baptised roused up in me again & I seemed once more to hear the eloquent voice of Geo. Thompson amid the crash of brick bats & the howls of the mob.

Dont think I undervalue Mr Garrison & his party. I yield to none in reverence for them. Political anti-slavery men are many of them but half galvanized. But the old organization of abolitionists though narrow & proscriptive in their spirit are at least as deep as the sea & as earnest as the stars. Would to heaven I could equal their enthusiasm & principle & yet avoid their faults. But here I am, chained to a narrow circle of cares & occupation which seems to offer me no outlet. My duties to my friends, my *own developement*, which I consider ought to be with each of us *collateral*, not subservient to that of others—my sense of personal independence with which I know that you will sympathize, my consciousness of my own deficiencies of genius & of culture which I desire so far as I can to remedy all seem to say to me, "You must stay where you are still longer—you must earn an independent position *first* & use it worthily afterwards." Is this mere selfish love of Money? Is it a feeling of false pride that I do not choose to be poor & dependant? Is it a lurking personal ambition or vanity? I hope not, though all these faults I detect in myself daily. I reason the matter over with myself & I think my position a correct one.

Yet still, as the inevitable river of Time sweeps life off year by year & sees nothing accomplished but the objects that perish with the using, I fret like a caged bird & feel as though I was guilty for not doing more. My life wants unity. Happy Lucy Stone! You at least have no such riddle to untie. Calm & happy in your self-imposed poverty & isolation you pursue your way—marked out by your judgment & approved by your success. You look at me & everybody else as more or less imperfect embodiments of Goodness & Virtue, but are too wise to let your sympathies be too much entered[?] for any individual. Well I am glad you can do this. I cannot & shall therefore try to get things so shaped as to live a Christian life yet, for a few years before I die at least.

A number of the anti-slavery friends who have heard through Mrs Ernst that you might possibly come out this fall enquired last evening whether you would be out here & seemed desirous of hearing you. Our meeting had unusual interest from the fact that a low loco-foco Criminal Judge Flinn of this City remanded into slavery under most aggravating circumstances three colored people who were brought voluntarily into the City by their master's agent, en route for the South. A writ of habeus corpus was got out & they were brought before Flinn by lawyer Joliffe a whole souled abolitionist and a brother in law of Flinn whose daughter he is educating. This occurred a few days since. Joliffe called a public meeting to take steps to impeach the Judge who has long forfeited public respect by ignorance & dissipation. From a fear of being identified with anti-slavery a large & respectable public meeting unanimous in condemnation could not get a chairman. But resolutions were passed & a committee of three appointed to collect evidence. Next morning Flinn attacked Joliffe in the market house & knocked him down without provocation. Mr Joliffe's health being poor, has been much injured by the excitement which his warm feelings have rendered inevitable & he has had an attack much resembling apoplexy. Last evening he was present however & presented Mrs Ernst with one of the broken fetters taken from the man whom he had vainly attempted to rescue, accompanying the gift with a most earnest & beautiful little speech. Mrs. E. though taken by surprise responded. This, in connection with Judge McLean's late shameful decision on the fugitive law has roused up a great deal of feeling which I hope will not soon be done away.

But I permitted myself to write to you on two accounts & as I will not inflict so long a letter as my last, I will state them. First, in case you accept as I hope you will, under existing circumstances, my suggestion to visit Cincinnati, I enclose an invitation from my sister Ellen, whom you know & who has just returned from the East to make our house your home just as though you were one of our number. . . . The other matter is that you speak of intending to spend Sunday & Monday, the 2^d & 3^d of October next at Niagara on your way to Cleveland. I never was there but once, for four hours in a heavy rain. Two days at Niagara in your company with you at leisure for a good talk would be *an event*. Will you certainly be there on those days & will you permit me to meet you there Sunday morning & accompany you thence to Cleveland? I do not want you to do so if you would rather be *alone*. But if you are willing I will try & get off from business Saturday morning & return from Cleveland home again. Forgive me this second long letter. I certainly try your patience sadly. I hope to hear from you before long. Please remember me to your parents & sisters & brother. Do not overexert yourself in your activity & believe me

Your friend Henry B. Blackwell

Rochester, N.Y. Sept. 24, 1853

Dear Mr. Blackwell:

Mr. Channing has just handed me your note. I expect to be at Niagara at the time specified, and am very willing that you should be there too, though I fear you will not find me very companionable. My soul is always silent before that great Presence; and while I have a world of feeling words always fail me. But we are friends, and can understand silence or speech.

I think you know me well enough to put the right construction upon my consent to meet you at Niagara. I am glad of the friendship of the good whether they be men or women, and sex shall never debar me, (with my consent) from the companionship of such. But believe me Mr. Henry Blackwell when I say, (and Heaven is my witness that I *mean* what I say) that, in the circumstances I have not the remotest desire of assuming any other relations than those I now sustain. I would incur my own heavy censure, if by fault of mine, you did not understand this. But since you do, I shall be very glad of an opportunity to have one good, long, frank talk with you. . . .

> Very sincerely your friend
> Lucy Stone

L ucy and Henry met at Niagara in early October, and for Henry at least, it was a highly romantic occasion. In a letter written months later he spoke of sitting at her feet by the whirlpool "looking down into its dark waters with a passionate & unshared & unsatisfied *yearning* in my heart." Whatever Lucy may have felt, she did not say. She wrote her mother that she had spent Sunday and Monday at Niagara, and had walked over the suspension bridge to the Canadian side. Niagara she described as "a wild, wonderful place," adding she would like to live there as she found the "eternal roar of water . . . so soothing and so grand!" But she didn't mention having any companionship.

From Niagara Lucy and Henry journeyed to Cleveland for the Fourth National Woman's Rights Convention. Henry was elected secretary of the convention, and prompted by his feminist beliefs and his love for Lucy, he gave his first woman's rights speech. "The interests of the sexes are inseparably connected," he said, "and in the elevation of the one lies the salvation of the other. Therefore, I claim a part in this last and grandest movement of the ages, for whatever concerns woman concerns the race." Afterward, Henry recalled that his address was considered to have been a very fine one, though at the time, the *Cleveland Plain Dealer* commented: "Mr. Blackwell spoke too long. He forgot it was a Women's Convention."

Henry also remembered that in the afternoon between the morning and evening meetings, he and Lucy walked to the bluff overlooking Lake Erie and watched the sunset, and "all was affectionate and tender." Lucy, however, related none of this in the letter she wrote her mother; she said only that Sam Brooke, the head of the Ohio Anti-Slavery Society and a former suitor of hers, and "Blackwell" had both attended and made speeches. But she did tell her mother that she was going on to Cincinnati to hold meetings with Lucretia Mott, and instructed her to forward her mail care of Henry B. Blackwell.

Throughout the remainder of October Lucy lectured in and around Cincinnati with Henry making all the arrangements. She stayed with the Blackwell family in Walnut Hills, and was as pleased with them as they were with her. Toward the end of the month Henry's brother Sam confided to his diary: "She is a most admirable woman. By her quiet decision, steady purpose and lofty principle, she reminds me strongly of Elizabeth; and by a certain precision and distinctness of utterance, and personal neatness and good judgement. We have quite adopted her."

From Cincinnati Lucy went on to Louisville, Kentucky. She was in slaveholding country now, and lying awake one night, she mistook the sound of a donkey braying for the cries of a slave being whipped. But she was greatly encouraged by her enthusiastic reception in Louisville and other Southern towns. The halls where she spoke were packed to overflowing, and the local papers printed favorable notices of her meetings.

While she was away from Cincinnati, Henry barraged her with letters and packages, and one letter in particular impressed her so much that she copied part of it in a letter to her sister Sarah, and asked her to preserve it. The letter was from Henry's sister Elizabeth, in answer to one of his about Lucy's resolve never to marry. It contained an eloquent expression of the high ideals with which more than a few young women invested the marriage relationship—ideals which were encouraged by the romantic literature of the period, but which were often difficult to achieve in reality. Thus Elizabeth wrote of wedded love: "This love to a noble soul, is indeed the creation of a new heaven and a new earth, it is a constant inspiration, the thought grows clearer, and larger, the affections expand under its influence, it is perpetually creative, and beautiful forms of truth and goodness spring forth, like crowds of angel children, from the true marriage love." She went on to say that she thought Lucy Stone was capable of this "grand good," and that, in her view, it was "a sin, a fearful mistake deliberately to shut the soul from this God given means of growth, this actual revelation of a heavenly life."

Yet while she celebrated married love in theory, in actual practice, Elizabeth was far from encouraging her younger brother to marry Lucy Stone. Lucy reported to Sarah that in another note which she had seen, Elizabeth had written that she would be very much disturbed if she thought Henry's future happiness depended on her. And she was quick to add that as far as she was concerned, Elizabeth need not worry: "I am more and more convinced that my road in life is a solitary one."

Still, she was deeply appreciative of all Henry's efforts in her behalf, and a new note of affection was apparent in her letters to "dear Harry."

New Albany [Ind.] Friday Nov. 11 1853

Dear Harry,

Your note mailed yesterday containing one from your excellent mother, & from Mrs. Guild has just come today to my hand. Thank you Harry for writing me so often. The little notes, while I am here a stranger, & alone, are doubly grateful. If you knew how much good they do me, you would not be ashamed of writing. But now that you have not only your own place, but perhaps also that of Sam to fill, I am afraid it gives you trouble for which I should be sorry. So Harry dear, though it is very pleasant to get a line from you, pray do not write when you ought to be asleep or resting. I have not recieved the package containing toothbrush &c [et cetera] but presume it will come today. I shall inquire for it. . . . It is very kind and thoughtful of you Harry to send my things, to plan so much, and look so carefully after my interests. I can make no return, but simply to thank you, and I do that most sincerely.

The Louisville people did not cheat me, I think. I had to pay the city five dollars an evening for a *lisence* to lecture. The posting of the large bills made up the sum. . . . I recieved at Louisville a note signed "many Ladies," asking me to give an *afternoon* lecture, (and choose my own subject), or they would be "compelled to forgo the pleasure of hearing me," I suppose because they cant go in the evening alone, or *think* they cant. I dont know whether I shall gratify them or not.

I did recieve your note of Friday last, just after the pamphlets came. I think I have lost no letters of yours. One of the clerks at the P.O. told me he would put everything for me in the box of the Louisville Hotel, while I remained there, and then, send here. He seemed very kind, and really to wish to do something to aid me. . . . .

My letters are all of *my* affairs, & *myself*. So you will be sure to brand me as a great *ego-tist*. And in view of the documents, how can I deny it? I am glad Alcott is with you. Much good may you get from him. I hope you will hear his "conversation" of friendship. Your mother & Ellen & Geo. all would like to hear that I think.

I have been having a fine indignation over an article in "Harper" for Nov. on Woman's Rights. He says, "There is danger that the laws giving separate property, and of course, the management of separate property, to the wife, may in time, vitally affect the oneness, which is so essential in the marriage idea." "The most serious importance of this modern Woman's Rights movement is derived, from its direct bearing upon the marriage relation & it will substitute for the marriage *union*, the unholy alliance of *concubinage*." Was there ever falsehood, meaner than that? But we can afford it, if he can. He sees clearly, that by our movement, the wife will have more freedom, and her husband less power over her. And he trembles for his throne. Well, he cant keep it. The new buds *will* push off the old leaves, and our refusal of consent will make no difference. Putnam for Nov. has an article "The American Ideal Woman" which contains a great deal of truth. It is surely some indication of gain, when such magazines criticize us. . . . .

H enry managed to visit Lucy at Louisville, at Madison, and finally at Chicago. This last meeting marked a turning point of sorts in their relationship, for Lucy acknowledged that her feelings for him went beyond those of ordinary friendship. But despite her growing love for him, she remained set against marriage, and for the time being at least, he didn't get another opportunity to plead his case in person.

While Lucy lectured in Ohio and Pennsylvania on her way back to Massachusetts, Henry traveled to Wisconsin to buy land for speculative purposes. A friend had told him that the state was offering land for sale at $1.25 an acre on thirty years' credit; and as Henry recalled, "Having plenty of youthful energy and very little money," he accepted his friend's suggestion that he go to Wisconsin and buy up some land for them, after first persuading several other friends and local merchants to join with them in purchasing about fifty thousand acres. There was, however, one hitch to the scheme: The buyers had to make an advance payment of ten percent in gold, and since there was as yet no railroad running to Madison, Henry had to devise another means of getting the money to the state capital. He secured an old-fashioned hair trunk, wrapped the six thousand dollars' worth of gold in layers of cotton batting, and took it with him on the stage to Madison.

Chicago Friday Dec. 30 [1853]

My dear Harry

I went last night to my lecture, through a most pelting snow-storm. An audience of 250 or so were gathered, I made the best discourse I could to them under the circumstances—returned to my room,—the winds wailing as though all the demons of despair were in pursuit of them, and listened for a little, to their dismal howl & then began more seriously than I had ever done before, to think of *us;*—our possible and impossible;—lost in the subject, time passed without note & by and by, the light burned out and left me, in total darkness. And then I went to a dreamless sleep. At eight in the morning, had a fire built, & soon came a rap at the door, to which I made no reply, and then, unbidden, a servant entered, and gave me your letter. I had not arisen, so I sat up in bed, and read it. . . . I am glad that your visit here gave you so much happiness. It was good for me too. I have only this regret, in regard to it, that the manifestation of the affection which I really feel for you, lures you to hopes which can never be realized. It would be as foolish, as it would be untrue, for me to pretend that I feel an ordinary friendship for you. Indeed Harry, I have made no pretences to you. When I loved you less than Charles & Nette, I told you so, and when I loved you more, than them I told you *as frankly*. You *are* dearer to me than they are, but all that you are to me, does not come near, my ideal of what is necessary, to make a marriage relation. . . . Harry, human love is a treasure, which ever enriches him who gives and him who recieves it; hence I have been glad that I could love you, and be loved by you, and have reverently accepted it, knowing that we should both be happier, and better for it. Wedded love is a pearl of still greater price which ever enriches him who gives and him who recieves it. I hope we may both, be able to find it but do not let us mock ourselves, by even a *good* counterfeit. If there were real affinity between us—the elements by which a true marriage could be made, I do not think that I should so instinctively recoil from the thought of it. But Harry we *are* capable of being friends, and in this relation, it will always be a joy to me, to be able to add sunshine to your lot.

But it is 9 o'clock and I was awake so late last night, that I feel the need of sleep, and must retire. Greeley lectured tonight, but I had so much to think and feel, that I preferred the quiet of my own room. I hope that you are in a better place, than when you wrote me. If you could come by telegraph, I would invite you here, for an hour, to my comfortable room, but since that cannot be, I will invoke the Good Angels, to be around you, to comfort and defend, and to nourish in you, all that is pure & true and noble. Good night my ever dear friend. God bless you, & prosper you.

> No. 42 Tremont House [Ohio]
> Sat. [January, 1854]

Good Morning Harry,

We have a snow storm, which will probably make my audience small again tonight. The papers say this morning, that my lectures "are said to be the best that have been delivered here this season." The people have listened well, and great discussion is being had at the homes, as I learn, by private individuals, which is just what we want. . . .

I saw the resolutions of the colored people here. Poor things! I pity them. Their lot is very like that of women. Why do I hate politics? Because they are based on falsehoods, and must necessarily result in injustice and corruption. The idea that a *majority* have a *right* to control the action of a minority is false, and its actualization is an atrocious usurpation. I believe in freedom; the majority of the people of this country do not; so they pass over me a fugitive slave law and compel my obedience or make me suffer. I am a friend of Peace; the majority are not; they make war against Mexico or Cuba, and force me to raise the supplies to carry it on. I am rich enough to send a ship to China, to import on my own account, but before I am allowed to do it, this government which has used its power either to make me suffer, or else to violate all my convictions of duty, taxes me to support its power and to pay for the *protection* it gives me. Harry, it is the most stupendous falsehood that was ever imposed upon human beings, and I should most deeply regret it to find you in its vortex. But people will have a government, you say, and shall it be left to the *bad*? The politician, as the creature of the public sentiment, never goes ahead of it, because he depends on it. He who creates and controls that public sentiment, is much greater than a politician, as the creator is greater than the thing created. To make the public sentiment on the side of all that is just and true and noble is the highest use of life, and that I should rejoice to have you do.

But Harry, in your choice of business for life do not ever raise the question whether I approve of that. Our spheres of duty, most likely, are wide apart, but we can be friends while each grandly lives out his own idea.

I shall be at Salem a week from today, and at Pittsburg all the next week. I do not know my address there.

Cincinnati January 22. 1854

Dearest Lucy

Here I am this cold pleasant Sunday morning back again from my hyperborean wanderings all safe & in good spirits. . . .

I had a very pleasant visit to Wisconsin altogether. The country & people were new & somewhat different from what I was used to. The climate clear & very cold—the ground covered with snow—the lakes & rivers all bridged with ice—the winds singing through the woods & prairies continually that mysterious song I never tire of hearing & never can fully comprehend. The wild country had its charm to me which cultivated & familiar human territory lacks. The people were New Englanders, New Yorkers, & Norwegians—mostly of the lower classes—hard, shrewd, energetic, & most abominably *profane*. I never heard so much swearing amongst all classes in the same time in my life. There is certainly a want of *sentiment* & *poetry* in these Northern organizations generally which the people of more genial latitudes possess. The frost & snow have got into their *temperaments* & chilled their souls a little. Yet I doubt not but they are really better husbands, wives, & parents after all than our more *sympathetic* & *enjoyable* people.

I entered altogether some 75 sections of land of 640 acres each—of which I shall myself retain 8 or 10 sections. As my commissions on the transactions will amount to about 1500$ over & above expenses, besides what I may make on my own purchases I am well satisfied. . . . But as I know these mere moneymaking considerations are ones which you take but little interest in, I ought to beg your pardon for taking up time in specifying results. . . .

Your letters dear Lucy, are very sweet to me—not the less so for their striking difference of tone & feeling on certain subjects. They are thus different because they are so frank, like yourself:—they speak your feeling at the moment. Now let me interpret your real feelings towards me to yourself, as I believe they are. You love me as you will never love anybody else in this world. I feel it & know it and am happy in that belief. But you see in me intellectual differences *which* in some respects you have been accustomed to associate in your own mind with moral inferiority & which you do not coincide with. You see probably in my character many faults & immaturities & inconsistencies which sometimes pain you. Above all you feel unwilling to *marry*. There is an *idea* of independence sacrificed. You are not willing to risk any compromise of your efficiency in influencing public opinion & not able to see how you can avoid doing so in marriage. Having *made up* your mind against matrimony for years you find it impossible to change it—& yet at times & when you are with me you would almost wish that it could be changed. I think it quite likely you will soon forget me in a measure Lucy. You passed, when you left Chicago beyond my influence—I can no longer do anything for you. I can no longer plan for your meetings nor visit with you, nor care for you. I never could do *much*, though your affection exaggerated the little I did. Now I can do *nothing*. For months I shall not see you. The little black picture is all I have left. You will soon cease to feel the mesmerism of my presence. Your old friends & old associations will drive me & mine out of your mind. In a few months you will probably look back at that Tuesday evening at Chicago with surprise & wonder you could ever have felt so towards me. The *ascetic* philosophy of Calvin will regain its full control over you & you will fix again & forever your determination to sacrifice the holiest & most beautiful human ties to a false & mistaken idea of the operation of the laws of Nature & of Duty.

You will go on through life laboring for the good of others & therefore happy—but with a consciousness at times of a *want* never satisfied. I think you will eventually discover your mistake. You will see that we owe a divided duty to *ourselves* & to *others*. That a philosophy which commands us to *suppress* our natural instincts is false & that a true life can never be one which is false to any portion of our human nature. Alcott said, when here, that the Reformer who has not obtained a home & *family*—partner & child—needs to commence the reform within himself. I believe that he is correct. You will some day believe it also. You see dearest Lucy that I am not deluding myself with false hopes. I am not very wise God knows—but wise enough to foresee the *probability* of your mind's taking the course I have indicated, now you and I are once more separated. I am also wise enough to reconcile myself to the inevitable as well as I may. I am too much of a man to pule & whine like a baby because you dont choose to marry me. I shall always find objects enough—worthy or foolish, to keep me busy. Life is not very long & a busy one is soon spent. A little more or less happiness matters little. If there is such a thing as Immortality I suppose you will change your mind hereafter—if not it will be all the same fifty years hence.

And yet I could wish things were otherwise. I read the book of life somewhat differently than yourself. I *should* like a *home* of my own—a wife whom I could entirely trust & love—a child to carry down my life through posterity to fight its way up into that better Future in which we all believe. I do not think that either you or I should be less efficient together than separate. I dont think *all work & no play* is the best mode of getting even the *most work* out of life. Above all I do not believe that we were created *only* for results ulterior to ourselves. I think sufficiently well of myself & of all human beings to believe that we were created as positive *ends* as well as means. We have a right to be happy *in & for ourselves.* If not, what a stupid thing to try to make *other people* happy. If *positive good* is no object to ourselves certainly it is not to others. But *what is positive good*? I think reason teaches us that it is only another name for *developement.* Happiness is the result—the *test* of and *proof* of it.

Therefore I think the very consciousness of a want in your nature only to be gratified by marriage is a proof of the duty of fulfilling it. I know that the argument is not necessarily that you should marry *me*. That is again another question. You say you do not love me enough to do so. Then I say—wait until you do. But do not resolve beforehand against marrying me. See me & think of me & give me a fair chance of being loved by you. You cannot love by your simple will any more than you can see. But you can let yourself love or prevent yourself from loving just as you can open, or shut your eyes. Dear Lucy love me if you can. I will endeavor to give you no cause ever to regret having ever done so. But why should I trouble you by saying over in this letter what I have said verbally so often to so little purpose to yourself? I ought to ask you to forgive me for not filling my letter with something else. You may forget me if you will. I shall not forget you. Day after tomorrow I leave for Indiana—in about two weeks or rather *three* weeks from this I shall be in Hutsonville. . . . Remember me to Mr Garrison & the friends we both know, when you see them. God bless you, Lucy.

Yours ever
Harry—

By February Lucy had returned to her home in West Brookfield, physically exhausted from the long, difficult months on the lecture circuit, and emotionally drained from the conflict she was undergoing with regard to marriage. Thus it was little wonder that she suffered a new attack of the excruciating headaches that had plagued her while a student at Oberlin.

Although she continued to struggle against the idea of marrying, there was one area where she allowed herself to change: Having worn bloomers since 1850, she was now ready to abandon the controversial costume. She wrote Susan B. Anthony, "About the long dress, it is all fudge to pretend that any Cause that deserves to live is impeded by the length of your skirt," and added that she planned to have some long and some short dresses to wear, depending on the occasion. Her letter provoked a highly emotional response from Miss Anthony: "Lucy, if you waver, and talk, yea, and resolve to make a long dress, why, then, who may not? If Lucy Stone, with all her reputation, her powers of eloquence, her loveliness of character that wins all who once hear the sound of her voice, cannot bear the martyrdom of the dress, who, I ask, can?" Susan was still struggling to endure this martyrdom, but Mrs. Stanton, who had already given up wearing bloomers herself, gave her hearty approval on the same sheet: "Lay aside the shorts. . . . By all means have the new dress made long."

In April Lucy was back in Cincinnati for an antislavery convention, in which Henry took an especially active part, offering many resolutions and speaking at length. Outside of the convention, he continued his pursuit of Lucy with mixed results. There was a memorable Sunday night ("I shall never forget Sunday night, shall you?"), followed by a lovers' quarrel, or at least "a lovers' *misunderstanding*," and then a reconciliation of sorts ("the night before you left us, we made that at least less sad").

After the convention Lucy lectured elsewhere in Ohio, but her inner turmoil was beginning to interfere with her efforts. For the first time, she spoke of dreading her lectures, and wrote that she longed to see him and have "one more talk in freedom," but felt they could not do so "without scandal." Although the mention of scandal might seem odd at this juncture, there was, in fact, already "talk" about them. That spring Lucy received letters from Susan B. Anthony and from her good friend, James Mott, saying they had heard rumors that she was to be married. Naturally, Lucy was anxious to discourage the spread of such rumors, but at the same time, her fear of scandal showed that despite her flagrant disregard of certain conventions, she was still very much the proper Victorian lady.

In another area as well, she bore out the stereotype. Along with "the horror of being a legal wife, and the suffocating sense of the want of that absolute freedom" which she now possessed, the sexual aspect of marriage was very disturbing to her. She wrote of "the revulsions of feeling which continually recur," and obviously meant sex because later on she said, "You say you know just as well as I do the revulsions of feeling, &c as far as a *man* can."

For his part, Henry seemed resigned to the fact that Lucy was not to be won overnight; on April 21 he wrote her sister Sarah: "Jacob you know waited patiently 14 years for Rachel—and if so mean a man could wait so long for a woman who does not seem to have had much to recommend her, I certainly ought to be able to do as much for a better woman."

⤳

Marshall Clark Co. Illinois Feby 12. 1854

My dear Lucy

I have this afternoon, on reaching this place, received your good, kind, *whole souled* letter. Thank you for it. It contains much that is true and, as I believe, some things that are not so—but I will not quarrel too much—even with what I think mistaken, while you so honestly & earnestly believe it.

So you are taking a little rest at last! Thank Heaven that you are & that you have a quiet home where "solitude broods like an angel." But I could hardly help laughing out at your *novel* description of the *solitude* you have sought—Shakespeare, Waverly, Passion Flowers, Daisy Burns, the newspapers the children & the grown people. Why—what you call *solitude* is a perfect *huzza*. The first two names call up in my mind (in spite of a poor memory) a *perfect host* of the ancient Past—& added to this you breathe in all the rush & whirl of the Present—the *Congressional* debates, the *Nebraska* conspiracy, the *Mitchell* treachery, the Turkish war—the whole turmoil of humanity & call the combination *solitude*. I pass over the additional accompaniments of brushing, sweeping, making snowpaths, &c . . . because, as you say, *change* of employment is sometimes the *best rest*.

No wonder you have suffered with headache dear Lucy—if your very *relaxation* shakes my stupid nerves to contemplate! I am *very sorry* to hear that you have suffered though, Lucy—Do take warning by it & not allow injudicious friends (like me) or yourself to work you so hard hereafter. Recollect that it is not good economy to spend the *principal* of Life when we should live on the *interest* of it instead. And this reminds me of your suggestion relative to lots in Toledo. You ask my opinion. . . . I do not think highly of Toledo myself. . . . If you wish to invest, I should advise you in preference to buy farming lands along the line of the new railroads now building through Illinois. . . . If you wish to buy *town* property I should advise either Chicago, Cincinnati, or better than all, New York, *even at the prices*, because these points are certain still to grow & increase.

So much for business—now then for something better! You do not know the pleasure I feel in the assurances of your affection for me which you so frankly express. I should be either more or less than human if I did not feel *ennobled* by being the subject of an affection so pure & elevated. Believe me, I will try hereafter to prove myself worthy of it. Still more happy do I feel at the possibility which you admit, of your feelings becoming hereafter still more strongly enlisted in my favor. While I do *not* believe *one word* of the practical fiction (as I deem it) that any two human beings are constituted *peculiarly* & in *all respects* fitted for each other—perfect counterparts, capable of a mystical & absolute union—I do believe that certain temperaments, tastes, & dispositions naturally attract, or repel, each other & that we are so constituted that we *need* to form an alliance the most pure & intimate possible, with one individual of the opposite sex. . . . To conceive oneself precluded from assuming it, because the existing laws of Society do not square with exact justice, is to subject oneself to a more abject *slavery* than ever actually existed. Will you permit the injustice of the world to enforce upon you a life of celibacy? The true mode of protest is to assume the natural relation & to reject the unnatural dependance. I say unnatural, because there is no degradation in dependance if it be *mutual* & *natural*. The infant is dependant on its mother, but it would be a foolish *baby* who would knock its brains out to escape from that relation.

Now you know that I fully admit the injustice of the present law of property as regards married people (& indeed *all others*, in a more or less degree). But as to the right of personal custody however true in old fashioned times—it is not *practically* so now at all & not even any longer true in theory. Consult any lawyer you can trust, in *any* state in the Union, or in England, as to whether a husband *can* control his wife's movements, or residence, & my life against a dime— *every* lawyer everywhere will tell you—no! Universal custom & experience *proves otherwise*—positive judicial decisions explicitly *deny* the right. No husband *can* prevent his wife's leaving him—except by refusing to support her or *holding on* to the *children*. As you refuse, in any case, to be supported—I suppose the first threat would have no terror.

As regards to the second—you are aware that the custom has now grown to be a law in many of our States that the children are awarded by the Judge to the party considered not in fault. And we should remember that in cases of marital separation—give the children to whom you will, there is hardship *somewhere*. It is *rather bad* for a father to give up a child. I hope you do not think that the male sex have *no* parental affection. I think in most cases, where there is fault on both sides the children should be divided. Where very gross criminality exists in Father or Mother, or both, the children should be removed from the one, or both. It is also true that *under existing circumstances* the fathers are generally best fitted both by position & by character to fulfill the trust beneficially to the children. And it is really true or is it not? that the welfare of the children should be made after all the paramount consideration?

The fact is—while people are imperfect & make unwise & unhappy marriages—there must be *some law* to judge between them. And let the law be what it will, cases of gross cruelty & injustice will sometimes recur under its provisions. Of course the law should be made as equitable as possible in its general provisions! But because these *are* general they will sometimes work badly. So do the laws of Nature in spite (if I may so say) of God's wisdom & benevolence. The fact is, unhappy marriages are like diseases. Medicines only mitigate the horrors—they cannot always do that.

You ask me if the laws placed a man in the same position on

marrying, as they do now woman—would I marry? I say frankly—I certainly *would*. I should indeed be cautious in entering into the relation & should first satisfy myself that you would not be likely to lock me up, or rather *attempt* so to do (for the *law* would soon get me out with a writ of habeas corpus, if you did)—2^d—I should require you to promise not to avail yourself of any unjust laws giving you control of *more than half* of my future earnings & 3^d I should place beyond your control all my present property. These I should do not *against you*, but from a sense of personal duty & with your full concurrence. Certainly Lucy I should not act unwisely. If the marriage were harmonious the laws *would not exist* so far as we were concerned, because its provisions *only apply* where appeal is made to it. If it proved discordant & you proceeded to lock me up, I should let myself out by habeas corpus & sue you for assault & battery. I should go into business in a friend's name (a very easy & common matter) & you never could get one dollar of my earnings. I should sue for divorce on the general grounds of gross cruelty & neglect &c & if the State did not grant divorce on those grounds at the worst I could easily move into one that did. I should steal at least half my children from you & put you to the trouble & expense of a law suit to get them back. If you succeeded I should shortly steal them again & give you the same trouble over & over till you compromised. In short I should be my own master in spite of much unjust annoyance.

Why then are women so terribly oppressed you may say? Because they have not, as a class, the education, the spirit, the energy, the disposition to be free! Give me a *free man*—he can never be made a slave. Give me a free woman—she never can be made one either. Surely you enormously exaggerate the scope & force of *external* laws at the expense of *internal* power when you lay such frightful & hopeless stress upon a few paltry enactments. The great evil I think, in our institutions lies *here*—that they so crush the spirit out of people that they do *not make themselves free*. . . . The first step from slavery is to seek freedom for *ourselves* . . . the next is to seek it for others & for all. I think when a woman has taken the *first* step she need not greatly fear ever to suffer from *dependance*. The only danger she should guard against is to avoid trying to play herself the despot—most intelligent, energetic women (& men too) do that thing. As to your proposition about prefering death to dishonor, that is all very good, but is in no respect a parrellel case. You didnt make

the external law & are in no sense responsible for it. The law of
marriage existed before Blackstone! I think a wise person *cannot* be
a conservative—neither a *radical* reformer. *Both* are *fanatics.* Fortunately though I have faults, I am so constituted that I am not likely
to err in this respect, but in others. You (in common with *all radicals*)
with all your ability & earnestness & *because of these*, have a tendency to err that way.

But I have written an immense letter, all logical & argumenta-
tive, which (in a letter) is great nonsense. . . . Lucy dear—if I *could*
express to you properly my view of matters & things you would see
that as to marrying *I am right* & *you are wrong* & you would marry
me and be all the freeer for doing so. Your views on the subject are
warped from the unfortunate impressions of your childhood. I hope
that your soul will be large enough eventually to *outgrow* these
impressions. Meantime dearest—love me all *you can* & believe me

Yours *ever* Harry

Boston Mar. 17 1854

Dear Harry
. . . I am glad that I am going to see you so soon, and that we
shall have a few days to talk a great deal. Your letter suggests *many*
things, about which both of us have much to say. But Harry dear
pray do not ever feel that you "should act more wisely to let differences of opinion drop out of sight between us." We *have* differences
of opinion, and if our love cannot be large enough to enable us, to
bear them pleasantly, it is a great deal better that we should know it.
You have seemed to me, all the more noble that you have not only,
not tried to conceal your differences from me, but have rather taken
pains that I should understand your true position. But in all honesty,
Harry I do not think that our agreement, or our disagreement, will
affect our *ultimate* relations. If ever, a little hope is born in me, that
somewhere, sometime, I may find and enjoy the complement of my
existence, the old reasons, (which I have so often repeated to you)
come back and with terrible pertinacity claim supremacy, and this
budding hope dies out. And my life's thread, I can see clearly, spin
on, very much as at present, until lost in the unseen. So Harry, tho'

I hope that *as friends*, we may help each other "to be wiser, to be better, and to be stronger," do not let any expectation in regard to me prevent you, if you can draw to your heart and life, what will bless you more than I should be able to (from the circumstances of my life) even though (which is not probable) we should find adaptation between us. But we will *talk* of this, only, in the meantime, do not *hope anything*. I am glad that we are to have one more opportunity of spoken expression. And *whatever* results from it, the regard we cherish makes, and will make us both better.

I hope your Nebraska meeting was not a failure. The New Hampshire election, gives some reason to hope that by the coalition majority, the Nebraska bill will be defeated. But if it is, it is only for a time. I hope you read in the speech of Stephens of Georgia, the cool insults to Northern men. I like to see the contempt which is *felt* spoken. If there is any manhood in Northern voters, it may wake it up. We are having a great discussion . . . on capital punishment in our Legislature. Garrison, Parker, Phillips against hanging, Dr. Beecher, and Rev. Mr. Waterbury in favor. It finishes this A.M. I go to hear [it]. The Rev. Mr. R. Storrs gave an anti slavery lecture last night at the Melodian. The last half, was grand.

What a magnificent delivery of fugitive at Milwaukee the other day. It wont do to get "sick of human nature" Harry, when it shows so much nobility.

I have read the bit of poetry you sent. It is beautiful, but it should not put the fulfillment of the soul's prophecy, and the heart's hope (for most people) beyond the grave. I will keep it. Do not work too hard. You feel a relentless necessity to make a fortune. But it is hardly worth while, "to kill one's self, to get a living." I shall go home the last of next week, and get a little rest before going to Cincinnati.

Affectionately yours
Lucy

Mt. Vernon [Ohio] Sunday Apr. 23 [1854]

Dear Harry
Your instinct I am sure will not tell you that I am not at Columbus. So *I* must do it. I am at the home of Mrs. Bloomer. Her men

printers, entered into "a solemn league and covenant" that they would not teach a woman to print, nor work in an office with one. Consequently the men were all discharged, and in the emergency, Mrs. Bloomer, sent a most imploring letter, for me to come and help vindicate the principle involved. And so I am here, and last night had a meeting, which I am sure will be good in its results. . . . I got your telegraphic despatch at my lecture on Friday evening. . . . The letter I got next morning. . . . I wish I could convey to you all, and just what, that letter brought to me. But perhaps I could not have done it, even if you had been with me. And it is no matter. I cannot answer it now. Thank you Harry, darling, for its words of kindness, of frankness, of disinterested love. If we ever meet again, and can forget to *feel*, we will talk like *figures* of your propositions, but I *cannot* write about them. Is it best for you to come east, this summer? I do not think it is. Not that I do not want to see you Harry dear, and that too, in the free home of my sister. [scratched out line] But can we not understand each other better by correspondence, when I get time to write? I think so. Still my dear, if you do come east, you may be sure of a glad greeting. It is right to put your mother's picture with mine, and sometime, when we meet, you may have the lock of hair you ask for to put in it. . . . I want you to believe, if you can, in the correspondence in H. C. Wrights book, as indicative of what should be between husband & wife. God bless you dearest, & help you to be a wise ruler over yourself.

Cincinnati April 25. 1854

Dear Lucy

I wrote you a long letter three or four days ago to Columbus & another Sunday to Zanesville & I am not going to inflict much of a one to day. . . . I wrote you my views about Wrights book rather freely for a letter, but I put two extra wafers to keep impertinent curiosity from a possibility of opening it. I have been writing & reading more than usual since you left us—business having slackened up for the summer. I do not quite know when I shall be able to come Eastward this summer—yet Lucy—I tell you truly I should feel heartsick if I thought that many long months would elapse without seeing you. With you I live, without you I vegetate. One week in the quiet hills of Massachusetts with you, at your sister's house, with no gossiping observers to watch over our movements, all by ourselves, with God and the Angels, the blue sky over our heads, the green earth beneath us, and the bright summer air around us,—I would ask no other heaven and invoke no other mediator but you, dear Lucy. God bless you.

Harry

[Zanesville, Ohio, April 25, 1854]
Tuesday evening 10 o'clock PM

My last lecture is over, until the 10th of May. And I am so glad! I have dreaded these lectures, more than I can tell. But they are past, and very well too. Thank fortune! Now, Harry dear, I wish you were here, for an hour, & I would tell you why, in *this* letter, I ask you to come east, and in the *last*, said I did not think it best. I said to myself, "it will cost Harry $50. to come east. It is not likely that he will get that value in return, for however much I love him, (and he is very dear to me,) the horror of being a legal wife, and the suffocating sense of the want of that absolute freedom which I now possess, together with the revulsions of feeling which continually recur, and the want of certainty that we are adapted, will never allow me to be his wife. And if he were sure that I would not be, he would not desire to come."

Now Harry, I have been all my life alone. I have planned and executed, without counsel, and without control. I have shared thought, and feeling, and life, with myself alone. I have made a path for my feet which I know is very useful; it brings me more intense & abundant happiness by far, than comes to the life of the majority of men. And it seems to me, I cannot risk it by any change. And when I ask, "*can* I *dare* to change," It rings an everlasting "*no*." And then I do not think it best, for you to spend time, and money, in vain. And so say, "dont come." I have lived alone, happily and well, and can still do it. I have always been superior to circumstances, and can continue so. My life has never seemed to me, a baffled one, only in hours that now and then come, when my love-life is consciously unshared. But such hours are only as the drop to the ocean. The great whole of my life is richly blest. Let it remain so. And then again, I say, "dont come." But when I know by your letters that you do not understand me, I long for *one more* talk in freedom, and blame me, for desiring it, at so much cost to you. If there were any way, to see you, without scandal, before I leave, but there is not. So do as you please. Come east, or not.

I sympathize most fully with you dear Harry, in your struggle, and desire to make your life wholly beautiful. What we earnestly strive after, we *can* attain. "All things are possible to him that *wills.*" We sometimes succeed in the *great* matters and fail in the lesser. "The *little* foxes spoil the vines." But I *expect,* that as you cultivate steadiness of purpose and deliberation, and love of & *trust in* the Truth, *without regard* to *consequences,* that you will find your life, most beautifully sphering itself about the Central Life, finding *all* its *true* relations, and in each, blessing, and being blessed. Good night and may all the good which a noble life deserves, be abundantly yours. . . .

With love to the household
Yours truly   Lucy

Cleveland Wednesday Apr. 26, 1854

Dear Harry

I wrote you this morning from Zanesville, where I got the Liberator which I will return by the mail that carries this. That was a very stupid being (I dont believe it was a woman) who wrote the article you desired me to read.

Garrison's reply, is very well. I never said however, that marriage is a state of slavery. A wife's position is capable of being made horrible enough; but chattelism is a still "lower depth" to which marriage, bad as it may be made, should never be compared. And I have carefully refrained from doing so.

To say that one who is not married is not competent to speak in regard to it, is about as absurd as it would be, to require a physician to have personally the small pox & fever, and every other disease, so that he might act from experience in the application of remedies. The great, universal laws of life, are written on every human being, and may be understood by all who are willing students.

I like "Mauprat" very much. George Sand, is a philosopher, and has studied deeply into the human soul. I like her "Edmee" greatly. I read coming up in the cars today to Mauprat's return to this country,—shall finish it tomorrow. I wish we were reading it together. And today in the cars, as passage after passage of exceeding beauty and truth came under my eye, I said again and again, "I wish Harry were here." I love to share with you what gives me instruction or pleasure.

I hope you will read in this Liberator which I return the article on "the exploration of the Amazon, and the designs of slave power." It seems to me that dissolution of the Union is the only alternative to save us from a long protracted slavery. If the people *could* only see that a government which provides for the dehumanizing of man, and gives more political power to those who are guilty of it, leaves its subjects *no choice*, but to repudiate; simple conformity to such a moral standard must inevitably destroy slavery. I wish, that as a nation we could see the safety, as well as duty, of implicit obedience to the *unchanging right*—that nothing which is *unjust, can* ultimately win. But the nation is made up of individuals, and as are the units, so must be the aggregate. . . .

I enclose a little scrap, which I found going the rounds of the papers. It seems as though I must be near my death, or *ought* to be, when my life begins to be written with pen. I think Sarah Pellet must have written it. The allusion to picking the chestnuts, brought vividly to my mind a time when I needed a school book which father thought a *girl* need not have, and I went with my little bare toes, and gathered chestnuts enough to buy one, and then felt a prouder sense of *triumph*, than I have ever known since. But that is all gone, and may be forgotten. It is eight o'clock, and your home circle are perhaps having a cosy time in the little back parlor. God bless *it*, and all of you. Hope you are well.

Cincinnati May 2. 1854

Dear Lucy

Quite unexpectedly to myself, I find that business will call me Eastward next week, so that I shall leave here for New York on Monday morning the 8th & consequently *shall be in N.Y.* on the 10th & of course shall be present at the anniversary of the American [Anti-Slavery] Society.

I do not know whether I shall take pains to get a letter from the Ladies here as a Delegate formally appointed, or not. I have no intention of *speaking* at the meeting. There will be speakers too many & too distinguished to make it either wise or modest for me to do so. I have my powers to cultivate & my reputation to make. But I shall greatly enjoy being present dear Lucy. Just one year ago, I stood in the Chinese Museum Hall divided between my sympathy with you, my admiration of Wendell Phillips & my horror at a villainous *yellow* bloomer which had placed itself with a great flaring straw hat on its head right down in front of me. After the morning meeting was over I stood in the doorway & saw you & Mrs Abby Foster go out together with a peculiar feeling which you little thought you would ever *share*. As Mrs Foster went out—she turned & said "Come along with me Lucy," & I felt quite to envy her the friendly familiar tone of intimacy which she used.

Really Lucy dear—a great deal has happened to me & to you *since this time last year*. In spite of *hardware* & its annoyances, I have lived more this last year than all my life before. Let me see—I heard you at the Anniversary. I *almost* heard you. I read your speech at Metropolitan Hall. I heard you at the Constitutional Convention. I saw you at the Anti-Slavery office. I saw you at the Boston Convention. I visited you (sublime impudence!) at West Brookfield. I got your *first* little letter at Walnut Hills. I met you at Niagara & sat at your feet by the whirlpool looking down into its dark waters with a passionate & unshared & unsatisfied *yearning* in my heart that you will never know, nor understand. I rode with you in that *sacred* night with a miserable hack for a temple & the stupid driver for a priest & you dear Lucy for my Divinity. I was with you at Cleveland & heard you speak & stood on the same platform of freedom & purity & aspiration. I stood with you in the dark cool night overlooking the Lake—with Charles Burleigh & Antoinette—your hand in mine & the great roar of the waves coming up & the winds sweeping over us—& Charles quoting poetry—while I was *living* it. I met you at Cincinnati—& again was with you at Smith & Nixon's Hall & heard Mrs Mott & yourself & then night after night I had the *privilege* of hearing you & being *with you afterwards*. And we planned your

Western trip together & rode in the buggy together & I saw you at Louisville & at Madison that happy Sunday & at Chicago that still happier Tuesday. And I got your kind letters at Madison & in Indiana & Illinois & counted the days till I should see you once more in Cincinnati. Then I met you at the cars & had that ride to Mrs. Ernst's by that very *circuitous route* up the Creek & back again. Then I saw you at the Convention & in the Committee & elsewhere & at last *that Sunday* at home. I shall never forget *Sunday night*, shall you? And then we had something which, if not a *lovers' quarrel*, was at least a lovers' *misunderstanding*—but the night before you left us, we made that at least less sad. And since you left me at the railroad I have had three letters full of affection, full of consolation. Surely dear Lucy the last year has not been wasted.

But these are only some of the *salient* points. You know not the hours which you have gladdened for me in the forest & the prairie. Your little black picture had been with me by day & by night & scarcely an hour has passed, by day, or by night, without your presence in my soul. Can you doubt the permanence & reality of my affection dear Lucy—after I have thought of you so often & so long? Should I not have grown *weary* of the same thought if it had not incorporated itself into my very being? Dear Lucy—believe me—I love you!

This is very curious—that I should write page after page of sentiment when I set out to be calm & cool & philosophical. I wanted to say to you that I shall be in New York on the 10th May. My business will probably occupy me a week or ten days afterwards. So that I cannot visit you till about the 18th or 20th of May. Will it be convenient to you—compatible with your other engagements to have me visit you then. If not, I want you to say so freely & frankly as it is your wont to speak. I have set out with the determination that my love shall *never fetter you* one iota—that I will never directly or indirectly impair your activity, but that I will compel you ten years hence to acknowledge "My acquaintance with Harry had been an advantage to me *every way*." So, if you want that time to prepare your future speeches, or lectures & cannot use me to read to you what you want to study for that end, I should like you to say so & I will *postpone* my visit till a better time. Or if you can give me only *one day*— I want you to say so—& I will religiously observe the limitation.

Surely we know each other too well to stand on the slightest ceremony with each other! . . . Good-bye—God Bless you—Harry.

P.S. Day after tomorrow May 4th is my birthday. I shall be *twenty
nine* years old. Not so far behind you Lucy after all!—and *much older
for my years*, thank heaven!

Cincinnati May 5. 1854
Saturday Evening—

Dearest Lucy
  . . . I have a thousand things I want to say to you. I have not
been thinking about matters for a year, without getting some ideas
which I want to communicate. I think in a good long, quiet, uninter-
rupted talk we can come to an understanding together on many
points. One or two things I want you in the outset to understand. I
do not want you to *fetter* yourself *one particle* for my sake. I do not
want you to forego *one sentiment* of independence, nor one attribute
of *personality*. I want only to help you, as best I can, in achieving a
really noble & *symettrical* Life. I want you also to *help me* to do the
same. We *can help* each other I am sure not merely as friends—nor
as lovers, but as husband & wife.
  I do not want that we should endorse the present unjust laws,
but by making our public & outside *contract*, enter a practical &
efficient protest against them—the only protest which can be understood & *imitated*. I do not want you to do this—till I can so place
myself as to unite our lives without inconveniencing, or retarding
either. Lucy—you say you can *understand* marriage as well by theory
as by experiment. You ask if it is necessary that a Doctor should have
the small pox to understand it. There is no analogy in the cases. Marriage is not a disease, but *celibacy* is. Marriage is the *normal* state of
mature human beings & brings with it experiences, insights, which
cannot be attained without it. I do not believe that man, or woman
can take perfectly *sane, rational* & true views of the relation of the
sexes to each other & to Society except by experimental marriage.
  But I will not enlarge on matters & things now—indeed I have
no time. . . . I hope you may see Elizabeth while in N.Y. I do not

think you either of you understand each other fully & I *know* she does not quite understand you. God bless you dear

Yours ever Harry!

I *hope* you will have an anniversary worthy of the Cause & of the Society. Remember me *especially* to Mr. *Garrison*—

New York May 12. 1854

Dear Lucy

. . . I attended the Convention diligently as a delegate from the Ladies Anti-Slavery Society—made a speech in opposition to the Resolution that the *one sole grand* aim of Abolitionists should be the Dissolution of the Union—which though no[t] much in accordance with the views of the Society, which I was presumptuous enough to criticize in several respects, was well received. I endeavored to speak temperately & wisely & at least served a good purpose, for the small thinly attended meeting which had been very dull before—became excited & I had the pleasure of being attacked by H. C. Wright, Redmond & some half dozen others. I furnished *texts* & am not thin skinned.

I have several things to say to you about the Convention when I see you. I am afraid Mrs Mott didnt like my speech much, for she told me afterwards when I shook hands with her, not having the opportunity before, that she doubted whether it was I, or my brother [Samuel Blackwell] but she wanted to shake hands with me *for the good service I did at Cleveland*.

But I have no time to write further. Dear Lucy, God bless you. I have had your papers forwarded to Gardiner as directed. Elizabeth sends her love.

Yours ever
Harry

Illness in the family had prevented Lucy from attending the antislavery meetings in New York, but later in May she went to Boston for the New England Anti-Slavery Convention, and there met Henry on the day that the fugitive slave Anthony Burns was taken back into bondage. It was a day that Henry would remember long afterward. The air was heavy with tension; already a huge protest meeting had been held in Fanueil Hall, and a small band of abolitionists had rushed on the courthouse in an unsuccessful attempt to free the arrested slave. In the course of the attempt, a volunteer deputy had been shot and killed, and fearing further violence, the United States marshal had called in a company of marines and one of artillerymen. Troops lined the streets from the courthouse to the wharf, and a cannon was pointed at several thousand spectators who had gathered to watch as Anthony Burns was escorted to the ship that was to take him back to the South. Lucy and Henry went out to Nahant, where they sat on the rocks overlooking the sea, and heard the firing of the cannons that signaled Burns's departure. Afterward, Lucy gave a rousing speech at the antislavery convention, in which she protested the incident, and called for the dissolution of the Union.

From Boston she and Henry went on to her sister's home in Gardner, where with "no gossiping observers" watching them, they tried to sort out their relationship. However, their privacy was not quite as complete as they might have wished; Lucy's niece Emma Lawrence, who later married Henry's brother George, remembered that "as a small intrusive child pleading to go with them, I was benevolently dragged up the beautiful hill behind our house on one of their walks, when he would certainly have preferred her company without mine."

Whatever actually passed between them during the Gardner visit, Henry was apparently encouraged, because Elizabeth Blackwell now wrote directly to Lucy to extend "the hand of sisterly friendship." She said that Henry had just left her, and that they had talked about Lucy and "the united future which probably lies before you."

In the remainder of her letter Elizabeth aired her views on woman's rights conventions, which she felt were a waste of time. It might seem odd that she—a pathbreaker in her right—should have felt so, but in many ways, Elizabeth's ideas of what was appropriate behavior were quite conventional. She had, for example, refused to walk in her graduation procession at medical school, because she considered it unladylike, and now, no doubt for much the same reason, she objected to woman's rights conventions.

Lucy wrote back to Elizabeth thanking her for her assurance of welcome within the Blackwell family circle, but added that "possible" rather than "probable" would have been a better word to use in reference to their "united future." She also disagreed with Elizabeth about the usefulness of woman's rights conventions. Elizabeth did not bother to reply, because, as she explained in a letter to Henry some six months later, "she waived any reference to you, and on other points we view life from such different sides, that I thought discussion would be unavailing until personal affection had linked us together." So ended the correspondence between the two women Henry loved most, and who he had hoped would be friends.

By mid-June he had returned to the West for the purpose of visiting his land in Bad Ax (now Vernon) County, Wisconsin. As a speculator and absentee landlord, he was bound to incur the anger of the settlers there, and although he managed to escape unharmed, he was well aware of the extent to which their hostility was justified.

❧

Milwaukee, Sunday June 18 1854

Dearest Lucy—

. . . I want to tell you about my journeyings since I last wrote for somehow I cannot feel satisfied unless I make you to some extent at least a partner in my daily life. I want you to know my doings & my thoughts & I want to know your's—for otherwise I only half live & by sympathy with you I seem to double my life. You know that last winter at the request of some friends I visited Wisconsin to enter land for them from the State on thirty years credit. . . . I retained for myself, my brother Sam & my partner Mr Ryland, the lands which I selected in *Bad Ax County*. . . . To see & examine these was the object of my present visit. . . . The Country we [Ryland and he] found very beautiful & diversified. The East side of the County is traversed by a river, *the Kickoopoo*, (beautiful name!), and is hilly and densely covered with a magnificent forest. . . . . West of the Kickapoo in the centre of the County are beautiful rolling prairies interspersed with groves of oak trees and *barrens* as they are called, that is, thickets of small oak bushes and hazel brush. From this part of the County several streams take their rise in large springs of clear *soft* sandstone water, as pure and bright as the water that I drank at your father's house. These streams run westward into the Mississippi forming great gorges and cutting the land into ridges covered with oak trees and valleys bare of trees—natural meadows of luxuriant grass watered by clear streams, which are all full of speckled trout and afford excellent mill power. . . . Through the centre of the County run a range of rocky mounds, often very picturesque and on the points of the hills & in the steep bluffs of the streams rock crops out everywhere, mostly sandstone. I never saw a new country with such good natural roads & in all respects so agreeable & healthy. It needs only the *people* to make it a most lovely residence.

I found that since I had entered my lands, a speculator named Ludington of this City had taken all the other *state* lands for sale on credit—& in so doing had entered out a number of actual settlers, who had neglected to secure their farms. There still remained U.S. government lands in plenty at 1²⁵ an acre, but they could not be bought *on credit* & the people were exceedingly indignant at it. I also had ignorantly entered out some ten or twelve settlers & one principal object of my visit was to arrange matters with them & let them keep their farms. Most of these were Norwegians and I settled the matter with them holding a kind of council on "Coon prairie" with an interpreter one fine day. Some, I let have their land at about cost, some, better off, I charged a small advance, with others I exchanged for other lands.

But so soon as it was known that I was in Viroqua several unprincipled village politicians resolved to take advantage of the universal feeling against speculators to give me trouble. The chairman of the meeting which was called to express their indignation was a fellow who keeps the only tavern in the town—which I had found so uncomfortable when there in the winter, that I did not go to it this time, to his great offence no doubt. I did not hear of the meeting till 'twas nearly over, but there was a good deal of abusive talk & it adjourned over from Saturday night to meet Monday night again. I heard all about the movement from friends in the little town, and expected trouble, but kept quiet, went on with my business and treated the whole matter with seeming unconcern. By Monday evening . . . there was quite a gathering of people in the town—all sorts of rumors and misrepresentations having been set afloat with regard to me. . . . I went to my friend McMichael who was evidently a good deal alarmed at the turn things were taking and told him that I wanted him to go with me to the meeting. He declined saying he felt unwell, but promised to come shortly, so I went alone. I found the Representative of the County in the midst of an inflammatory speech—which was received with great applause. He alluded to my presence in the town & made several very false charges, which brought out cries of "tar & feathers, ride him on a rail" &c. I then rose & stated that I was present & should speak for myself when he was through. This made him much more moderate & careful & afterwards I spoke for nearly an hour explaining my position & views—showing the absurdity of condemning an individual for doing what they would all gladly do if they were able & avowing my own opposition to land monopoly &c &c. I endeavored to say nothing but what was strictly true & wise though I confess the logic whereby I proved to my own satisfaction at the time that I was not a land monopolist, looks rather one sided to me at present. However I produced a very good effect & though several efforts were made to reply, Mr. Ryland and Mr. McMichael, who had subsequently come in, followed me up & the meeting passed some general resolutions & adjourned in great good humor. . . .

Altogether the affair was quite an amusing episode, but Lucy it seems as though in the present constitution of Society, do what we will, we cannot advance our own interests without doing a certain injustice to others. If I am able to keep these lands a few years they will make me rich, but meantime I am certainly impeding the settlement & prosperity of the Country round me. I see no way of avoiding this, unless I go out myself to live there, build mills, establish a store & so forth thereby compensating for the land holding. By doing this too I could in a few years exert a controlling influence in the County and become rich & under certain circumstances I could enjoy the position. But when I reflect that I should then of necessity become a man of business absorbed to a great extent in mills, railroads, and agriculture—I shrink from a move which at my age fixes my sphere for life. . . . This morning, Sunday, I went out to look at this handsome, flourishing young City, intending to take the Steamboat for Chicago at 9 AM. Unfortunately my watch was too slow & I got back just in time to be too late. I must now wait here till tomorrow morning & shall occupy the rest of the day in a desperate attempt to prepare a poem for our club on 4th July. I feel bound not to disappoint them, because they have voted to exclude liquors and invite ladies— in great measure, as I believe, out of complaisance to me. . . . Lucy I wish you could have been with me to see Lake Michigan this morning from the high bluffs above the town & that you could have bathed with me in its cold blue water. God bless you dear. Love to sister Sarah & to little Emma. I am trying to be faithful to my promise of *sincerity* & remain yours ever

Harry

Gardner [Mass.] July 23 [1854]

Dear Harry

This note, which I snatch a moment just at sunset to write, is to tell you that I got yours from Lafayette, and that if you do not hear from me at Marshall, it will be because I cannot command the time. . . .

I hope you will get the letter I wrote you at Logansport. I mailed it on the third of July. It covered six pages of large letter sheet. If it is lost, you will be saved the vexation of reading my bad writing. You will let me know whether you get it, and if you do not, I will give you its substance again. Believe me dear Harry we do *not* belong together as husband and wife. If we did, I should not so often feel my spirit protesting against it. It seems to me that everything connected with our acquaintance has been preparing the way, for us to be better helpers and friends, and that *this* is the *only* relation which we can truly sustain. But I cannot write more now. If I get time I will write you fully at Marshall.

Wishing you health, happiness and *every good*—Yours affectionately

H enry advocated "forcible rescue" of slaves, and late in the summer of 1854 he was given an opportunity to act on his belief. Shortly after his return from a collecting trip in Indiana, he went to Salem, Ohio, for the annual convention of the Western Anti-Slavery Society. Since Salem was a stronghold of Garrisonian abolition, the mood at the convention was quite militant. Henry was in the midst of reciting a poem written specially for the occasion when the news came that a young slave girl was on the train scheduled to pass through Salem at six o'clock that evening. The supreme court of Ohio had already ruled that slaves brought into the state by their masters could be freed if they expressed a desire to be so, and now it seemed the perfect time to test that ruling.

❧

Cincinnati Sept. 1. 1854

Dear Lucy

Today ought to be Autumn but cant make it out! Thermometer 95 in the shade. Nothing worth living for but ice water & water melons. Business so dull that the whole City has nothing to do but gossip & I . . . the subject of that gossip—Heavens what a fate! Well business will revive—gossip will die out—the sun will get over his fever & the earth will become moistened with rain. Let us take things more easily—"twill be all the same a hundred years hence."

To speak in plain prose Lucy dear—having nothing to do this hot day I have sate myself down in our office to write to you, whom in spite of all your warnings & rejections & presentiments I cannot help loving as my own soul & thinking of as my *wife* that is & is to be. Dear Lucy your letter of 28 August has just reached me congratulating me on my return home. I did not stay long there however, for having received an invitation from the Western A.S. [Anti-Slavery] Society to attend their annual convention at Salem, I went up last week in company with Mrs. Ernst, Mrs. Coleman, & Christian Donaldson. . . . The Convention lasted Saturday, Sunday, and Monday.

I spoke four times during the three days. 1st on the duty of resistance to unjust laws; on the second day, in a large tent, with a very large audience, on the Nebraska Bill, and again in the afternoon in defence of political abolitionists against some sweeping and unjust charges of that excellent Ishmailite, Henry C. Wright. On Monday, Edmund Quincy having introduced a preamble and resolutions on behalf of the majority of the Business Committee—C. Donaldson and I dissenting—declaring the non-voting and covenant with death & agreement with Hell platform spoke in support of them in the forenoon, and Mr. Donaldson gave his reasons for voting. After dinner, I gave my reasons for voting as a duty, and for not advocating or desiring a dissolution of the Union. I spoke for fifty minutes with marked attention and some applause, and though the resolutions were adopted by an almost unanimous vote, I *think* I stated our case so as to command respect, if not acquiescence.

During the afternoon session, a despatch from Alleghany City (opposite Pittsburg) was received, stating that at 6 PM the train going West, through Salem, would contain a colored girl with her master & mistress, on her way to Tennessee, & requesting us to stop her. You know that being voluntarily brought into the State, she was *legally free*. Accordingly, after adjournment of Convention, a meeting of about 1200 persons assembled at the depot & were addressed by Charles Burleigh; a committee of four were appointed to see the Conductor & ask the girl if she wanted her freedom. The committee selected a respectable colored man to act as spokesman & when the cars arrived I found myself along with them. We found the little girl *only 8 years old* with her mistress & baby & the colored man asked her whose child she was. Getting no answer he asked the lady who promptly told him " 'twas none of his business." The committee then enquired of the lady, & found she and her husband were on their way to Tennessee, & that the child was their slave. The child was asked if she wished to be free & replied yes whereupon I told the owners, the husband having meanwhile come in, that the child was now legally free under our laws & must go with us. I took the child's arm, & commenced lifting her from the seat, seeing that the passengers in the cars seemed to sympathize with the owners, & that there was no time to be lost. At that moment a young Cincinnatian of the name of Keyes collared me & remonstrated with me. I let go of the child, who was instantly caught up by the other members of the committee & passed out & carried swiftly off into the town in the arms of a colored man, and shook him off. So soon as I found the child safe, I returned & explained to the astonished Tennesseans the motives of our conduct & after a very animated & angry discussion of a few minutes the bell rang, the cars started & the assembled multitude gave 9 hearty cheers.

In the evening we had a spirited & crowded meeting at the Town Hall. Dr Thomas, one of the committee, stated the facts, I then spoke—Chas Burleigh followed we had songs & at the request of the audience I named Miss Topsy, who appeared on the platform, *Abby Kelley Salem*—the Christian name from the lady who has done so much in that section of the Country, & the surname from the place which had the honor of saving her. A Hunker [?] Whig lawyer spoke well in favor of a resolution endorsing our action, and the audience passed it unanimously. But on my return home I find the matter very much misrepresented in the papers, as was to be expected. The Gazette gave a tolerably fair account; the other papers, which I send you in the form of extracts, are very abusive. I have however, published my statement of the facts and have sent to Salem for a corroboration of them.

Altogether, it is rather an amusing affair, & I do not regret the part I took in it, notwithstanding I regret the odium and misunderstanding which attaches to anything of the kind. The worst attack upon me is today, in the Commercial, signed "an eye witness." It is written by a member of our Club, & asserts that I assaulted the lady, scratched her neck, & tumbled the baby on the floor. Christian Donaldson will reply in Monday's paper, with an equally flat denial of all this. And if I succeed in obtaining a contradiction signed by the citizens of Salem, I hope eventually to set the matter right. Meanwhile I have at least the comfort of success. We saved the child & vindicated the state. This systematic publication of falsehood was threatened me beforehand if I would not produce the child & have the matter decided by its wishes, with the promise of free papers if the child wished to be free. I told the parties that she was free already & wanted no papers & that they might publish me as much as they pleased.

So you see, Lucy, that with all my love of approbation, I am not, at present, on the road to popularity, apparently. What you say in your letter about the importance of perfect sincerity and fixed anti-slavery principle is very true. I am not willing to admit, however, that the Disunionists are necessarily more radically or consistently anti-slavery than myself. But why cavil about means? Our aim is the same and we all work towards it in our own way. I agree with you in regarding the operations of Emigrants Aid Societies in settling Kansas, as very hopeful. I begin to hope that she will come in as a free state. . . .

Harry

Because of his part in the slave rescue, Henry was indicted for kidnapping, but as the lawyer in whose hands the case was placed was a member of the Cincinnati Club, and a personal friend of Henry's, the case was never brought to trial. Henry was also in some personal danger: In Memphis a reward of $10,000 was offered for his capture "dead or alive," and in the months that followed, southern men often stopped into the hardware store so that they would be able to recognize him if he ever dared cross the border into Kentucky. Moreover, since many of the store's customers were proslavery, Henry's role in the rescue brought a drop in business—much to the displeasure of his partners. Even his own family, for all their abolitionist sympathies, weren't overjoyed with the part he had played. Ellen wrote Lucy that she didn't think "the use of force justifiable, except in cases where the person concerned appeals . . . for help," and Elizabeth confided to Emily that Henry appeared "to be ruining himself through injurious influences acting on his morbid craving for distinction." By "injurious influences," she clearly meant Lucy, because, in fact, it was Henry's love for Lucy and his desire to prove himself worthy of her that had finally impelled him to action; and his heroic gesture impressed her more than anything he had said or done previously.

[West Brookfield, Mass.] Sunday—Sept. 3. 1854

Dear Harry

We are enjoying a pleasant September Sunday. It has rained constantly during the last three days—too late however to do the crops any good. Even the leaves of our forest trees are falling. But I did not sit down to write of crops, weather, or withered foliage. Am generally thankful for pen & ink, but between us in our present position I hate them. Indeed Harry, I *must* see you. Our interview cannot, in *justice to you* be postponed until Jan. The Woman's Rights Convention at Philadelphia closes on Friday Oct. 20. I will go to Pittsburg the next day, and meet you there, if you can leave your business, and we will spend the Sunday Oct. 22 in trying to come to some permanent understanding.

If there *can* be a true marriage between us, it is as much for *my* happiness & interest to assume it, as for yours. And if there *cannot* be, it will be your gain, not less than mine to avoid it. Do you suppose dear Harry that now, when I believe I have a *right* to the marriage relation, after having spent half my days on the barren desert of an unshared life, that I would voluntarily shut myself up to its utter loneliness, still longer, if I knew any true door of escape? O no! Believe me Harry, if my love for you had in it, that *glad* self-*surrender*, & boundless trust, which are a part of the very essence of that glorified affection which *is* a wedded love, no hereditary tendency, no disease, no nothing except yourself should or *could* prevent my public recognition of it. Had I been Jane Eyre, I would have turned from that half-finished ceremony, and the dumb lips of the priest, to the love-altar in my own soul, and there, (not only as *our right*, but as a *sacred* duty imposed by our mutual love,) with Angel Witnesses & God to bless, I would have consecrated myself to the solemn, yet joyful duty, of keeping those altar-fires forever bright and pure, and would have been calm and happy, in that confidence which conscious integrity always gives. The mere existence of *such* love is *proof* of its right to be. All other questions may be conditional, but *this*, is independent of everything. A wedded-love exists, *therefore* it is right. It seems to me that there should be not a doubt in regard to its *quality*, any more than one doubts whether the sun shines. It may be, that I am deluded in regard to this, just as I now *know* I was, relative to my right to be ever married; but, as, *with those convictions*, it would have been wrong for me to act contrary to them. So now, I have no choice, but to wait for full assurance. If it ever comes to me, for *you*, or for any other, I shall accept it, as the *best* blessing of my life—for an unmarried life, made the best possible, is yet only a half-life.

After I came to know that I had a right to be a wife, and you so persistently and generously sought me to be yours, being conscious (as I still am of a very sincere affection for you,) [I] determined that nothing on my part, should prevent its full growth. To that end, I determined to be entirely frank with you, and revealed all that pertained to me, and mine, with a frankness and trust, such as I never gave to any other—but that kingdom of Heaven did not come by observation, or by being sought, and desired. The old paining hesitation lingered, and lingers yet. It does seem to me that there must be some inherent want of affinity, which is the basis of it. But Harry, dear I do not like to *write* about it. Let us have one more candid honest conversation. It will be better than a thousand letters. Meanwhile, as we neither of us, wish to get what is not ours, nor to reject what does belong to us, I think we cannot fail when we meet of coming to the right conclusion. . . . I saw by the papers, that the meeting at Salem had a *grand finale*, in the peaceful rescue of a little slave. What a change in her destiny! I would rather have been a helper in her rescue, with its conscious approval, than to be President of any slaveholding confederacy. The papers said she was immediately christened "Abby Kelly Salem." But I shall learn the particulars soon. I am giving a few lectures, just around here. We are all well. Sarah sends kind remembrance. Love to you and yours

I sent Jacques. He and Sylvia seem to me like statuary wrought from the choisest marble, which only needed a *master* artist to make them perfect.

[West Brookfield, Mass.] Sept. 10, 1854

Dear Harry

It is Sunday noon. The low sad patter of rain driven by fitful gusts of wind, so continuous for the last 2 days, has created in me a lone drear feeling, which will dissipate perhaps, as I write you. I am very glad & proud too, dear Harry of the part you took in that rescue. Your statement of the facts was well. But do not *defend* the deed. It is its own best defense, and *needs* no other. The newspaper bitterness will pass away and their falsehood be forgotten while deep down in the hearts of all who know of the rescue, will live ever, real esteem for those who made it. Many who are not capable of a noble act themselves do yet respect all the more those who are.

What an exciting scene it must have been! How much of intense thought, feeling & action, were crowded in that little space of time! What a change in one human destiny! What material for pleasant memories, was furnished to many! God bless you all, as he will, & as every worthy deed does ever! It is possible your enemies may try to make this matter interfere with your business. But even then you will be richer with your self respect, even though you may have less in dollars. The only safe wealth after all is that which "does not perish with the using."

I am glad that you spoke at Salem, your full political anti slavery conviction. I should have despised you, if you could have pretended to what you do not believe. But I hope your attitude of defense will not close your mind to the real arguments that are on the other side. The anti slavery political action, does indeed seem to me, a great waste of power. Equally clear is it that a dissolution of the Union, would bring freedom to the slaves, and wealth to the North, while persistence in a Union cemented by wrong as you yourself admit, is creating in this nation, moral blindness, and moral bankruptcy, which are appalling, & would be discouraging, if we did not *know* that *truth must EVENTUALLY* triumph. I *should* love to see our country, "The heir of all ages and the youngest born of time" realizing the beautiful ideal of freedom & equality which our fathers painted in their sublime Declaration of Independence. But when can we hope for it, if the only influence to that end, is a political party which admits that the Constitution robs the slave of his vote, and gives to his master, and still consents to swear support to such a constitution. But you say, that, will become a nullity. Not while such a moral cancer is eating out our vitality. It can be done only, by covering every proslavery clause with moral abhorrence. Sometime we must have one more talk on the subject. Today I am not in the mood of writing about it. But "Let *others* praise the Union."

In about two hours I start for a lone drive of seven miles, to give a lecture. The rain will give me a small audience, but I must keep the appointment. . . . I hope to meet you at Pittsburg. I will wear a long dress there. You do not desire true relations for yourself and me, Harry, more earnestly than I do. You can scarcely tell me anything I do not know about the unfitness of a single life. I have tried it longer than you. I know how every joy in life, may be intensified by being shared, & every pain made less. I exceedingly desire true relations for both of us [scratched-out sentence]. I have born an isolated life, until I know how to do it, and to be very compatible in it. Wishing you health of body & soul.

Yours very truly,
Lucy

[West Brookfield, Mass.] Sunday Oct. 8 [1854]

Dear Harry

I received last week your letter of the 27 ult.,— also the newspaper manuscripts, another letter, and also one from Ellen enclosed. . . . Thank you for them all, and for the wish you indicate that by reading what you write, I may know *you* better, which I very much wish to do. Yet the glimpses which your paper gives, I have caught before. It shows your versatility of talent, and in some other things assures me, of the correctness of opinions I have been forming. May be, Harry, your natural place, is that of an editor. You have certainly done very well in this sheet. I will return it by the mail of tomorrow from Boston, where I shall be, and *there*, will be no curious searcher into our correspondence.

In your letter of the 27. you say you think I overestimate, the natural defects of my being—and that I can more easily forgive and forget *yours*, than my own. If I have spoken oftener to you of mine, it was because I did not want you to be ignorant of them, or to forget them. And that if they could alienate or weaken your love for me, it should be *now* rather than hereafter. But I do *not* exaggerate them, and if you ever know me as well as I know myself, you will *then* see that I do not. I told you of my very limited literary culture, which is entirely true, though it is due I think not to any want of taste or capacity for literature but to the *want of opportunity*. I do not think that the *essential elements* of my being, are poor and barren—for with no external helps & everything to contend against, I have yet wrought out for myself, a far better life, than thousands who have every facility. With *their* advantages I know that I might have been far better, and more harmoniously developed than I am. Yet I do contemplate with proud satisfaction, my lone struggle with Destiny and my victory too, so far as it *is* a victory. And for the future, I shall still seek after knowledge and symmetry of being. And unless I make some fatal mistake, shall continue to improve long years yet, I hope. You say again that "Age is the greatest actual barrier" but hope it is not *so* great since I "lay dormant" while you were having a kind of hot-house growth.

Harry, excessive toil, and excessive grief, gave me a *premature* womanhood, and so, by a natural law premature physical decay, will come all the sooner. Do not forget either that a man, is younger than a woman of the *same* age.

If I have not often spoken to you of your defects it is because I knew that you did not *need* to be reminded of *them;* at least, between us, they were for *my* consideration, though for *you* to cure. I have *tried* to regard them, as I would if they were my own. . . . Nor do I think that faults, deficiencies, age, or differences of opinion, should interfere in the least, with those between whom a wedded life is possible. Not that it will be blind to any or all of these—but each will fit himself gladly to those which cannot be changed, and help kindly and lovingly to remove the others. We at least, have this advantage over younger lovers, who always fancy the object of their affection perfect; who, as the illusion vanishes, awake sadly to the reality and wear a life-long disappointment. We know *some* of our defects, and may by mutual help cure them, *if* that all-hallowing love *ever* comes to me, through which alone, we can accept, or share a common destiny. But it is useless to *write;* one hour's conversation, will be worth an ocean of letters. And I will see you before long, somewhere.

In regard to the Salem rescue—I can scarcely tell you, how the radiance of the halo I had thrown around your action there has been *dimmed* by your last letters. When you wrote me of the rescue,—of the falsehood & systematic abuse which followed you, and that it was threatened beforehand, and quietly added: "all which does not break my sleep of nights"—I said to myself, "here is a noble deed which

Harry did not do from *impulse*. In the two or three hours that inter-
vened between the receipt of the despatch, and the arrival of the
train, he had time for reflection, and after counting the cost, deliberately made up his mind to abide by his highest convictions. And
now I have found in him, that of which I *feared* he was *constitutionally defective*, viz. the ability to *sacrifice* all that must be sacrificed,
and to accept the *consequences* of the carrying out of his *real* ideas,
at *whatever cost*!! I felt *nearer* to you then, dear Harry in all that
constitutes nearness, than I ever did before, and if you had been
indeed my husband, I would have gathered you to my heart of hearts,
with more lovefull trust, and tenderness than ever, sure that such
high heroism, and great *fidelity* to *yourself*, might be trusted to the
utmost; and it trembled in my heart, and on my pen to tell you so—
but I thought of my *own* defects and waited, until you were so abused
by others that I could not avoid telling you how much dearer you
were to me for that act. Then in a day or two, I received yours,
regretting the "needless loss of influence," the "obloquy," the "indis-
cretion," &c &c. I felt no anger, or reproach, but a saddened sense
of something *lost* and gone, has attended me ever since. I had so
much *wished* to find in you, that simple faith in the right, that "let
justice be done if the Heavens fall," that perhaps I was *too ready* to
seize upon anything which indicated it.

If you were to die tomorrow, *this* act, is perhaps the only one of
all your life, that the historian would think it worth while to record.
And when the future Gibbon, shall write "the Decline & Fall" of our
country, the anti slavery epoch, will form no unimportant part,—the
rescue at Syracuse & at Salem, will find a record, and *then* when
party prejudice, and hostility to the anti slavery movement are forgotten, these events will be seen, in their *true grandeur*. And your
children's children will be *proud* to tell that *you* formed a part of
those acts. My one regret dear Harry in regard to it is, that regret is
possible to you—And still you do not think that a temporizing policy,
or ideas of mere expediency affect, or create your present feelings in
regard to it. Do not deceive yourself, nor blame me dear Harry, because I persist in calling, or trying to call your attention, to this really
most serious defect in your character. The deep intense, constant
yearning which I feel that you should be *sound* in this *vital* part
shows me how very dear you are to me. Do not think that I love to

tantalize and pain you, or that I wish to dictate. Heaven knows that I do neither. But I *do* desire more than I can *express*, that the *future* pages of your book of life, shall not be scarred, because you could not trust God, that when He established true principles, He made it sure that the *best* influence should attend conformity to them. . . . Pray do not be willing to deceive yourself. You *see* your need of greater self-control, and you will strive for, and attain *that*. I *wish* you could see how much *more* you need to strive here. I will not write about it. But when I see you dear Harry, *may* I speak to you, *about you*, just as *freely* as I *think*? You have often said that if I were your wife, I should help you to a better life. Let me as your *friend* speak plainly.

I go this evening, a few miles to lecture & tomorrow commence my winter's pilgrimage. I wish you could see our forests. They seem more beautiful than ever. The dark ever-greens scattered through this region, heighten the contrast. I wish the moral world were *as* beautiful. It will, some day when we are all true, be infinitely more so.

I will write to you from Philadelphia whether I will go to Cincinnati, and *when*.

With much love, and the hope that, as we know that we are not perfect, we must strive to become so.

Lucy

[West Brookfield, Mass.] Tuesday Oct. 10 1854

Dear Harry

Here I am at my own home, whither I came yesterday. . . . I returned you yesterday, from Boston, your paper, with notes to Ellen and yourself.

Do not think dear Harry, from what I wrote you then, that I have *no* satisfaction in your part of the rescue, or that I think *you* have none. I almost regret that I *wrote* you anything in regard to it— that I had not reserved all I thought, until I could *speak* it. But you will not misunderstand me, I hope. I do not want to be *one-sided*, but I want that we should both be *right sided*. But we are going to be very frank, and very candid and very honest, with ourselves and with each other when we meet. And *then* we shall not misunderstand nor mistake. I reciprocate fully your wish that I sang like Jenny Lind, and were the perfection of grace & beauty &c and especially that I were ten years younger. But in all except the last, I expect somewhere in the ages, to find myself greatly improved. Next to the being perfect, the best thing is to *wish* to *become* so. . . .

Mother sits by me, and asks to whom I am writing, and when I tell her, she quotes, "young men's vows are soon forgotten." Her experience, in life, and in the world, makes her distrustful as it well may. I only wonder that *trust* is any longer possible to the human soul. And yet how necessary it is to trust!

Your state election is today. And you think you have voted as an intelligent slave would wish you to. Well do what *you* think is right.

Yours affectionately

338 Arch St. Phila, Pa.
Oct. 22, 1854

Dear Harry

This very beautiful Sunday, I hoped to spend somewhere with you, but the fates forbade, and according to your fatalistic theory, it is all for the best, so I submit.

Our Convention is over, and well over too. From first to last there has been no discord or disorder. We have had crowded sessions, and when the last closed at 10 o'clock on Friday evening, I felt that it had been good for us to be there. The press, without exception, I believe, has been respectful and fair. Mr. Higginson aided us greatly by his speeches and counsel. He is a very noble man. One of the anointed. We took upwards of $700. at the door, and sold $50. of valuable tracts, which I have just had stereotyped. So the good seed is being sown; it will grow and bear fruit when we are dead. Our lot as workers is scarcely less good than theirs who will enjoy the results of our labors.

I have been trying to plan to meet you. Nette will scarcely have left you, before Mr. Garrison will be in the city. I dont want to meet either of them. . . . If Nette could spend Sunday with Mrs. Ernst, and not return to your house, I would be there Sunday evening, and thus save a day, but as I do not know that such arrangements can be made, it will probably be best for me to fix Monday evening, to meet you at Cincinnati, if you prefer to have me go there rather than stop at Pittsburg. . . . I shall expect a line to tell me what you think is best. If I do not hear from you, in time to reply, I will telegraph you, over the signature "John Jones."

I want to see you. I want this suspense which haunts me, sleeping & waking, over. The subject had not been absent from my mind an hour, since you left me last June. Bewildered and fearful, I see nothing clearly, and dread lest *any* step shall be a wrong one. Like Ajax, I yearn for *light*, and would be half-willing to forgo it forever after, if I might but KNOW now just what is right, and true. I love and value *alike*, your happiness, & mine. A false step may peril & destroy both, yet I can seek guidance nowhere. It is pitiful to be so blind and weak! Farewell.

L. S.

Wilmington Del.
Oct. 26 1854

Dear Harry

I have just got your letter of the 21inst., and hasten to say by this morning's mail, that I rather you should meet me at Pittsburgh. . . .

I am sure it will be impossible to escape Nette, and Mr. Garrison & the Anti Slavery Bazaar. We shall not need more than one day. And you can return to Cincinnati in time to look after your anti slavery meetings—at least so much as Sam does not care for in your absence. . . . I should love to go to your home, and see Ellen & your mother & brothers but it is *you* now that I want to see, and where we can be entirely alone. . . . I am sorry to interfere in any way with your business, or your arrangements for lectures. But I *cannot* go to Cincinnati. I thought I did not care, but I will not go denying people, and I *cannot* see them.

I have not time to add another word.

Very affectionately
Lucy

At Pittsburgh Lucy and Henry finally came to an understanding: They were to be married, though the time and place of the actual ceremony had yet to be fixed. Considering the hectic nature of both their lives, this wasn't easy to do. Henry went back to Cincinnati, but soon left on a collecting trip in Indiana, while Lucy gave a few more lectures in Pennsylvania, returned briefly to her home in Massachusetts, and then set off on a lecture tour of New England, which brought her back to Boston toward the end of December for a round of antislavery meetings.

⧞

Chambersburgh [Pa.] Sunday Nov. 5-1854

My dear Harry

This clear, cold, still beautiful Sunday I am alone in a quiet Baptist family, who say grace at all their meals, and who regard the ordinance of baptism as essential to salvation. A clergyman dwells in the family, and this morning he favored me with text, verse, and commentary to prove the Divine obligation to be immersed. I quietly expressed the opinion, that a *true life*, irrespective of all forms could alone render one acceptable to God. *That*, he said, would do for those who had no Bible, but not for those who *had*. After an hour spent in the discussion of this *grave* question, he proposed to give me an account of his conversion—said he *knew* I *should be interested* in it, and then proceeded, for another hour, until he was obliged to go, to preach,—greatly to my relief. But, as I had only to *appear* to listen, I kept thinking of something else, much more than of what he was saying. I dont know, but it seems to me that God must have infinite merriment, over the foibles of some of his creatures.

I have had two meetings here, which paid me over expenses, about $75. I should have had a third this evening, but the good people here, do not know, (some of them) that the Sabbath was made for man. So after having engaged the Court House, I was told by the door keeper, as I entered the Court House, last evening, that he "had conscientious scruples about opening the house on Sunday, and that he could not do it. I told him I was sorry, but should be still

more sorry to have him do, what he thought was wrong, and that he
need not do it. I would employ some one else. Whereupon he said
the commissioners would not allow anyone else to light it. So I sent
a messenger to them, but while they did not object on their *own
account*, they thought it would not do to set the example of "paid
lectures on the Sabbath." And so I have the evening to rest, which is
better for *me*. And the discussion which is growing out of it, will be
better for *them*, than the lecture. My friends, (and they are the larger
number) say, "What is the difference in principle—*you* collect money
on Sunday, at class meeting & conference to pay your preacher. Miss
Stone does no more" &c. &c. It will do them good. I am glad, on the
whole. . . . .

8½ o'clock. I was interrupted with calls. . . . Some 20 young
men, who had come in 15 miles from the country expecting to hear
a lecture, called, so at least, they might have a *sight of me*. We spent
an hour, in a warm discussion on color phobia, started by some one,
who said, that the people did not like a remark I made the evening
before, viz. that a negro was as good as a white man. And he advised
me not to prejudice my own cause, by adding the rights of "niggers"
to it. A very animated, warm, but very respectful discussion ensued,
in which I took the ground of absolute equality of natural rights. One
man said the blacks were a different order of beings—had not the
same creator &c. I charged him at once with being an infidel (the
same had been circulated about me). I told him the Bible declared,
that God had made of one blood &c. which he denied, and hence, he
was an infidel, for he did not believe the Bible. He said he did not
believe that part of it—and so, said I you *are* an infidel &c. &c. Justice & truth were on my side, and made apparent too. I told them,
my next lecture there, should be on prejudice against color. They
said they would give it a candid hearing, but they wished all the
blacks were out of the country. That Cumberland Valley, so beautiful
in scenery, and rich in soil, *ought* to produce more harmonious &
beautiful spirits. It will some day. I thank the Good Father that he
allows *hope* to live on forever. . . .

Harry dear, I think I wronged you at Pittsburgh, when I told
you I did not believe you were honest. I *do* think you are true to
your own convictions, and *that* is to be honest—but I do not think
your stand point is the highest. But I *know* that you do aspire for a

noble and manly life, and I feel a quiet confidence, that your future
will be worthy your father's son.

Good night. God bless you.

Terre Haute [Ind.] Dec. 10. 1854

Dearest!

    "De profundis clamavi" Lucy! Lucy "awaite me!"—Which is,
being interpreted,—I have written to you from the depths of Hoosierdom & Suckerdom & I trust you will get my letters! For three
weeks I have been making a pack horse of myself riding up & down
through the length & breath of the Wabash Country from Lafayette
to Terre Haute & from Indianapolis to Springfield. I have collected
15000$ & uttered (inaudibly) 15000 maledictions upon the roads, the
people & the business. As a natural consequence I have acquired the
appetite of a wolf, the digestion of an ostrich, the stupidity of a jackass
& the solemnity of an owl. One more week & I *trust* I shall be at
home. After all—there is no place like home. I *will quit travelling*! If
there is a hut on the earth, or a hole in the ground, or a crooked
branch in a tree, I will take possession & defy all the powers of Earth
or Hell to get me out for a year. The "imponderable fluids" electricity
& such like, may keep up their everlasting vibrations if they will—
but for myself being a ponderous solid I intend to *settle down & be
at rest*. Dear Lucy—all this means simply—I am very tired of running
about & am looking forward with great glee to spending a quiet
Christmas on Walnut Hills. By the way—Marian is to be with us.
Wont you come too. . . .

    I have very little to say. I have built as many castles in the air
lately as a diet of sausage & short cake & forty miles a day on a horse
will permit. I suppose I shall plead guilty to putting *you* into each of
my castles however much they differ in other respects. Sometimes I
plan to live in New York where the great panorama of human life
flashes by most rapidly & shines most—sometimes I plan to live at
Chicago & use my present hard earned acquaintances in fertile &
wealthy Illinois to build up a wholesale grocery business there on the
flat shore of blue Lake Michigan. Would you like to live in Chicago
Lucy? I hope to be home this day week or next day. Write me as

soon as you get this & tell us whether you will be with us at Christmas? Good bye dear

> Yours ever & a day after
> Harry

> Cincinnati December 22ᵈ 1854

My own dearest Lucy

 . . . I had travelled on horseback 45 miles over very rough roads, but on a beautiful day—crossed the Wabash on a flat boat with my horse with some difficulty the ice running & rode 7 miles by Starlight over the prairie into town. There I recᵈ a budget of letters from various quarters & among them those two welcome ones from you. . . . My dear Lucy thank you a hundred times for all the strong, warm, beautiful love & confidence which fill & animate those letters. I hope to show my thanks in something better than words in all the actions & feelings of my future life. Dear Lucy dont fear but that I will return you love for love to the fullest extent that your soul is capable of putting forth. You say that some one told you you had the capacity of love of 20 women. If so I will give you the love of as many men. I will *try* to be to you *all* that a man *should* be to the woman he loves—*can* I say more than that?

 In your last letter you tell me of the pain you experienced at the idea of being placed in the *legal* position of wife. I am *very sorry* that you should thus suffer. But surely there is no *degradation* in being unjustly treated by *others*. The true degradation & disgrace rests not with the victim but with the oppressors. In this case the *disgrace* is more *mine* than *yours*. The Law by clothing me with unjust powers puts me in the position of the wrongdoer but it only puts you in that of the wrong sufferer & so my case is morally the most painful. But after all what is the Law? It is *nothing*, unless *appealed to*. It is merely "a rule of civil action" in case of such appeal. It exists only where it is invoked. And even there, by taking proper steps we can anticipate & alter its possible action. But dear Lucy unjust as is the Law, the *position* of a *wife* is based in Nature & is therefore *honorable*. All the perversions of Men cannot make the *married woman* other than a woman in a true relation to herself, to her husband & to her kind. So do not let this matter trouble you. . . .

Dear Lucy, we will live a pure & rational life. We will not be selfish, or impatient with each other in anything. We will advise together & each live out our own nature freely & frankly. . . . But Lucy dear—do not feel *constrained* to marry me. Even now—or even on the very day itself, if you feel pain & shrinking postpone it just as long & as often as you please. Now you are my wife in sight of God by the divine tie of affection, I can wait as long as you please for its manifestation in this way. Dear Lucy you will break no faith & violate no compact if you leave me at any time either before, or after marriage. You are your own mistress & always will remain so. You speak of "Lucy Stone that was." You are the same Lucy that was & always will be. Dont feel badly on my a/c [account]. Dear Lucy—I would rather wait *ten years* & have no children than give you *any* unhappiness. I hope that what I have said about the legal position being no disgrace will seem as forcible to you as it does to me. I want you *never* to feel badly again about our affair. If you could quite understand my feelings towards you you would not. Still when you do feel so, tell me about it. I shall write to Elizabeth to-day & tell her how matters stand. She would feel much hurt if the news reached her through Dr Hunt, or any other quarter. . . .

As to your property dear—it will be necessary I suppose to settle all your *personal* property on yourself. This includes your money in the hands of our firm & all other than real estate in fee simple. I do not know the law of Ohio, or Mass., but the best way will be to put it into the hands of trustees for your benefit. . . . Then we will engage to *share earnings* on both sides—you to get half of mine & I half of yours, so long as we live together. If we ever separate—each to relinquish all claim to the others subsequent earnings & each to take half the children you having the choice. If the separation is from wrong conduct—the right to control children to be decided by arbitrators—one each selected by you & me & one more selected by them. In case of death either party may will his or her property to whomsoever he pleases unless there are children—in which case enough to support & educate them, shall be reserved. Unless separation take place the surviving partner shall be the executor & guardian.

In case of death after separation, unless gross misconduct on either part has been the cause—the survivor takes the children previously held by the other partner & becomes their guardian—otherwise—the deceased partner shall have a guardian nominated by him or her in the will. Neither partner shall be liable for any debts contracted & liabilities incurred by the other partner previous to marriage—nor (except for maintenance if necessary) shall have any claim to property acquired by the other partner previous to marriage—nor shall the private property of either partner be liable for debts of the other. You shall choose when, where & how often you shall become a mother. Neither partner shall attempt to fix the residence, employment, or habits of the other—nor shall either partner feel bound to live together any longer than is agreeable to both. All earnings *subsequent* to marriage during its harmonious continuance to be liable for family expenses equally, but all *surplus* of joint earnings to be annually divided & placed to the credit of each. It will require some reflection to plan out *exactly* the conditions which in case of domestic difficulties would be exactly equitable. I think however that the true idea of marriage is a business partnership in pecuniary matters like that existing between members of our firm. You & I will be *joint proprietors* of *everything* except the results of previous labors. In case of there being an only child—& the separation involving no moral turpitude on either side we should share its possession taking turns. For the sake of a good example we will draw up a contract specifying our course under all these various contingencies of separation by dissention or death. But I *feel* & *know* so well that the first at least *cannot* happen, that it seems almost farcical for *us* so to specify.

Think over my suggestions on the previous pages. The appropriation of *joint earnings* to family expenses & the *division* of *surplus* is clearly the only equitable provision. Even among birds it is the office of the male to bring food & assistance to the female while she is rearing the family. To give the woman the charge of self support in *addition* to that of nurturing her offspring would be a monstrous injustice to Woman far worse than the present imperfect system even if it were not, as it would be, a physical impossibility. The surplus, where any exists, should be carried to the individual credits & be under the sole disposal of each. I see no difficulty in the law for a *loving* marriage. I have just indicated it. But in case of separation & alienation no possible ingenuity can devise a rule under which injustice *may* not be done, nay *must* not be done to one & often to both parties. But I think the agreement, as I have stated it, would be the best possible. Of course the infant should under any case except habitual vice of the grossest description, be guaranteed to the mother. I like your idea of simple habits & a quiet mode of domestic life. Unless in Association, luxury would cost more than it comes to. I have no relish for display. We shall find our happiness in *comfort* not *show* & in nobler things than costly gewgaws.

Speaking of property reminds me that I have just ascertained a most excellent place for investing for you any money which you may have to spare. The government lands at 2^{50} per acre on the Central R. Road in Illinois are almost all taken up, but I know of some two, or three sections of excellent land still vacant on the line of the Chicago branch about 100 miles South of that city & near some of my own. . . . If you will rely on my judgment in such matters which is remarkably good—send me what money you want to invest in a Draft on N.Y., or Boston & I will at once select the land for you in person—get the Certifs made out in your name & remit them to you. . . .

Dear Lucy I must close my long letter. I want to meet you & take you into my arms again more than words can express. God bless you & keep you my own little wife—& believe me ever yours

Harry

Cincinnati Dec. 23. 1854

Dearest Lucy

. . . You talk about our plans & future home & express a very wise & natural preference for the superior social & intellectual privileges of the East. We will not be hasty in our decisions, nor premature. The first thing is to get clear where I am. The next will be to take a free breath & look around. I am in no hurry. I have the same preference for the East on many a/s. It is in the view of my *Future* that I doubt a little the wisdom of going East. I have the foundation of a fortune laid in the West & see an opening for myself & brothers in Chicago that does not present itself in New York. . . .

But if, on consultation, the plan of going there seems to you

undesirable we will give it up. I will, if necessary, sacrifice even ambition to *love*—& with you I shall be rich enough anywhere. . . . My
preference for Chicago was simply this. There, upon a smaller Capital
than East, Sam & George & I might commence a wholesale grocery
business with our Illinois customers & one of us could run down occasionally & plant out & superintend a magnificent orchard of apples
& peaches upon a beautiful high rolling tract of prairie from which,
with a good glass, you can see the R.Road 40 miles North & 40 miles
South. . . . Thus I think that in five years at latest I might retire
from business with a permanent income from the orchard, far more
than sufficient, while my Wis. lands would pay off all my debts. But
as a mere *place to live* I should certainly prefer the East. There is a
superior culture there which will perhaps more than counterbalance
the *breadth* & freedom & progressive energy of the West. I confess
I like the spirit of the Western people much better than that of those
in the East. They *know more* though they do not know any one thing
so thoroughly. They are liberal & neither so *indifferent* nor so *hide-
bound* as people in older & poorer communities. . . .

And so, dear Lucy, you have been buying little things for "our
home." You want its outward & its inward beauty to correspond! So
do I. But whether it has the Mountains & the Ocean outside & the
thousand little comforts inside, or not—we will make it rich with love
& bright with ideas & warm with earnestness & noble with hope &
aspiration & great principles. We will try to be true to universal interests & not to forget the *Race* in our own little objects & cares.

I wrote to Elizabeth to-day telling her about our next Spring's
intentions. Lucy dear cannot you arrange to marry me on the 10th of
February next. On many a/cs I wish that we were married. . . .
What time in January do you expect to visit us? Let me know at once
for I expect to have to spend the greater part of January in Indiana
& I will endeavor to arrange to be at home at the time you appoint.

[Boston] Dec. 25 10 o'clock PM [1854]

Harry dearest I sent you by tonight's mail a little bit of a letter, very
unsatisfactory to me,—Indeed all my letters grow more and more so
to me,—I *want to be with you,* and have scope for that fullness of
expression, which my soul all the time yearns for. But I have a round

of meetings that must be *first* held. And then, my own dear darling Harry, while we are happy in each others society, we will help each other, as far as we *can* render aid in all that will give us the noblest life. I know that in some departments you can aid me very materially. And I look forward, with calm, deep happiness and high hope of an opportunity for more symmetrical developement than I have hitherto had and I am not selfishly seeking my alone good. I will *try* in every way I can to aid you, and to make your life too more symmetrical. Dear Harry we can, and will help each other, & we will be *forever better*, for our wedded love. Mr. Garrison was here this evening, and spoke of our marriage. He said, after wishing us all blessings, "I like Harry. He has great freedom of thought, would not put a shackle upon anybody's freest thought, and is very true to his own convictions. I used to go to see his father when he lived in Jersey. He was a man of great worth of character, dignified, refined, cultivated & true as steel." He said many other things, which I have not time to write. But it is *very* satisfactory to me to know Mr. Garrison, and other dear friends of mine here, feel attracted to you, and esteem you. I hope that your friends too will be able [to] regard me kindly. . . .

I am spending some to get things for us [to] keep house with— silver forks, spoons, blankets, sheets, towels, &c &c. . . . I get valuable things, for they will be cheaper in the end The little stool which I drew today, will be a pretty ornament for our parlor. Mr Garrison said that when it was announced that 1 had drawn it, the hall rang with a shout, which showed how glad they were to have me have it. Its price was five dollars—but I must stop. It is half past 10.—Christmas eve is almost over. I wish we were to spend its remnant together! I hope I do not weary you with so many letters. I should love to write you every day—but if I do not write you very often hereafter—it is because I am reading various things which I ought to have read years ago—but could not,—but if I read them now—it will be all the pleasanter for us when we *live* together. May it be indeed a *living*, and not a stagnation! Sarah will go to Cincinnati soon. Her husband likes [it] there, very much. Her illness was caused by a premature birth—A little boy—too young to have a funeral for— but we both shed a tear for it. You must not of course speak to her of it. I hope you have had a good day dearest. . . .

Most truly yours.

Months before Lucy had agreed to marry him, Henry had suggested making a protest against the unjust laws in regard to marriage, and now he again brought up the idea. It wasn't original to him: In 1832 Robert Dale Owen, the reformer and son of the founder of the utopian community of New Harmony, had denounced the unfairness of marriage laws at his wedding, and so had Theodore Weld and Angelina Grimké in 1838, and the English couple, John Stuart Mill and Harriet Taylor, in 1851. But the idea was very much in keeping with Lucy's oft-stated aversion to the legal position of a wife, and showed Henry's sensitivity to her feelings in the matter.

However, on another point, he was surprisingly insensitive. A close-knit family, the Blackwells were accustomed to sharing everything that pertained to their lives. Thus when he first began to court Lucy, Henry had wasted no time writing Elizabeth about her, and then forwarding Elizabeth's letter on to Lucy. Now that they were to be married, he did the same—despite the fact that Elizabeth greeted the news of their engagement with marked coolness. "Your engagement with Lucy is a thing we have long expected & so perhaps ought to be familiar with," she wrote, "& yet it seemed to take me by surprise to-day, as if I had never heard of the matter." She went on to say that Lucy had as yet only come before her "in the eccentricities and accidents of the American phase of this nineteenth century, in bloomerism, abolitionism, woman's rightism," but that she was ready to welcome as a sister-in-law the "immortal Lucy who will live and bloom in rich humanity where there is no slave, no caste, no mud."

Along with Elizabeth's letter, Henry sent Lucy a letter from his oldest sister, Anna, who was living in Europe and hadn't yet been informed of their engagement. However, this didn't stop Anna from writing what Henry himself described as "a tirade against Yankee women." And in fact, her letter proved more upsetting to Lucy than Elizabeth's, because it stirred up feelings of inferiority that were associated with the defects of her "literary culture."

≈

Cincinnati Jany 3. [1855]

My own dear sweet Lucy

I have just rec^d your letter enclosing Dft. [draft] for investment—& feel as I always do when I read your letters—that I am the most fortunate & favored of all living men to have thus won the love of a woman so pure & true & noble. Dear Lucy I shall have to wear out that footstool you drew at the fair in sitting at your feet & laying my head upon your faithful lap. I will *try* to be worthy of you & to imitate your disinterested & generous unselfishness of affection. I am sorry you should still feel as though *martyrdom* would demand *refraining* from marriage rather than *suffering* the law's injustice. . . . Why Lucy dear—You even now occupy a position similar in *kind* & differing only in *degree*. The law now says—You are not *fully* a citizen—You shall not *vote* shall not make laws, nor say who shall make them. You suffer this injustice for the same reason as you will the other. You *cannot help it*. "Ah, but I *can* avoid it in the one case and not in the other"—you will perhaps say. You *can* indeed avoid it *in both cases*, but in both it *costs too much*. You can avoid the political injustice you now suffer by retiring from civilization to some uninhabited, or barbarous country where individualism is the only law. You can avoid the additional injustice attached to marriage by *violating* the *divine law* which says *marry*, or by going to the same barbarous wilderness—& *in no other ways*, but these two.

Now then, if we could find a little band of men & women who, *to make a perfect State* would withdraw to some unclaimed wilderness & there found a nobler New England—I am ready to go. But I do not think any human laws have such claims upon my obedience as to *compel me* to go. I have a perfect right to stay & set the laws at defiance. We have a right to be a law unto ourselves. Would it not be a *slavish* doctrine to preach that we *ought* to sentence ourselves to celibacy because men have enacted injustice into a statute. But Lucy dear I want to make a *protest* distinct and *emphatic* against the laws. I wish, as a husband, to *renounce* all the privileges which the law confers upon me, which are not strictly *mutual* & I intend to do so. Help me to draw one up. When we marry, I will publicly state before our friends a brief enumeration of these usurpations & distinctly pledge myself to never avail myself of them *under any circumstances.* Surely *such a marriage* will not degrade you, dearest—Lucy, I *wish* I could take the position of the wife under the law & give you that of a husband. I would rather submit to the injustice a hundred times, than subject you to it.

I am about to make a trip into Wisconsin. A number of my friends want to buy more land & I can make sufficient commission to justify going up. Moreover I take a wild pleasure in travelling in Winter through an almost uninhabited Country *well* wrapped up with clothes impenetrable to the cold & buffalo overshoes on my feet & a compass in my pocket—mounted on a good horse & surveying a new Country & a strange climate. I feel happier than anywhere else except in your arms. . . .

I enclose Anna's letter to me & also to the family. Ellen wished me not to send it saying that you do not know Anna well enough to understand her & that it would make you feel unpleasantly. But I know you well enough to know better & inasmuch as Anna has not the *remotest idea* of you & my engagement, nor *any reference to it whatever*, you cannot feel any *personal* hurt from her strictures on Americans. Anna suffered very much in this Country. . . . & since she has returned to England & been placed in happier circumstances she looks back at America with a very natural though not very wise aversion. . . . I also enclose Elizabeth's reply to my letter announcing our approaching marriage. Dear Lucy—Goodbye God bless you my own little wife & unite us as soon as may be—meanwhile believe me—

> Ever your own—
> Harry—

Boston—Jan. 18-1855

Dearest Harry

   . . . Do not fear that I shall not understand Anna. She is much like you, and knowing you, I can interpret her. With her high culture, and artistic life, it is the most natural thing in the world that she should desire the same excellencies in the wife of her brother.

And it would be a *great deal better for him*, if *it could be so*. I know the *worth* of those things, not as she does, from *possessing* them, but from the *want* of them. But I have a real desire to improve, and doing the best I can, with you all to help me, the time may come when I shall come nearer her ideal, and my own too. I wish I had a rich and varied culture, with personal wealth and beauty, and every good—but these have been all outside the rocky path over which I have toiled. I have very little, of that which the world values, to carry you, dear Harry, but *such as I have,* and *all* that I have—the *unselfish* love, of an individual heart are *yours*. You will never be proud of my polished exterior, nor of my brilliant intellect, nor of my high culture. But in the circle in which you will move, you will of necessity, often feel that I am inferior to it—you will be pained, and your love of approbation will suffer, many times, because I shall be ever on the unpopular side of unpopular reforms. Our moral stand point, and our view of what is intrinsically worthy of pursuit are so different, that we shall each, many times feel alone. I have so little literary culture, and no artistic, that in all these respects you will feel sorely *uncompanioned,* for I am sadly deficient. But I will try and surround you with those who shall supply what I lack, so far as these things are concerned; and will *try* as far as I can to supply the wants of your *heart*.

But as you said to me, in a letter the other day, "do not feel constrained to marry me, even on the day itself, if you cannot do so freely." So I say to you, do not let our engagement or anything that has passed, make you feel *any obligation,* to me. I know how much you and your family have acquired, which I have not. I am glad for them; it is worth a great deal. I know that it will be impossible for you not to *feel* the difference, and painfully, too. I know too that if we have little ones, it will not be possible for me to gain much, for many years, in the respects in which I am so deficient. So, dear Harry, in view of it all, if anywhere, even in the most silent corner of your heart, there lingers the *faintest* wish, that we sustained no relation, but that of friendship—I would *infinitely* rather it should all be dropped—it will be for the highest good of both.

I am not writing this, on account of anything in Anna's letter. I love and value her all the more on account of her earnest interest in your welfare. And her wish that you should have a cultivated wife, is surely sensible. You *ought* to have. But I am not so, and *may never* become so. My culture has been mainly of my moral nature. I want to be situated for the future, where I can make progress in other respects. Early in our acquaintance I told you of my deficiencies (perhaps there was no need, they are apparent)—and they have ever been in my mind as an objection to our marriage. So my dear Harry, be *honest* with yourself, and *frank* with me. And let no false sense of honor, or of what people will say, prevent you from being *entirely* true to yourself.

But we will talk of it, when we meet, and of the *business* too. I have thought a great deal of what will be best. I know that you have a good business talent, and have no doubt that in that department, you might "excel," or that you could accumulate largely, of the treasures that perish with the using. And that you could have the distinction of being called a rich man. As he who makes two spires of grass grow where only one grew before, is a benefactor—so he who *creates* wealth is a benefactor. But there are plenty of people who can make money—not so many who can bring the world a high *thought,* that shall make its *immortal* part better;—fewer still, whose life of sublime devotion to the highest right, leaves an example, which, by its *imperishable worth,* wins followers, and so makes the world *better,* if not in money, at least better in morals. I hoped that we should be able to give ourselves to the great *moral* movements of the age— But of all of this, we will speak when we meet. . . . I think you will not misunderstand me, or this letter my dear Harry. If you do, I will make it all plain when I come to see you.

> Very truly yours my own Harry
> Lucy

When they met in Cincinnati toward the end of January, Henry was able to assure Lucy that he did indeed still want to marry her, and throughout February, while she lectured in Michigan and he was off in "the depths of Hoosierdom" on another collecting trip, they used the mails to discuss various plans for the future, the protest, and the where and when of their wedding. But by early March it began to look as if their marriage might not take place at all. Henry's concern that Lucy was overexerting herself with lecturing changed to genuine alarm when he learned that she was again suffering from the "hard headache." This time the attack was more serious than ever, and Lucy herself feared for her sanity.

Lucy's illness was clearly related to her impending marriage. Marriage was such a powerful determinant of the future course of a woman's life that more than a few thoughtful women of the period suffered a highly emotional reaction, or "marriage trauma," in regard to it. So Lucy's response wasn't necessarily unusual or extreme. Nor was it out of character: She had long ago determined to "call no man master," and now on the eve of her capitulation, she was torn by conflicting feelings. While she was filled with a romantic yearning for union with her soul's complement, she also feared the self-annihilation that seemed to go hand in hand with marriage. The legal disabilities of being a wife continued to weigh upon her, as did her sexual phobias. Victorian reticence on this subject did not permit very explicit discussion of her feelings. She preferred to confide in her sister Sarah rather than Henry, and he was reluctant to write very much about it in his own letters. Yet the problem was there and it was complicated by the question of offspring. Lucy wanted very much to have children, but was afraid that because of her advanced age—she was now thirty-seven—any children they had would be born defective.

Henry, of course, tried to be as reassuring as possible, but there was only so much he could say. The demons that Lucy was battling were at once powerful, and deeply personal.

❧

Adrian [Mich.] Feb. 1ˢᵗ 1855

. . . Dear Harry I do so love you. My heart warms towards you all the time. I shall be *so* glad when it becomes possible for us to be ever together! I want to be with you, and am half disposed to drop, or rather *not* make appointments for many meetings hereabouts, and be married at once, and then go with you to Wisconsin, and while you go to see the land, I will lecture in Milwaukee & Madison. O no! that will never do. I had better hold the meetings, as I at first proposed. But my heart *yearns* towards you *all the time*, so deeply,—so intensely—and [I] only pray this deep earnest love may last forever. Dearest I cant write. I am at a private home, and three lady visitors are in the room, other company is just now coming in, and two children are trying to show me all their playthings. So you must *understand* what I would write, and wait until next Sunday. Give much love to the friends at Walnut Hills, and be sure that for yourself the largest and warmest room in my heart is *all* for *you*—dearest—

Ever yours
Lucy

Cincinnati Feby. 6. 1855

Dear Little Lucy

I hope you wont be offended by the *diminutive*, which I so often attach to your name. It is an expression of love which, I know not why, seeks to *surround* and *embrace* the object of affection & so, I suppose, conceives of it as small, in order, (not being *very* large myself), to encircle it. Your Adrian note reached me last evening. Spofford & George & I were walking rapidly homeward in order to spend the Monday evening as usual together in reading & talking over some subject, or author. Just as we had passed the street in which stands the Post Office a *feeling* came over me that there was a letter from you lying in our box for me. I told them I expected a letter at the office & would get it & rejoin them—went to the office & there, sure enough, was just one letter, which proved to be your's from Adrian. On reaching home while Mr & Mrs Spofford & the folks talked awaiting supper, I read it & you do not know how much *good* it did me. Every letter seems a guarantee of your love. I feel *assured* that your true heart beats steadily *for me* & though I ought to know it & do know it without the letter, yet it makes me realize it more thoroughly.

So you escaped the snow drifts & the frost. I feel quite anxious about you & only wish I could be ever by your side, by day & night, to watch over you. For *my* sake dear Lucy, watch over *yourself—keep warm*, make the people give you fire in your bedroom, get regular meals & wrap up well—also take regular exercise. I want to *keep* you well. Also if you catch cold try not to speak much till you recover your voice, for that is a great danger, and above all dearest, do not let any doubts, or forebodings about our *future* cause you pain, or anxiety. Be sure that I have but one desire—*your happiness* & *prosperity*. I will try to so act towards you that your love & trust will grow daily more perfect—& to so live that I shall be more worthy of your love every day. Surely if I am *true* to you & to myself, I *cannot* do you harm! . . .

You ask me to write out a protest against marriage laws. I will try & send you in a few days the result of my deliberations. But I hope to accept *your* form rather than my own. It should be *brief, distinct* & *comprehensive*—so as to be read, understood & remembered.

I am very glad dear Lucy that I can reveal, in spite of my imperfections, something of Divinity to your soul. I should like to stand in your heart & mind as a perpetual reminder of the nobler qualities of Man, as you must represent to me the highest elements of Womanhood.

You promise to be true to me if all the world forsake me. I hope you may never be so situated. It would be ten thousand pities if your honorable name should ever be associated even involuntarily & innocently, with the errors & crimes of anybody. If I thought you could ever be called upon to go through such an ordeal, though I *know* that you would be as *true* as *steel*, I would see you *once more* & then go into the wilds of South America, or the human wilderness of Europe, or Asia, or else build up a better reputation in Australia & leave you to find a fitter mate. But I do not think that a *possibility*, certainly not a *probability*, exists of such a misfortune. If it *do come* we will counsel together as to what is right—& if I may—I will defend myself—if not—I will suffer in *silence* what the law inflicts & then shame *law* & *facts* by a life which shall disarm criticism. But *acknowledge* guilt, I think I never shall nor ought! However I have looked that spectre too often in the face to feel alarm, or lose my presence of mind—come what may! . . .

Yours ever

Feby. 13. 1855
Terre Haute Indiana

Dear Lucy

I wrote to you last Sunday evening enclosing a copy of a protest, such as seemed to be needed & proper as a declaration of principle & a model for imitation. . . . I have this evening sent a copy to Elizabeth of the protest requesting her criticism. She has very good taste & may make some suggestions of value. I am curious to see *your* protest & trust you have perhaps prepared one before the receipt of mine—as I should like to observe the different workings of our minds when considering the same subject. Marian does not like the clause anticipatory of *possible* future disagreements, but I say, we should have one, because though we probably shall never need it, yet it is in cases *only* of death, *or* disagreement, when the law *can* step in to work injustice & therefore for *others*, if not for ourselves, we ought to have arbitration on principle of *equity* substituted for the unjust *law*. At least, so I think—what say you? I have altered *ownership &*
use in second specific grievance, to ownership, *or* use—to prevent a possible cavil from those who may say that the fee simple of real estate remains in the wife, though she loses the *use* during the husband's life. I attach the last contract clause to avoid the unpleasant impression produced upon the mind, by the contemplation of possible discord & also suggesting indirectly the absurdity of promising to love, honor & cherish with the qualification of *ability* to do so. . . .

We will try to live so beautifully & so actively that every night we can compare notes together all by ourselves in one another's arms & say "we have not lived to-day *in vain!*" We will plan together, lay out each our own work, help each other to do it & report progress every night. I know not what sphere of action I shall undertake. I should quit business altogether, realize what I have . . . invest it at 10% interest & live on the income, which with economy would support us. But then I would *study three years* & then *speak* in *public*— not before. I could by that time find out whether I was fit for the career of an *intellectual* leader of men. But I suppose I must not postpone the settlement of these old debts—and to settle them I must re-enter the gambling shop of commerce & trust to energy & Providence to draw a Prize. . . .

Harry

Ann Arbor [Mich.], Feb. 26, 1855

Dear Harry

Your letter with the "protest" received. The protest I like in the main. I shall prepare a form when I get home. . . . I would like first, the things against which we would protest—just as you have done. Then follow that with a concise statement of what we regard as just and equal, in all cases which will cover that of possible disagreement, without at all implying that we anticipate any such trouble for ourselves. The promise to love, honor &c &c, I shall never make. Those things are dependent upon the qualities that can inspire them, and if they cease all promises are vain. When I go home, and am rested, I will send you a copy of it. I shall rejoice as much as you, dearest, when we can fully share our life. . . .

Lucy

Cincinnati Monday March 6. 1855

Dearest Lucy

I have only this morning received your letters. . . . I feel very uneasy that you may be *sick* & hope that if so, you have written for me to come to you. Why these letters have taken *a whole week* in coming I find it hard to understand, but the Mails like every other department of Gov. are shamefully mismanaged. . . .

Dear Lucy—you make the common error of New England people. You work too hard & will wear yourself out, if you do not set a guard over yourself. Let me be that guard dear Lucy for it is a sin and a shame that you should thus try your excellent constitution. I have never been celebrated for my own special care of myself but I will pay more attention hereafter *for your sake* & I want you to do the same for *mine*. . . .

My own dear love, *take your own time & place* for our marriage. Suppose we make the place West Brookfield & the time my birthday May 4th. I shall be 30 years old that day & having then arrived at years of discretion may very properly do a discreet thing, the *discreetest* of my life, by making my future rich & beautiful by allying it with your's. But I only propose that day, in case you prefer it. If you can pleasantly make an *earlier* appointment, I need not say that every day is counted, which keeps me from you. You tell me in your little note not to write till I hear from you again. Yet I feel so uneasy at the result of this week which has elapsed since that note was written with the "hard headache" & the weary frame, that I know not how to delay & shall send this letter off at a venture. . . .

Dear Lucy—we *know each other* & we *know* that we are *one*. It was not for nothing that my heart leaped towards you & yearned for you when I first saw you in our store six years ago. You are the only being on Earth that I fully sympathize with & I assure you that the better you know me, the more you will feel, that with all my errors & deficiencies you have not thrown away your love. . . . We can either marry at Brookfield, at New York, or at Cincinnati & just as soon as you choose. But dear Lucy I am not at all anxious that you shd [should] *promise* to love, honor & cherish me, for I know your heart. I have no preference for any particular form, or place. My home is in *you*—my marriage is already solemnised. As for your plan of making a stock farm in Illinois—I expect some day to realize that, but not just now, for it will require the investment of much money and the superintendence of a reliable person, neither of which are yet forthcoming. Good bye dearest—God bless you—Write me how you come on & if you are sick let me come & nurse you. I am ever your own

Harry—

Walnut Hills Sunday Afternoon
Mch. 18. 1855

Dearest Lucy

. . . Since you received my despatches in Canada, you have felt *pained* at the idea of having caused me anxiety by what you have written. Do not feel so! I have not suffered *much*, not one tenth part of what you have & when you suffer, I *wish* to suffer with you. And you surely *did not write* anything which would have caused me any anxiety if my thoughts had been less fixed upon you & my knowledge of your character less intimate. You say that you expressed your sufferings & fears more fully to Sarah than to me. Dearest—hereafter,

please do not, from any fear of giving me pain, refrain from letting
me know *all* that occurs & all that you feel. I can comprehend you,
be sure—& as I will conceal nothing from you, do you suppress nothing from me. As for the struggle in your mind at times about the
propriety of our trying to have children—I will only ask you to *postpone* that question altogether till we are married. THEN we will earnestly & carefully consider it *together* & do as we feel to be *right*
afterwards. You know dearest Lucy, that I am too proud & too *aris-
tocratic* ("in a certain fine sense," as Alcott would say) to be willing
to have any but fine, noble children & if we cannot fairly and reasonably hope from the laws of Nature & the *facts* in such cases to have
such ones, we will *wait till we can*. But I know some things, which I
will not tell you till I see you, which make me hope & believe that
you may become a cheerful & happy Mother by me, as you shall, *in
any event*, be a loved & cherished & happy wife. Now, dear Lucy, if
it be possible & so far as you can, put aside the dark presentiments
& fears & disgusts which so naturally come over you at times. Think
only of *me* & of the *need of you* which I feel & the good & happiness
we can both confer upon each other if we will & let us come together,
so soon as possible. . . . Sarah wants you, little Emma wants you—
Mother & sisters & brothers want you & oh Lucy dear—more than
all of these a *hundred times*, I want you. We can be married here as
soon as we choose, at Mother's house, & either publish it at the time,
or a month afterwards in either the Eastern, or Western papers, or
both simultaneously, as we prefer. No one, but ourselves need know
of our marriage till after the Convention if you choose.

As for that Convention—altho. I am doing & shall do all in my
power to aid it, I do not intend to take any active part in it, *as a
speaker* this year, if I can help. My partners feel desirous of my not
doing so, until we can make a change & dissolve the firm. Of course
the odium which attaches to me from the Salem affair has been to a
certain extent injurious to our business & much more so to its *reputation* (for purposes of selling out) than to its actual condition. . . . I
hope you do not understand me, dear Lucy, as regretting that affair,
or as willing to compromise one iota of independent thought & action
from sordid motives. On the contrary, I will endeavor soon to assume
a position where I shall have no partners to object to my course, as
an injustice to themselves.

Only three, or four days ago, I was obliged very much to offend them by getting out a writ of habeas corpus for two slaves, who were brought to the City on the Maysville Steamboat & thence transferred across our Landing to the Louisville mail Boat "Jacob Strader." These men were chained round the body & to each other & were being transferred from Dover Ky to Missouri, by a man, who had bought them only two days before. I only heard of it at 10 AM & the Strader was to leave at 12. Two colored men had called at the Store to consult me about it, but I had been out till then. I went direct to Jolliffe's office & omitted to take my informants with me—so was compelled to make the affidavit myself. The writ was granted by Judge Storer. Jolliffe & I went to the Landing & saw the deputy Sheriffs on board. The Capt. denied the presence of the slaves, but on search they were found & taken to jail. I called on them with a young free colored man in the afternoon & represented the advantages of freedom. I found them both desirous to be free & *not* to go to Missouri. But the claimants & their friends got the trial postponed 2 days successively & meantime talked to them & bribed the jailer, turnkeys &c till they got the poor fellows bewildered & intimidated—representing that there were hundreds of men in Cincinnati out of work—that they would be starved to death or put on the chain gang &c &c. However we sent friends to see them on our side & day before yesterday & yesterday the case was very ably & fully argued on both sides. The question is an *important* one, which we have wanted for a long time to bring up. It is this—Does a slave become legally free if while being carried from one slave state to another on the Ohio River, the steamboat incidentally lands on the Ohio shore. We contend that the jurisdiction of Ohio extends to low water mark—that a slave brought by his owner or agents to the bank of the river on a steamboat comes within our State & under our law & so becomes a free man. The other side contend that the Ohio River, being a national highway is free to the citizens of all States with their property. . . .

If, as we confidently anticipate, the decision is in our favor an important principle will be established. We learn however that in that case, the men are to be immediately arrested & taken before an infamous Fugitive Slave Commissioner named Pendery & by him in defiance of State Law even, to be remanded. The decision is to be on Wednesday next & we shall try to get the poor fellows clear. I was too busy to attend the actual trial. Senator Chase (just returned from Washington), Judges Walker & Stallo & Mr Jolliffe, four very able men are said to have spoken nobly on our side. Of course the "Enquirer" came out with an infamous half column of abuse against me as a "public nuisance," a destroyer of the business of the City, a British renegade, a negro thief &c &c & invoked a mob & a coat of tar & feathers &c &c—all which I shall be well satisfied to endure, if we can get Ohio *one step nearer* a free State, than before.

I have read the various speeches of Chase, Sumner, Seward, Phillips & others to which you refer. Also a very good one of Henry Wilson's defining his position, which strikes me as manly & ingenuous, except the opinion that Mass. would (in the absence of Federal usurpation) enforce the fugitive clause of the Constitution—that was *very mean*, or at least *intentionally ambiguous*. I wish you saw the "Nat. Era" regularly. Dr. Baileys articles against the Know Nothings are grand & conclusive. . . .

Dear Lucy—how I wish I could have been with you & watched over you in your trouble at Hutsonville & at Bellville, But it is probably owing to that very illness of your's that I owe my love for you & your's for me, for it was your bringing in the little Draft on C. Donaldson to our store that first made me see you & I *loved you at sight*. Years afterwards I came East—*almost wholly* to know you, for I had never forgotten you. Write soon, dearest Love & tell me whether you can come on to me & *when*. I *hope* you can come soon dearest, for I *want* you & am ever your own

Harry—

On March 21 a frantic Henry wrote to Lucy's brother Bowman at West Brookfield. According to him, Lucy had "been more than once on the verge of brain fever during the past few weeks," and he was concerned lest she hadn't reached home safely. But about a week later, she wrote from West Brookfield to assure him that she was indeed feeling better. On the same day—March 29—she also wrote to her closest friend, Antoinette Brown, about her forthcoming wedding:

The *day* is not set. I have not been quite well, and so it is delayed. But when it is fixed, I will write you, so that you may think of me, and fancy, if you can what of thought and feeling goes on, under the surface. If the ceremony is in New York we want you to harden your heart enough to help in so cruel an operation as putting Lucy Stone to death. But it will be all according to law, so you need fear no punishment. I *expect* however to go to Cincinnati & have the ruin completed there.

Then, unable to maintain her bantering tone any longer, she broke down and laid bare the reality of her suffering: "Dear Nette—I am tired. My head aches—so excuse, for I must get rested, and strong."

West Brookfield Mar. 29 [1855]

Dear Harry

I write [to] let you know that I am still better. My head is so that I have now scarcely a fear of insanity. I feel the power of *self control*, and as long as I can do that, there is no danger. . . .

I wrote to you yesterday, that perhaps the 12th Apr. would be the day. I fear I cant be ready by that time. If I were *well*, I could and would go to you then. Sam J. May is to attend the Convention. He is a good man, perhaps it will be as well to wait until that time. But as soon as I can feel sure of being well, I can determine at once. I am sorry to tantalize you in this way—but I think it will cost you less to wait while I am here, for me to be well, than it will to recieve me tired and not well. But I am getting stronger every day, and perhaps in *three* weeks can be with you, but we had better leave it unsettled for the present, not because I am childish, but simply because I cannot tell, how long it will be, before I shall be fit.

I am glad that business is better, and that you have so much, that you cant leave—*provided* it is business that will pay. I am glad you do not care for that miserable "Enquirer." I am sure that by every noble soul, you will be more esteemed, for the aid you render the outcast slave. I saw the N.Y. Tribune account of it. It is well to have these legal points tested. Do you think, that after all your over and over committal to the Anti Slavery cause, that a good speech at the convention would make you any more obnoxious? But you must judge what is best. You know all the circumstances better than I do.

You ask me to write you "all." Dearest Harry some day, when I am stronger, I will either write or tell you *everything* I have thought, and felt. You say you know just as well as I do the revulsions of feeling &c as far as a *man* can. I have no doubt that you do *understand*. I am glad my dear, that you can never *feel*. But I am calmer, happier, and as for months I have loved you alone, deeply, and truly, so I still do. And from our mutual love, we will yet, I trust, realize much of happiness. Do not be troubled for me—take good care of your health, and be sure that I shall be cared for here.

We have plenty of helpers. If I am *any* worse, we will write you. If you do not hear so often, know that silence, is proof of getting better.

With *much* love
Lucy

Cincinnati April 2. 1855

Dear Lucy

. . . I think it is entirely unnecessary to allow the Convention here to affect the time, or place of our marriage. Every one will appreciate your withdrawal from it, who knows, or thinks anything about the matter—& if they did not, it would be none of their business. . . . As to the *protest* dear Lucy, it was my proposal & I adhere to the idea of making it. It commends itself to my judgment & to my feelings. I do not sympathize with Elizabeth's objections though they possess a certain force on the score of mere *taste*. I think that under any circumstances I should prefer to make it & in the present case, your well known position will relieve the publication from the charge of *egotism*, which is the principal argument which would otherwise lie against making it. . . .

I do greatly *want* you with me. I think it will be *better* with us both when we are fully & permanently *united*. I am *very* glad you

are better. I trust that those terrible headaches will not return. . . .
You say that your Father & Mother have just celebrated their *golden
wedding*. That is as it should be. You say "our's will not last so long."
I am not so sure of that! I have a great preference for living to the
age of four score years & I surely think that you will not be so wanting in politeness & consideration as to go to the next world before
me. You say you shall try to write me about Dr M's theory, if you
feel able so to do. Do not do so, dear Lucy. We can talk that matter
over together when the proper time comes & believe me—*nature*
will soon teach us much more than any theory good, or bad. You
surely can *trust* me, for, admitting that Dr. M's opinion be true, until
you can see it to be so, you shall have your own way without any
attempt on my part to influence you otherwise. I think that you un-
derrate the force & virtue of *instinct* when guided by *affection* &
love. . . .

I am sorry you feel so much pain at placing your property in
your sister's hands. I think you should feel pleasure at thus foiling the
unjust laws relative to your property & retaining *substantially* the self
control which is formally denied. Why *you* should feel *humiliated* by
the unjust legislation on this subject I cannot understand. . . . But
I will not multiply words. If you feel so much pain in settling your
property—leave that matter till we can do so *together* previous to our
marriage. It can be done equally well at Boston, or Cincinnati. As to
the other subject of uneasiness, your fear as to the *quality* of our
children, should we have any—I have some things to say to you about
that, when we meet, which I *am sure* will make you feel much happier & better satisfied on that score. I postpone it till we meet, because I do not like *writing* on that subject. Dearest little wife—God
bless you—Take the best care of yourself, try to be lazy for once. Let
me know whether I shall come for you & believe me. Ever your own
in life or death

Harry

West Brookfield Apr. 8, 1855

Dear Harry
. . . I see that the last day of the Convention falls on Friday—
which is "an unlucky day." It wont do to be married on Saturday, so

Sunday evening April 29, at Walnut Hills, I think will be the best time & place. We will have no strangers—no formality of joining hands, but in a quiet, home-like way assume the life to which our love prompts. You shall read the Protest and Nette or Mr. May shall simply say that we are husband & wife. Wont that be enough & right? . . . . I wish that I was wiser, better, better developed, better fitted to be a wife better fitted to be *your* wife. But Harry, cheerfully, hopefully, I will carry you *all* that I have, the *best* that I have, and if a *real* wish to contribute to *your happiness,* and an *earnest effort* to do so, and to enrich your life, *can* produce these results, we shall never regret our love. I *want* in *every* way to make your life happier. It will be a joy to me, to know that I do you good. We will be *mutual* helpers, in all that is truly worthy. Together we will acquire knowledge, cultivate a love of the beautiful in Nature and Art; of the Right because it is right. We will teach absolute sincerity to sit on our lips, and in our lives. Our love, pure and fresh like the sunlight each morning shall greet us, and never know either weariness, decay, or disgust. Our happiness (now unspeakable) dear Harry will be just in proportion to our goodness. The more truly good we are, the more real happiness shall we share. It will *depend* upon *ourselves.* There is no irresistible Destiny. "Our own hands sow thick the seeds that spring to weeds or flowers." We will sow the right seeds, and then cannot fail of a joyful harvest. . . .

I enclose a copy of a Protest slightly modified from yours. I shall show it to Wendell Phillips and get his criticism. I shall show him yours also, and then if we must, we will compare, and revise, and make it right. . . .

I shall not write you until my return from Boston in about ten days. I shall be very busy, and will not assume anything which *can* be omitted, for I am not quite strong and well yet, but every day getting better I think.

It will be *very pleasant* if Ellen is at home with us this summer. But she must not stay on my account as Emily did for Marian. I am not so childish as that, quite. I shall carry no *furniture, except the box* for the corner. If you are *determined* to live to four score years, I shall then be *so near a hundred,* that though it may not seem polite, I still think that kindness to you, would then require that I should ask to go up higher, and I intend *always* to be kind. My Mother sends her love to yours, and hopes they both will be happier, in the increased happiness of their children.

The slave girl went free, thank God!

With much love yours
Lucy

Cincinnati April 13. 1855

Dearest Lucy

. . . This morning, I received your good letter of the 8th inst, enclosing your form of protest and proposing Walnut Hills April 29th, as the place & time. Of course dear Lucy I accept, with all proper & natural feelings of delight & hope, the proposal—& consider it *settled, provided* that you do not rather accept *mine* as follows. Suppose that I leave Cincinnati, *Friday morning Apl. 27*[th] & reach West Brookfield Saturday afternoon the 28th. That I there meet Elizabeth & Marian, who come up from N. York & wait for me at the hotel & either that evening, or next morning (as may be most convenient to your friends) that I drive them over in a carriage to your well known, though only once seen home. That we spend Sunday together at your brother's walking over the hills & looking at the distant mountains & that either Sunday evening, or early Monday morning we marry & start Westward. . . .

My reasons for proposing this course rather than the other one are—1st *The appearance of the affair*—a smaller matter of course than any *strong* consideration of convenience, or propriety, but still, one not to be overlooked. I do not want to do *anything* to give the Public, who are to be, through the Protest, acquainted with the fact of our wedding, any unpleasant, or unfavorable idea of its tone & spirit. I do not wish to seem forgetful of the fact that you *have* a *home* & *family ties* of your own, of which you are not ashamed & to which you do not feel indifferent. I do not think that it would make any difference in the case of a lady unknown, but in *you*, to come a thousand miles *to me* might seem a violation of the customary etiquette of good taste which might strengthen many silly, or misinformed people (the last class a very large one) in the idea that you are really the migratory, unfeminine, ungraceful contemner of proprieties which

newspaper criticism & common gossip pronounce woman's-rights ladies to be. Therefore I should like everything connected with the
externals of our wedding to be strictly unexceptionable, so that the
fact of our protest may have its full weight & no chance afforded for
illnatured remark.

2^d I would like that you should not take the long journey *alone*.
I feel uneasy at the idea of your setting out, after the fatigue & excitement of packing & leavetaking with the idea of the wedding still
before you, to ride so far, just recovering from a severe illness—indeed not yet quite recovered. It will be more prudent, more pleasant
for you—better every way that the little tired head should have my
shoulder to rest upon & that you should know before leaving your
accustomed friends & places that I was with you to try to compensate
for all.

So I really think & feel that, unless you *prefer* the other plan
very much, I had better come on for you. . . . If we marry Monday
morning, we might spend our first night at *Niagara* & not, as before,
be compelled to separate & listen to the roar of the torrent
alone. . . .

Again Massachusetts is at present (with the sole exception
perhaps of New York) the most hopeful State for the speedy amelio-
ration of legislation on the Woman question—the more hopeful, because her women are more intelligent & moral & therefore better
fitted to exercise their rights if conceded & more likely to desire
them. You are better known there. It is your home. You owe your
native State your protest & her laws being still more rigid & unjust
than our's, it is still more needed there. I hope you will not think
that I undervalue your goodness in proposing to come *here*. I appreciate your independence, your considerate, disinterested, self-sacrificing affection. But, dearest, since you have found it necessary to
postpone the wedding until a period when, I can, without inconvenience come on, let *me* further modify the plan in the manner above
proposed. . . .

Dearest little Lucy keep up your courage! Dont let evil
forebodings & fears find any hold on you. Trust in God, in yourself,
& in me. Dont overwork yourself in body, or mind. *Try to be lazy* as
you promised & believe me my own little wife

Ever yours
Harry

Cincinnati April 20. 1855

Dear Lucy

I rec^d your despatch yesterday evening, dated Boston, saying you were sick again—& made up my mind to start this (Friday) morning, in which case I should have reached Boston Saturday night. I made arrangements to do so, but on going home in the evening, Mother & Ellen persuaded me not to start until I should receive the letter which the despatch said was on the way. Against my own judgment, which tells me I *ought* to have gone on, I have concluded to remain here therefore till I hear from you which I ought to do to-morrow (Saturday). I shall be guided dearest Lucy in my movements by the contents of your letter which will probably express some wish with regard to them. But it seems to me positively *unnatural* that you should be sick & suffering in Boston & I a thousand miles off unable to nurse, or care for you. But dear Lucy whatever be the state of health in which this letter may find you—whether better, or worse in mind or body—believe that I am with you in spirit & will be with you in body just as soon as you intimate a wish that I should do so.

Dearest Lucy—I greatly fear that you have suffered pain in contemplation of our marriage, which you have suppressed in your letters—that you have brought on this new attack by anxiety & premature fatigue. If this be so, for my sake & for your own—try to dismiss such thoughts from your mind. If you cannot do this—then telegraph me to come on *at once* & when we are *together* & you can tell me just how you feel & what you fear, believe me *all will be right*. The Convention can very well spare me. Its preliminaries are all arranged. The hall is engaged & several speakers are *sure* to be here. Therefore, as I am too busy to be able to give the thought requisite to accomplish much in speaking—& shall spend Sunday next at any rate in drafting resolutions &c—I may just as well come on & be with you without waiting for the Convention to terminate. I feel at present in a state of painful suspense as to your condition & a vague impression fills my mind that *I ought to be with you*. Dear Lucy with a heart full of love & regret for your sufferings I am still as ever—

Your own for time and eternity—
Harry—

Perhaps because she realized that the strain of the trip to Cincinnati might be too much for her in her weakened condition, Lucy agreed to have Henry come for her, and their wedding date was set for May 1, 1855, at her family's home in West Brookfield. Thomas Wentworth Higginson, a Unitarian minister, abolitionist, and long-time friend of Lucy's, agreed to perform the ceremony, but besides Higginson, his wife, and another abolitionist friend, Charles Burleigh, there were no other outsiders. Antoinette Brown had been invited but did not come, nor did Henry's sisters, Marian and Elizabeth, who were both living in New York. Shortly before the wedding Elizabeth wrote to say that Marian would not be able to attend because of ill health, and she herself chose not to appear.

So it was a small party that traveled by train to West Brookfield the day before the wedding. Henry met them at the station and then, as Higginson recalled, they rode through a rocky, hilly landscape until they reached "a high little farmhouse, round which the misty sky shut closely down, revealing only rocks and barns and cattle." Lucy's parents were there and so was her brother Bowman and his family, but her sister Sarah didn't come from Cincinnati nor did her oldest brother Frank who also lived elsewhere.

The ceremony took place the next morning before breakfast in a room decorated quite conventionally with orange blossoms and "cloth of gold" roses in vases. Lucy was dressed in a silk "ashes of roses color" gown, while Henry wore "the proper white waistcoat." Before the ceremony they stood together and Henry read the final version of the protest they had agreed upon:

> While acknowledging our mutual affection by publicly assuming the relationship of husband and wife, yet in justice to ourselves and a great principle, we deem it a duty to declare that this act on our part implies no sanction of, nor promise of voluntary obedience to such of the present laws of marriage, as refuse to recognize the wife as an independent, rational being, while they confer upon the husband an injurious and unnatural superiority, investing him with legal powers which no honorable man would exercise, and which no man should possess. We protest especially against the laws which give to the husband:

1. The custody of the wife's person.

2. The exclusive control and guardianship of their children.

3. The sole ownership of her personal, and use of her real estate, unless previously settled upon her, or placed in the hands of trustees, as in the case of minors, lunatics, and idiots.

4. The absolute right to the product of her industry.

5. Also against laws which give to the widower so much larger and more permanent an interest in the property of his deceased wife, than they give to the widow in that of her deceased husband;

6. Finally, against the whole system by which "the legal existence of the wife is suspended during marriage," so that in most States, she neither has a legal part in the choice of her residence, nor can she make a will, nor sue or be sued in her own name, nor inherit property.

We believe that personal independence and equal human rights can never be forfeited, except for crime; that marriage should be an equal and permanent partnership, and so recognized by law; that until it is so recognized, married partners should provide against the radical injustice of present laws, by every means in their power.

We believe that where domestic difficulties arise, no appeal should be made to legal tribunals under existing laws, but that all difficulties should be submitted to the equitable adjustment of arbitrators mutually chosen.

Thus reverencing law, we enter our protest against rules and customs which are unworthy of the name, since they violate justice, the essence of all law.

After the wedding Higginson sent a copy of the protest, along with an accompanying letter, to *The Worcester Spy*. Both the protest and Higginson's letter were also published in *The Liberator*. Thus given wide currency, the Stone-Blackwell protest became an important model for imitation.

The actual ceremony differed only from the usual one in that the word "obey," but not the words "love and honor," was omitted. When it was over, there were tears on Lucy's part, and wedding cake. As the newlyweds were about to leave, Father Stone warned that "it would not all be sunshine for them," and then they were off for New York where they were to spend the night at Elizabeth's house. A party had been planned in their honor, but Lucy was too ill to join in the festivities. Instead she went immediately to bed with a severe headache.

One can well guess "what of thought and feeling" was going on inside her, and what a tremendous effort of will it must have taken simply to get through her wedding day. Nine months later she wrote her mother: "I know you all felt a little badly, at our wedding, because Henry was a stranger, and you did not know what I was risking, nor what future I might be making. But I have learned to love and trust him vastly more than at the wedding." Yet if at the time, she still had serious doubts about Henry and their marriage, she was at least spared the physical intimacy she dreaded on their wedding night. In another letter to her mother written just after the wedding, she explained that Henry came up to their room after the party, and thoughtfully didn't wake her.

As for the bridegroom, he must have felt relieved that the wedding had taken place at all. Beforehand, he wrote his brother Sam telling him how pleased he was to find Lucy active and animated, and said he hoped that "the trouble in her head" wouldn't return. But whatever fears for the future he may have harbored, he hid them behind a comic mask when he wrote of his marriage to his good friend Ainsworth Spofford: "I have just entangled myself beyond the possibility of release. . . . I lose no time in conveying information of the frightful casualty. . . . Enter Lucy Stone in silk dress and H.B.B. (of unenviable notoriety) in a mulberry coat and white vest. . . . Tears and wedding cake by all the Company—Departure of the Company— the Unenviable and the Bride taking cars for N.Y. . . . P.P.S. Ora pro nobis!"

TWO

A Model Couple
1855-1864

I am trying to be a good wife and mother. I have
wanted to tell you how hard I am trying, but I have
tried before and my miserable failures hitherto, make
me silent now.
> Lucy Stone to Henry Blackwell, May 21, 1858

Little wife—trust your husband's *better nature a little
longer*.
> Henry Blackwell to Lucy Stone, September 8, 1857

The first months of their life together did much to dispel the fears that had haunted Lucy before her wedding. She was no longer suffering "revulsions of feeling": Although the language of physical passion was alien to her, she did allow herself to admit during one separation that she envied Henry's traveling companion "his privilege by your pillow," and in another letter wrote: "My heart *yearns* for you . . . when I lie down at night, tho' I sleep more soundly alone." Moreover, she was relieved to find that she had lost none of her freedom by marrying. From the Blackwell home in Walnut Hills, where she and Henry went immediately after their wedding, she wrote Susan B. Anthony at the end of May: "Of my husband (since the honeymoon is over) I can speak truly now; if I please, but will only tell you how he treated me last evening when after reading your letter, I asked him if I might go to the Convention at Saratoga. Only think of it, he did not give me permission, but told me to ask Lucy Stone! I cant get him to govern me at all." That summer she did return to the East for the woman's rights convention at Saratoga Springs.

Henry, meanwhile, played a small but nonetheless important role in Ohio politics. The state's antislavery contingent was divided into two factions, the Liberty party and the anti-Catholic, antiforeigner American party, popularly known as the Know-Nothings. These two factions came into conflict at a mass convention held in Cincinnati to nominate delegates to the state convention of the newly emergent Republican party, and in the ensuing turmoil, the convention was almost broken up. However, an eloquent speech from Henry saved the situation. He appealed to both sides to join forces, and the coalition thus formed was crucial in securing the nomination of the abolitionist Salmon P. Chase, who went on to be elected governor of Ohio.

In the fall of 1855 Henry and Lucy were reunited, and it was Lucy's turn to make one of the more memorable speeches of her career at the National Woman's Rights Convention, held in Cincinnati that year. Responding to a previous speaker who referred to the woman's movement as being composed of a few disappointed women, Lucy said: "From the first years to which my memory stretches I have been a disappointed woman. . . . In education, in marriage, in religion, in everything disappointment is the lot of women. It shall be the business of my life to deepen that disappointment in every woman's heart until she bows down to it no longer."

Yet in her own marriage, she clearly wasn't disappointed. In January she wrote her mother: "I have one of the best husbands in the world. He is *always* kind and good, and never yet in any way, by word or act, has been otherwise. He is here only evenings . . . and I listen for his footsteps at about 7 o'clock, glad always to hear it." But not long afterward, she and Henry were again separated: She set off on a lecture tour of Illinois and Indiana, while he went on another collecting trip for the hardware business.

During this time two people very close to Lucy and Henry were married. Samuel Blackwell and Antoinette Brown first met in 1854 in South Butler, New York, where as a newly ordained minister, Antoinette had her own pulpit. Sam stopped to visit her on Henry's recommendation, and their three-hour "confab" on woman's rights and other subjects blossomed into a lengthy correspondence, and finally marriage on January 24, 1856.

Lucy's jubilation prompted one of her few jokes; Sam, she said, could "rejoice in the fact that he alone of all men has a Divine wife." Yet while she delighted in the union of her best friend and her brother-in-law, Susan B. Anthony did not. Their common spinsterhood had created a special bond among the three women, and now that Lucy and Antoinette were married, Susan felt betrayed and abandoned. She wrote reproachful letters to both, provoking the following retort from Lucy:

> But it is very absurd of you, you naughty thing, to feel that
> you are left *alone*. Are all the married ones dead and gone?
> Have we neither life, character, nor use? You are a little
> wretch to even *intimate* that we are nothing now. Let me
> tell you as a secret that if you are ever married, you will
> find that there is just as much of you, as before. You wont
> even miss the shadow of the old identity, nor will anybody
> else. So just quit thinking that you are left in possession of
> the whole world alone—for we shall claim our share, and

what is better still, we shall get it too. . . . I wish we had
another brother for you, Susan. Would we not have a grand
household then?

Early in February while Lucy was away lecturing, Cincinnati was
stirred up by another fugitive-slave incident. Margaret Garner, her
husband, their four children, and her husband's family managed to
escape from Kentucky to Cincinnati, but there they were appre-
hended. As the officers approached the house where they were hid-
ing, Margaret Garner killed one of her children by cutting its throat,
and tried unsuccessfully to kill the other two by striking them on the
head with a shovel. Learning of the case while she was gone, Lucy
plunged into it upon her return to Cincinnati. She visited Margaret
Garner in prison, and was so moved by her plight that she beseeched
the jailer to give the slave mother a knife to kill herself, as the woman
preferred death to a life of slavery. She also made a speech in the
woman's behalf when she was brought to trial, and appealed to her
owner to release her. Many years later Henry recalled Lucy's part in
the Margaret Garner affair with great admiration: "I have always regarded Lucy's action, she being a comparative stranger in an intensely proslavery community, as one of the finest incidents of her
life." But despite Lucy's intervention, the woman and her family
were taken back into bondage.

The incident intensified Lucy and Henry's dislike of Cincinnati;
however, by the spring of 1856, they were able to leave that city for
good. Henry and Sam had found a new partner to take over their
share in the hardware business, the Walnut Hills home was to be
sold, and its various occupants were preparing to move to the East.

⁂

[Walnut Hills, summer, 1855]

Dearest Lucy
. . . So you have made some engagements to lecture. Dear
Lucy I shall be very glad that you are speaking, provided you do not
find the excitement unpleasant, or injurious. But do not *risk* the pos-

sibility of bringing on a return of the terrible suffering of last winter. Be *very* moderate & very careful of yourself. I rather fear that the excitement may be bad for you. And Lucy dear—do not let the idea of your *Appleton investment* affect *in the least* your plans, or proceedings—because, you can pay for it out of the *interest* on your money in our hands entirely independent of your lectures. I do not want any feeling of the necessity of *gain* to affect the spontaneity of your labors. It seems to me an element which is unworthy to enter into your calculations. Dear Lucy—do not let your *marriage* make you feel *less free*. If you are not willing that your husband should *support you*—at least do not think it will ever be necessary to *support* him. Surely dear—Lucy Stone Blackwell is more independent in her pecuniary position than was Lucy Stone. . . . If you desire to lecture this fall I will organize for you a little tour to Wisconsin—there are some 12 towns—say Waukegan, Kenosha, Racine, Milwaukee, Madison, Janesville, Watertown, Waupun, Fond du Lac, Sheboygan, Appleton & Green Bay, which would be worth visiting—but I should advise selecting only five—say Racine, Milwaukee, Madison, Janesville & Watertown, and give to each three lectures leaving at least two days to rest between each course. This would consume nearly a month & we ought not to be separated longer. Dearest when I become free from business, we will lecture *together*—that is, if it seems best & you are willing—meanwhile you must not overtax yourself & wear yourself out. Remember, my child, you are *older* than me already & you must not live so fast as to prevent my catching up. You say that when you see how much work is to be done, it seems to you selfish to desire a quiet home & children & friends—that we ought to renounce these & work till we die. I have sometimes felt so—but I know that this is not a wise feeling. The noblest *preaching* is *incomplete without* the noble life to exemplify it. To reform others we must try to reform ourselves, by assuming the natural relations of humanity & acting our part well therein. I have often thought Christ's recorded life extremely *imperfect,* as an *example,* because he did not show forth either the *son,* the *husband,* or the *father.* Moreover this life of renunciation is *suicidal.* How can we speak of what we do not know? Does not Mrs Mott possess more *weight,* because she has the matronly dignity & experience of her past life? I believe dearest Lucy— that we human beings require in our lives *alternation* of thought &

employment. As sleep is necessary to the body—so are periods of relaxation to the soul. [The remainder of this letter is missing.]

Cincinnati Sept 12. 1855

My own dear little wife

I hope you will forgive me for calling you *little,* for I use the word as one of *endearment* & not as a diminutive by any means. I write almost every day & no sooner despatch my letter than I want to write again. Not that I have anything to say in the way of news, but because *I love you with my whole soul,* Lucy dear—& I *want* you should know it. I always feel, while reading & after reading, your good letters, a more vivid & delightful realization of the love *you* bear me. I trust dearest, that you always feel so, after reading mine. . . . I am sorry that my letters are not better, but I always write in haste & doubtless often say foolish things, which cause you pain. For instance, I spoke a little depreciatingly the other day of our excellent friend Chas Burleigh. Now dearest, please do me one little net of justice. Reserve any remark like that, which *might pain* you, *only* because I have failed to express myself clearly & well, till we next are in our own quiet bed *together* & then let me explain to you what I really wanted to say & did not. I suggest this dear Lucy, because it often occurs to me after I have sent my letters—"I wonder if Lucy will misunderstand anything I have said & so think I mean something else?"

Lucy dear—how I *wish,* I were as prudent & considerate as you. But *you shall teach me* to be so, for I will try to be worthy of you, my own love. Lucy dear—I will be satisfied with my letters, if they can only make you feel & see *how perfect* is my love *for you.* You sometimes speak *depreciatingly* of our union & seem to *doubt* a little, whether we are *in all respects* adapted. I hope dear, that *my* defects do not too much pain you—for to *me,* you have *none.* I would not willingly *overstate* my feelings to you. But Lucy dear—*if* you have defects, I am not conscious of them. To me, you are all I want, all I need, all I desire.

Chas Burleigh says you are not beautiful. To me, your person is *perfectly* lovely. When I *first* knew you I used sometimes to wish you had a prettier nose, I remember. But now, I would not have your nose altered for the world! For, dear Lucy—your love, your affection, your fidelity, your honor, your womanly good-sense, your cheerfulness, your sensitiveness, your generosity are not *lost* upon me. I *reverence* you, as well as *love* you & I only *long* for opportunities to manifest to you the love which fills my soul. And I want you to understand dear Lucy that you may *trust* my love—"love is love, for evermore"—If you ever take the small-pox (as you deserve to, for not getting yourself vaccinated), if you ever become sick—& ever *irritable* & *cross*—if you ever join the "free lovers" & practice their vices— if you get into *any misfortune*, no matter how sad, I will watch over you dearest, like a Mother over her child & I *will never forsake you*, SO HELP ME GOD!! Dear Lucy—is it nothing to have inspired a wayward, unsettled, impulsive nature with such a *principle* of love as this? [The remainder of this letter is missing.]

Cincinnati Sept. 17. 1855

My own dear wife

I spent yesterday (Sunday) as pleasantly as I can spend any day *without you*, in reading Mrs. Nichols' "Mary Lyndon." It is a singular book, morbid, rather coarse with all its maudlin sentimentality—very one-sided & I fear, *not* very truthful. Yet there is a great deal of *power* & much shrewd observation—in fact Mrs Nichols is no ordinary woman—she possesses a great deal of talent & a little genius. Her book is spoiled however by the *wretched trash* which is the only name fit to designate the correspondence between herself & Nichols. How she can have been so deceived & still continue so deceived by an *artificial* person like her husband is astonishing. His letters are *made up*—their sentiments fictitious, their expressions overstrained, he is not in earnest, except in his wish to deceive her—in which he evidently succeeded.

The best part of the book is, I think, her descriptions of her meeting with Lang, Lynde, & Mooney, the transcendentalist trio at Greenwood. Lang is of course *Charles Lane* & Mooney [Bronson] *Alcott*, but who is this *Lynde*, whom she represents as her first love— I should like to know. Also her description of her New York life—

first in the boarding house & afterwards in the houshold on 13th St. is well given. *There,* I can verify her sketch very much by my own observation. Dr. Ellery & his two sisters are Dr Edgeworth Lazarus & his sisters Margaret & Ellen. The crazy brother & sister were Frank Webber & sister—he was then part editor of the Whig review. Her "Anna" is of course my sister Anna. Her bringing her thus before the public in connection with herself, without even the disguise of name, after she had slandered & betrayed her—& after Anna had, in consequence, withdrawn entirely from her society & friendship with disgust & abhorrence is a most unpardonable piece of impertinence. Her sketch of Anna's brilliant social qualities is not at all overdrawn, but she entirely overlooks her generous & magnanimous goodness & disinterested benevolence, of which she had received many proofs.

I would not judge Mrs Nichols harshly, but I have no *confidence* in the truthfulness of her book. Her *facts* may or may not be *fables*— she is not reliable. Observe how faultlessly Christian, she describes herself & with what a malicious meaning her *apologies* for her enemies are filled. I fancy if *Mr Hervey* could tell his story, he would show us a very different portrait of their connection & its dissolution. Her "Angelic" Eva—I remember as one of the most disagreeable depraved young girls I ever knew. I shall write to Ellen to take a copy of this book to Europe & show it to Anna.

But, enough of that—I am told that Nichols is coming to Cincinnati to establish an office for the promulgation of his views. I hope it will not be so, for he will do much harm, become a *nuisance,* be persecuted & mobbed probably & then flourish after a fashion for some years & do much more harm, on the strength of the natural sympathy thereby aroused. I trust that these "free lovers" will not thrust their immoralities before the public in the "Womans Rights" disguise which they are trying to assume. I suspect a plan of that kind. It would be an infinite shame & pity to allow the just claims of women to liberty of person, to rights of property, to industrial, social & political equality, to be associated with a conspiracy against purity & virtue & all the holiest relations of life. But I believe you & Nette & Phillips & Higginson & Mrs Mott will prevent such a degradation.

Dear Lucy I calculate that you will be at Boston the day after tomorrow at the Convention & that this letter will reach you at Francis Jackson's. I hope you will have a good meeting & advance the Cause.

You have my most hearty approval & warmest sympathy in your objects & efforts. . . . I think of you by day & by night continually & kiss your miniature before I go to bed & when I get up—but it is a poor substitute for my own dear Lucy in her *living* presence. Once more—God bless you.

Yours ever
Harry

Utica Saturday Night Oct. 13. 1855

Dearest Lucy
. . . I have done up a good deal of reading. Read half of Mary Wolstoncraft's "Rights of Women"—all of report of Worcester Convention & all of *Ruth*. The latter is an *excellent* story. The sentiment seems to me a *little morbid*. Poor Ruth was in no sense a *sinner* & her consequent self-humiliation & abasement, however, concievable were *superstitious*, not called for. There was far too little *self assertion*, too exclusively an *affectional* life in her—but it is a *lovely* character—all the more natural for its faults—for they are the peculiar faults of women. Women are so fettered & dwarfed intellectually that they are compelled to live too exclusively in the region of sentiment & of affection at present. Many of Ruth's traits reminded me of *you*. I hope however that you will not recognize *much* of Donne alias Bellingham in *me*. I think the interest of the story is *intense*, but like that of many of our best woman-novelists' books it is painful, monotonous & morbid. What a frightful protest against the prevalent sexual code of morals the whole story presents. What *argument* for downtrodden, unfortunate women, can equal in *cogency* the simple sketch of Ruth *innocent* becoming Ruth (not *fallen* but) *the husbandless Mother*. And when we reflect upon the usual fate of women so situated both elsewhere & *here* in America—even Modern Times with its license seems less revolting than present Society with its accursed Puritanism & sweeping condemnation.

Dear Lucy—In Ruths beautiful *goodness*—in her generous self-abnegation & faithful affection she *faintly* resembles you. But when I contrast your broader views & stronger individuality I can say with truth that I think my own dear wife, worth a hundred thousand ideal

Ruths. And I want to end my letter by telling you dear Lucy *how entirely* I love you & how I miss you by day & by night, while I am away from you. . . . I want you to live *50 years*! & for me to live 50 years & one day in order to manifest in my life that wealth of appreciation & affection for you which no *words* have power to express— And so good-night—sweet sleep & pleasant dreams rest on your soul till my return. Good-bye

Yours—Harry—

Forrest [Ind.]—Thursday Morning Jan 24 1856

Dearest Harry

It is eight o'clock. I have just eaten my breakfast, and now sit in the little room where I slept, before a stove filled with green wood, which will be ready to burn, about the time I leave. . . .

I read last evening, from Godey's Ladies book the advice of some old wives to a young one, warning her never to keep house, for her husband would find fault with everything, and never be at home, if he could help it &c. It was very rich, showing the defects on the male & female sides, in a manner to profit both. . . .

Sam, and Nette enjoyed their first night together, I suppose, last night. They will have a beautiful calm life, full of loving trust. I wish they had more of this world's goods.

Be sure and take all things to make you warm, and comfortable, my Love, while you are absent. It was too bad that I had to leave before you did. But when we get *our home*, we will *live together*. . . .

Love to Mother
Forever & forever yours
Lucy

Ft. Wayne Friday Jan. 25. 1856

My own dearest

. . . The cars from Cincinnati yesterday, were an hour & a half behind the time, and I began seriously to fear that I would not be able to get here in time for the lecture. But as soon as the train came in sight, I sent a despatch to Mr. Gray, and at Lima, recieved one from him, on the cars, asking if I could go "right from the cars to the lecture?" I said "yes" & went into the saloon, changed my dress, arranged my hair &c, but we arrived in time to give me a half hour. There had been a great deal of opposition and last Tuesday, when they expected me, from my first appointment, two calico balls were got up for the same evening. Mr. Gray said the whole town was in a ferment, &c &c. All this he told me before the lecture. Of course, the opposition must be killed, and the first evening must do it. So I went full of faith and hope. A large audience had assembled. And, Harry, brave good sensitive, critical husband of mine, you would not have been ashamed of your wife. I gave them a good lecture. At times the house rang with cheers, and then again, was still as the grave, with a deeper feeling. Before the first half-hour, the truth had triumphed. It was such an *infinite blessing* to feel again the old inspiration & *faith* in *myself,* and to see the audience swayed as the wind, the grain. I would not write this, even to you my own dearest Love, only you know how I have feared, and because *you will love to rejoice with me.*

As I stepped on the cars to come here, there stood Mr. Pierpont. I offered him my hand, which he took, but by a bewildered look, showed he did not recognize me, & I said "Mr. Pierpont does not know me." My voice made him remember, and he exclaimed, "O bless my heart. I'm a good mind to kiss you right here before all the people. Are you well, are you well?" Yes said I, "very well, only I am greatly provoked, at this lazy train. Why did you not hurry it on." "Because I did not know you were here" said he. Then he inquired for you, told me his wife had died since he saw me, &c &c. Then he asked for Nette. I told him, she had the day before been married to my husbands brother, and added par nobile fratrum, to which he exclaimed "par nobile sororum"! And then after a moment, added "So she has gone down into the abyss too"—haunted evidently with the idea that marriage is the annihilation of a wife. We must *prove* the contrary.

There was a little scene in the sitting room of the hotel, which I believe I shall write you, it was so rich. No I wont, I can *tell* it you so much better, but I have laughed a dozen times since thinking of it. When you are less busy, and I am at your side, I'll tell it you. I am at an excellent hotel—had beef boiled & venison, and eggs for breakfast—for dinner, turkey, beef, roast & boiled, stewed oysters, tomatoes, cranberrys, pies &c. Wont you take a bit with me? Take good care of yourself, for both our sakes. Let me know where to address you. Send me short letters. The Good Father prosper you & bring you back to me, and me to you strong and well.

Ever yours
Lucy

Dayton [Ohio] Wednesday Jan. 30 [1856]

Dearest Harry

   . . . All three of my lectures, were such as they *used* to be, and the papers came out, quite in Louisville style. I am *so* glad to find again the old inspiration, and it comes to me more & more. I cleared there $130, over all expenses. . . . Harry dear you *are* the *best husband* in the world. In the midst of all the extra care, hurry, and perplexity of business, you stop to look after all my little affairs, even to the *counting my tickets*, doing everything you can to save me trouble. How shall I ever pay you, for all your thoughtful kindness? I will *love you*, as I do, with *all my heart*, and in future try and be as careful for you, & *not leave the leggings for Mother to mend!* Be sure I did not know they needed it, but I *ought* to have known. . . .

   Sam and Nette, follow *our* plan of making the most of the time they are together! Well, God make their love, as good to them, as ours is, to us. Sam will think us less lazy perhaps than he used to. I never think of them, without *wishing* for *you*, as I do, a thousand times besides. I quite envy Mr. Ostrom, his privilege by your pillow! Every night, when I lie down, I do so miss the sheltering love of your arms and the near personal presence! My own dear husband we *must not* in future be separate so much. I feel a constant sense of loss. God bless & keep us for each other.

   For one half moment the other day, I thought I should be killed. And the one thought that pained me was for *you*. In coming from Ft. Wayne there were but two passenger cars; the rear one, into which

I first went, as you asked me always to do, was so filthy and full of tobacco users, that I went in the front one. We had been on about an hour, when at once we felt, a sudden jerk, and then saw the baggage car, like a frightened creature, rear high in air, and with a wild plunge, it went down the bank. As it stood there poised, for a brief moment, there seemed nothing to hinder our car from taking the same course, but the upset of the other released ours. And only one person was slightly injured. The whole was due to the port. [porter] springing the switch.

I found on my arrival here, that Mr. Bloodwell had done the advertising very badly. For all this big town, he had but 50 posters, and there had been but a single notice, in the advertising column, except in the Gazette, whose editor knew me at home, and he had given me, a good local notice. I immediately filled up all the posters I had, and had them put up, but John G. Saxe was to lecture that evening—there was a very attractive bill at the theater and sleigh rides were abundant, &c &c. My audience only paid $16. Hall $10. Advertising $5. door helper $1. so that my hotel expenses will be so much out of pocket. Tonight Mrs. McCready reads & acts. A troupe of negro singers are to be here through the week, and as but one lecture was advertised, and the week is so full of attractions I conclude not to speak again, until I go to Springfield & Urbana. . . .

Saxe called on me last night after my lecture, and staid until nearly 11 o'clock. Camilla Russo, and Mrs. McCready remained also. We had a pleasant time. Yesterday PM I rode out with the last named to the Lunatic Asylum. Camilla played and Mrs. M.C. acted for the inmates. It was a nice time—but the best of all times, I have had with *Bryant's poems*. They have been a well spring of water to me. *He* is a true poet. Thank you again darling for that *grand Christmas gift*. We'll read more of them together sometime. . . . Yes Harry we will have a library—and make an annual appropriation to it. I want to lecture all the rest of the season, and save as much as I can, for us. . . . "God bless you *my own dearest husband*, and keep you body and soul, healthy and happy, and progressive is the aspiration and prayer of your own wife."

Lucy

I shall look for little bits of letters at Richmond & Winchester.

Mattoon Coles Co. Ills Feby. 1st/56

Dearest Lucy

I have thought of you every day since last Monday, when I left home and have wished to write, but have found it impossible. I went down to Aurora Monday Morning & at 2 PM met Mr. Ostrom at Lawrenceburg, having walked 4 miles with saddlebags on shoulder to do so. We reached Terre Haute Monday evening, stopped at the Prairie House, the cleanest, neatest, & most comfortable hotel in Indiana. There, with a cosy fire & comfortable beds, we took as much comfort as is possible to me, *without* you. Next morning came over to Paris & after spending the day there, at 3 P.M., we set out on hired horses, for Oakland, 20 miles distant. Scarcely had we started when we encountered a furious gale of wind full of snow, which came thundering over the vast bleak prairie blinding & half stunning us. As we advanced it grew rapidly colder & when we reached our stopping place, I found my knees so stiff that I could scarcely alight & poor Ostrom had to be *lifted* off his horse.

However a good supper & sound sleep in a comfortable bed made all right again and next morning we set out about 10 o'clock after arranging my business there—with the thermometer at zero—and a clear sharp North West wind sweeping over us to cross a 17 mile prairie. It was a glorious exhilerating ride. . . . Yesterday was milder & we rode 40 miles from Bourbon to Sullivan & thence to Shelbyville. . . . At Shelbyville we experienced our greatest *hardship* in the shape of a most *filthy* tavern—so abominably nasty that poor Ostrom pleaded sickness & declined going to the breakfast table—his supper the evening previous, having rather acted as an *emetic*, than a cordial. For myself being more used to such things, I resolutely ate three shortcakes & drank a cup of muddy coffee—carefully refraining to see the little girl with dirty hands and a running sore on her arm, who acted as waiter & blind to the woman combing insects out of the child's head within three feet of me. I regarded my greasy plate with a *general* glance, which declined to note the *smear* which blurred it & handled my knife & fork, as though they were not really extremely sticky and glutinous. The old landlord sat opposite & coughed & spit tobacco juice all around him, the landlady blew her nose with her finger & wiped it with the back of her hand, in the intervals of pouring out the coffee, but I preserved my equanimity & ate the proper quantity of hot biscuit, although I well knew that the dough had supplied the place of soap to the hands of the fair manufacturer thereof. Such is the virtue of equestrianism in frosty weather! As for the beds, it is sufficient to say that Ostrom kept his stockings on for *fear of dirtying his feet* & I caught a slight cold by exposing my shoulders because I could not endure the bedclothes in the vicinity of my face, while I put my head into the palm of my hand & kept it there all night to prevent its coming in contact with the pillow. However we have a nice place here & shall have almost every day hence forward. . . .

Yours ever
Harry

Richmond, Ind. Sunday Feb. 3, 1856

Dearest Harry

I suppose this clear, cold, beautiful Sunday finds you where the wild wind twirls your locks, freshens your cheeks, and I hope does not chill you. I am in a small room, with green & brown carpet, blue curtains, red table spread & a bit of whale bone for the door latch, while one broken pane of glass keeps the stove quarrelling with the temperature of the room, but I am very comfortable and happy. . . . A heavy snow storm began in the middle of the forenoon but I reached Dayton safely. The great snowflakes came down beautifully, but gave me a small audience so that for the two lectures my expenses were $5 more than the receipts, but I gave *good lectures* thank God! made some friends, & the papers all spoke well. . . .

Dear husband of mine here alone today I have been thinking of you, more grateful than ever, that God has given me *you* to *love,* you and no one else. . . . When I am with you, I read every day some little new page of you, and when I am absent, I study what they mean, and the more I know you the more I love you. And wherever I am, *always* I feel the hallowed presence of *this which I cherish* for you, and my heart *yearns* for you now as I write, and when I lie down at night, tho' I sleep more soundly alone, I yet miss you sorely. . . .

I suppose you have seen the notice of that horrible slave capture in Cincinnati where the heroic mother killed her child. No hall could be had for a meeting of sympathy, and the Gazette talked in an exceedingly doughface style of the impropriety of holding meetings which might cause the halls to be destroyed, &c &c. My brain burned at the thought that *anybody* could for one moment weigh the safety of property in the scale with that which might have secured LIBERTY to those who have proved so well that they deserve it. I recieved a letter yesterday from Mr. Jolliffe asking me to accept the guardianship . . . of one of the wounded little ones. I wrote him, that I hoped they would all get their freedom, in which case, *such* a mother, was all the guardian they needed, but that I was willing to aid in any way I could, tho' such guardianship needed to be there, and now—and my arrangements would keep me for some time absent. . . . After lecture Sunday evening. A small audience but a real good lecture, and many came to thank me, cleared $11. . . .

Ever yours
Lucy

Terre Haute Ind. Feb. 7. 1856
Thursday evening 10 o'clock PM

Dearest Lucy
    . . . I enclose a letter from Mother to me & one from Anna to me & you. I shall tell Mother when I write her, that I can have no secrets from you—and that I will send you both Anna's bane & her antidote. Anna is certainly wrong & Mother right however, in regard to the *permanent* natural fact that the husband must, as a general thing earn the support of his wife and children. This, in no sense, militates against the personal independence of the wife, who is an equal partner in the matrimonial firm—& any other arrangement would be a gross injustice & cruel imposition upon the wife. Surely dearest Lucy, it would not pain you, nor annoy you, if you were without money to share mine with *me*. You *could not* feel humbled, or subservient in accepting my earnings any more than in accepting my caresses—since you know they would be valueless to me unless you shared them. *Any* marriage not consecrated by love is mon-

strous—& the *presence* of love, makes dependance *mutual* & financial details simply *trivial*.

What Anna says about the superiority of the short dress & your disinterestedness in giving it up *for my sake* gives me mingled pain & pleasure—pleasure in the thought of your *love* which has prompted you to change it & pain that you should think it necessary to my happiness to do so. Dearest Lucy—I shall have to go on my knees to you to induce you to resume the short dress. If your judgment still decides that you had better wear it—I would infinitely rather you should do so. I am *not* so thin skinned as you imagine & am quite willing to *help* you wear it & indeed to help you carry out your own convictions in every way. I want you to feel & know that I *aid* you, not retard you. So dearest, I am desirous to meet you next Saturday night two weeks in the short dress & pants. I shall find nothing disagreably masculine *within* the dress & so can easily overlook externals.

I have not seen the Cincinnati papers since I left, so I only know about the slave case by *hearsay*. But I do not comprehend the Gazzette's remark quoted by you, about the impropriety of endangering *Halls*. Cincinnati is mean enough, God knows, or she would not permit the *question* of those unfortunate people's right to *themselves*, to be even *tried*. But I cannot believe that the current of sympathy in the Community can be *with* the *masters*. Still less do I believe that a meeting of sympathy would be mobbed. Had I been at home, I feel it in my bones that we *would have had* a meeting somewhere. If no hall could be got, in a church. If no church could be had, in the market-house. I shall regret nothing so much in leaving Cincinnati, as leaving a place where the great question of human liberty is so often brought up & where the friends of freedom are so few and so much needed. Good-night dearest my own Lucy. God bless you.

Yours ever
Harry

Cincinnati 9½ PM Apl. 3. 1856

My dear Wife
I have only time to write a single line, or two—telling you that we are all well—& enclosing a letter . . . from your friend Sholes—

also a minority report, which is *sound doctrine,* but not quite so well written as is his letter to you. The latter is really very fine. . . .

Yesterday I enclosed you the Liberator, which, together with *three* other letters should reach you at Sidney. I am glad that you *concur* with me in calling some parts of Hale's speech *reprehensible.* I wonder why he should so belittle himself & so *weaken* himself and his party! Whether I ever go into politics is doubtful. Whether I should succeed in that profession is perhaps improbable.

But if I ever do—I *think* I shall never be found *crouching* & *whining* to slaveholders, or doughfaces. I believe in *aggressive,* frank, energetic political action. No *truce* with slavery. No parleying with crime. No courtesy with man stealing, woman-whipping, & child-selling! Lucy dear—can there not be an *honest* politician?

Yes—there can be!—just as there *may* be an honest merchant, or lawyer. The temptations are immense, but *not* invincible. Put Jesus Christ into either politics, profession, or business & he would both *succeed* by his *wisdom* & be *true* by his *virtue.*

But I am not Jesus Christ—& so I may as well *beware of myself.*

Good-bye—God bless you. I shall think of you next Sunday & long for you—but shall wait patiently till the Good Father reunite us.

Dear Lucy—love me & trust me & believe me. Ever your own

Harry

[Walnut Hills] 4 o'clock Sunday Afternoon Apl. 12/56

Dearest Lucy

I commenced a letter yesterday afternoon at the store, but tore it up, remembering that today being Sunday, it would not leave at any rate until Monday morning & hoping that today I could send you a better one. But I have been busy all day reading Dickens' "Bleak House" which I have not before got hold of & at dinner Mother presented us with a heavenly apple pudding. So, being at present somewhat like a boa constrictor after he has swallowed a sheep, you must excuse any *torpor* which may creep into this epistle. . . .

I enclose herewith an article from the Newport (Ky) News describing a spirited antislavery meeting lately held by C. M. Clay and his friends in Ky. The Editor has just returned highly encouraged. At his request, I wrote an article for him to appear on tomorrow as an editorial, nominating Clay for the Presidency. Not that I think he would be the best possible selection, or one likely to be made, but I approve of his name being presented in the only antislavery Paper in Ky. as a true man, *deserving* of the position. You must not mention my having written the article, as it is of course prepared, as coming from a Kentuckian & is addressed specially to Kentuckians. I will show you the article when you return.

Yesterday evening Sam & I attended the Club & had our names quietly erased from membership. We had a very spirited & interesting debate on *Colonization*. Mr. Force first spoke strongly & pleasantly in its favor urging its beneficial results upon both colored Americans & Africans. I replied in a speech of 25 minutes, which I think was a good one. I opposed the scheme because it was so *unnecessary* & repugnant to the people themselves, because both the end proposed & the means used are *bad*, because it is necessary to the slave that free men of color should *stay here* & to free men of color to perfect in contact with whites the civilization so imperfectly attained as yet &c &c &c. We had some six or eight speeches, all good, on both sides & I think *showed up* Colonization pretty thoroughly. . . .

May God bless you & fill your soul with hope & faith & courage & your body with health & vigor and bring you back safely to my arms.

> Goodbye little wife
> & believe me *Ever Yours*
> Harry

P.S. Sam has been working in the garden yesterday & day before in a broad brimmed straw hat & linen coat looking quite patriarchal. He has tied up the raspberries, planted a lot of potatoes & chopped several of his toes with an axe. The injury however is *not* very serious.

> Our room, Walnut Hills Sat. AM Apr. 26, 56

Dearest Harry,

Your little note, in a letter to Sam, reached me two days ago. You are a good child Harry,—here by your presence and absent by your letters, and in a thousand ways you do me good. . . . I shall be packing tomorrow, then bid goodbye here. . . . Then if we do not find a place to live, in Wisconsin, we will go East together, and see what is there. . . . We must hallow the little place that *is to* be our *home*, with earnest effort at self-improvement, with noble aims, *and* good resolutions coined into deeds. It seems to me, that in the little spot, (God guard it!) unknown to us, yet existing *somewhere*, in actual fact, we shall be able to live nearer our ideal, to make more of our time, and to achieve what is more worthy of us. In the long rail road rides, when speculation steps from your mind, you will have time perhaps to fix some definite plans for *your* future. The place where our home is, must depend much on that. If we could have land enough to grow so large a part of our subsistince, that we *need not* depend upon the public—with a little income from rents, or interest, and be free to study, to think, to grow unitary, and symmetrical, and be ready to give occasional help to any great Cause, and perhaps to rear some "little olive plants around our table"—this seems to me the most desirable way of living. It is surely free from all the meanness of trade, & as society is, it seems to me, is the only way, which is both innocent and honorable. But we will talk of it when we meet again, and when, I hope we shall be separated less my dear.

Just one year ago, this room was getting ready for us to occupy, and now for us to leave. Where, & how, will another year find us? Spite of me, a little sadness and regret, will steal over me, as I count the hours, to the time, when this room consecrated by our first wedded love, will be ours no longer. I wish you were with me dearest. It would not seem so sad, if we went out, as we came in, *together*. But 'tis no matter, for after all it is best. . . .

Yours forever
Lucy

I shall keep the anniversaries of our wedding & your birth, in silence, and alone, which is next best to having them with you.

Lyons, Iowa, April 29. 1856

Dearest Lucy

I reached here Saturday night, or rather Sunday morning at 12½ o'clock. I had delightful weather during the week & attended to con-

siderable collecting business on my way. I found George absent &
apparently permanently located at La Crosse. Everything here is in
a ferment—the community being equally divided between land speculators crying up their lots & strangers prospecting, or moving in.
Quite a rich developement of human nature going on. *Man the
Schemer* is quite prominent. Every one sees visions of indefinite
wealth ahead & is willing to submit meanwhile to every privation &
labor. The river & the Country are *beautiful*. The climate windy &
bracing. I think well of the place & its prospects. . . .

This afternoon I go to La Crosse to see George. If I can get hold
of those tracts about which he wrote, or others equally favorable,
without putting myself in the power of any strangers by relying upon
them in any way, I shall invest in the name of my Cincinnati friends,
not otherwise. . . . Meanwhile dear Lucy, I keep perfectly cool &
am in no danger of catching the speculative fever. My excitability will
be reserved for other objects than land speculation. . . . I thought of
you on Saturday as coming home from the Refuge & packing up *our*
clothes & things. And yesterday (Monday) morning I thought of you
as starting with Sarah. To-day, I think you are at Niagara *having a
good time*. . . .

Believe me dear Lucy I want to be *with* you & shall make my
absence as brief as possible.

God bless you—Farewell
Yours ever
Harry

May 18. 1856
Cincinnati Sunday Afternoon

Dearest Lucy

I hope, if nothing unforeseen prevent, to start East on Tuesday
morning. In that case, I shall probably go direct to West Brookfield,
and if—as is quite probable, I find you at Gardner—I shall cross over
in a buggy & join my own dear little wife, with a joy which I *know*,
you will share. Then dearest, I will explain to you fully the present
position of affairs & we will run down to N. York together—there see
Eliz. & M. . . . & other friends & thence go to Wisconsin appraise

& offer our lands for sale & then either make a temporary stay there for money-making purposes, or come back Eastward as our UNITED judgment shall decide. . . .

What a horrible aspect the Kansas matter begins to assume! I feel half disposed to throw over every private consideration & buy a "Sharpe's rifle" & "Colt revolver" & be off to Lawrence to counsel *moderation*, but to assist *anyhow*.

What say you—Shall we throw ourselves into the Crusade?

Ever your own
Harry

P.S. Wherever we go & whatever we do henceforth dear Lucy—let us not separate any more but live & act *together*.

For a while at least, Lucy and Henry did manage to live and act together. At the end of May she met him in Chicago, and they set off in a horse and buggy for Wisconsin. They owned some six thousand acres of land there, but before they could sell it or trade it for land in the East, it had to be surveyed and certified.

Their journey into Wisconsin was a rugged one. The roads were bad and sometimes virtually nonexistent, and accommodations along the way left much to be desired. Henry wrote his brother Sam that at one farmhouse where they stopped for the night, "Lucy was horrified by having to sleep in dirty sheets & two girls & a dog kept passing through our room, disturbing our conjugal reflections very much." The situation at Viroqua, their destination in Bad Ax County, was scarcely better. At first they boarded at a local hotel, but as Henry remembered, "Lucy accustomed to the exquisite clean linen of a New England farmer's home, found this mode of living too uncomfortable, so we rented a room & boarded ourselves."

They spent about three months in Wisconsin. Henry was busy surveying his land most of the time; however they were both able to give some lectures. Lucy's Fourth of July address in Viroqua was especially memorable: In the middle of her speech the platform on which she was standing collapsed, but with characteristic aplomb, she drew a moral from the mishap: "So will this country fall unless slavery is abolished."

Yet more than anything else, her feminism was fired by what she saw of the lot of frontier women. To her brother Bowman she wrote: "The women work out as much or more than the men, and are never allowed more than four days after the birth of a child, before they have to go out to milk, and in the family nearest us, the wife slept in an out-house all winter, because her husband who lay snug by the fire, said, when the baby was born, and it was a *girl*, 'if she will have girls, cold is good enough for her,' and he is a very good specimen of the whole." Scenes such as this spurred her to a new level of feminist militancy, which for the first time challenged the foundations of her abolitionist faith. As she confessed in a letter to her family: "But truly, I care less and less every day which triumphs, freedom or slavery. In either case, all the women of the land are yet subjects, ruled over by the white male population, and from my heart deeper and deeper breathes the prayer that slavery may yet crush every white man into the same condition in which the white men have placed women. Then we will struggle up together out of our common wrong, but until the goad pierces them as it does us, they will never know that we are hurt."

During this time, Lucy acted to rid herself of a personal mark of bondage. While a student at Oberlin, she had come upon the words in a textbook, "Women are more sunk by marriage than men," and when, playing the devil's advocate, she asked her professor why this was so, he replied that it was because married women lost their names and became identified with their husbands' families. His answer made a strong impression on Lucy; according to Antoinette Brown, she brooded over the matter for days afterward. Yet though she regarded a wife's loss of her name as a terrible injustice, she wasn't ready to do anything about it at the time of her own marriage. Instead she settled for a halfway measure: Like Elizabeth Cady Stanton, who used her maiden name along with her married name, she would be called Lucy Stone Blackwell. This was the name that appeared on her wedding card, in the announcement of her marriage in *The Liberator*, and in various other notices of meetings she attended during the first year of her marriage. Lucy may have hesitated to take the final step and call herself Lucy Stone because, in spite of all Henry's attempts at reassurance, she harbored strong doubts as to whether she could, in fact, go on being Lucy Stone after she was married. She also may have waited until she had had an opportunity to post herself on the legal side of the question. She did consult three different lawyers and was assured that there was no law requiring a wife to take her husband's name.

Whatever the reasons for her hesitation, by July of 1856 she was ready to proclaim herself "Lucy Stone (only)." She instructed Susan B. Anthony to leave off the Blackwell from her name in the announcement of a forthcoming woman's rights convention, and when, several months later, she discovered that her request hadn't been complied with, she reacted emotionally. To Susan she wrote: "At first it made me faint and sick until a flood of tears relieved me. . . . O! Susan it seems to me, that it has wrought a wrong on me that it will take many years to wear out. . . . I have lost something which has darkened all my heavens. Hereafter, I shall work, but with less of hope and courage."

The extremeness of Lucy's reaction showed how crucial to her sense of self her name was. As Lucy Stone she had defied the conventional notions of woman's sphere, first by going to college, and then by becoming a public lecturer. The name was associated with both her early struggles and later triumphs; it stood for all she had gained, and all she had feared to lose in marriage. Just when she wanted the world to know that Lucy Stone had survived marriage with her separate identity intact, it came as a cruel blow to discover that the recognition of her latest, and in many ways most important, victory had been denied. Moreover, the cruelty may have been intentional, since Susan B. Anthony had never been pleased with Lucy's marriage.

No wonder then that Lucy felt wounded and betrayed, but as she had promised Susan, she continued to work for woman's rights. When Henry's business in the West was finished, he and Lucy moved to New York, where they stayed with his sister Elizabeth at her combined residence and dispensary on East Fifteenth Street. It was, in Henry's words, "a somewhat crowded and impecunious household," for besides Lucy and Henry, Hannah Blackwell, Marian,

Emily, Sam and Nette and their new daughter Florence, and Dr. Marie Zakrzewska from Cleveland also moved in with Elizabeth and Kitty, the Irish orphan girl she had adopted three years earlier. Lucy and Henry found themselves relegated to a tiny attic room, but as before, they were both away from home much of the time.

When they moved east, the Stone-Blackwells were land-rich. In addition to their several thousand acres in Bad Ax County, they had Lucy's land in Appleton, Wisconsin, acreage in Clinton and Lyons, Iowa, and a farm near Chicago, which Henry and Sam had taken in exchange for their share in the hardware business when they sold out. But until they could sell some of this land, they were cash-poor, and so Henry had to find an occupation that would bring in some money. He traded off some of his western land for an interest in an agricultural book publishing company, in which Augustus Moore, an old friend from Cincinnati, also had a share. As the company's traveling representative, he returned to the West in the winter of 1857 to set up farmers' libraries that would be well-stocked with the firm's books. For her part, Lucy kept to her usual hectic schedule of lecturing in different parts of the country—despite the fact that she thought she might be pregnant.

⁓

Harrisburg, Pa. Sunday Jan. 4, 1857

Harry darling! A week ago today at this hour, 9½ I was close by your side in the little attic, and so happy to be there! Now if I could only have you here too, in this large well furnished room, with its warm fire, and view of beautiful hills, I should be most gladly grateful. Will it not be a great blessing that we shall both know how to value, when we *can* LIVE together in our own home?

I imagine you will be getting ready today to start on your wanderings. I wish I could help you. I hope you have a *large warm* shawl, and will take the *woolen* stockings, and that in *every way*, you will have a successful trip. And when you return, I will try and be in N.Y. to give you the warm welcome which now is always in my heart for you. The last time I was here was when on my way to meet you at Pittsburg. I wish I could tell you how differently I feel towards you *now* from what I did then. Then, there was a strange sad distrust of us both. And now my heart turns more full of trust & tenderness to you than I can express. And every day is getting back more & more the old faith in myself & brave courage too, which before helped me to work out all that which made *me* better, and was good for others too. Out of a full heart I thank God for *your* generous *love,* which is giving me back my former self, but more & better. And may He help us to be *always helps* to each other. I do not know dear Harry that I ought to write you in this way, for I know that your thoughts are *full* of business, and necessarily so. But you must write me about it. And let me share as fully as I can. . . .

One afternoon, in company with some ladies, I climbed the hills, on *this* side the river. They are bald and bare, and the soil slid under our feet, so that we had a most vigorous circulation before we reached the top. But once there, you have a view that more than pays the toil. The valley of the Juniata inexpressibly beautiful—the river like a silver thread winding through it—and the whole, like Jerusalem girt about with mountains, covered with cedars goodly as those of Lebanon. I wished for *you* there dearest, and thought how Marian & Sarah would enjoy it—and was disturbed only by the excessive garrulity of an old lady who amused herself by regaling me with tales of the ignorance of the inhabitants of the place. . . .

I have read Lalla Rookh. You know all about that; the life of Horace Greeley also. . . . Last, I have read Aurora Leigh! O, Harry, *that* is the book! It preaches, but its genius makes the preaching attractive, and the sermons are such as many souls are waiting for. It is full of philosophy, poetry, humanity and true religion. I like it very much. We will read it together, sometime. Next I am going to read an autobiography of a female slave. It is written by a Miss Griffith of Louisville, the little poet that Prentice petted so much. She called on me at Louisville; is a very pleasant person. All her property is in slaves. She is now in Philadelphia preparing free papers for them, and has commenced getting her own living by writing a book. The Motts, of whom I borrowed it, like it, and her, very much. I get a good deal of time to read, and should more, only that so many women who are boarding at the hotels, having nothing in the world to do, come in to see me, to pass the time, to get a new sensation and a little variety. Poor things! I pity them and I get sermons from them all, and somethings for my lectures, and more than all, a deeper detestation of our social systems which seem contrived to crush all real nobility out of woman with a deadly and destructive certainty and perforce, to make her an empty nothing. God give me patience and willingness to work on against this strong setting tide of evil!

Lucy

Chicago Ills. Feby. 11. 1857

Dearest Lucy

. . . I hoped to find a letter here from you, but none has come. I should not begrudge a high price for one, to assure me of your health & safety. After the *strong probability* that exists of your being in *so different a position* from what you were, two short months ago, you may readily imagine that my heart yearns towards you with a painful sentiment of solicitude on your behalf. Lucy dear—if I could take all the pain & suspense, I would not let you have *one pang.* I would gladly take it all for your sake. It may be however that you are spared the dangers and deprived of the hopes of maternity before this reaches you. You may have found that your expectation was groundless. In that case, dear Wife, do not mourn, nor despond—for I will love you *all the better* if possible, from my sympathy with your loneliness. My dear Lucy—Be happy *for my sake.* But, if you find your belief confirmed—*remember that I love you* & be content to give me this *last proof* of *your affection.* I will try to deserve it, by doing all I can to act bravely & nobly. I wish you knew how I long to be with you—how I *count the days,* till we shall again be in each other's arms. . . .

I have enjoyed my visit to Madison. After the first day, I went to the house of Mr. F. Y. Kilgore formerly of Wilbraham, Mass., who knows & esteems you. He says he thinks you have done more good than *any living woman.* . . . At his house I found some four of the members of the legislature boarding—two of them very influential men. One of these Mr. David Williams, chairman of the House Comm. on Agr., I especially liked. He is one of the broadest, most sound-minded, symmetrical men I have seen. A large man weighs about 225 lbs—a farmer's son & a farmer—who has educated himself & done it in the intervals of his healthy, independent labor. He says he owns a good farm & has all the comforts of life—but is not rich and could not be, if he tried; for he cannot take enough interest in accumulation—his mind is not in it. He is not brilliant nor eloquent, nor quick—but he is simple, earnest, calm, contented, wide & large in all his views & feelings & knows many things.

I feel more & more convinced that the *hope of the World* lies in Agriculture. A man who does not live on his own land is a factitious & artificial being. If I had to choose my past, I would have been born & bred a farmer & stick to the trade. . . .

Dear Lucy I have written you a long letter with very little in it—but you will read it with interest for my sake—Please take the *very best care* of yourself, till I come home to help you. Do not feel nervous, nor anxious, nor worried, but keep a brave heart & try to realize that my soul's arms surround you with an *inexpressible love*. . . . I intend never to feel unwell any more till you die of old age & then I will die & we will both be buried in the same coffin. Meanwhile my own dear little wife—I am—

Ever your own—body & soul
Harry

At the old home. [West Brookfield] Mar. 4, 1857

My own dear Husband

I sent you a line written at the station to let you know how unexpectedly I had come here, when that very day I hoped to be with you. But as the legislative committee would grant a hearing, it seemed a pity to incur the expense of going to New York to return so soon, especially as we are not able to afford it. So I robbed my heart for the sake of the $12 which will help to get indispensables for the dear, little home which is *somewhere,* and which will be all the dearer when we find it, from the fact that we have been so long without a local habitation. . . .

Dearest Harry I wish I could see you half an hour. It seems as if I might be brave a long time after, if only for one little minute I might look into your eyes. Please God, I will be with you before long. But Harry love, I have now an invitation to go with [Wendell] Phillips to Maine, to the Augusta Legislative Committee who are also ready to hear what may be said for woman's right of suffrage. They want us next Tuesday, Mar. 13, and I have concluded to go. They have referred our Memorial to a select committee, and some of the best men in the State are on it, and Harry dear, *if* in the hour that is before me I should go out of my body, or have it left a wreck, *this* work will be worthy work to leave as my *last*; an immortal cause will gain by it. I am not hurting myself, and shall take the best of care. I think I can be home certainly by next week, and then I shall not go far any more this spring. I rested five days with Sarah, and here I have a fire in my chamber, and have quite a time preparing my best thought—with it best dress for Friday. If we get us a home soon, I will be as quiet as you desire. . . .

> With dearest love
> Lucy

On April 1 Lucy and Henry finally acquired a home of their own—a cottage with an acre of land in Orange, New Jersey, which was purchased in Lucy's name. To meet the asking price of $5,000, they made a down payment of $500, which Lucy borrowed from a friend, traded off 240 acres of their western lands, now valued at $10 an acre, and secured a bond and mortgage for the remaining $2,100.

However, Lucy's delight in at last having a home of her own was marred by the fact that Henry wasn't there to share it with her; a week after they moved in, he left for the West on business, and was away throughout the spring and part of the summer. Lonely in the new house, Lucy, nevertheless, kept true to her promise to remain quiet, and her inactivity brought further rebukes from Susan B. Anthony. In July when Lucy wrote Susan that she couldn't attend a forthcoming convention in Providence because she was soon to be a mother, the latter could hardly contain her irritation. "Lucy, *neither* of us have *time*—for much *personal* matters," she replied angrily.

Although her friend's reproaches caused her pain, Lucy was determined not to stir that summer. She was afraid that if she dashed about from lecture to lecture and convention to convention, she would endanger her life and that of the unborn infant. For like many nineteenth-century women Lucy faced childbirth with a certain amount of dread. Her younger sister Sarah had already lost a child at birth, and she had been present when her brother Luther's widow had suffered a miscarriage. At thirty-nine Lucy was considerably older than either woman, or indeed, than most women when they had their first child. Moreover, she was concerned that the ruggedness of her life as an itinerant agitator had impaired her general health and childbearing capacity. So it was not surprising that she embraced the Victorian notion of confinement. By July she was in her seventh month of pregnancy—the time when middle-class women were advised to take to their beds and remain there until a month after delivery. Lucy probably didn't take this advice literally—after all, she was alone in the house with no servants to wait on her—but she did make an effort to restrict her movements.

Henry was at least there during the last month or so. In early August he returned from the West, dissatisfied with the management of the agricultural book business. He left the company, and found employment closer to home in New York, as a bookkeeper for the Vanderbilt steamship lines.

ⱷ

Orange, N.J. July 20, 1857

Dear Susan

I have waited for your second letter that I might answer them both in one. And 1st of business—I had a letter last night from a friend near Providence (Mrs. Elizabeth Chace of Valley Falls) who says the preliminary work can be done without trouble for the convention if it is held in Providence, and she thinks it would be well to hold it here. She is a daughter of Arnold Buffum—a sister [-in-law] of Marcus Spring, and is the soul and source of all the antislavery meetings that have been held in Providence this season. She is very efficient and a Mr. Hathaway has stood by her this winter and is ready to help our convention. . . . But you and Mr. Higginson must decide the question, as you will have the responsibility, for *I* cannot attend the convention wherever it is held. Before it comes, I expect to be a mother, and so necessarily absent. I shall write Mr. Higginson about Providence and leave it to you two, to manage. I will do what I can, but as two persons so far apart, cant work together, you had better assume the *entire* care of it. . . . I will send out the call—and aid in securing speakers as much as I can. If you are ever in my situation, you will find that swollen feet, and hands, & general discomforts are not good assistants in any work. . . . By the way, did you know that Mr. Eddy had taken those two little girls of his wife, from Mr. Jackson's on pretence of a ride & gone to France with them? The rascal!

Of course, you must use your own judgment about the time & place to discuss the marriage question. But when it *is done*, it seems to me, we must not call it, "woman's rights" for the simple reason, that it concerns men, just as much. Two days, & the previous evening will be none too much, for the good of the cause, *provided you have speakers enough*. I *hope* the convention will be all it ought to be, and I have no doubt it will. I shall try & send a letter. I dont believe Nette can go. She is very poorly. Now about that other matter. Who are the people that say "Susan says &c!" The *last*, & which was the immediate cause of my writing you anything about it, was a letter from Mr. Higginson, in which he says you saw me in N.Y. and thought I "did not appear quite right" &c. It was not the first time that such *intimation* had come to me,—and when it came to me *there*—my cup ran over. I felt that whether I held more or fewer meetings, gave more or less money—went less or more to help you *you*, next to Nette, of all persons in the world should not distrust me. And when others told me, as from you what you have put into 7 out of 10, of all the letters you have written since my marriage I had every reason to believe them. And when last winter you wrote Nette and me under one cover, and used this expression, "I am terribly afraid lest what everybody says will be true, that like other wives, you will flat out and do nothing. Nette will be excused because she has a baby, but Lucy—" I asked Nette what you *could* mean by it. She made some cool, philosophic answer, But to me it seemed cruel.

My legal position as wife deprives me of the power to use a cent of all the money I have earned, or may earn, only as I get it through a third person. I cant sell legally what I have acquired without Harry's consent. If I sign any transfer of his property I am ever insulted by being "examined separately and apart from my husband" to know if it is by my own free will—my right to my name even is questioned and with all this smart, added to that I suffered as a *woman*, before I was a wife. You were "terribly afraid" that in such doting ease, I should become nothing. O Susan, it was as wrong to you as to me. I cannot understand it. And when Mr. Crosby told me, what you quoted in your last but one, how could I help believe it, when it was only a little broader statement, of what the very last letter I had then received from you said, when I had declined attending your last winter anti slavery meetings, and in which you assured me that "Good Mr. May is grieved that you should say no to *me*"—I felt wounded, grieved, hurt, almost as I never was before. I wrote you about it, but concluded that I would be as silent to you, as to Mr. Crosby, to whom I did not open my lips. That it was womanish to mind it. Still I could not *help* minding it, and when we met in N.Y. I felt a mountain of ice between us. I felt that without any reason, you had lost all faith in me, and I wondered at the kiss you profferred. But I am in no state of body or mind to write about it. I still believe that *you* are the same brave faithful worker, that I always have, and in my heart, are just as earnest blessings and God speeds for you, as ever—but I must make the path for my own feet. I have no advice or explanation to make to *anybody*.

With best wishes
Lucy

5 Bowling Green N. York Sept. 8. 1857

Dearest Lucy

I have been thinking with inexpressible emotions over our past lives & *past life* together. I look out from the dark, mysterious shadow in which our present life is veiled & see more clearly the defects of my character & purpose which have thrown so many obstacles in your path & so much bitterness into your cup. Lucy dear—*however* this great crisis may eventuate, whether it result, as I hope & believe, in *our* assumption of new duties & cares, or whether in leaving me *alone* in this strange, uncongenial world—I will try to *meet* my responsibilities *worthily & well*. Dearest! you have made me *very happy* in spite of surface cares & excitements, in feeling for you a *love* and *esteem*, such as you may well prize from your husband. You have ennobled my life. I fear that I have *not* ennobled *your's*! But Lucy dear—I hope to be your's *always & forever*. I cannot at once change the habits & faults of my whole life, but henceforth you shall see me *ascend & improve*. If God give me the great *privilege* & honor & blessing of your *personal society*, I will try to show my gratitude by living *nobly* in act & thought. If otherwise—I will stay in the world, awaiting the reunion—longing to join you—& working for the great cause of human progress, which you have helped, with all the ability which I possess. And if from beyond the grave, it be indeed permitted to influence and inspire—dear Lucy—you shall always find an *open* heart & an expectant longing.

Little wife—trust your husband's *better nature a little longer*. Forgive the *weary way* I have forced you to travel. Accept my renewed & solemn pledge to struggle for that *internal nobility of purpose*, which can alone eventuate in permanent nobility of *life*.

My own love—what can I say to comfort you in your lonely sufferings—what can I do to benefit you! I know of nothing better than to promise to live bravely & honestly and to subject mere material aims to loftier purposes. Lucy—I feel that after all, I *have* something in me, which I may live to bring out, & which is akin to your own aspirations. Whenever I wipe out the debts which I owe—I will *devote myself* to developing in myself & in others the *best purposes*. I hope you may live long to help me do so. In any event—my own wife—take courage! God is near you—he will not desert you. No *final* failure is possible to you. And your husband will be *true to you*. God bless you—

> I am forever yours
> Harry

Almost a week later, on September 14, Lucy gave birth to a healthy baby girl. Emily Blackwell came out from New York to deliver the baby, and Henry himself was at home at the time. But while the birth was relatively easy, the choice of a name for the new child was not. Ostensibly, it was the first name that caused the most difficulty, but the real issue at stake had to do with the child's surname: Was she to be named Stone after her mother or Blackwell after her father? Henry was willing that the child bear her mother's surname, since Lucy was the one who had "suffered to bring the child into the world," but Lucy felt this would be unjust to Henry since the child was half his, and also unjust to the child, for it would cast doubt on her legitimacy. So the child was given the surname of Blackwell and the middle name of Stone, yet for nine months the first name remained a blank. Then Lucy and Henry chose the name of Sarah; however, when both Lucy's sister Sarah, and Henry's sister Ellen—who had been named Sarah Ellen, but had quickly dropped the "Sarah"—protested, they switched to Alice, and Alice the child's name remained.

During the first year after the baby's birth, Henry continued to be absent from home for extended periods of time. Unhappy with his bookkeeping position, he went back to the agricultural book publishing firm after Augustus Moore bought out the original owner. In December of 1857 he was away on business when Lucy decided to register another public protest against woman's inferior status. At a woman's rights convention several years before, she had urged women not to pay taxes while denied the vote, and now she was ready to act upon this revolutionary principle herself. When the tax bill for their house arrived, she returned it to the tax collector with a note explaining that she wouldn't pay the tax while "women suffer taxation, and yet have no representation, which is not only unjust to one-half the adult population, but is contrary to our theory of government." The state of New Jersey responded by ordering a public auction of certain of Lucy's household goods, and on January 22, two tables, four chairs, a stand, and two pictures—one of the New York reformer Gerrit Smith and the other of Ohio's abolitionist governor, Salmon Chase—were sold to pay the delinquent taxes. A neighbor bought the furniture and returned it to Lucy, but this in no way undermined the symbolic value of her protest. At the time it generated a great deal of publicity, and thereby helped call attention to the woman's movement.

Henry was also away for several months in the spring and summer of 1858, and it was during this period that he met Lincoln for the first and only time. While in Springfield, he went with the Illinois superintendent of schools to consult Lincoln on a point of law, and found him "as he was coming out of the Court House with his law books under his arm—a tall, middle-aged man with kind eyes and a frank, quiet manner who impressed one with sincerity, sense, and benevolence." Henry recalled that Lincoln "had then attained only local celebrity." But that very year Lincoln was to capture the national imagination with his "house divided" speech, and later, with his debates with Stephen A. Douglas.

This separation was especially difficult for Lucy. Ill and exhausted much of the time, she was trying to resume her public career while keeping up the household in New Jersey and caring for their baby. These conflicting demands on her time and energy created a strain that was evident in more than a few of her letters. At the beginning of April she wrote Susan B. Anthony that she wouldn't make a set speech at a forthcoming woman's rights convention because she couldn't speak well while nursing the baby; and perhaps in anticipation of another angry outburst, added rather defiantly, "I shall not take any responsibility about another convention till I have had my ten daughters."

∽

Dunkirk N.Y. 5 P.M. March 3/58

Dear Lucy

. . . It is a great relief to me to think of you as having *help* with you—though I fear it is somewhat inefficient. And now for two, or three items of business—

1st As regards your lectures—I saw Mr Tilton yesterday. He was very friendly & especially desirous that you should be at his wife's party tomorrow evening, but I told him I did not think you could be there. I would advise you to postpone any positive arrangements for your lectures in Jersey City & Brooklyn, until you are actually *located* at *Elizabeth's*, with a girl to nurse the baby during your absences under *Mother's supervision*. Then, take the requisite time to make well planned arrangements. Have the lectures thoroughly advertised & noticed in the local columns of the New York papers as well as those in J.C. & Brooklyn. Give the subject in full "the social and industrial disabilities of Woman" &c. Let the lectures be noticed *at least twice* in the Herald, Times, Tribune & Post before they commence & each morning of the day when you deliver them. If all these preliminaries are *properly* & *thoroughly* attended to, you will have good audiences. I wish that I could be at home to help you. From Elizabeth's by stages & cars &c, with sufficient time to work in—say *a week at least*—you can work personally which is far better than by agent. . . .

I have just finished reading the Atlantic Monthly for March. It is *by very far* the best number that has yet appeared. . . . There are two stories illustrative to womanly self devotion & constancy—*both admirable* & I think *true to nature*. . . . Altogether it is a number worth your reading. I will mail it to you from Chicago. . . . Goodnight dearest Lucy—Give *our* baby twelve kisses & tell her I long for her & for you with a deep, true love—God bless you both & my Mother is the prayer of yours ever

Harry

Springfield Ills. March 12, 1858

Dear Lucy

. . . Everyone here is reading Seward's speech. It is being much read by the *Douglass* Democrats, who are having quite an anti-slavery revival. There is a deadly feud here between the Douglass men and the Lecompton men & a strong probability of a permanent breach in the party.

Everything is *excessively dull* out here. No money—all waiting till spring comes & moves the *produce* now lying on the farms & in the warehouses. The weather is *beautiful*—clear, mild & bright. . . .

I am glad to say that my leg is getting better daily. Today for the first time for two weeks I can walk up stairs without making one foot draw up the other. No new boils & a reasonable hope of escape from that infliction. I hope you will receive a vigorous, healthy husband on my return from the West in exchange for the insignificant cripple that gave you so much trouble this Spring.

Dear Lucy—It is both your fault (or rather *misfortune*) & *my own*, to look too much at the dark side of things & too little at the *cheerful* & *sanguine* one. Let us hope for a happy reunion & for many loving & useful years of sympathy & happiness with our little girl & our little home. Dearest good night. God bless you.

Yours ever
Harry—

Janesville Wis. March 25. 1858

Dearest Lucy

This morning I despatched a letter to you from Chicago written late last night when I felt a little blue. But when I rose this morning the sun shone brightly—the air was delicious & I took my seat in the cars after going down to Carnes & Wilson's with a letter from you in my cap. The air in the car was hot & disagreeable, so I went out upon the platform behind & sat on the steps & read your letter twice & then *sunned myself* for a full hour & thought of you the dear wife at home & our little blue-eyed treasure which you have watched over so tenderly & faithfully.

Poor Lucy I have kept you ever since our marriage in so *unsatisfied* a condition. I have carried you off to Cincinnati & Chicago & Wisconsin & New York & New Jersey—have given you no rest or permanent home—have separated you from your mother & brothers & sisters & friends—have fettered you in your public carreer of usefulness & fame—have given you anxiety, pain, poverty, sickness, privations manifold—have vexed & pained you to the very heart often & have been a drag instead of a helpmate to you—& yet *you love me*—Poor Lucikin! I fear it is on the principle that all men love & prize *what has cost them dear*.

Well—Lucy—be that as it may, I *am glad* you love me. I am sure I have wished & do wish to make your life all you could wish it & God knows—I would sacrifice every personal preference to accomplish that end if it were necessary. I do hope that I may be permitted by the great superintending Intelligence which stands behind these inflexible Laws & directs their workings, to live long enough to vindicate the sincerity & constancy of my affection for you by a *wiser* management of our affairs. At any rate, it is a blessed knowledge that *we love each other*—not as most people do who are married & have children—but with all the *enthusiasm* & devotion of younger lovers. I am sure dearest that familiarity in our case has *not* bred contempt, that we are glad we are linked forever together & true to each other in our heart of hearts. Lucy dear—I shall doubtless make many mistakes & commit many errors, but you must forgive them for *I love you very dearly*.

And so our little one grows & plays & rejoices in the new world she is beginning to observe & understand! Dear little child! May we both be spared to give her all the help that parents can give their children. I am sure that the responsibilities of our position will make us very anxious to live nobly & to infuse into her little soul none but brave & true thoughts. I shall feel more sincere & earnest & try harder to make my life what it ought to be—for her sake & for your's. I believe that in the economy of nature—the sense of parentage is intended to be a spur to aspiration under the discouragements to which we are subject as we realize our defects & the terrible *imbecilities* & *blemishes* which mar every character. When the first flush of youthful ardor is over—this yearning pity & sympathy for our poor little children comes to our aid & reveals to us our better selves. Lucy dear—we shall both be *better* for our child's sake & I hope & trust that she will be better for our's. For myself I am ashamed that I ever whine over little ailments & misfortunes when I have a wife & child whom I love so dearly. . . .

I am glad Higginson approves of your course in Orange—*still more glad that I do*. I am glad that Abby Hutchinson enjoys her musical revival. . . . I am reading the Atlantic for April & shall forward it in a day, or two. Lucy dear please observe Mr. Higginson's wise suggestion. *Do not overwork* or allow *anything* to induce you to task yourself unduly. Especially about the garden I *fear* for you.

Please Lucy employ help & *dont break your back* sowing seeds & planting—$25 more or less will not affect me—but a little strain, or a cold or any personal injury inflicted on yourself will do so. For my sake dearest wife be very careful of Lucy Stone. . . .

Orange kitchen April 4, 1858

My dear Harry,

I got your note & its extra enclosure to Mrs. Johnson last night. One other, which says I am a fool for loving you when you have dragged me off &c. Thank you for both. We will talk of the plans of both when we meet. . . . Baby is outgrowing all her clothes and she is so pretty in all her actions. I have just asked her to send you ten kisses & a half & she smiled a hearty assent. It is too bad that you are away from her! She give me a world of weariness & trouble, but I *love* her. . . .

I have heard nothing from Mother, and feel anxious. I am well & so is *our* baby. I hope you will find her daguerreotype. . . . I hope you wont be badgered out of your life by people talking to you of me. It is a pity to have a notorious wife. I am sorry for you . . . Isn't the anti-Lecompton triumph grand! Dearest Harry take good care of yourself. Dont get discouraged. We shall live on & through all. . . .

Ever aff.
Lucy Stone

Orange Sunday Apr. 25, 1858
In the little kitchen with Mother & baby

Dear Harry,

. . . Mrs. Johnson took care of baby Thursday night & I lectured in N.Y. to a good audience & am to have $50 for it. I staid with Elizabeth that night. But kept awake, thinking of the dear child, & vowing I would never leave her again. She took a dreadful cold . . . which has made me very anxious, but Mother who is with me, says that the worst of it is over. She is a dear child, Harry, and every day I love her more. You will see that she has changed a great deal. . . .

You will remember the 1ˢᵗ May. Let our spiritual telegraph answer this year dear Harry. It is less expensive, and quite as sure. I wish you could be with me, but still I am rather proud to see you persevere with Augustus' business. It is better than to yield to the feeling of least hunger that would send one rushing home. I am very glad you are well dear husband of mine. Try and take good care of yourself. I am well too and have no new boils. I have put half the garden into grass—the peas are up & everything doing well. . . .

It is 9½ o'clock PM. Mother has gone to bed, and so has baby, and now here alone, I so wish for you Harry! I *love you*, and am trying to make the little home pleasant for you to come to dearest— and to be myself what a wife & mother should be.

Good bye dearest

Chicago Ills. Saturday Night May 1ˢᵗ 1858

Dearest Lucy

It is late. All day long, with frequent thoughts of you & our dear little one passing through my mind, I have been scheming & pushing this library project for Augustus. It is bed time. I shall not sit up to write the letter tonight—but feeling *so sure* that you have been thinking of me & so almost sure that you have been writing to me—I cannot help writing these first few lines to tell you how *thankfully* & *hopefully* I hail the return of the *most sacred* & *fortunate* day of my life. Dear Lucy, if you only could *know* & *realize* all I feel for you— you would *know* that we are *married* in soul & forever. I *know it*. God bless you my own wife. Your picture lies open on my desk before me—your picture & Baby's. For the last time of many, I have read the little note which seems to me to have been written *both by you & by baby*—so well it expresses the little infant soul—& have prayed God to bless you both, my *treasures* at my golden mile- Stone. Lucy dear—please God! I will *never* leave you & baby again for so long an absence. Forgive me this once. It was *not for myself* that I did so. Good-night. Would to God—I were with you in our little Orange home! Sleep, sweet & peaceful & refreshing, rest on you both, till the Sunday sun dawns on Orange. . . .

I thank you dearest wife for the care you are taking of *our baby*. It is a great shame & pity that I have had to leave you all the burthen & weariness of it. Yet I would gladly take it, if I could, in order to see the pleasant smile in her bright blue eyes & to hear her little pleasant voice. That brief experience of mine with our baby has been a *precious one* to me. It seems like a *dream*. I did not know what a father's love meant before. I shall never forget it now. I sometimes ask myself—"Have I really a wife & child?" And then as the thought of you & baby comes over me, I am siezed with a perfect *despair* at being separated from you & feel like cursing library, business, my own folly & western lands the root of all evil. . . . But, dear Lucy, the hope of rejoining you & little baby comes over me again at times as sweet as the breath of flowers. Let us *hope* & *love* & wait patiently. The sun will rise at last.

I am reading Irving's life of Washington—a delightful book. What is so inspiring as the life of a *great man*? And what man so great as he, who like Washington makes *duty* & *wisdom* his supreme objects—who has learned to control all his wandering & irregular impulses & to move onwards in a steady, consistent, noble life. Lucy dear I *have it in me*—you shall help me to *bring it out*. Last night the Democrats burned tar barrels here in rejoicing over Lecompton—just where, a few weeks ago, the Republicans did the same over its temporary defeat. Yet we shall see that this is but a *fatal victory* to them—one of the drops added to that great cup of humiliation prepared for the North, which the Slave Power will have to drink at last. I hope you get the Tribune regularly. I *am glad of your lecture in New York*. I see you are asked to repeat it in Brooklyn. It may be well to do so. But you had better take Baby with you if you do. You will feel better. Take the girl with you to carry her. The $1^{50} is not worth the anxiety of the separation.

Lucy dear—I want to be made one of the *Vice Presidents* of the next Woman's Convention. I shall write a short letter to it, which if you like, *you may read yourself*, or get read by some one else. I *wish* I could be there.

I have been praying God for one thing specially of late. It is that I may be permitted to get our matters into such a shape that we may have a little *quiet* simple home somewhere, where we may rear our little children, (if He gives us more than one) & whence we may work for the Woman's cause. To *get Woman the right of suffrage in Massachusetts!* that must be our aim. There, where the standard of womanhood is highest—where *character* is most prized because most developed—where human rights are household words & where the revolutionary spirit burns most brightly—there we will *win for woman absolute equality before God & the Law*.

This is no momentary vision. It has been *growing on me* a long time—let us realize it. Goodbye dearest Lucy—God bless you—Kiss our little one many times for me—I love her & love you *truly* & *fervently*—

Yours ever dear—
Harry—

P.S. Get good help at any price! Dont economize too closely.

Orange, in the kitchen 5 PM Sunday May 9, 1858

Dearest husband of mine,

Where are you today? I do not know but hope you are safe in the keeping of the great Father. I got your letter written on tho anniversary of our wedding. Thank you darling for all its words of love & trust & hope & aspiration. May they all be ever true! MY letter [for] that occasion is not written—will be sometime I hope. . . . You speak of regretting that the burden of Baby is left to me alone—I do get tired—arms, feet, & back every day—but my regret is that you are losing the miracle of the unfolding child. It is wonderful—and you will scarcely believe your eyes when you see her. I hope your letter to the Convention will be in time. . . . I hope your present determination to work for suffrage for women, sometime, will last. Next to freedom for the slave comes as the other immortal idea for this age—woman's equality. They are the two things that history will record of the present time. We will talk of it.

I dont know that I can go to the Convention—for I certainly will not leave *your baby* with the girl I have. Mother told me that she would care for her, but she has concluded now to go into N.Y. herself

& I shall not be needed thank God! so it is no matter whether I go or not. If I go home, I will write you. Mrs. Browning has a wonderful poem "Isobel" in the Liberator. Read it if you see it. This has been written by snatches. It is nine o'clock now. Good-night dearest.

Lucy

[Orange, N.J., May 21, 1858]

Dearest Harry,

It is a gloriously beautiful morning—the 21st of May and as the wretched boil I told you of in my last burst last night, I hope to get off to Father's next Wednesday. . . . I wish you could see our Sarah now. She is trying to creep—and *moves backward*, and around. She has the most radient little face, I ever saw and *is* a very promising child. I never feel her little cheek beside of mine,—never hear her quick coming breath—or her sweet baby voice, without the earnest purpose to gather to myself more symmetry of being—to sustain all my relations better—to be to her the example and so the guide she will need.

I *am* trying to be a good wife and mother. I have wanted to tell you how hard I am trying, but I *have* tried before and my miserable failures hitherto, make me silent now. But if I have conquered myself, or gained anything in all these weary weeks you will find it in my actions. I *hope* to be more to you, and better—when you come to me. I am glad too darling, that you feel the lack of dignity in the *running* to the station &c and that you will *try* to mend it. I will have the breakfast earlier, and we may, after all, be a model family yet. We will be patient with each other. I will try and have more time to read—and to go out with you, when I can, and not neglect Sarah.

Chicago Ills. June 1. 1858

Dearest Lucy

Thank God, June has come & I may now hope that *within this very month*, I may rejoin you & baby to *stay* & not to leave you, let me hope, any more.

You can hardly imagine how *long* & *weary* the past three months seem. As I lay last night in bed, the time seemed *years* & I fairly *bemoaned* myself—it seems *so inexpressibly sad* to be thus severed from all I love. Hereafter *nothing* must induce me thus to leave you—not even friendship & nothing else would have induced me to go this time.

I think you can hardly have felt this separation so keenly as I— (I hope you have not) because you have had little Sarah to nurse & care for. I have had nothing but business. I have done my best to keep up my spirits—I have not allowed myself to be idle. Whenever the weight has grown too oppressive, I have occupied myself incessantly & thus *forced* myself away from memories & longings I dared not to indulge. But I dont believe I *could stand* another six weeks of this deprivation from you & I must try to keep "a great patience" till the time of my release arrives. I learn from A.O.M. that it rained heavily & incessantly on the day you had intended to leave Orange. I hope you postponed your departure until it cleared up. Lucy dearest—let me hear from you when your first hurry of greeting your mother is over & when you have visited Bowman & Samantha & the *little folks*. I wish I were with you to carry little Sara to the Rock House & to the top of the Mountain & to ramble alone with you & her over the breezy fragrant hills of your childhood. Lucy Stone *I love you. . . .*

Good bye dearest. I write in haste.

Love to all our friends & *especially* to your father & mother.

Yours ever
H. B. Blackwell

I *am well*.

Take care little Sara do not *catch cold*.

Gardner Sunday June 2^d 1858

Dear husband of mine

It is 8½ o'clock AM. We, (Baby & I) are on a small grass flat, back of the barn, Baby asleep in a wicker wagon that has carried both Sarah's children. She has two teeth and is nearly sick with the worst cold she ever had. She creeps & climbs, and gets in a perspiration, and then takes cold. I dont see how I can prevent it. Poor thing! She wheezes with every breath but the cough seems loose[?] & I hope will soon be better. I shall take the best care I can of her—& you Harry dear must hurry away from that steaming heat & intolerable dampness—dont stay an hour after it is possible to leave. I hope to see you within *two* weeks. You have been so long absent darling that your coming seems more strange, than your being away. I can hardly *believe* that you will be with us again. May the protecting Angels have you in their keeping!

Now that your exile is so nearly over, dear Harry I want to tell you, that in no other absence have I ever felt your loss so much, never longed so for you, never needed you, as I have during these 4 weary months. I was glad that constant change, saved you from the gnawing hunger that I felt. I *hope* that we may not need to be so separated again & yet I do not like to have you tell Augustus that you *never* will go again—you may be obliged to unsay it. Better say nothing, *but act* when the time comes. . . .

I am much obliged for your kind wish that I should rest. But Harry no one who takes care of a baby *can* rest. I have not *felt* rested for months—you may take care of baby *one* day, and you will understand it—and if you add to that, the making [of clothes], mending, washing, ironing &c, for her & you, there will be little time for reading or rest. . . .

> Ever aff.
> Lucy—

Henry didn't return until July, and the next winter he was forced to go back to Chicago on business. But this time, unable to endure another lengthy separation, Lucy and Alice joined him. They boarded with several different families in nearby Evanston, which Henry remembered as "a very pleasant village with a beautiful grove and public park extending to the Lake shore, where we had a bath house." Every evening when he came home from work, Lucy and Alice met him at the station, and as he approached, "the child ran forward. . . . It was a pretty picture."

Yet it was also during this period that Lucy had a miscarriage and lost a baby boy. She reacted to her loss by immersing herself in Alice at the expense of her public career. Ever since the spring of 1858 when Alice had caught cold while Lucy was off lecturing in Brooklyn, she had made few public appearances, and now her resolve to devote herself solely to motherhood was even more firmly fixed. As she wrote Nette in February of 1859:

> I wish I felt the old impulse & power to lecture, both for the sake of cherished principles & to help Harry with the heavy burden he has to bear,—but I am afraid, & dare not trust Lucy Stone. I went to hear E. P. Whipple lecture on Joan d'Arc. It was very inspiring, & for the hour I felt as though all things were possible to me. But when I came home & looked in Alice's sleeping face & thought of the possible evil that might befall her if my guardian eye was turned away, I shrank like a snail into its shell, & saw that for these years I can only be a mother—no trivial thing either.

Nette herself was maintaining an active preaching and lecturing schedule despite the fact that she too had lost her second child. Later she would describe Lucy as "an almost too careful and self-sacrificing mother."

In the summer of 1859 Lucy and Henry returned to the East. Augustus Moore's health had failed, and when he sold out his part in the agricultural book publishing company to two other men, Henry left the business as well, and went into real estate. He and Lucy moved into another house next door to the first one in Orange, New Jersey, and he opened up real estate offices in both Orange and New York. While he was at the New York office, Lucy frequently took charge of the Orange office, and even took customers out to show them property herself. In addition to renting and selling houses to other people, Henry also engaged in trading his western lands for various mortgaged properties in New Jersey, and as this involved a considerable outlay for taxes and interest, he decided to transfer the real estate business to his brother George, and go back to work on a salaried basis. George proceeded to expand the business, and eventually realized Henry's own early dream of becoming a millionaire. Henry, meanwhile, took a position first with a manufacturer of kitchen ranges in New York, and then as a salesman and bookkeeper for Dennis Harris, his father's former employee in the sugar refining business.

By this time he and Lucy had moved to a house with twenty acres of land in West Bloomfield (now Montclair), New Jersey, and every morning Henry made the hour-and-a-half commute into the city, while Lucy tried to augment their income by growing produce and selling it. But as Henry later recalled: "Our abundant crop of cherries and apples scarcely paid for the gathering and the hired help. . . . We had not learned that it was cheaper to let the land lie untilled & leave the fruit ungathered."

Occupied with her "farm" and her child, Lucy remained on the periphery of both the antislavery and woman's rights movements. After John Brown's raid on the arsenal at Harpers Ferry and his subsequent arrest and execution, she and Henry were among the eight signers of a petition to the governor of Kansas, applying for the remains of two of Brown's associates, as they were to be relinquished for burial if claimed by friends. In the area of woman's rights, Lucy also corresponded with Elizabeth Cady Stanton about the propriety of discussing marriage and divorce at the National Woman's Rights Convention to be held in New York in May of 1860.

Lucy advocated divorce on the grounds of drunkenness, and also as a means of ending a loveless marriage: "that a true love may grow up in the soul of the injured one from the full enjoyment of which no legal bond has a right to keep her." Moreover, she recognized the crucial importance of the marriage question. In 1856 she wrote Nette:

> It is clear to me that the question underlies this whole movement and all our little skirmishing for better laws, and the right to vote, will yet be swallowed up, in the real question, viz. has woman, as wife, a right to herself? It is very little to me, to have the right to vote, to own property &c if I may not keep my body, and its uses, in my absolute right. Not one wife in a thousand can do that now, & so long as she suffers this bondage, all other rights will not help her to her true position.

Yet she felt they weren't ready to discuss the question at a forthcoming woman's rights convention, and later told Susan B. Anthony to use her "own judgment about the time & place to discuss the marriage question," adding, "But when *it is* done, it seems to me, we must not call it 'woman's rights' for the simple reason that it concerns men, just as much." Now she urged Mrs. Stanton to call a separate convention to discuss marriage and divorce, and when Mrs. Stanton refused, continued to express her misgivings: "It is a great grave topic that one shudders to grapple, but its hour is coming. . . . God touch your lips if you speak on it."

As Lucy had feared, the hour for discussing this "great grave topic" had not yet arrived. When Mrs. Stanton offered resolutions calling for more liberal divorce laws at the May convention, she was bitterly attacked by Antoinette Brown Blackwell, who regarded matrimony as a bond made in heaven and therefore indissoluble; and then more moderately by Wendell Phillips and Garrison, who argued that divorce was not a woman's rights issue, but the problem of both sexes. Lucy took no part in this heated exchange. Although she had told Mrs. Stanton she would attend the convention, she apparently changed her mind. She may have felt that she couldn't leave Alice, and she may also have wished to avoid a public confrontation on such a controversial issue. Whatever her motives, her absence from the convention and her subsequent failure to support the stand taken by Mrs. Stanton and Miss Anthony contributed to a growing coolness between them.

The following spring the whole country was shaken by the outbreak of civil war. In Montclair, Henry observed "an absolute breach of neighborly sympathy" between those who supported the war, and those known as Copperheads, who opposed it. Along with other pro-Union men, he formed a Union League to counteract the secret antiwar societies that were springing up everywhere. But his support of the war effort stopped short of actual fighting: When he was drafted in the latter part of the war, he became one of the "three-hundred-dollar men," so called because under the provisions of the draft, men of means were allowed to pay this sum for substitutes to serve in their place.

Lucy's own role during the early years of the war was limited. While others like Dorothea Dix, Clara Barton, and Henry's sister

Elizabeth devoted all their time and energy to organizing massive relief efforts, she was simply one of the many anonymous women who picked lint for bandages. She was still absorbed in motherhood in these years, but even if she had wanted to play an active public role, there was no cause which could enlist her considerable talents as a propagandist. The war had brought a temporary halt to the woman's rights movement, and in the first years of the conflict, antislavery remained in doubt. Fearful of disturbing the delicate balance of support necessary to maintain the war effort, Lincoln made it clear that his chief aim was to preserve the Union rather than free the slaves.

So Lucy and Henry bided their time. Tired of the inconvenience of living so far from the city, they rented the Montclair house, and moved into New York in the fall of 1862, boarding on Gramercy Park. That summer they vacationed at West Brookfield, and returned to New York for the winter to board at another location farther uptown.

During the period they were living in New York, Lucy finally found a cause she could support. Responding to a call issued by Mrs. Stanton and Miss Anthony "for a meeting of the Loyal Women of the Nation," she attended the convention held in New York on May 14, 1863, and was elected its president. The purpose of the convention was to launch a huge petition campaign in support of a constitutional amendment abolishing slavery, and to this end the Woman's Loyal National League was established, with offices at Cooper Institute. Miss Anthony was the only worker to receive a minimal salary, while Lucy and others donated their services on a part-time volunteer basis. On February 9, 1864, the mammoth petition, known as the Prayer of One Hundred Thousand, was presented to the Senate by the abolitionist senator, Charles Sumner, and that summer, after the Thirteenth Amendment had passed the Senate, the Woman's Loyal League closed its offices.

Throughout the summer, fall, and winter of 1864 Lucy and Henry lived apart. He spent the summer working in New York for Dennis Harris, and then in the fall left his job to campaign for Lincoln's reelection, and in the winter went to the West to see to the sale of some of their land. Lucy went first to West Brookfield, and afterward joined her sister's family in Gardner. It was a time of extreme psychological and emotional stress for her. Indeed, not since the months immediately preceding her marriage had she seemed as close to total breakdown. She fluctuated between periods of deep depression and raging headaches, and periods of light-headed euphoria, when she wandered about feeling a "dreamy peace." Her disturbed mental state had a number of causes. At forty-six she was undergoing menopause—a phase which was regarded as a severe drain on a woman's health and stamina and which was, in fact, disorienting to many women. In Lucy's case the onset of menopause marked a real turning point in her life. Alice was growing up and since there would be no more babies to take her place, the time when Lucy need "only be a mother" was rapidly coming to an end. She faced this prospect with mixed emotions. During the eight years she had devoted herself exclusively to Alice, she had lost much of the self-confidence that had made her such a successful public speaker. Now the thought of sallying forth as she once had filled her with dread, yet she was well aware how much remained to be accomplished in the area of woman's rights.

Also contributing to her mental turmoil was the fact that her father was dying. (Her mother had passed away four years earlier.) Throughout the summer he lingered on, until finally on the last day of September he died, leaving Lucy with a legacy of unresolved emotions. Even on his deathbed Francis Stone continued to show a definite preference for his sons over his daughters, and his behavior must have rekindled old feelings of resentment on her part. It was perhaps inevitable that some of this anger should be directed at Henry. Hence the request that she have the income of her own property, and that in the future their properties remain separate.

Lucy's letters of this period contain much discussion of real estate and other purely mundane matters. Yet underneath the surface lurks an awareness that they have reached a crisis point in their marriage: She has lost the strong sense of identity she possessed before they were married, and in order to regain it, she feels she must live apart from Henry. She loves him and hopes that they may be permanently reunited, but the future is uncertain. As she says in one of her letters: "If all our future is made rich, by this separation we shall be glad, when it is past, that we braved it through, or if not, we shall at least feel, that we tried to get safely over a bridge that, after all broke."

〰

West Brookfield, Sep. 14, 1860

Dearest Harry

This is our one wee darling's birthday, and today at two o'clock PM my good Mother went to her other children. Peacefully, without terror, or apparent pain. We have but one mother now. Let us do for her everything we can.

I long for *you* when my heart is so bruised. But I know she will meet a large circle of long-loved friends, and I rejoice for her. "It is not she that is bad off," Eddy says, "but we." We love and loved her for the generous self-forgetting that never was absent from her, and we respect her for the wealth of truth that was part of her soul. May we deserve as well from our children, as she does from hers.

Poor father feels it intensely. I pity him, so old, alone, and needing sympathy and help all the time. I dont know when I shall go home. The funeral is on Sunday. Then father will need to have me a few days, and if I go to see Aunt Hetty, I shant see you before week after next. . . .

Love to you all
Lucy

Box 299 PO. New York July 23/61

Dear Lucy

No news from you & Alice yet! Of course, as you expected me to be at Green Pond [New Jersey], you would not write & I dont expect a letter at present. But when you get this, write—only half a dozen words will suffice—say merely—"Alice is well—I am well." Do this, twice a week if you have a chance. Yesterday, was a terrible day in New York. The bad news, grossly exaggerated, kept coming in & hundreds surrounded the bulletin boards at all the offices. I rejoice to say that Mr Haskell & Mr Judd have both had despatches from their sons "I am safe." I send you papers today. The loss seems to have been about 500 to 1000 men & some *very valuable* cannons worth even more to us than the men. But it was a disgraceful panic

& if the enemy had only had the sense & courage they would have driven the whole army into the Potomac.

Love to all
Harry

P.S. I spent Sunday quietly at home, Saturday night & Monday night I took tea at Mothers. I have slept at home every night since you left—& usually take my breakfast in New York (coffee & muffins 12½ cts) my dinner at home & my tea wherever I happen to be. The cat is *hungry* & *friendly*. Tell little Alice that the squash vines are growing so fast that they are running over almost everything in the garden—that the tomatoes are getting as large as her mug & that Papa sleeps alone in Mama's bed. . . .

West Brookfield Tuesday June 14^d [1864]

Dear Harry

. . . I hope you had a good time . . . at the Highlands. *We* went strawberrying, and got about 2 dozen—enough to give Alice a little strawberry and cream & sugar. She laughs & enjoys all the little messages you send her,—but when I ask her to write, she says she spells so wrong! But I think, she *will* write, next Sat. I kept her from school 2 days last week, as she seemed tired with the long walks. The rest, made her all right—and at this moment she is burying her kitty, in the new mown hay in the garden, while Nette & Maggie, do the same. When the cats dont mew, *they* do—so there is plenty of music. There are no brooks or ponds, large enough to drown her, so dont be anxious on that score.

Your study of "Mill," has decided your plan about being out of debt. I agree with you, in the main. But in troubled times like the present, and such as will follow, no investments are safer, or better, than, improved unincumbered real estate. . . . Now my advice is, that you give up your position with Mr. Harris—go West, attend personally to the sale now in hand. . . . then go on, and see what can be done with the other lands—sell them if possible,—then come home. . . . The change will have given you rest,—put you in good frame [?] to write, or rather prepare an excellent campaign speech or two, which shall be full of reverence for human rights,—and like the last sermon we heard from Mr. Frothingham make every one who hears, wish to be nobler, and better. I have no doubt, you could be paid as a campaign speaker. But whether you could or not, we *owe* to these troubled hours, *our* contribution of the best we have to give. . . . I wish I were able to help too. Maybe I shall, by and by, for I think I am getting better here. At any rate, I shall try my best. Everything here, is simple, unpretending, moral, while all the wide surroundings are beautiful—and one *ought* to get better of ones badness.

Harry dear if you *should* be drafted, you must buy a substitute at any price—*Draw on my credit if necessary!!!!* I wish this infernal war were over. But the nation does not deserve peace till it respects human rights. Father is better for several days. But since he cant see, he is not as comfortable. . . .

Children's voices stopped the pencil, at this point. It is now 8½ o'clock, Wednesday, morning. You are doubtless on the cars going to business. We have had breakfast—the dishes are washed—beds made—the two rooms, swept, and dusted—Alice gone to school. . . .

I hope you will consider seriously my proposition to lecture this Fall. . . .

It is a beautiful morning, a little cloudy, but the air is sweet with the breath of clover, the honeysuckle (I hope mine prosper) & the syringa. I shall rejoice in the ride over the hill—when the prospect seems finer to me each time I see it.

I have the Sat. Tribunes, for which thanks. I believe I left the Apr. No. of the Atlantic and Sylvias Lovers at Mrs. Palmers. If you are in that neighborhood, perhaps you will call. Father is not quite as well this morning but at present he seems [as] likely to live as any of us. In haste.

Yours truly
Lucy

West Brookfield Tuesday [June] 21st [1864]

. . . Your proposition to come here, on the 4 July, *I* should be glad to realize,—unless there is something that can give you more variety, and pleasure. . . . There are plenty of spare beds here, (each of the families having one)—I had the simplicity to suppose, that you would prefer to sleep with your "family," you little naughty boy! . . .

Father is having a poor time now. He has spells of total blindness—a great weakness. We have had a homoepathic Dr. for him once, but nothing can make an old man young. Since he cant read, he dont want to live. I get the papers you send, and am quite proud of your promptness. . . . If the Standard of the week before is not lost, I should like that. It contained a letter from Mrs. Stanton. I have not yet had time to read the *Stanton custom house affair.* . . .

If you could work for true principles in the pending election, and after that, as a missionary at large, I should like it. There will be a strong tide of vice and general immorality created by the war & everybody's influence will be needed against it. Your long practice with the Cincinnati Club, has given you freedom of utterance, and your respect, for what is right, will give power to what you say. I wish I felt in myself, the power to do anything. Perhaps I shall—Who knows?

Harry dear, if you can come up for the 4th &c. I wish you would. We want to see you *very much*—only you ought to have a better change, & one with more good in it.

I want to send you some money to buy paper with, so that you need not *cross write* all your letters!!!

When you collect my rent, from Mr. Makin, will you please pay it to Mr. Browning, and cancel my mortgage to him. Then my little place [the Montclair property] will be clear. I suppose the wretched people there, are eating our cherries (May they choke them!) But we wont go back there to live & be worried again. If you should come here, I wish you would bring Mr. Frothinghams Stories of the Patriarchs, & his parables—also "Ten acres enough" &c. Dont get them, at the last moment, and so lose the cars. But when you have made up your mind to come,—*then* get the books. I visited the school to-day and saw Alice, (one of 30) in the spelling class. I shall keep her at home tomorrow for the sake of her eyes, which seem weak. Love to Mother. . . .

Aff.
Lucy

West Brookfield, Mass. July 12/64

Dear Susan

Yours of 20th ult. went to Gardner, whither I have not been. My Father's poor health has kept me here since the day I saw you in N.J. He is in his 85th year and since I came home has so lost his sight that he cant read, or help himself in the way he used to—and some one must be most of the time with him. I have a niece now teaching, who I hope will take my place when her school closes.

You went to the old farm and found it sad. But you have your mother, Susan, and that is more. Here is the old farm with its wild hills, and rocks, and dear little streams, but mother is not here, and tho' 16 people sleep under this roof—only two "gray care encumbered" people are left of those who played here long years ago with me—good, excellent people, all of them, but they are not *my* people. So that I feel almost a stranger in this very room where I was born. But enough of that.

My head is decidedly better here. I escaped the last month, with only one day's headache, and none of the mental confusion that has so tormented me before. The quiet of the farm,—the old associations,—the total change, are worth a world to me. And if I can only survive the inevitable change of constitution and be right side up, at the end of it, I shall pray again for the return of that great impulse that drove me into the world, with words that *must* be spoken.

My early experience in trying to lecture with others will always deter me from committing a similar folly. I have always wondered at the patience with which Pillsbury bore my presence at his meetings (perhaps I helped draw) for I never made a decent speech when his great knitting brow was within the sound of my voice. And it was only when I went alone that I accomplished anything. So, Susan, even if I were free, I should not go to the meetings you are planning. I must begin by myself till my feet are firm under me, *then*, once in a while I can attend a convention. Now dont feel badly about it. I *know I am right*. I was *unspeakably* disappointed in the Cleveland platform. I expected the largest anti slavery utterance instead of the announcement that slavery is dead. Not before the convention could I have believed that Fremont would consent to a fellowship with such a man as John Cochran. It is as true as ever that we cant touch pitch and not be defiled, and bad as Mr. Lincoln is, a union with him and his supporters, seems to be *less bad* than a union with peace Democrats. All that I see of the New Nation too, I dislike. Its spirit is bad. It hates Lincoln and so tries to win the credit of the North for *his* sake. Its love of country is less than its hate of Lincoln. Pray dont work for that party Susan! You will be sure to be sorry for it. Radical anti slavery is our work,—its weapons are ours. The tools of politicians are dead weights in our hands.

Isnt it pitiful to see Mr. Garrison who 30 years ago hadn't a shadow of excuse for anybody who had the smallest smell of pro-slavery about him,—now vain of a letter from Montgomery Blair, stand pelting Phillips whose wholesome criticism seems to be all there is of anti slavery at that office. It is surely better that one who has battled bravely for the right should die before his time in triumph than live to make himself a fool.

I feel proud of Wendell Phillips but I am sorrier than I can tell that he touches the Cleveland people. His true place is outside of all parties,—an advocate of great principles—a critic of parties and persons—his power would be as it was, without limit. . . .

I wonder if there is any way to make Mr. Garrison see that his fulsome laudation of Mr. Lincoln is right against the slave. Oh, if he could only cry out as in the earlier days!

Mr. Chase is out, and I suppose driven out by Lincoln. Well now, let the Rebs take Washington, kill Lincoln and the Blairs and install Jeff Davis. That will bring the abolitionists to their senses.

How is Mrs. Stanton? I want to write to her, but as I do all the *work*,—cook, wash, iron, sweep, dust, *everything*, and teach Alice an hour a day, I get little time. Give my love to her and tell her not to work for a party that dare not put her name to the call for its convention for but a single day. Write me now and then Susan. I hope you are getting strong and rested, and that you will be able to work and not die. With kind regards to your mother and Mary

Affectionately,
Lucy Stone

West Brookfield Friday July 22 [1864]

In my little room, at the west window. 6 o'clock PM seated in the large rocking chair, where you took your last lunch with us.

So you did not get the letter I mailed you on Monday, Harry dearest, for which I am very sorry for tho' the letter wasnt much, it came from *us*, and told you we were well. *I* look for a letter from you every mail, and tho' I dont *expect* one, I am a little disappointed when I find there is none, and am a good deal glad when there is one. I quite agree with you, that tis a pity for us to live separate. I would rather live with you somewhere, than with anybody else anywhere, darling. But we will abide our lot, this year—save what we can—and gain strength, & courage, and patience, and hope, and all graces & virtues, for future use.

Here, with fewer cares, & almost nothing to vex me, I hope to get back, somewhere near to the state of soul & spirit, in which I was, when you first found me. And then, when we meet, to begin new. We shall perhaps come nearer our ideal of what a wedded home life, ought to be.

Sat. 6 o'clock PM

Alice is very sorry you did not get our letter of Monday. She had *written* a sentence, and made many kisses with long tails. . . . I *always* write you on Sunday so there is something wrong when you do not hear on Tuesday. . . . I suppose your merry company are now at Lake Hopatcong. I hope you will be refreshed, by the change my little boy. I have felt very near to you all day, darling dear, and have wandered around, with a dreamy peace in my soul, glad that in all the world, no one is so dear to me as you—and thankful, for this strange union, which draws me by pleasant, tender ties to you. Let us try to correct all our faults, for each others sake Harry, and let us be made perfect, not through suffering, but through love.

This morning I got your letter of yesterday, with its serious business proposition, to me, which I as seriously answer—that you cannot know how necessary, how *indispensable*, it is, for me, to live in some quiet corner, free from criticism, or scrutiny, where I shall be able *perhaps*, to find that better self of me, which during all the years of my poverty-stricken girlhood, steadily aspired to a life of worthy use—and which, with a patience that no delay wearied, and courage, that no difficulty ever daunted, carried me, serene, and self-respecting to the port, I had toiled to reach, and then, kept me there, to work, with the same courage & patience. O no Harry! for the sake of us three, I must keep in some quiet "Cleft of the Rock" till the Angels of healing make me whole again. And you, Harry, unless you feel a great power urging you to public speech, had far better be silent. Now our little child wants to be "read to." So good night dearest.

Sunday evening

You have had your plunge in the Lake, and I hope, a grand merry time so that you will be better all the week for it. I think your lecture is in *your* trunk. Can it be in the bag of papers? It seems to me that I put it in your box of paper collars. I am glad of the papers. *They come from you. . . .* I have seen a meager report of the Greeley & Sanders correspondence. Mr. Lincoln's reply is good. Give him credit. Aunt Hetty is down upon me for a criticism I made of Fremont. Father is not quite as well. Let me know when to look for Spofford.

Ever truly your wife

West Brookfield Sunday July 31, 1864

Dear Harrykin

. . . It is my opinion . . . that you will never be satisfied to discontinue for any length of time, the business to which you have all your life been accustomed, and it is perhaps not wise that you should and we must shape our lives accordingly. But for the present, it seems to be best, to adhere to our original plan—viz. that Alice and I should stay in the country for this year. . . . I dont believe I could live, shut up with Alice in a suite of rooms, all next winter. And I want to make the most of the rest and liesure & quiet of this year, and next too, if I find this change is really good for me. I would *rather* live with you, Harry dear, *a great deal*. But I *need* to be hidden, and shielded, and comforted by the large silence of the country. And if all our future is made rich, by this separation we shall be glad, when it is past, that we braved it through, or if not, we shall at least feel, that we tried to get safely over a bridge that, after all broke. . . .

I hope you have a pleasant time with Spofford, tho' you make so brief mention of him, that I can infer nothing. What does he think of old Abe? And what of the Fremont faction? Did you find your lecture? How do you abide this dreadful weather? We had a little rain a week ago, with cool days. But it is burning hot now. Thermometer 90 degrees in the shade. Springs dry everywhere but here. . . . I wish we could live together. I want you all the time, for speech, and for silence, for rest, and sympathy, and all good things Harry dear. Alice is a good child and really tries to be good. She learns rapidly, and will soon read for herself anything. . . . Father is poorly today— Alice quite well and I am ditto. The papers come 3 at a time. Cant you send them daily? I see the Atlantic is out. Last, not least, I would not buy Elizabeth's half the farm, nor hurry to sell it. It is a safe investment. We can wait. With good wishes for all your people

> Ever your own wife

West Brookfield Aug. 9th [1864]

Dearest Dee

. . . If you buy 10-40's [government bonds] I wish you would buy the amount of my mortgage, in *my name*, and let the interest be paid to me. I will return the bond. It is more important to me than you have ever known, that I should have the income of my property. Now that there is no reason why I should not, I greatly prefer to arrange so that our properties may be separate.

You can get a rest from business now my dear, and I rejoice for your sake. Wont it be delightful to feel that you are free! Dont ever again, get on a treadmill. I think there will be no need. I can go this week or next, to Martha's Vineyard. I shall go tomorrow to Gardner.

I think Father will do very well with Clara.

Alice is well. But I have a headache today, and am not in mood to write.

> So good bye dearest
> Ever your own wife

Gardner, Sept. 4, 1864

My dear Harry

We are now completely settled. . . . Spofford's criticism of your lecture, I think is good. He would give you more credit as a writer, if he knew that you wrote that lecture after the day's fatigue, with an ulcerated throat, and mainly after midnight. You write well, Harry, when you have a fair chance, and nobody must say that you do not. Perhaps you speak better. Perhaps you are wise to "plunge into this fall campaign." *Somebody* needs to speak for freedom & justice. At any rate, I shall be glad to have you rid of the connexion with Mr. Harris, and *I have no doubt*, that you might be very useful during the canvass this fall. It will be a pleasant change for you. And if you earn no money, it is no matter. We do not need it. . . .

I am glad that the Convention at Chicago has come out so square footed for the old order. It will be easier, to work against them. I have not yet read carefully, either the speeches or resolutions. . . . I think you will find no difficulty in getting a substitute. There are men enough, who would go, if they are paid for it. . . .

We reached Boston, and finished our lunch at 12½. Then I went to the Anti Slavery office, and dear old Mr. Walcutt insisted upon my going to dinner with him, at the new home, he has recently purchased. . . . Geo. Thompson boards with them. We had an excellent time. It was good to be there. Mr. Garrison was that day, moving to a new house he has bought in Roxbury, where his son Wm. (who is this week to be married to a daughter of Martha C. Wright of Auburn) will live in the house with him. . . . Charles Sumner is at the heart of the movement to get Fremont, & Lincoln to resign. But Mr. Walcutt thinks the Lincolnites wont even notice it. Pillsbury is tired of politics, and Phillips of the Fremont movement. . . .

We left Boston at 5 PM and reached here at 8. . . . Henry told me there was a package for me from you in the hall, whereupon he introduced me to a *barrel*. The intimation of "something" that had been sent to Alice prepared me for a basket of peaches. But when we opened the barrel next morning, and drew out the abundant supplies, which were totally unexpected,—a huge ham, a box of tea, smoked tongue, salmon, sugar, white and brown, &c &c, I felt like sitting down at once to write a treatise on "Housekeeping Made Easy" for the benefit of all young wives. The beginning and the end should be this: "Choose a provident and thoughtful husband, who voluntarily will take all the burden on himself. " Harry darling, I am unspeakably obliged to you for this thoughtful kindness. I came here fairly dreading to make necessary purchases in this little ridiculous town, where petty gossip retails everything that occurs. You have saved me all necessity. Accept a thousand thanks. Sarah has fitted me out with housekeeping materials and the little machine is fairly in motion. I have more goods than the laws of N.Y. allow a widow . . . in the main we are very comfortable. I get from Sarah, tomatoes, corn, beans, cucumbers, squash, potatoes, and apples. We have had a great supply of blackberries, and they are still unexhausted.

Alice will begin school tomorrow. The school is graded, and Sarah thinks highly of the teacher. So I hope the child will be able to go all day. She seems remarkably well, has a great appetite and no end to play. . . . I think you must send her a letter of greeting for her birthday, on the 14th. I propose to make a small party for her. . . .

We shall be *very glad* to welcome you here, Harry dear, at any time, when *you wish* to come. Alice danced first on one foot, and then on the other, and ended with a vigorous clapping of hands when I told her, that *perhaps* you would come. She woke & cried for you, the first night we were at Aunt Hetty's, and always assures me that she loves you most. I shall not soon have occasion to send so long a letter, so excuse this.

Truly your wife
Lucy Stone

Gardner, Sep. 20 1864

This is the day of the draft, Harry dear, which I hope you may escape! Yours of the 16th came Saturday. So you are really getting ready in earnest for the campaign. No doubt you are,

> "Yearning for the excitement that the coming
>   weeks will yield,
> Eager-hearted as a boy when first he leaves
>   his father's field."

Success to you darling! I have no doubt this Fall's work will do you good in every way, and others good also. The consciousness of power *to do* blesses the very marrow of one's bones. I expect to see you, when the campaign is over, fresher, fairer, fitter, stronger, and looking ten years younger than now. So swinging my hat, and shouting hurrah! again I say "Success to you, my own darling Harry!"

Sage advice must follow, that First, in all your speeches, be sure that your *facts* are *facts*. Dont overstate. Second, avoid as far as possible, all personalities. Urge to right action, for high moral considerations, mainly, but from a lower material plane, only just so much as may be necessary, to build a bridge to the plans above, and God bless your work.

I suggest also that you get new stockings, that will be warm and require no darning; that you have a muffler for your throat. Some bore will always be with you after the lecture who will be disposed to continue the discussion. Put your mouth in your muffler, and tell him that you cant talk on account of your throat, which you must respect if you would keep yourself able to speak through the campaign. Dont forget your blanket shawl, which is in a band-box at Elizabeth's. If you travel nights you will need it, or if you ride from a lecture. Please attend to these bodily suggestions, my little boy. I know from experience how necessary they are.

I am very, very glad for you, that you will soon be off the treadmill of business, which you need never resume, (in the same way) and that you will *feel* free. I think you were quite right to take the $50 from Tilton. I wonder if you could not write some things for his paper this fall, which might be a stepping stone to a permanent engagement. . . .

Alice trots to school night and morning, is well, improves, and tries to be good, and enjoys herself. Yesterday we were up on the mountain, and in a pine grove, and had a delightful time. Alice climbed (higher than she ever did) up an old yellow pine, and when I shouted "Well done!", she wished Papa was here to see.

I think you wont get here till after the canvass, but we shall welcome you just as gladly then. I have just finished "Very Hard Cash." It is better than "Love Me Little, Love Me Long," but too full of tragedy. If McClellan's letter divided the Democrats, it will be the best thing that could happen.

> Affectionately
> Lucy

Gardner Tuesday Oct. 4th [1864]

Harry dearest

I have two letters from you with an enclosure of Spofford. You did not say a word of your throat. You must tell me, in *every* letter how you are. You can hardly know how anxious I am, lest the unusual effort of speaking and the inevitable exposure should make you completely sick. I hope you will heed the united advice of Spofford and your wife, not to attempt to speak more than 2 times a week. . . .

We laid father's body in its final rest, beside of Mother's on Sat.—accompanied only by our nearest neighbors. One old man who said he had known father, more than 60 years, and who is himself over 80, was one of the bearers. There were three others, over 76. The funeral was as little disagreeable, as so sad an occasion can be. No strangers were present—only friends, & neighbors. Father's face was placid—almost beautiful. He was glad to die & we felt that it was best. But the old home, and father's house, will never be the same again to any of us. We came back from the grave to the empty rooms, with a sense of loneliness, which only they know as have felt it. All day Sunday as the dismal rain patterred on the windows of the deserted rooms, where we were arranging & deciding various matters, the tears kept gushing—the present and the past so sadly mingling. We all seemed to stand on another round, in life's ladder, & to feel that those below were *broken*.

We came here yesterday. The children took the back seat, and so amused themselves. The day was cool and cloudy, all the better for our ride. The whole distance, was one grand picture gallery— vastly finer than when you rode with us. I am glad to have spent this fall in New England to refresh my remembrance of its gorgeous autumn beauty. Ten years in warmer latitudes, made me half forget the grandeur and glory which every autumn cover all New England.

Henry, says your lecture was spoken very highly of by the best people present, so take heart Harry darling I am glad that Spofford feels so cordial and friendly. I hope you will go to Washington.

Alice has gone to school today, is very well. Glad that you call her little coon. . . . Invariably in the morning, she expresses the wish that Papa was with us. With love to you, and best wishes for all whom you love.

Very truly
Your wife

Gardner Monday Oct. 10 [1864]

Dearest Harrykin

. . . Your first nights meeting, and the past midnight bedtime, quite remind me of my own "old lang syne." Success to you! If cautions did any good, I should say something about care after your "regular sweats"—and too much speaking. But I know it is of no use, so shall be silent. I shall think of you every night as trying to enlighten the good people of Jersey. Much good may it do. We had ice and frozen ground last night, and a cold wind today. . . . Alice is well, and in great glee because her teacher today gave her a colored certificate. Her school lasts only three weeks longer, and there will be no winter school, for small bipeds. So I shall have to teach her.

Good by Harry dear
Sarah sends love.
God bless you—
Ever your own wife

Gardner Oct. 23ᵈ/64

Dear Mrs. Blackwell

I have been wishing a long time, Mother dear, to rejoice with you, on account of Harry's freedom from business and also that he is out of debt, with several thousands in his pocket. I think he need never again be in bondage to any man, and only hope that he may now find some pursuit which he will thoroughly enjoy.

I wish you would all join with me in urging him to try a change of climate this winter, for his health.

His throat was in a sad state when he was here, and I never before saw him, so literally "skin & bone"—He said he was not well, that "in the morning, he felt brave enough to face a lion, but in the afternoon, he would run from a sheep"—Poor fellow! All these years of hard work, have told on his constitution. Now he has liesure and means, to try what a change of climate will do, to make all his future years, full of health and strength. An old acquaintance of mine, from Brookfield went as a private to the war (S. Carolina). He suffered horribly from catarrh, for many years. He returned, entirely cured. The simple change of latitude wrought the cure.

I wish the Dr. would seriously consider, and advise with Harry, on this matter. The trouble in his throat is becoming serious. And *something* must be done for it. I tremble all the time lest constant speaking, should increase the evil. Of course, you hear from him, how much he enjoys the campaign. *Any* change would be grateful, after Mr. Harris, and sugar.

Harry told you, of my fathers death. He would have been 85, on the 11th of Nov. All the summer, especially when he could no longer see to read, he seemed to be just *waiting*, and was glad when he knew that his last hour drew near. He was confined to his bed, a little more than a fortnight. My two brothers were constantly with him, which was a great comfort to him. He said "how good you are" to them.

His mind was clear, and in perfect peace, except one night, when a great horror came upon him, and he thought [he] was not fit to die, but with the morning light, came peace, which continued to the end. He had a dread, of a hard death struggle such as he once witnessed, and told my brothers, that they must not leave him for a moment, but must anticipate his wants, when he could not speak. The last night we thought, he was not conscious and Sarah was to sit by him, as my brothers were weary. Very soon after they left, Father opened his eyes, & looked around. Soon he did the same again. He missed my brother who came to him, and asked "Do you want anything father." The poor old man put his arm around my brothers neck, asking better than words that, he would stay with him. They did not leave him again. About 2 o'clock at night, the last day of Sept., in answer to a question, he said "All is peace," and soon passed quietly away. He survived Mother 4 years, and fourteen days. We put autumn leaves, round his pale face, which was sweeter, and more placid, than I ever saw it in his life, and laid his body, by that of our Mother. He had filled up a long life, and his last years were his best.

I cannot tell you, the sense of loneliness & loss, we all felt when we returned from the grave to the house, which had been the *home* of the family, for 50 years. The house, and the beautiful hills, remain, but the *home* is gone—wrinkles and grey hairs cover the remnant of those now scattered, who used to gather there. We too, shall soon go to our last sleep.

Pardon me, Mother dear for this long writing, of what perhaps, nay, surely, cannot interest you much.

Alice has grown very much this summer, and often speaks affectionately of you, and all her Blackwell relatives, including Kitty. I have kept her from school the last week. The scarlet fever prevails here, and several of the school children have it, and were taken at school. I think it better to keep her out. The disease takes a mild type. I have heard of no deaths. . . . I am glad you are to be in the parlor, this winter. It will save you from many a weary step. With kind wishes to all the household.

> Very truly yours
> Lucy Stone

Gardner Chamber Sunday Dec. 4/64

I think of you today dearest Harry, as riding with Frank, or Ryland, over the old familiar hills, and through accustomed streets, seeing well-known faces and familiar objects—rejoicing in the glorious wind, and clear sunshine of the blessed day. May it add health & strength to your body,—marrow to your bones, and good every way! God bless you darling mine, and save you from the perils of robbers, of travel, of disease, and bring you safe to us again! . . .

I believe we shall on the whole, be better satisfied to rent our Bloomfield place. It will give us another year of rest. We will take up our abode either at Nantucket, Martha's Vineyard, or Labrador. We will fish, learn to boat, & swim, read, study, think, and grow *together*. I believe we ought to contrive to take Marian with us somewhere, and help her try to ease the torment of her stomach. If she could rent her house for the summer, she and Mother might be with us,—where, free from the bother of housekeeping, we could be free to take care of, and help each other.

I have been getting immense satisfaction from Parker's Life. How he continued to make the most of his time, and the best of anything! And more than all, to keep his soul patient, grand, brave. I have written Abby Hutchinson that she must straightaway get it, and bless herself with it. If you see the Independent of last week, I wish you would read [Henry Ward] Beecher's sermon. It was preached on the Sixth of Nov. It is very rich, and just pat for the time, tho' it make me sick and faint, to see how he assumes that we have a true Christian Democracy, which recognizes the equal political rights of *all* the people. Good Rev. Andrew did just the same, at Springfield. Men & such wide-seeing good men, forget that *all the women* are disfranchised—what hope is there for the rest? The *right*, and the *claim*, of the Women, is so far out of sight, that these men, *hunting for justice*, forget that every man's wife, mother, and daughter has no political existence, and so state the false fact, that in this country, a true Christian democracy gives equal political rights to all. Harry, you and I, will work together (Moses, and Mrs. Moses) to make this country a democracy without sham or humbug.

Emmerson has delivered the first of his series of lectures in Boston, on Education. The first thing he says, is to make one independent. He "so must be taught, to swim, row a boat,—harness a horse, and to cook his own supper." This mastered, he can do all things for himself. I am anticipating with a great deal of satisfaction, our stay in Boston this winter. It will be like a perpetual benediction to be in the society of those with whose labors and sympathies, I have so long shared. . . .

I am sorry the trip West will be so expensive. But since it cant be helped, we wont whine over it, especially since we are not poor. Alice is very well, and has been with me up the mountain. . . .

Gardner Sat. Dec 17/64

My dear Husband
Your letter written and mailed on the 12th inst from Chicago reached me yesterday. I had not heard from you since the date of Dec. 7. Generally I get a letter every two or three days, & so long time had passed, and no letter came, that I had fully made up my mind, if no letter came yesterday, I should today write both to Frank Donaldson, and to Gen. Sherwood—so sure did it seem that some evil had happened to you. Emma brought me the letter which I siezed, my heart in my throat and tears in my eyes so infinitely glad to get *any* tidings. There you were tired, cold, and just ready to start on a still colder trip for *my sake*. How I longed to put my arms all around you, to warm and comfort you! O! Harry darling, I love you dearly, I can almost measure how much, by the sense of pain, and loss, which the not hearing from you made me suffer. I shall be glad

enough dear little child, when we can spend the winter together. Still I do not wish you to hurry your visit from Washington, but take a good time there, and at N. York, for I am not selfish in my love. . . .

We are all hoping that Sherman has got to the coast, and all indignant that the Canadian authorities have released the raiders.

We are making varieties of little things for Christmas—all secretly.

I have bought another half cord of wood. The intense cold weather consumed the pile right away. Our room took fire the other day. We sat with our back to the fire. We smelled smoke, and on looking, found a strong current issuing from each side of the fire, under which the boards had caught. I poured the contents of my pitcher—and still the fire came out. I ripped up the pine [?] and to my dismay, saw the fire blazing under the floor. I ran for an ax & cut off the first board, dashed under water, and so made an end of it. The next day Henry mended it. It is now safe. He also laid a tier of brick up the back of the fireplace, so that the fire comes more outward. He also laid brick through the draft way. So the loss was gain, in the end.

Alice spent the day yesterday with another little Alice, and was made very happy by it. She is very well, as we all are now that I have heard from you, tho' the date was nearly a week ago. God bless you dearest. I hope the boil did not torment you.

Ever & forever your own wife

Gardner Dec. 22 1864

My dear Harrykin

This is your mother's birthday, wild, cold—the world covered with snow, and for the first time since you left my old colored woman has not shown her face, so I am maid of all work, and have but little time.

I must wish you a merry Christmas, and Happy New Year, and tell you that we are well. We have sent Alice's ambrotype to N.Y. against Christmas—one for Grandma, one for Kitty, and one for Florence, and now I enclose one for you, which I had taken with Emma, for myself but, it is a good likeness of the child, and I thought I should be glad to greet you with it at Spofford's on Christmas if you are there, at that time, or whenever you do reach here. Alice claims it for her own, so you will please bring it carefully for her. We are rejoicing in the great victories, and in the fact that the rebels seem seriously disposed to give freedom to the slaves. . . .

There is to be a new draft I see. Who will be caught by it? I think I shall go to Boston about New Years. The schools will begin there and Alice must be ready.

Ever affy
Lucy

Gray-Haired Champions

1866~1893

For the abundant and unselfish work you have done for women Harry dear you know how thoroughly I appreciate it and how grateful I am for it.
    Lucy Stone to Henry Blackwell, February 20, 1887

I think of you every day & wish you could be here without fatigue or exposure to meet these fresh sympathetic, young western audiences which are an inspiration.
    Henry Blackwell to Lucy Stone, August 26, 1890

T he bridge did not after all break, although it continued to be a bit wobbly for the next few years. Instead of going to Boston for the winter of 1865, Lucy and Alice were reunited with Henry in New Jersey, where they at first rented and later bought a house in Roseville, now a part of Newark. During this period they adopted an orphan girl named Annie Gleason. Ostensibly, the purpose of the adoption was to provide a playmate for Alice, but the real reason must have been to give Lucy the second daughter she couldn't herself have. And in fact, while Alice apparently didn't get on very well with Annie, whom Henry described as "active, noisy, hasty-tempered, rollicking, affectionate," Lucy "soon became tenderly attached" to her. Nevertheless, she and Henry seem to have agreed that it would be better, for the time being at least, to place Annie elsewhere. She lived with a succession of other families until she died of spinal meningitis in 1870.

Henry wanted more children as much as Lucy, but he also realized how important it was for her to return to the field of public speaking. Since she was hesitant to go forth alone, he put aside his business interests for the moment and joined her on the lecture platform. His support and encouragement came at a critical juncture; otherwise, she might have continued to flounder, but as it was, she gradually regained her old self-confidence, and took her place alongside other feminists in the drive for "a true Christian democracy" with equal political rights for all.

With Emancipation achieved, the abolitionists had regrouped around a push for black suffrage, and taking their cue from their old allies, feminists concentrated their efforts on getting the vote for women; the woman's rights movement became the woman suffrage movement. Moreover, in the early days of Reconstruction, as the abolitionists assumed political power through alliance with the Radical Republicans in Congress, feminists were hopeful of victory. Their strategy was to make woman suffrage and black suffrage inseparable demands.

Thus, in January of 1866 Lucy and Susan B. Anthony presented a meeting of the American Anti-Slavery Society in Boston with a proposal inviting them to join with the woman's rights movement in a single national organization dedicated to universal suffrage. But Wendell Phillips, who had assumed the leadership of the society after Garrison's resignation, kept the question from being put to a vote, and so the women had to wait until May when the Eleventh National Woman's Rights Convention—the first since the war—met in New York. At this convention feminists and their abolitionist supporters formed the American Equal Rights Association, with universal suffrage as its goal. Silver-haired Lucretia Mott, now in her seventies, was elected president of the new organization, Henry Blackwell recording secretary, and Lucy Stone, a member of the executive committee—although neither of them actually attended the convention.

That spring, however, they did travel to Washington to try to persuade Charles Sumner, author of the Fourteenth Amendment, protecting the political and civil rights of the freedmen, to omit the word "male" from the amendment, as it would be the first time this word appeared in the Constitution in connection with the right to vote. Henry recalled that Sumner received them courteously enough, but refused to change the wording of the amendment, claiming that he had already sat up one night and rewritten the offending clause fourteen times before concluding that he couldn't in any other way express his meaning. So, in June of 1866 the Fourteenth Amendment was ratified as it stood.

Sumner, along with other Radical Republicans and many abolitionists, now took the stand that it was "the negro's hour," and that women must wait until black males had been enfranchised before pressing their claims. Nevertheless, Lucy, Henry, and other feminists kept up the fight for woman suffrage on the state level. In January of 1867 Henry addressed a message to the Southern legislatures, "What the South Can Do: How the Southern States Can Make Themselves Masters of the Situation." Pointing out that there were more white women in the South than blacks of either sex, he urged woman suffrage as a means of maintaining white supremacy. This line of reasoning, with its racist overtones, was to become the major argument in favor of woman suffrage in the South, but for the time being its impact was limited. In March Lucy made an appeal before a committee of the New Jersey legislature for the removal of the words "white male" from the state constitution. (Given the vote in 1776, women and blacks were later disenfranchised in 1807.) Her appeal was voted down, thirty-two to twenty-three, but two other major state contests loomed ahead: one in New York and the other in Kansas.

In Kansas the legislature had approved the submission to the voters of two separate referenda—one removing the word "white" from the state constitution, and the other removing the word "male." Feminists regarded the campaign as a crucial one, since it marked the first time the question of woman suffrage had come before the people of a state. However, they were reasonably confident of success: Not only did Kansas have a strong abolitionist tradition, but the state also boasted an excellent record on woman's rights, having earlier passed liberal legislation in that area.

Lucy and Henry set off for Kansas late in March of 1867, and spent a grueling three months there. They traversed the state, holding meetings in every county seat; and at one point, after being exposed to a heavy rain, Lucy caught a bad cold, which—in Henry's words—"permanently impaired the power of her beautiful voice." In the East the Republican press was strangely silent about the campaign, while within the state itself certain Republican leaders were openly hostile, one going so far as to accuse Lucy Stone and "that seed wart she carries around with her—called Blackwell" of being free-lovers. But their generally warm reception by the people of Kansas gave them cause for hope. In late May Sam Wood, a prominent local organizer, telegraphed the American Equal Rights Association: "With the help of God and Lucy Stone, we shall carry Kansas! The world moves!" Characteristically, Henry's own enthusiasm for Kansas led him to invest in several hundred acres of land in the state.

Returning to the East early in the summer, Lucy and Henry continued to work on the Kansas campaign. Without taking time even to change from her "plain, worn, gray Kansas travelling dress," Lucy went directly to Boston to plead with Wendell Phillips to lend his support. Afterward, she visited Horace Greeley and Theodore Tilton in New York in an effort to get them to endorse the woman suffrage amendment in their respective papers, *The New York Tribune* and *The Independent*. Henry did his part with an "Appeal to the Voters of Kansas," which he circulated in the hopes of collecting signatures from prominent abolitionists and Republicans. But it was becoming increasingly apparent that most abolitionists and Republicans would not stand behind the demand for woman's enfranchisement. In New York a constitutional convention rejected a proposition calling for woman suffrage, but approved another measure recommending the removal of a $250 property qualification tax on black men. Encouraged by the New York decision, the antifeminist element in the Kansas Republican party succeeded in ousting Sam Wood, and the local equal rights organization fell apart.

Lucy and Henry had gone to Martha's Vineyard for a much needed rest, but were soon back in New York, working in the office of the Equal Rights Association, at Susan B. Anthony's request. Susan herself spent much of the summer raising money so that she and Mrs. Stanton could join Olympia Brown, the Universalist minister and feminist who had taken over the field in Kansas after Lucy's and Henry's departure. But despite strenuous efforts on the part of all three women, it was clear to Henry when he returned to Kansas in October that the campaign was in serious trouble.

✑

New York May 12. 1866

Dearest Lucikin

I send you by today's mail a Tribune containing the proceedings of the Nat^l Woman's Rights Convention. It evidently went off well & the speeches are excellent. What do you say to our making the following experiment? Take our carriage June 1st with a good horse which I will buy in N. York putting them on board the Hartford Steamer & driving thence to Gardner. Lay out a list of say 25 Massachusetts towns. Advertise the giving of as many lectures on Woman's Rights by yourself & me. Admission free. You shall speak *first* in all cases, but if you prefer only for a short time, or as long as you feel like. I will follow filling up all gaps & weaving in any [things] you may omit. Then, if you choose, you shall close—or not. In short, I will act as your *supporter* & *aid* & we will see whether we cannot do your great work a real service. Lucy dear—I am *sure* that if you

Lucy Stone
at the time of her marriage.
(Library of Congress)

Henry Blackwell
as a young man.
(Library of Congress)

Portion of Henry Blackwell's first letter to Lucy Stone,
showing his habit of cross-writing his letters. *(Library of Congress)*

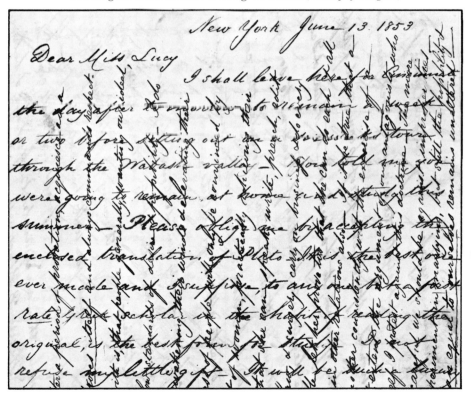

Clockwise, from top: Antoinette Brown Blackwell in 1852 before her marriage *(Schlesinger Library, Radcliffe College);* Samuel Blackwell *(Schlesinger Library, Radcliffe College);* Elizabeth Blackwell *(Schlesinger Library, Radcliffe College);* Sarah Stone Lawrence and her daughter Emma *(Schlesinger Library, Radcliffe College);* Alice Stone Blackwell in childhood *(Schlesinger Library, Radcliffe College).* *Center:* Lucy Stone and her daughter, Alice Stone Blackwell, in 1858 *(Library of Congress).*

Lucy Stone, circa 1870.
(Sophia Smith Collection, Smith College)

Henry Blackwell, 1866.
(Schlesinger Library, Radcliffe College)

Letter written by Lucy Stone to Henry Blackwell on the occasion of their twenty-fourth wedding anniversary, 1879. *(Library of Congress)*

The Woman's Journal,

No. 4 PARK STREET.

Boston, Apr 30 1879

Harry dear

I hope you get the line I left for you at the office. I was sorry not to see you to hear how you had succeeded in raising money. and also to beg you to read in the evening something that will help free your mind from the care

Lucy Stone in 1893.
(Sophia Smith Collection, Smith College)

Henry Blackwell at Chilmark, Martha's
Vineyard, 1908. *(Library of Congress)*

Alice Stone Blackwell in middle age.
(Sophia Smith Collection, Smith College)

feel able & willing to make the trial good will come of it! If your head aches & you dont find the spirit move you will see that I will come up *well* to the rescue, & if you are in *good mood*, I will *gladly* make myself *brief* & *witty* in a ten minutes speech you taking *the whole time*. Let us try to sing the New Song of Humanity *together*.

Dont let this suggestion vex you. If the hour for its accomplishment is not yet come—we can afford to wait. . . .

The weather is beautiful. I am *very* well. Have lately read Victor Hugo's "Toilers of the Sea" a fine story which I will bring you. Am now reading the May Atlantic which I will also bring you. Meanwhile my dear *wife* & *sweet heart* I am counting the days till we meet again & have the *holy* & *pure* joy of feeling our unity of soul—for we now *know* that we are *one*—forever—in sickness or in health in joy & in sorrow & our love will grow in the future as it has in the past. Kiss our dear little Alice & realize that I am

Ever your own Harry

New York Post office box 299 Jan. 24-1867

My dear Mrs. [Abby Kelley] Foster

I sit down to write you, with a feeling of despair which never came to me before where a principle is involved.

We have just returned from Philadelphia, where we went to assist in forming an Equal Suffrage Association. Geo. Thompson was there, and said "he did not think it would make any practical difference whether women voted or not." Edward M. Davis said "he sympathised with the Equal suffrage movement but he would take no position in it, that involved work. All his *work*, should be for the Negro." Eight colored men gathered around us during the recess, and said they thought women were well enough represented by their husbands &c. Robert Purvis alone, of them all, said "he should be ashamed to ask suffrage for himself and not at the same time, ask it for women, and he marveled at the patience of women, who were silent as to their own claims, while the great mass of the Negroes for whom they worked, would give their influence like a dead weight against the equality of women with them." Lucretia Mott, clear eyed as ever gave her voice, and her money, for universal justice.

But you, and Phillips, & Garrison, and the brave workers, who for thirty years, have said "let justice be done, if the heavens fall," now smitten by a strange blindness, believe that the nation's peril can be averted, if it can be induced to accept the poor half loaf, of justice for the Negro, poisoned by its lack of justice for every woman in the land. As if the application of a *universal* principle to a single class, *could* suffice for the necessity of this hour!

The broad principle of universal justice put into the foundation of our Temple of Liberty, is the *only* thing that can save it. They who today, stand saying, "this is the Negroes hour," are just in the position of those mistaken men, who after the war of revolution, said, "dont let us meddle with slavery. It is a bad thing, and will die of itself. But the business of this hour is to get a union." They got the union, and we know the results.

Now, as then, those who hold the life of the nation in their hands, do not see, that the path of justice, is the *only* path of peace and safety. They will not even ask for it, and we shall go on, drifting among breakers with no pilot to guide, where the anointed eye sees the clear channel in which we might ride in safety.

O Abby, it is a terrible mistake you are all making. . . . There is no other name given, by which this country *can* be saved, but that of *woman*. The Nation does not know it, and will not learn, Greeley says, "*dont* stir your question." Oliver Johnson sits in Theodore Tiltons chair, and snubs Mrs. Stanton and every one of us, not even opening our replies to Tayler Lewis. During a whole year, till very lately, has the Anti Slavery Standard thought it necessary to apologize, if it gave an item looking toward justice for woman. The "World" refuses to publish anything, because "its position would be misunderstood." So we get no access to the public ear. Susan Anthony gets no money from the Hovey fund, for her work in N.Y. The Greeks, abroad are remembered, and I hope they, and there "Isles" will be saved, but "the Greeks at our door," are forgotten. But the penalty for that forgetting, is not for Woman alone, or for this country alone, but also, for that great multitude whose longing eyes are trained from all shores to our own, for an example of a government, which derives its just powers from the consent of the governed. They alas will be disappointed, as shall we. But the mills of God grind very slow, and as we sow, so must we reap.

Here is a kiss for the hem of your garment, and all good wishes for you, and yours, but the tears are in my eyes, and a wail goes through my heart akin to that which I should feel, if I saw my little daughter drowning before my eyes with no power to help her.

> Very truly
> Lucy Stone

Junction City, Kansas, April 21, 1867

Dear Friends, E. C. Stanton and Susan B. Anthony:

You will be glad to know that Lucy and I are going over the length and breadth of this State speaking every day, and sometimes twice, journeying from twenty-five to forty miles daily, sometimes in a carriage and sometimes in an open wagon, with or without springs. We climb hills and dash down ravines, ford creeks, and ferry over rivers, rattle across limestone ledges, struggle through muddy bottoms, fight the high winds on the high rolling upland prairies, and address the most astonishing (and astonished) audiences in the most extraordinary places. To-night it may be a log school house, to-morrow a stone church; next day a store with planks for seats, and in one place, if it had not rained, we should have held forth in an unfinished court house, with only four stone walls but no roof whatever.

The people are a queer mixture of roughness and intelligence, recklessness and conservatism. One swears at women who want to wear the breeches; another wonders whether we ever heard of a fellow named Paul; a third is not going to put women on an equality with niggers. One woman told Lucy that no decent woman would be running over the country talking nigger and woman. Her brother told Lucy that "he had had a woman who was under the sod, but that if she had ever said she wanted to vote he would have pounded her to death!" . . .

I think we shall probably succeed in Kansas next fall if the State is thoroughly canvassed, not else. We are fortunate in having Col. Sam N. Wood as an organizer and worker. We owe everything to Wood, and he is really a thoroughly noble, good fellow, and a hero. He is a short, rather thick set, somewhat awkward, and "slouchy" man, extremely careless in his dress, blunt and abrupt in his manner, with a queer inexpressive face, little blue eyes which can look dull or flash fire or twinkle with the wickedest fun. He is so witty, sarcastic, and cutting, that he is a terrible foe, and will put the laugh even on his best friends. The son of a Quaker mother, he held the baby while his wife acted as one of the officers, and his mother another, in a Woman's Rights Convention seventeen years ago. Wood has helped off more runaway slaves than any man in Kansas. He has always been *true* both to the negro and the woman. But the negroes dislike and distrust him because he has never allowed the word white to be struck out, unless the word male should be struck out also. He takes exactly Mrs. Stanton's ground, that the colored men and women shall enter the kingdom *together,* if at all. So, while he advocates both, he fully realizes the wider scope and far greater grandeur of the battle for *woman.* . . . It is worth a journey to Kansas to know him for he is an original and a genius. If he should die next month I should consider the election lost. But if he live, and we all in the East drop other work and spend September and October in Kansas, we shall succeed. I am glad to say that our friend D. R. Anthony is out for both propositions in the *Leavenworth Bulletin.* But his sympathies are so especially with the negro question that we must have Susan out here to strengthen his hands. We must have Mrs. Stanton, Susan, Mrs. Gage, and Anna Dickinson, this fall. Also Ben Wade and Carl Schurz, if possible. We must also try to get 10,000 each of Mrs. Stanton's address, of Lucy Stone's address, and of Mrs. Mills article on the Enfranchisement of Women, printed for us by the Hovey Fund.

Kansas is to be the *battle ground* for 1867. *It must not be allowed to fail.*

The politicians here, except Wood and Robinson, are generally "on the fence." But they dare not oppose us openly. And the Democratic leaders are quite disposed to take us up. If the Republicans come out against us the Democrats will take us up. Do not let anything prevent your being here September 1 *for the campaign,* which will end in November. There will be a big fight and a great excitement. After the fight is over Mrs. Stanton will never have *use* for *notes* or *written* speeches any more.

Yours truly,
Henry B. Blackwell

Fort Scott, May 1, 1867

Dear Susan:

I have just this moment read your letter, and received the tracts; the "testimonies" I mean. We took 250 pounds of tracts with us, and we have sowed them thick; and Susan, the crop will be impartial suffrage in the fall. It will carry, beyond a doubt, in this State. . . . There is no time to write here. We ride all day, and lecture every night, and sometimes at noon too. . . . As to the [*National Anti-Slavery*] *Standard*, I don't count upon it at all. Even if you get it, the circulation is so limited that it amounts almost to nothing. I have not seen a copy in all Kansas. But the *Tribune* and the *Independent* alone could, if they would urge *universal* suffrage, as they do negro suffrage, carry this whole nation upon the only just plane of equal human rights. What a power to hold, and not use! I could not sleep the other night, just thinking of it; and if I had got up and written the thought that burned my very soul, I do believe that Greeley and Tilton would have echoed the cry of the old crusaders, "God wills it;" and rushing to our half-sustained standard, would plant it high and firm on immutable principles. *They* MUST take it up. I shall see them the very first thing when I go home. . . .

We have crowded meetings everywhere. I speak as well as ever, thank God! The audiences move to tears or laughter, just as in the old time. Harry makes capital speeches, and get a louder cheer always than I do, though I believe I move a deeper feeling. The papers all over the State are discussing pro and con. The whole thing is working just right. . . . I do not want to stay here after the 4th, but Wood and Harry have arranged other meetings, up to the 18th or 20th of May, so we shan't be back even for the Boston meetings.

Very truly,
Lucy Stone

Park Row [New York] Friday [Oct. 11] 12 o'clock [1867]

Dear Harry

I enclose the autograph of Clarke, but I would not show it unless he denies it.

If S.B.A. [Susan B. Anthony] pushes to know about funds, tell her we paid a good deal from our private money—and that Phillips is *willing* we should draw from the Jackson fund, so much as we will give our personal guarantee for.

I am sorry you have such a melancholy day to ride, and that [you] will only see Kansas, when it wears the sear, and yellow leaf.

As soon as you left the house, Alice came, and gave me a large kiss and hug, without speaking a word—just to show that she felt with me, our common loss, in your absence. Poor little soul! Take good care of yourself, *dearly beloved*. [William Cullen] Bryant writes that he has not the least objection to our use of his letter—Good! I find a letter asking for one tract, and another asking for two, each enclosing 10 cts. That is about the amt. of business here. I have engaged a lyceum lecture in Brooklyn Dec. 26, and take the proceeds.

Ever aff—Love to
Mrs Robinson

Sunday Oct. 13-1867
Our chamber [Newark, N.J.]

Dear Harry

I suppose you are in St. Louis, today. I hope it is as fine there, as it is here, where the day is half of cloud, and half of shine. . . .

Horace Greeley has sent me a letter, which is in answer to mine asking him to print the address of the women of Kansas in the weekly and semi weekly Tribune. The Standard this week, quotes a letter from Greeley from the Pall Mall Gazette—in which he takes the ground that the home, and the vote for women dont agree—I'll send it you. . . .

Yesterdays Tribune, has a report of the social science association meeting held in Boston, with a very good editorial calling attention to it, in which everything we need *except* the ballott is urged for us. I'll send that too.

I have two characteristic letters from Susan. In one, she gives us a cuff after this fashion—"I fear your release of Parker [Pillsbury] is "penny wise, and pound poor." He surely has brought us a good deal of money, and the work he does, pays richly." Isnt that rich, after *her urgent* solicitation that we should hurry from the Vineyard, because Parker could not stay in the office, and after Parker himself told us and Patton that he *must* be relieved!!!

Our children & Sam's had a walk this morning, and now we all go again to the woods over the canal this PM.

Marian's school begins on Thursday, and I suppose Alice will have to go, tho' I never did a thing with so much reluctance. She *needs* to be thrown with many children, & the putting her alone with Floy [Florence Blackwell], only increases her natural tendency to isolate herself. I am thankful that Frances will not be a pupil. With much love—Ever mine

Lucy

Lawrence Kansas Oct. 25. 1867

Dearest Lucikin

I have just returned from a trip to S. N Wood at Cottonwood Falls. Things have been as we feared. He became discouraged, went home early in August & has not done anything since. He was taken sick & nearly died, was in bed three weeks—his wife & children were then sick. He was out of money. The mail to Cottonwood was *robbed* & he never got any letters till a few days ago *for six weeks* The campaign was left to run itself & of course it ran into the ground. Had not Mrs S. & Susan come out & Olympia Brown made the most heroic & persevering fight ever known, it would have been a *complete fizzle*. As it is, *we are beat*. It is only a question whether our vote will be large enough to give us respect & bring the case up again hereafter. I predict *to you* a vote of about 5000. It may exceed that. If it reaches 10000 we are *virtually* triumphant. Negro Suffrage is in *great* danger. I think it will carry by *a small vote*. But most people think it is sure to be beat.

Wood is not dishonest, nor without excuse. He is perhaps not be be blamed, yet I confess I *am disappointed*. I got no money from him. He says it is all spent & $150 besides of his own money. Baker of Topeka went down with me, carried me there with his horse & buggy—got no money, but Wood promises to pay him & will probably eventually do so. Baker says that he is sure Wood *expected* strong backing & large pecuniary aid & was disappointed at not receiving them. But I think the disappointment was quite as much due to the fact that the people were not *up to it* & could not be brought up to it in a single campaign, however vigorous. My impression is that whatever may be our vote, the practical steps which I have taken in regard of printing tickets, writing to every County, and getting out circulars will result *in doubling our actual vote*.

And it is really *very important* to get as heavy a vote as possible. . . .

With kisses for little Alice for whom I have plenty of pleasant things to tell to her when I return

I remain
darling dee
Ever your own
Harry

As Henry had predicted, the campaign that had begun so hopefully ended in defeat: Black suffrage was voted down 19,421 to 10,483, and woman suffrage, 19,857 to 9,070. Still, Lucy and Henry weren't totally disheartened; after all, more than 9,000 men had voted in favor of woman suffrage, and in the future they hoped (incorrectly, as it turned out) to build on this vote. In their view, both amendments would have received a higher vote had not Mrs. Stanton and Miss Anthony made the error of turning to the Democrats, and to one Democrat in particular for aid.

George Francis Train was one of the more colorful minor figures of the postwar era. Copperhead, financier, railroad promoter, Fenian, suffragist, and the first man to be arrested under the Comstock Law for sending obscene materials in the mail, Train dressed like a dandy in brass-buttoned coats, patent-leather shoes, and lavender kid gloves. He also spiced his speeches with barroom jokes, including tantalizing suggestions as to how he and his traveling companion, the staid Miss Anthony, were spending their nights. But if his buffoonery was hardly in keeping with the high moral tone of the campaign, neither was his overt racism. For Train combined appeals for woman suffrage with scathing attacks on black people. He volunteered his services in Kansas, because he was conducting a one-man campaign for the presidency at the time, and jumped at the chance for additional publicity. For their part, Mrs. Stanton and Miss Anthony accepted his help because to a very large extent their desperation had made them reckless. Abandoned by their traditional allies, they were ready to welcome any offer of support—even if it involved a repudiation of their abolitionist faith.

However, as far as Lucy and Henry were concerned, there was no excuse for such irresponsible behavior. They felt that Miss Anthony and Mrs. Stanton should have first consulted with the American Equal Rights Association before joining forces with Train, and even accused Miss Anthony of squandering on him equal rights funds that should have gone to other workers. The charge was a serious one, since Miss Anthony prided herself on her complete honesty in financial matters, and it left a residue of personal bitterness.

Despite this criticism Mrs. Stanton and Miss Anthony accepted Train's offer of an all-expenses-paid lecture tour from Kansas back to the East, and of financial backing for a woman suffrage paper. On January 8, 1868, the first issue of *The Revolution* appeared. The new paper's name was in keeping with its goal of radical change in every aspect of women's lives, and its motto, "Principle, not policy—justice, not favors—men their rights and nothing more—women their rights and nothing less" was indicative of the break with both abolition and Republicanism. Mrs. Stanton and Parker Pillsbury, one of the few abolitionists who had remained loyal to the feminists throughout, were the editors; Miss Anthony was the publisher and business manager; and Train and David M. Mellis, financial editor of *The New York World*, were the financial backers. By agreement, the feminists were to have the front part of the sixteen-page weekly, while Train and Mellis used the back pages to advocate their peculiar financial and political ideas.

The Revolution was a highly effective feminist organ. The paper supported woman suffrage, called for better wages and working conditions for women, and printed articles on a wide range of subjects related to their oppression—poverty, prostitution, marriage and divorce, and the role of the Church in subjugating women. But at the same time, *The Revolution* widened the split within the feminist ranks. Lucy, Henry, and other Equal Rights leaders bridled at Mrs. Stanton's and Miss Anthony's continued collaboration with Train, at the paper's anti-Republican stance, and at its outspoken advocacy of such controversial issues as divorce. Two opposing factions were beginning to take shape.

Meanwhile, Lucy and Henry continued to push for suffrage on the state level. In April of 1868 Lucy, still suffering from headaches and periods of depression, went before the Massachusetts state legislature to plead the case for woman suffrage. The following November she and Henry returned to the Boston area to attend the founding convention of the New England Woman Suffrage Association. The delegates to this convention included well-known abolitionists, Republican leaders, and several prominent literary women. Julia Ward Howe, successful writer and the epitome of New England gentility, was elected president of the association, and Lucy Stone, a member of its executive committee.

The focus of the new organization was clear from the start: Although Lucy and a few others made eloquent appeals in behalf of woman's right to political power, the bulk of the membership put the freedmen first, and women second. Thus when the Fifteenth Amendment, providing that "The right . . . to vote shall not be . . . abridged . . . on account of race, color, or previous condition of servitude," came under discussion in Congress, the New England association supported the amendment. Mrs. Stanton and Miss Anthony, however, did not. In January of 1869 they called a woman suffrage convention in Washington—the first to be held in the capital—and petitioned Congress to include the word "sex" in the amendment, or failing that, to follow the Fifteenth Amendment with a Sixteenth Amendment, giving women the vote. Lucy was noticeably absent from this convention, and *The Revolution* criticized her in an article entitled "Stones Holding Their Peace."

The debate over the Fifteenth Amendment intensified the breach between the two factions. The final rupture came at the annual meeting of the American Equal Rights Association in May of 1869. There Stephen Foster, Abby Kelley Foster's abolitionist husband, demanded that Miss Anthony and Mrs. Stanton step down as officers of the association—Mrs. Stanton was a vice-president and

Miss Anthony was on the executive committee. He charged that they had "publicly repudiated the principles of the society," by associating with such an avowed racist as Train, and by opposing the Fifteenth Amendment. The black abolitionist Frederick Douglass also joined loudly in the attack, but Lucy and Henry defended Miss Anthony and Mrs. Stanton against the charges of racism, and tried to steer a middle course between the extreme militancy of the abolitionists on the one hand, and of the feminists, on the other. "We are lost if we turn away from the middle principle and argue for one class," Lucy said. Yet it could not be otherwise, and forced to choose, Lucy and Henry cast their lot with the abolitionists. They joined with the majority of the delegates at the convention in passing a resolution in favor of the Fifteenth Amendment, and refused to rally behind a drive for a Sixteenth Amendment, enfranchising women.

Finding themselves outvoted and under attack, Miss Anthony and Mrs. Stanton withdrew from the American Equal Rights Association, and two days later formed their own organization, the National Woman Suffrage Association, at a reception for women delegates that was hosted by *The Revolution*. Deliberately excluded from this new organization, Lucy, Henry, and other members of the New England Woman Suffrage Association acted quickly to form their own organization. Throughout the summer they corresponded with reformers all over the country, urging them to come to Cleveland in the fall to assist in the formation of a nationwide suffrage association that was to be organized on a delegate basis with equal state representation.

∽

Plymouth Wed Aprl/68

Dear Harry

I reached Boston at 9 o'clock. Slept at the Adams house, and next morning in a driving snow storm, met Olympia, and went to the State House, had a good hearing, about which I must tell you, and came down here with Mrs. Spooner, heard Phillips lecture &c. . . . Mrs. Spooner's house is very near the ocean and all this morning the tide has been running, with the wonderful colors, crests, & colored shadows, and *my* shadows have fled. Only I have headaches all the time, and did yesterday, tho' it did not spoil my speech. But with this bright clear sky, and sweet ocean air, and more than all the presence of these old friends who have real sympathy with me, and my ideas, I *must* get better.

I speak at Pembroke Friday night, and shall go to Gardner on Sat. Several members of the House want to have me repeat my address before the whole body next week if they can arrange it. I was invited to ever so many places and really might lecture all the time. . . .

Love to Mother & all—but most for you.

Affy—
Lucy

Boston Sat. Apr. 11 [1868]

Harry darling

I wrote you from Plymouth, and also had a note from you there.

The weather has been really awful. Both meetings have been held in a storm, but each paid $2.00 more than the expense. After the hearing had on Tuesday—I was invited to be heard by the representatives in the Green Room—next Wed. at 10 o'clock. I enclose the order. Perhaps you can get it into the Post—with some friendly notice of the first hearing. . . .

God bless you Harry dear and give you the large patience you need with me. My blues are gone. I wish they may never return to trouble me or you. Dont fret about business. We shall do well enough.

I shall probably get home on Thursday or Friday.

Love to you dearest
and to the children & Grandma

Newark N.J. Mar. 24 69

My dear Mrs. Field

Thank you for so promptly sending me the letters of Mr. Sumner.

I herewith return them, and agree with you that there is nothing in them, to make it desirable we should publish them, even if we had not his express wish that they should not be.

I wish he felt moved to give our cause, the great, brave help he rendered to the slave.

Nevertheless we must be forever grateful for what he *has* done for human rights, even tho' it does not tell directly for us. I think God rarely gives to one man, or one set of men, more than *one*, great moral victory to win. Hence we see the old abolitionists generally, shrink from the van of our movement, tho' they are in hearty sympathy with it. If Mr. Sumner "dont want to be in this fight," as he told me, in my heart, I yet say "God bless him"! Our victory is sure to come. And I can endure anything but recreancy to principle.

I think I would send petitions to Geo. W. Julian. He has really *done* more this winter, than any other member for us. And promptly after Grant's inauguration introduced three bills for woman suffrage in the District [of Columbia] in [territories of the U.S.], and an amendment to the constitution, securing woman suffrage. I am delighted that Grant asks *Quaker* help for the Indian.

I *hope* WE may be better acquainted. I am sure I should love you very much.

> Cordially yours
> Luoy Stone

Newark, Apr. 9, 1869

Rev. Sam J. May
My dear Friend

I came home last night from a lecturing tour in Maine, Massachusetts, and Rhode Island, and as I looked through the last number of the "Advocate," and saw your announcement of the good work being done in Onondaga Co. [New York], for women, my heart gave a glad gush of gratitude for the host of helpers, true men and women who are rallying everywhere to establish justice without distinction of sex. So here are my thanks to you, dear Mr. May, larger thanks than I can express that your honored name stands as President of this new Society. It is a guaranty which makes us all feel safe.

Our cause goes bravely on, and we have abundant reason "to thank God and take courage." You will be glad to know that we stand quite a fair chance in Massachusetts of getting the word "male" (what shall I say?) "squelched."

Wendell Phillips and Mrs. Howe did excellent service last week, before the Joint Special Committee of the Mass. Legislature; next week Hon. Geo. F. Hoar is heard before the same Committee for the same Cause. The Legislature is largely Republican and temperance, and from such material much is to be hoped.

Susan Anthony has us all in The Revolution. She called a meeting of the Executive Committee of the American Equal Rights Society while I was absent at the Springfield Convention (tho' I am chairman of the Executive Committee) issued a Call with names of all the officers of the Society, and published it in the Revolution the next week, as tho' it were the organ of our Association! . . .

> With cordial good wishes
> Lucy Stone

> Newark N.J.
> Oct. 6-69

Rev. James Freeman Clarke
Dear Sir

It is decided to hold the Convention to form an American Woman Suffrage Association at Cleveland on the 17 & 18 of Nov.

Can you not be present to help organize?

Our cause suffers today from the lack of the organizing talent of MEN, in its management. Col. [Thomas Wentworth] Higginson has promised to be there, and we need you to help him.

If we can only organize wisely and well, with half our officers men, of the right kind, there will be no end to the good, that will come of it.

There has been no event of such large significance since the formation of the American Anti Slavery Soc. It is even greater than that, as it concerns not a class, but the race.

It should be organized by men and women whose names will command confidence, & win cooperation and sympathy.

I hope you will not say nay, but if necessary, let other things give way, for this very serious business!

We can only pay expenses. I wish it were possible to do more.

As soon as you can decide, please let me know, as we wish to advertize the names of those who will take part in the convention.

The Call, carefully drawn up by Col. Higginson, will be out I think on Sat. next.

Yours respectfully
Lucy Stone

[Newark, N.J.] Oct. 19-1869

Dear Mrs. Stanton

Enclosed I send you a copy of the call for a convention to form an American Woman Suffrage association. I wish I could have had a quiet hour with you, to talk about it. I *hope* you will see it as I do, that with two societies each, in harmony with itself, each having the benefit of national names, each attracting those who naturally belong to it, we shall secure the hearty active cooperation of *all* the friends of the cause, better than either could do alone. People will differ, as to what they consider the best methods & means. The true wisdom is not to ignore, but to provide for the fact. So far as I have influence, this soc. shall never be an enemy or antagonist of yours in any way. It will simply fill a field and combine forces, which yours does not. I shall rejoice when any of the onerous [?] works are carried, no matter who does it.

Your little girls, and mine will reap the easy harvest which it costs so much to sow.

With sincere good will
Truly your friend
Lucy Stone

Eastport Maine
Oct 31-69

Dear Nette

The point from which I write is 18 hours by steamboat beyond all railroads . . . so you can see how far away I am. I came down here to lecture for Woman Suffrage, and have had two meetings, as I had to wait over Sunday—the boat not returning till Monday.

I write especially to ask if the N. Jersey State Soc. will make you a delegate to the Cleveland Convention—will you not go? I am afraid we shall not get rid of the N. York host unless those who know the real need of doing so are there.

Col. Higginson either influenced by Theodore Tilton, or from a feeling (what shall I say) of mistaken magnanimity perhaps, told Mrs. Stanton and Susan, that he expected to see them at Cleveland. They neither of them intended to go. I do not know that they will. But it will be so dreadful an incubus to take them up again! tho' perhaps there will be no help for it if they go. But I do very much wish you could plan to be there, so that we may counsel. . . .

You know Alice goes to Newburyport this week. I think it the best thing for her, but I feel crushed and torn and homeless. But I shall make myself very busy. Harry will join me at Newburyport, and we shall set to raise the $10,000 to start a paper. I suppose you know the N.E. Woman Suffrage Association propose to take the "Agitator"—call it the "Woman's Journal" with Mrs. Livermore, Mrs. Howe, T. W. Higginson & Mr. Garrison as editors—if we can raise the money. If we do, I shall try and work through the paper, for the future, and quit this lecturing field altogether. It is not consistent with any home life, or any proper care of my family. I feel it more and more, and shall certainly not continue this mode of work—tho' it is my natural way. But I long for a snug home, by myself from which I can send out, what I think in some shape not so effective for me perhaps, but on the whole better, under the circumstances. If I were only a ready writer I should be so glad! I hope you are nicely settled for the winter, but you will miss Sam, so much more than before he gave his time to the family as the last year.

> With much love
> Lucy

> Box 299 PO New York Sunday
> Nov 1. 1869

Dear Lucikin

It is 3 PM—a beautiful fall afternoon. I have just returned from a conference with Jackson Davis & wife, who will go to Cleveland with the Gages & ourselves & who will go with us to Wilmington on the 12th inst to help form a Delaware Woman Suffrage Association.

Learning from Fielder Israel & John Cameron, that Mrs Stanton & Susan B.A. had written to them "appointing Nov. 9. & proposing to come and help them organize their society"—I informed them how matters stood & they promptly wrote Miss A. that they could not get along without Lucy Stone & that the 12th Nov was the day fixed upon. I have written to the Vineland [New Jersey] people to send a delegation & as it is important to get Pennsylvania in line, I have also written to Mary Grew proposing to get up a meeting there on the 10th to select delegates to go from Pa.

The Revolution is out against us & says that Gerrit Smith, Henry Ward Beecher, Geo. Wm. Curtis, and others would not have signed the call if they had known its real meaning. But Gerrit Smith writes a cordial letter which I bring with me. Alice's dresses and cloak are all brought home—& I will see that everything is put up tomorrow in readiness. I am going to see Tilton tomorrow to try to make him see how necessary it is to influence Mrs S. & Susan to *stay away from Cleveland* & not to fight us, either. I think I have made Mrs Tilton see it. I had a very pleasant half hour's interview with Mr G W Curtis yesterday afternoon, to try to get him at Vt [Vermont] to address the legislature. He cannot go. I spoke to him about taking the Presidency of the Am Asn if elected. He has taken it into consideration.

When I see you, I shall have a great deal to tell you & a perfect raft of letters & papers to look over with you. I think all is shaping well. I have written to Whipple to see Mr Phillips & if he cannot go to Vermont to see Mr Garrison in accordance with a request to that effect from Jas Hutchinson Jr. I have written a reply to Mr Tilton's article called "A Flaw in the Cornerstone" which I shall ask him to insert. The N Jersey Society are all right & the proper delegates appointed.

The Report in the Tribune of the Hartford Convention is by the young lady "Nellie Hutchinson" whom Mr. Higginson suggested as office Editor of our paper. I hope you have seen the report—specially of Mr Garrison's speech. I send you a pretty little poem by her. About half the description would apply very well to you but the wrinkles & grey hair & faded dress do not apply.

I judge from the last Revolution that John Neal is planning to get up a Maine Society in the interest of Mrs Stanton. Can you not head if off & have one formed in connection with the *Am.* W.S. As^{n}.? In haste—Ever your own

H B Blackwell

Susan B. Anthony did come to the Cleveland convention, and made no secret of her displeasure with it even as she gave it her blessing: "Though this Convention, by its action, shall nullify the National Association of which I am a member, and though it shall tread its heel upon *The Revolution*, to carry on which I have struggled as never mortal woman or mortal man struggled for any cause . . . though you here assembled declare that the other is null and void . . . and should be ground to dust—still . . . I will thank God for this Convention." Thus, with her grudging approval, the convention went on with its work of establishing another national suffrage organization. Called the American Woman Suffrage Association, it differed from the National in ways that reflected the divergent style, temperament, and background of its leaders.

Unlike the National, which was primarily a woman's organization (men could join and even hold office, but the majority of the National's members and all of its officers were women), the American eagerly welcomed men into its ranks. Its constitution stipulated an equal number of male and female officers, and alternating male and female presidents. The well-known minister and reformer Henry Ward Beecher was elected the first president, and Henry Blackwell, one of the secretaries. In the American no action could be taken without a vote by accredited delegates to the association's conventions, while in the National decisions were made and executed by a small group of leaders meeting weekly in New York. The American worked chiefly for state and municipal suffrage; the National, for the passage of a federal suffrage amendment. Finally, while the American limited itself specifically to the question of suffrage, the National—in the beginning at least—was willing to address itself to any issue, however controversial, that related to woman's rights.

With the formation of the American Woman Suffrage Association, the Stone-Blackwells moved from New Jersey to Boston, and that city became their permanent base. The reasons for the move were both personal and political. Many of Lucy's closest friends from her days as an antislavery lecturer—Garrison, Phillips, Samuel May, and Higginson—lived in or around Boston, and the city was also the home of the New England Woman Suffrage Association. New York, on the other hand, was dominated by the Anthony-Stanton faction; *The Revolution* had its offices there, and since Lucy didn't believe the city could support two suffrage papers, Boston seemed the logical place from which to launch a paper reflecting the more conservative views of the American association.

Like *The Revolution*, *The Woman's Journal* addressed itself to woman's rights issues other than suffrage, but unlike the other paper, it tended to steer clear of any issue that might alienate potential supporters of woman's enfranchisement. It didn't take up the cause of blue-collar working women, nor did it attempt to shake up the status quo by advocating easy divorce or by attacking religion as an instrument of woman's oppression.

The paper was financed by a joint-stock company with two hundred shares of fifty dollars each. Henry purchased the largest number of shares and Lucy sold the remainder to friends and supporters. Mary A. Livermore merged her paper, *The Agitator*, with *The Woman's Journal*, and became its editor, with Lucy, Julia Ward Howe, Garrison, and Higginson as the associate editors. Henry was the business manager, but when Garrison resigned during the first year, he dutifully took his place as associate editor, although according to his daughter Alice, he had never wanted to serve as an editor.

The Woman's Journal was to become the longest-lived suffrage paper in the country—a monument to the dedication and tenacity of two generations of Stone-Blackwells. It was also to provide Lucy with an occupation that was more "consistent" with home life and the care of her family; yet in the beginning it caused the disruption of that family: Alice was sent away to boarding school in Newburyport, Massachusetts, while Lucy and Henry moved into makeshift quarters above the *Journal*'s offices on the ground floor of the New England Woman's Club building at 3 Tremont Place. By the time Alice rejoined them several months later, the paper was firmly established as her chief rival for her parents' time and attention. Not only were Lucy and Henry preoccupied with the paper, but they were also away from home a great deal of the time. The first issue of the *Journal* appeared on January 8, 1870; at the beginning of February Lucy embarked on a speaking tour which took her from Vermont to Illinois and Ohio, and then back to Vermont again by way of Vineland, New Jersey. In March she went to New York for a business meeting of the executive committee of the still-extant American Equal Rights Association, returning the next month for a conference called by Theodore Tilton for the purpose of forming a united suffrage association. Lucy, Higginson, and George W. Curtis went as unofficial representatives of the American. But when they rejected Tilton's proposal for a new suffrage organization with a constitution patterned after the National's, and with himself as president, he formed the Union Suffrage Society without them. His next move was to engineer a merger first with the old Equal Rights Association, and then with the National at their May meeting in New York.

June found Lucy lecturing in Indiana, and in August Henry was called away from home by the illness and death of his mother. From Lawrence, Long Island, where his mother had spent the last months of her life, he wrote to say that his brother George was "fairly overwhelmed with grief at her loss." He seemed to find relief from his own strong sense of bereavement by focusing his attention on such matters as the price of lots in Greenwood Cemetery and the problem of renting the Roseville home.

In November of 1870 the American held its annual convention in Cleveland, and despite Susan B. Anthony's presence and impassioned plea for union, the association voted against a merger with the Union Suffrage Society—much to Lucy's and Henry's relief. The latter organization fell apart not long afterward when the National decided to resume its former name and separate identity.

With the American and *The Woman's Journal* established on a more or less secure footing (a huge deficit had forced *The Revolution* to cease publication the previous May), Lucy and Henry could afford to take care of some personal business. Toward the end of 1870 they moved out of their rooms above the *Journal's* offices to a seventeen-room house on Pope's Hill in the Dorchester district of Boston. The new house commanded fine views of the Neponset River, Dorchester

Bay, and Boston Harbor; its ample grounds were laid out with fruit trees, flowers, and lawn, and after the Stone-Blackwell family moved in, Lucy started a vegetable garden and kept a cow and chickens.

Now that they were again settled in a home of their own, and Lucy was launched on a new career, Henry sought an outlet for his own restless energies. On February 5, 1871, Alice wrote to Elizabeth Blackwell's adopted child and her good friend Kitty: "Papa has really gone to San Domingo. He has engaged to write enough letters to various newspapers to pay his passage, and has also, I believe, an eye to some private speculations there." Henry's visit was made in conjunction with that of a presidential commission sent to investigate conditions on the island with a view toward annexing it to the United States. Debt-ridden and unstable, the current government of Santo Domingo was in favor of the plan, as was President Ulysses S. Grant, influenced by his private secretary, Orville Babcock, and by American big business, which was anxious to exploit the island's considerable resources. Henry, too, became an ardent exponent of annexation; the following November he wrote a long letter to Charles Sumner, the chief opponent of the treaty in the Senate. In that letter he argued that annexation would promote the "moral and material interests" of both the United States and Santo Domingo, and that the world would "be benefited by planting free institutions and Northern thrift and energy in the heart of the Tropics, and by the consequent reduction in the cost of the great Tropical staples."

While Henry was absorbed with Santo Domingo, a new threat to the cause of suffrage appeared in the person of Victoria Woodhull, a notorious New York stockbroker, newspaper editor, clairvoyant, and free-love advocate. Mrs. Woodhull first attracted the attention of the New York suffragists when in January of 1871 she presented a memorial to Congress in behalf of woman suffrage. Arguing that the Fourteenth and Fifteenth amendments gave women the right to vote, she urged Congress to pass enabling legislation. Miss Anthony and two other suffragists who heard Mrs. Woodhull speak were so impressed with her eloquence that they invited her and her sister, Tennie C. Claflin, to speak at the National's May Anniversary in New York. Since Mrs. Woodhull's avant-garde opinions were well-known in New York, her presence at the suffrage convention created a sensation. But ignoring the uproar and the inevitable connection people made between suffrage and free love, Mrs. Stanton and other members of the National took her up eagerly.

Lucy was very much disturbed by this turn of events. She regarded the "Woodhull & Claflin tribe" as a "real curse," and made certain that the American was spared any association with it. Unfortunately, Mrs. Woodhull wasn't the only difficulty with which she had to contend; at the beginning of 1872 Mrs. Livermore left the *Journal* for the more lucrative field of lyceum lecturing, and with her gone, most of the burden of the paper devolved on Lucy and Henry. Moreover, Mrs. Livermore's departure couldn't have come at a worse time: In December while Lucy and Henry were attending a suffrage convention in Washington, D.C., their Dorchester house caught fire, and was almost completely destroyed. Their loss was substantial in both a financial and personal sense, for along with the house, its furnishings, silverware and other valuables, they lost letters, papers, and other memorabilia. Fortunately, the loss in the latter category turned out not to be as great as they originally thought. Although at the time Henry wrote his sister Elizabeth that all his "letters and papers of 30 years" had been destroyed in the fire, many of these were, in fact, saved. In the wake of the disaster, Lucy favored selling what remained of the house and taking lodgings in Boston close to the *Journal*, but Henry was determined to rebuild the house and his will carried the day: They moved into a small house at the bottom of the hill while the repair work went on.

It was a tense time for both of them. In February of 1872 Alice complained to her diary: "Mamma is getting to be just like Aunt Sarah snarling all the time. I could stand it well enough . . . but that Papa looks so tired and worn that I think I should cry if I didn't feel like swearing." Part of the tension may have been due to the fact that Henry was contemplating another trip to Santo Domingo, and Lucy felt that she could ill afford to lose him during this trying period. In any event, they seem to have reached some sort of an understanding because Henry did leave for Santo Domingo toward the end of March, and Lucy's letters to him while he was away showed a greater tolerance of his need for "change and variety, sunshine and birds."

Strong opposition in the Senate had killed the treaty of annexation, but several prominent businessmen were in the process of forming a company for the development of the island, and Henry was anxious to be included in its charter. One of the members of the original presidential commission, the reformer Dr. Samuel Gridley Howe, showed a similar interest in the island's potential. He, too, made a second trip to Santo Domingo, this time accompanied by his wife, Julia Ward Howe, whose very favorable impressions of the island were published in *The Woman's Journal*.

By May Henry had returned from Santo Domingo, and was again caught up in the suffrage movement. That month both the American and the National held meetings in New York, and at the latter convention Mrs. Woodhull announced the creation of a new party, the Equal Rights party, with herself as its candidate for the presidency. At this juncture, a horrified Susan B. Anthony acted quickly to sever the National's connection with Mrs. Woodhull, who then went on to make a wild bid for the presidency under the banner of free love and other eccentric causes.

Regarding the election of 1872, Lucy and Henry were content to work through traditional channels. The year before, Henry had succeeded in getting the Massachusetts Republican Convention to endorse woman suffrage at least in principle, and now he attended the Republican National Convention, held in Philadelphia in June, for the same purpose. His chances were helped by the fact that Grant was known to look favorably upon woman suffrage, and was besides a personal friend of Mrs. Livermore.

∽

[Boston] Nov 17. 1870

Rev James Freeman Clarke
Dear Sir

Mr Tilton, Mrs Stanton, Miss Anthony, and others of the N. York Society are going to Cleveland to try to force us into combination with them. They have been stirring up some of our Western members who are ignorant of the facts to join them there.

It is very *important* that Mass should be represented. Mrs Howe is trying to see you in order to induce you to go *if possible*.

I am authorized by the Mass Ex. Com to find delegates & if you will act in that capacity I will hand you credentials at Cleveland.

It will be best to start Sunday night. But early Monday AM will bring you to Cleveland Tuesday morning.

Mr Beecher will not be willing to serve another term tho very kind & cordial. We think of electing Mr Julian in his place if our opponents do not put Mrs Stanton or Mr Tilton upon us inspite of ourselves.

If you cannot go, please write a letter to my wife Lucy Stone—care of Mrs Hannah M. Clarke Cleveland O. expressing your opinion that we should not merge the American WS As^n in any other & that we should stick to the question of *Suffrage* & not complicate the cause with marriage, divorce & other outside questions.

By so doing, you will give us material aid & much oblige.

Yours truly
Henry B. Blackwell

Cleveland Nov. 27, 1870

Dear Harry

. . . I attended the Cuh. [Cuyahoga] Co. Soc. meeting here yesterday. Susan was there, & John Gage. Susan told how she got money from Train, how I would not work with him, &c &c. I stated the real ground of difference and urged that in any action they took they should make suffrage the main issue. Bradwell had reported before S got in. It was a small meeting. Not more than 100. present. I saw Judge Waite and his wife. They did not ask me to go with them. So I am at my cousins. But we had a frank friendly talk, and before next June, they will see the right thing to do. Harper's Weekly Nov. 26. has an article from [George Wm.] Curtis which puts it clean and right. There will now be clear dividing lines and we shall go on better than ever.

Aff.
Lucy

Boston, Mar. 19 1871

Dear Mrs. Janney

You will see by the last No. of the Journal, that Mrs. Livermore's article looks toward an affiliation with Mrs. Hooker, who is the sworn ally of Susan, and Mrs. Stanton and who in connection with Paulina Davis and Josephine Griffing, have done their best to defeat, and undermine, the A.W.S.A.

Now I regret her article, and think it so much better, for us to keep clear of other organizations at least, till they prove, that their work is good.

Now, if you agree with me in this view, will you not write a private, friendly note to Mrs. Livermore, and suggest that it seems best to you, not to strike hands, with those people at Washington. They were our late enemies. We dont know that they are our friends. The attempt to get names to a Declaration, is poor work, as not one woman, in ten thousand, will or can send her name, even if she cares much for Suffrage.

Do not mention to *any one* that I suggested this to you. But it is easier to stop a small leak, than a great hole.

How sudden the death of Mrs. Tilden! In haste, with much love

Lucy Stone

[Boston] Nov. 7 1871

Dear Friend Wildman

I have your letter, & certainly rejoice that all your delegates are right. . . . I expect Mrs. Cole, Mrs. Cutler, and Mrs. Longley, Mrs. Campbell, and Mrs. Churchill. Mrs. Livermore will not be there. She says her arrangement with Mr. Pugh to lecture in his "Star Cause" precludes the possibility of attending our annual meeting, as she is pledged not to speak in Phil^a except for him. I should let every other lecture go, for the sake of the annual meeting of the A.W.S. Association. I have tried to get Mrs. L. to do so, but she thinks she cant. I hope Mr. Furness, will come in and speak, even if he is not announced. We *need* every clean soul to help us, now when such a flood of what is fatal to the peace, and purity of the family, is rolled in on our question. Please say to dear good, clear eyed, Mary Grew, that my one wish, in regard to Mrs. Woodhull is, that [neither] she nor her ideas, may be so much as heard of at our meeting. I suppose we ought to have two large posters, at the Hall door, on the days of the meeting. We shall also need to make an effort to raise money. . . .

Very truly yours
Lucy Stone

New York March 20 1872

Dearest Lucikin

I reached N York at 7 AM took breakfast at Second Avenue & have been busy all day. Mr Spofford expresses himself as quite willing that I should be included among the corporators & will write Col. Fabens to that effect. He called with me on Mr Barlow & I made several suggestions as to the form which might be included which were well received, but at Mr Spofford's suggestion, I was introduced merely as a friend of Dr Howe & the point of my proposed interest was not named to him. . . . Aaron Powell will have a meeting in Steinway Hall tuesday & *thinks* he would like to have it for a temperance celebration on wednesday. If we let him have the hall on wednesday, we could hold our meeting *on* thursday. So I will see Steinway & Co & engage the hall for wednesday *or* thursday, & you had better decide which day of the two you would prefer. . . .

I am horribly *home sick*. I think of you as tired & worried & feel ashamed not to be helping you. Aaron Powell says that Mrs Woodhull & her set of odds & ends are going to hold a grand political convention & make a Presidential nomination. Mrs Hooker wrote to him to try & engage Steinway Hall for it, but Aaron says the proprietors wont let them have it, as the last meeting held here was very disreputable. . . .

Tonight I shall sleep at Second Avenue. Tomorrow night either on the briny deep, or on the Sound homeward bound. I really hardly know which. If I dont go down I have little hope of being included in the new charter—If I do, little fear of being left out. . . .

With ever so much love to you & Alicekin & kind regards to the household I remain

Ever yours Harry

P.S. In no case, move into the new house until the plaster is THOROUGHLY DRY. I have known many people die in consequence of moving in *too soon*. It will be *far better* to board a few weeks in Boston, than to run any risk.

Puerto Plata Apl. 1. 1872

Dearest Lucikin

. . . We had a stormy & slow voyage. For the first time I saw a *real* storm at sea & I have no desire to see another one. A huge wave carried off a part of the railing of the upper deck & deluged the state rooms & main cabin with water. The delay thus caused by the storm, made us reach the reefs that surround Turk's Island at night, which obliged us to wait until next morning at daylight. We reached Puerto Plata on the evening of Good Friday too late to enter the harbor until Saturday morning.

There is no business doing because it is "Holy Week"—which begins with Good Friday the anniversary of the crucifixion—and continues for a week. . . . On Saturday the entrance of Christ's *soul* into heaven was celebrated. I attended church which was crowded & the scene gay & bright as flowers, clean clothes & smiling faces could make it. At many of the street corners poor Judas Iscariot hung suspended in effigy & after Mass the soldiers marched round & shot him down to the great delight of everybody. I found my friend Martino Castillo very ill—but amused myself by visiting some neighboring plantations & by making acquaintance with merchants & other residents of the city. The place is growing, & a spirit of commercial activity & enterprize is aroused which makes the place much more cheerful & attractive than last year. The beautiful mountain scenery & superb climate make up for many deficiencies. . . .

I am more and more struck with the abnormal and semi-barbarous character of the present life of the West Indies. The resident foreigners are mostly unmarried men who spend a few years here in order to make money & who look forward to returning to Europe. Therefore they do not bring their female relatives & took no root in the country. Instead of importing *society* they bring only vices & the chief of these are drinking & licentiousness that are very general. Only *colonization* by resident American landowners will ever develope this beautiful island & only the example of American *family life* will ever redeem the country from its present immorality. The feeling here in favor of annexation is perceptibly stronger. The merchants now, as a class, are decidedly in its favor. Tell Alice that I have taken two glorious rides on horseback upon Mr Castillo's fine horse in company with several other gentlemen & wished much that she could have gone with me. These spirited but gentle little animals, as sure footed & active as cats, would just suit her & I really must try to get her one, some day, so that she may scamper about the country. . . .

Whether this trip of mine will have definite results in enabling me to carry out my plan of opening up a colonization enterprize from New England to this country hereafter, I cannot yet tell. If the island is annexed, this will be a useful and feasible matter. . . .

I hope you are throwing the detail of getting out the paper upon Miss Eastman & Mr Smith with Emma's aid. I try not to think about it, because I dread the care and worry which you *may* be exposed to, from having the paper on your hands—with inexperienced assistants. I do not know how much trouble you may have had during the past fortnight, but I hope by the time you get this, I shall be on my way home, if not already there. My conviction that a visit to S.D. at this particular time, is necessary in order to have a part in its future developement, was the only thing that made me seem to forget the pressing nature of our Boston engagements. Whatever may be the result of my visit here, I shall not have to reproach myself with want of the proper effort at the proper time, and I can hardly think that a month's absence will have any very ruinous result. . . .

Tell me just how things are at home—just how important my immediate return is—& whether I had better wait at N.Y. *now,* or if necessary, come down later. And, in any case dearest Lucikin, remember that you & Alice are never out of my thoughts & that I remain now as ever,

Your own
Harry

Harrison Square [Boston] Apr. 11 1872

Dear Harrykin

As it is possible you may return, as you thought you should, by the 19th I send a line to the care of Spofford Co. to let you know in advance, that we are all well, that the house goes on well, but so slowly, that we are told by Mr. Harris, we cannot get into it before June. The weather first cold, and then rainy put everything back. But it will be a nice house when it is done. . . .

The Journal has gone on very well. I am so glad to find that I can do it. Now you shall never have the drudgery of it again. I never wanted you to, and always felt that it was too bad that my work should burden & chafe your shoulders, but I did not know how to prevent it. You shall be as free Harry darling, when you come home, as you have always needed to be. I hope you have accomplished all you wanted by this trip, and that you found a great deal of rest & comfort, and health. It has not been hard for me. . . .

I wish you would see about the halls in N.Y. for our May meeting. We have both Apollo and Lyric Hall by mistake. I have written Lyric to release us, but have not heard. Ed Eggleston, Mr. Garrison, and Mr. Livermore have promised to attend the N.Y. meeting. I wait answers from others. Iowa has "gone back" on Woman Suffrage! It is too bad! Greeley has joined the Cincinnati Convention, which now assumes large importance.

We shall be very glad to have you with us, Harry dearest & we miss you all the time, and every where. When you are back, I want you to feel that you are not *bound* and *limited* by this place, and by us. You NEED change, variety, sunshine & birds. I have not always known it. But now that I DO know it, it shall not be my fault, if you do not have all the freedom & variety you want. We will both of us, give you the warmest welcome when you choose to stay with us, and we will cheerfully second any of your plans that will give you the larger sphere your nature needs. I have been so glad that you did really *take* this little bit of change, and have taken solid comfort, in thinking that the man in all the world whom I love, and care for, was getting health and rest, and for a little while, at least, doing what gave him pleasure. So Harry darling, here is a kiss for you, and larger love than often falls to the lot of any man, either to have or to endure.

L.S.

Phila. June 5. 1872

Dearest Lucikin

I have done all I can to get our resolution through, but the prospect is not promising. The Committee on Resolutions contains about 40 members, one from each State and Territory. None of these were selected until yesterday PM, and several not until this morning; each State delegation having a right to name its man.

Dr Loring, true to his promise, got a name changed so as to give us a friend on the Committee—Coggeswell of Yarmouth. He has taken the resolution and will urge its adoption, but will not make a minority report in case he is out-voted, as he probably will be. I felt over-joyed when I found that Ex-Governor R B Hayes was the member of the Committee from Ohio. But though he greeted me very cordially and promised to have the resolution brought before the Committee, he said he was acting in a representative capacity, and that while he felt a personal sympathy with the object, he knew that his constituents did not and should not be in favor of putting it in. This has greatly disappointed me. I have seen some 15 or more of the Committee—only one bitterly opposed, and he from Rhode Island. But not one thoroughly prepared to fight for it, and most afraid of it. I have sent a brief note, enclosing copies of the resolution to each member of the Committee and asking each to urge its adoption. This is all that can be done. If the Committee do not report it, I am trying to get some one in the Convention to move its adoption, but doubt whether I can find a mover, and dont believe it will be carried if I should succeed in finding one.

Hayes asked me if I would rather have the Massachusetts resolution with the last clause left out than nothing. At first I said, "No, that if no allusion was made to suffrage, it would have no value." But on reflection, I said, "Anything is better than nothing, but in case the last clause is omitted, change the phraseology of what precedes."

To-morrow AM I shall know the fate of my attempt. I tried to persuade Gerrit Smith who is here in great glory and honor, to offer our resolution. He could probably carry it through. But he called on the New York member for me and urged him to support the resolution.

Miss Anthony is here in a very reasonable mood. She has ad-

dressed a letter to the President of the Convention asking for a recognition of Woman Suffrage. I dont know whether it will be read or
not. I attended a meeting of the Radical Club at E M Davis' office
during the recess of the Convention this PM. Miss Anthony brought
a letter to you from Mrs Stanton which I enclose, and am glad of
its kindly tone. I shall return to New York to-morrow night, and shall
take the Stonnington boat Friday P.M. . . .

H. B. Blackwell

Thanks to Henry's efforts, the Republican party adopted the
following resolution: "The Republican party is mindful of
its obligations to the loyal women of America for their noble devotion to the cause of freedom; their admission to
wider fields of usefulness is viewed with satisfaction; and the honest
demands of any class of citizens for additional rights should be treated
with respectful consideration." Since no specific commitment was
made to suffrage, the gain was slight, but as Henry put it, anything
was better than nothing. He and Lucy personally appealed to Miss
Anthony and Mrs. Stanton to join them in a united effort in support
of the Republicans. Disenchanted with Mrs. Woodhull, and also with
the Liberal Republican and Democratic candidacy of Horace Greeley,
who maintained that woman suffrage and free love were one and the
same, the two leaders agreed. Huge pro-Republican rallies were
staged in Boston, Worcester, and Springfield; prominent members of
both the American and the National went on the stump for Grant;
and in November Miss Anthony marched to the polls and voted for
him. As expected, she was prosecuted, tried, declared guilty, and
fined in what became one of the most famous cases in the annals of
the suffrage movement.

Throughout the summer and fall before the election, Henry did
his part by writing article after article in support of the Republicans
for the *Journal*, but even in the heat of the campaign, Santo Domingo
wasn't entirely forgotten. On September 10, 1872, Alice recorded in
her diary, "Papa brought out a Colonel Fabin, a gentleman with an

aquiline nose, gray curly hair, and a very pleasant smile." She was charmed by the suave promoter. "He is about the first man I ever saw who knows how to talk," she wrote. "His conversation actually wiled one away from the charms of 'A brave lady.' . . . He told about his camels and I shut the book and listened until he and Papa got upon the subject of consuls and politics."

Henry and Colonel Fabens had much to talk about besides the latter's camels. In a few months' time, a scheme which *The New York Times* called "the most ambitious of its kind in the commercial annals of the United States" would be unveiled before the general public. But for the plan to work, Henry still believed that annexation must come first. He wrote Orville Babcock to this effect; and in a lecture he gave in Boston on Santo Domingo, he argued that with this tropical territory in the possession of the United States, products such as cocoa, coffee, and sugar could be delivered in Boston "at a fraction of the cost," and that it was "a matter of philanthropy to reduce the price of the necessities of life."

But annexation or not, the other investors in the scheme were anxious to close the deal with the government of Santo Domingo. In late December commissioners of the Samana Bay Company, a joint-stock venture with a capital of $20 million, negotiated a ninety-nine-year lease of the peninsula at an annual rent of $150,000 in gold, with extensive rights and privileges. Among these were the right to engage in trade and manufacture; to build railroads and telegraph lines; to sell or lease real estate; to establish a bank; to buy, build, or charter ships; and to organize a police force. In short, the company was installed on the island as a sort of "republic within a republic." Colonel Fabens was to serve as governor of Samana, and Dr. Howe as resident director of this "model state," whose programs for charity, correction, and education were to be modeled after those of Massachusetts.

It seemed a highly promising enterprise; yet by the fall of 1873 the company was already in a precarious position. Not only were there stirrings of revolution on the island, but when a financial panic hit Wall Street in September, the company was hard pressed for funds to meet its next year's annual rent. Three of its commissioners went to England in an effort to negotiate a loan, while in the United States the company appealed to the Navy to lease from it the island

of Alerantado as a coaling station. It planned to use the money from
the lease to pay its annual rent, and also hoped that the presence of
a U.S. force at Samana would dampen revolutionary ardor on the
island. Henry went to Washington to try to persuade the government
to take action. Failing intervention by the U.S. government, he
seems to have considered the possibility of using private force to save
the situation, because in reply to a letter of his (unfortunately not
among his papers), Colonel Fabens wrote in December: "Your suggestion as to the shipment of arms doesn't strike me as practicable.
But it is a matter for consideration."

In the meantime, events moved toward a swift conclusion. By
the end of December a revolutionary junta had assumed power on
the island; the English loan fell through; the Navy failed to act on the
lease of the island of Alerantado; and citing nonpayment of rent, the
revolutionary government annulled the treaty with the Samana Bay
Company. Early in April of 1874 Dr. Howe was at Samana when the
Dominican government's sole warship entered the harbor, and its officers demanded the lowering of the American flag, and the departure
of all those connected with the company. In a letter published in *The
New York Times*, Howe called the Dominican government's action
"an unlawful act of robbery," and maintained that the company had
a claim on the U.S. government "for protection and retribution." But
in fact, the company had no such claim; it had entered into possession
of Samana at its own risk, and thus subsequent efforts to get the U.S.
government to take up the company's case were doomed to failure.

During this period the suffrage movement was having its own
troubles. The spirit of cooperation between the American and the
National hadn't lasted long, and beginning in the late fall of 1872, the
entire movement was shaken by a scandal involving three of its prin-
cipals—Henry Ward Beecher, Theodore Tilton, and Tilton's wife
Elizabeth. Two years before, Elizabeth Tilton had confessed to her
husband that she had had an affair with Beecher. Tilton had confided
in Mrs. Stanton, and she in turn had unwisely related the story to
Victoria Woodhull. When the latter found herself abandoned by her
former suffragist friends, she had no scruples about revealing the affair in her newspaper, *Woodhull and Claflin's Weekly*. The exposure
produced denials, charges, and countercharges from all involved.
Elizabeth Tilton finally left her husband, and he responded by suing

Beecher for alienation of his wife's affections. As the scandal dragged on, people all over the country took sides; within the suffrage ranks, the leaders of the National tended to believe in Beecher's guilt, while those of the American thought him innocent.

In the early stages of the scandal, the *Journal* expressed its "disgust at the unmanly conduct" of Theodore Tilton for standing by while his wife's reputation was sullied, and also published a letter from Beecher denying the charges. But on the whole, the paper maintained a policy of judicious silence. By the summer of 1874, however, its editors decided the time had come to take a more definite stand. In an article entitled "The Tilton-Woodhull Conspiracy," Henry called the scandal "a wicked attempt . . . by the advocates of free love to destroy the reputation of an estimable lady and an eminent Christian man"—who had been devoting his leisure time to writing a life of Christ. The *Journal* also published lengthy denials of the fresh charges made by Tilton from both his wife and Beecher, and a biting attack on Tilton's character from the usually ladylike pen of Julia Ward Howe, which was used in Beecher's defense at his trial before his own Plymouth Church.

To Lucy the greatest victim of the whole ugly affair was Elizabeth Tilton. As she editorialized on August 29, 1874, "Of all the persons in the sad scene which has been passing before our eyes, Mrs. Tilton seems to me to be wronged and injured more than any other, and at the same time to be the most innocent." She could not believe that a woman she had known for sixteen years, who appeared to love her husband deeply, whose "house was a model of neatness, good taste, and good order," and who "never gave her children over to servants," was capable of adultery. To even admit such a possibility was too threatening to her own notions of love and the sancitity of marriage. For as Alice later observed of her mother, she devoured romantic stories with all the enthusiasm of a girl of sixteen, but could never bear to read anything involving marital infidelity.

On a political level the aftershocks of the Beecher-Tilton affair coincided with a major woman suffrage referendum campaign in Michigan in the fall of 1874. Both the National and the American sent workers into the state, but it soon became apparent that because of the scandal and the continued association of suffrage with free love, the campaign was in serious trouble.

∽

March 30, 1874
At home

My dear Mrs. Campbell

I am very glad to see that the Ill. State Society have made you chairman of their Ex. Com. Glad, too, that you have got the right side of that crooked stick, Mrs. Swisshelm.

You will have hard work, but if anybody can bring that State into shape, you can.

The Journal shall help you all it can, and all reports of your work, will be very welcome.

Alice was out of school five weeks with bronchitis, & now she is out again with whooping cough. . . . We are to have a grand 4th of July meeting in the grove at Framingham, and have a subscription festival in May. There are committees that have both in charge, so that the burden does not come on us.

It seems as though we ought to make a great deal of capital from both of them. Our cause has a wider hearing today than it ever had. The women on the school board,—the Smith cows, Abby Foster's house—and last, the rum crusade [Prohibition], all call attention to the woman question, & have made new friends & workers for us. And it is high time. H.B.B. is so tired & overworked that I look every day to see him give out, & my rheumatic joints will lay me up effectually one of these days. You will be needed in Michigan, where the question will be voted on next Fall. I am afraid Susan will go there. Miss Eastman says she will go without fee or reward. Mr. Hudson of the Detroit Tribune has taken it up in earnest, wants tracts by the thousand, wants to have the whole state organized &c. I have written them your address. . . . If Mich. or Iowa should call, I think it more to help there, than in Ill., so I hope you will be ready, if there is need. I wish I were young. How I would work, but alas! the rheumatism stiffens all my joints, and my active days are over. . . .

With kind regards to your husband
Most cordially
Lucy Stone

June 13, 1874
At home

My dear Mrs. Campbell

I have your letters. Am glad you went to the Fort Wayne meeting, & that it was a good one. But they have *no cause* to say that we do not publish for them. We are only too glad to report all good work, & we have published a great deal for them. . . . I am ever so sorry about Mrs. Hazlett, Stanton & Michigan! It is a thousand pities that a great cause must be gibbeted by its friends. I see the Michigan papers criticize & blame Mrs. Stanton, but in one case, at least, she explained what she had really said, and that was well enough. But her attacks on the Republican party are making enemies, and there is no need of it. I was sorry when I found that Mrs. S. was to be in Michigan, for she is utterly indiscreet. But it seems to me that, in another way Mrs. Hazlett will do as much harm. Between the two, will *the cause* be ground to powder? I hope not, for if only one State will give suffrage, the rest cannot keep long behind. I was amazed at what you said about the pay of Mrs. Stanton. I read it after having that very day traveled about Boston to rich men, to raise money for Michigan, where I had promised to go for nothing. Somehow, it took away my courage for doing the disagreeable work. . . .

> With kindest regards to you all
> including the baby
> I am yours truly
> L. Stone

Boston, Thursday Sept 3 1874

Dearest Luciken

I send you by today's mail a lot of newspapers containing an a/c of Beecher's acquittal by Plymouth Church & Society—&c &c—We are all well. Emily proposes to go home by cars tomorrow. George will remain a little longer. . . . No news. . . . Several friends have written thanking you for your article on Mrs Tilton. It has been recopied by several papers. The Zion's Herald, & Commonwealth give complimentary notices of it. Mr Henry Wilson, Vice PS. [President] asked me to thank you for having written it. The Committee of Plymouth Church quote from Mrs Howe's editorial in their report acquitting Beecher. . . .

This Beecher-Tilton affair is playing the deuce with WS in Michigan. No chance of success this year I fancy! Well—the Lord reigns.

If you can let me know when you will return, I will meet you & will continue to send my own letters & papers till I hear but will retain your correspondence till I hear from you. Love to Alice & Kitty

Yours H B Blackwell

Boston, Sept. 8 1874

My dear Mrs. Field

I feel extremely desirous that some helping hand shall be given to Elisabeth Tilton so that she shall never get into the grip of Theodore.

She has no money, nor resource of any kind, so far as I know. And her heart, aching for her children, may yield again to the power of her old tormentor if something is not done for her.

I do not mean, charity, but that some plan may be made by which she can support herself, and at least, the younger children, & have them with her. I do not know what to advise, but I feel sure that *you*, with your noble band of coworkers, will know what to do to help her. She needs *occupation* to save her from utter misery.

Pray see her, and find something for her to do that will have a money value.

Tilton has no legal right to the children, since he disclaims being their father, but I fear he will give her all the trouble he can.

Is it asking too much, that you will let me know whether anything, and what, is being done for her?

If I were not overborne with work, and drained of money, I would go to see you about it.

But I hope plans are already made for the poor woman, and that she will come into them.

Very truly   Lucy Stone

Michigan's woman suffrage proposition was defeated, but as the Centennial approached and the territory of Colorado applied for statehood, Lucy and others hoped that the new state constitution would enfranchise women. She had originally advised women not to participate in the Centennial celebration in Philadelphia, arguing that it should be a time for mourning rather than rejoicing, since women were still governed without their consent and taxed without representation. Yet she later relented, and decided to take part. Her contribution to the Philadelphia Exposition was an exhibit of "Protests of Women against Taxation," which included her own refusal to pay taxes in Orange, New Jersey. However, her exhibit was hung so high that it was virtually impossible to read.

While Lucy worked on the arrangements for the American's meeting in Philadelphia, Henry and his brother Sam went to Cincinnati to push for the adoption of a prosuffrage plank at the Republican National Convention. He returned with another favorable but purposely vague resolution, and then in July he, Lucy, and Alice went to Philadelphia for the festivities. In August, Lucy corresponded with Mrs. Stanton about a history of the woman suffrage movement, for which she and Miss Anthony were busily gathering materials. Given the degree of distrust and dislike that remained between her and the other two women, her refusal to be very cooperative wasn't surprising. Yet it meant that the American's role in the suffrage movement was largely neglected in the book that was eventually published. Mrs. Stanton and Miss Anthony had originally planned to omit any mention of the American whatsoever, but when Mrs. Stanton's daughter Harriet insisted that it wouldn't look well to do so, they let her write a brief chapter on the development of the American.

⟨∼⟩

Boston, Jan. 5, 1876

My dear Mrs. Campbell:

I trust that the great plea made at the Convention on the 10th inst. will be for woman suffrage in the new Constitution of Colorado.

The Commissioners who are to frame it have the rare opportunity to achieve by peaceful means, what our Revolutionary fathers fought seven years to obtain. A hundred years are gone, and the people of the civilized world stop to pay special honor to the memory of men who declared that "taxation without representation is tyranny," that "the consent of the governed is the basis of a just government."

These two great principles wait to be applied to women.

If it was tyranny to tax the colonists a century ago, and deny them representation, it is tyranny to do the same to women now. If it was wrong then to govern men without their consent, it is wrong now, to govern women without their consent. No part of the new Constitution of Colorado in this Centennial year, can be more appropriate, or have more historic credit a hundred years hence, than that part which shall secure for women the right to a voice in making the laws they will be required to obey, and in the amount and use of the taxes they will have to pay.

The women of Colorado should not cease to remind the Commissioners of their high duty in this respect.

Ever truly yours
Lucy Stone

Cincinnati June 13/76
Tuesday Morning 8 AM
343 Race St

Dear Lucy

We reached Cincinnati somewhat dusty and hot at 5.30 AM yesterday (Monday) morning. We stayed in our sleeping car till after all the other passengers had left then washed & changed our clothes and went off to breakfast at a restaurant—after which we looked up lodgings in a quiet familys small house—where we have a room with two beds & breakfast for $1.25 per day. . . . We have met many old friends. . . . I have seen a number of the delegates & am pushing our "plank." I think the chances of *Hayes* are decidedly better than those of any other candidate as, in my judgment, neither Blaine nor Bristow can get the nomination in which case their supporters have

to combine forces against Conkling and Morton on a third man—&
Hayes is the second choice of most of the Blaine and Bristow men.

Yours affy & in haste
Henry B Blackwell

[Cincinnati] Friday 9 AM [June 16] 1876

Dear Lucy

The Convention prolongs itself. Yesterday on motion of Geo F.
Hoar, Mrs Spencer of Washington, DC, spoke for 5 minutes. She
was not heard but looked well & did no harm. She had previously
gone before the Platform Committee with a resolution which simply
affirmed that the right of suffrage *inheres* in all citizens. I begged her
to add "irrespective of sex" assuring her that unless that was done the
public would never dream that women were included. Lizzie Boynton Harbert was with her & agreed with me. Our resolution was
adopted except the last clause for which "respectful consideration"
was substituted. It looks as tho Blaine would be nominated, with
Hayes for Vice P. . . .

Tomorrow evening we shall start homeward & I hope to see you
tuesday morning. Till then, with love to all & agreeable observations
to my Cub, believe me, dear Lucy, as ever,

Yours,
Henry B Blackwell

At Home July 19-1876

My dear Mrs. Campbell

Mrs. Livermore was in our office day before yesterday. I had not
seen her before, since she returned from California. Among other
things she told me, she found you, tired and ill. I suppose it is the
result of your hard work, and anxiety. I do most sincerely hope the
rest of the summer will restore you. I would not do a bit of public
work. If God can wait for Colorado to be just to Women we can. At
any rate, so precious a life as yours must be saved to rejoice when

the victory is won. So take it easy this summer my dear Mrs. Campbell. Enjoy the white tips of the Mts. and the bold, beautiful views. It is terribly hot here. But we are hard at work all the same. After the meeting in Philadelphia, we staid a week, to see the Great Exposition. . . . It is a great sight to see, and there is a great deal to learn. But it was very hot, and the being on our feet all day made it very hard. The water did not agree with us, and Harry had diarrhea which became dysentery, after we reached home. He was very ill for a week but yesterday he went to the office for the first time, and is now about as well as ever. . . .

Nearly every body here has quartered for the summer by the sea, or in the mountains. But if we left the Journal would stop. The money for it, is shorter than usual, and we do not quite see how we are to get through the year. But I suppose we shall some way.

Every body seems to be short of money, but those who have any go to the Centennial with it. It seems a most shameful shame that this hundredth year of our national existence should find women, as we are politically, & legally. You will see by the Woman's Journal, what a cute thing Mrs. Stanton and Susan did on the 4th July. They told John Hutchinson that they "meant to go down to history with doings of the 4th July 1876"—and so they will. By the use of Lucretia Mott's name, they got the use of the church of Dr. Furness, and they made a really good meeting, and good will come of it. I have dreaded the effect of their presence in Philadelphia. But they seem to be on their good behavior. Give my regards to Mr. Campbell, and for yourself a great deal of love, and pray rest, and get strong dear Mrs. Campbell, and let all the work go.

Ever truly yours
Lucy Stone

Dorchester, Aug. 3, 1876

Mrs. Stanton

I have erased the closing line in the notice of the "Universal Encyclopedia" as it was not true. I have never lived in Kansas. I have nothing to add.

I do not add my name to the "Declaration" because, as I had

nothing to do with its presentation, it would be wrong to say so. I think it is an admirable paper and my only regret about it was the sensational manner of presenting it.

In regard to the History of the Woman's Rights Movement, I do not think it *can* be written by any one who is alive today. Your "wing" surely are not competent to write the history of "our wing," nor should we be of yours, even if we thought best to take the time while the war goes on; rations, recruits and all are to get as we go.

There will come a time when this greatest of all the world movements will have made history and *then* it can be written. I do not wish to have any hand in the present one.

The complete set of the Woman's Journal can be sent you for the purpose you desire, at three dollars a volume, The regular price is five dollars. Six volumes would cost eighteen dollars. Do you want them?

Lucy Stone

Gardner Tues. Aug. 22, 1876

Harry dear

I shall send my editorial by the 8 o'clock mail tomorrow morning. You will surely get it in the noon mail. I have called it "In the country." It is gossipy, and so easy to write. . . . The Herald article chalanges the Woman's Journal, but it does not seem to me that we are called upon to take notice of it. Especially after the articles of T.W.H. [Higginson] always explaining that we dont think women are better than men, or that their suffrage will bring the millennium. I should let it go utterly. . . .

It seems mean almost to be here in this quiet resting place, while you are tugging so hard elsewhere, but Alice is better for it, and so are all of us. . . . I am glad you had a quiet day. Sometimes one gets as much rest by the absence of others as by change of the place. I will answer Maria Mitchell and agree to speak suffrage for the Congress, and be glad of the chance. . . . I enclose a few scraps as news items. . . .

Ever aff.
L. S.

Boston, Aug. 30, 1876

Mrs. Stanton

Madam

Your postal card asking me for the number of Legislatures I have addressed on Woman's Rights and the dates of those addresses is received. I have never kept a diary, or any record of my work, and so am unable to furnish you the required dates.

I made my first speech in the pulpit of my brother, in Gardner, Mass., in 1847. I commenced my regular public work for Anti Slavery and Woman's Rights in 1848. I have continued it to the best of my ability ever since, except when the care of my child and the War prevented.

Mrs. Stanton

In your postal card you say "must be referred to" in the history you are writing. If you will publish the letter [above], it will be a sufficient reference. I cannot furnish a "biographical sketch" and trust you will not try to make one.

Yours with ceaseless regret that any "wing" of suffragists should attempt to write the history of the other.

Lucy Stone

Boston, Nov. 29, 1876

My dear Mrs. Hussey

Your letter is just at hand. We never had those photographs copied. It would have cost seven dollars a hundred and there were seven to copy, and we had no $49 to pay for them, when we were not *sure* we should get it back. It was too bad, for each face was proof of womanliness, even with the title L.L.D. [Doctor of Laws]. But we are always unable to do things just for lack of money.

The Congress, I think is doing its very best. It has made a great deal of progress. And there has been a great deal to contend with. They began, afraid to say the word suffrage. And in three years, they are ready to have a paper on that subject. Dont let us condemn, but give them time. . . .

As to joining the temperance workers, I cannot advise. To *me* the suffrage work seems so immeasurably above, and broader, lifting *all women* up to a plane where they can work for temperance, and every other good thing, at such infinite advantage over their present plane, that I grudge the taking of a straw's weight of help away from it. You have on your shoulders, the suffrage work, the Contagious Diseases Acts, and your family. If you add anything more wont you fail? . . . But you must judge. Miss Willard is coming on grandly. I rejoice in her every day. But dont let her take you from your moorings. . . .

I wonder if you could be responsible to raise $100 for the Journal for the next year? We *must* have help from somewhere, and the Orange and Newport people if you were to *ask* them might easily make up that sum.

Ever truly yours
Lucy Stone

The year 1877 found Henry embarked on a business venture with a reformist as well as a money-making motive behind it. Like his father before him, he hoped to make sugar from beets, and thus destroy the sugarcane market, and with it the continued existence of slavery in the West Indies. In February he went to Washington to obtain a patent for a method he had devised for manufacturing glucose, and in March, he made another trip to Santo Domingo. That fall he and Lucy went to Colorado, where the voters were to decide on woman suffrage in October. As in the Kansas campaign a decade earlier, they maintained an exhausting schedule, crisscrossing the state by stage coach, speaking in a different town each day, and having to endure rather primitive accommodations in some of the remote mining towns where they stopped for the night. And as in the Kansas campaign, woman suffrage was defeated by a three-to-one vote.

Not long after their return Henry went to Portland, Maine, to organize and manage the Maine Sugar Beet Company—an activity that kept him away from home for long periods throughout 1878 and

1879. Their daughter Alice was now a student at Boston University—one of two women among twenty-six men in the class of 1881—and Lucy's concern lest Alice and the other students be exposed to any immorality through their reading led her to write the president of the university about the Greek and Latin books in use. While a student at Oberlin years before, she had been active in the college's Female Reform Society, and now in middle age, she had lost none of her prudery. She supported Anthony Comstock in his antivice crusade and warned the *Journal*'s readers about the British actress Sarah Bernhardt, because she had had four children out of wedlock.

In the summer of 1879 Henry traveled to Europe to purchase sugar refining equipment in Germany. Ever since they were first married, he and Lucy had talked of a European trip, but now as Lucy's overpowering sense of duty to the cause kept her bound to Boston and the *Journal*, Alice went in her place.

Lucy, meanwhile, was embroiled in a controversy connected with her refusal to use her husband's name. In nearly twenty-five years of married life, her insistence on being called Lucy Stone had created certain difficulties. To avoid misunderstandings when she and Henry traveled together, she had to sign hotel registers as "Lucy Stone, wife of Henry B. Blackwell," and since most judges, lawyers, and other bureaucrats refused to accept her maiden name, she was forced to use this form in signing legal documents. The only administrative area where her use of her maiden name went unchallenged was that of taxes: The various states where she resided were perfectly willing to accept her tax money under whatever name she chose to use.

Although an important principle was involved in a wife's right to her name, Lucy did not publicly campaign for this right in the pages of the *Journal*, perhaps because she didn't want to hinder the cause of suffrage by linking it with another unpopular cause, and also because there were, in fact, no laws requiring wives to take their husbands' names. But if she thought that, in her case at least, the battle had already been won, she was proved wrong in the spring of 1879 when she tried to register to vote. In April Massachusetts passed a bill giving women the right to vote for members of the school committee. Lucy went to the assessor's office, paid the required two-dollar poll tax, and took her receipted bill to the board of registrars.

However, late in May she received a communication from the assessor's office to the effect that she must amend her application to be assessed because it had been made under the name of Lucy Stone, or she couldn't register. She wrote back to say "that my name *is* Lucy Stone, and nothing more. I have been called by it more than 60 years, and there is no doubt whatever about it. If the use of a foot- or cart-path 20 years gives the right of way, surely the use of a name three times 20 years should secure the right to its use. There is no law requiring a wife to take her husband's name." She was perfectly right on the last point, but this didn't prevent the board of registrars from extending its decision in her case to a general ruling made in August that "a married woman must vote bearing her husband's surname." Armed with this ruling, the board wrote to inform Lucy on November 25 that her registration as "Lucy Stone" had been annulled, and her name struck from the voting list. Only if she signed her name Lucy Blackwell would she be permitted to register. Lucy tried to circumvent the ruling by offering to use the form "Lucy Stone, wife of Henry B. Blackwell," but the Board promptly replied that her proposed form of registration was unacceptable.

The board's decision infuriated Henry as well as Lucy. Alice later said that she had never seen her father more indignant than on this occasion. He suggested that he and Alice go before the registrar and swear that they had known Lucy Stone for twenty years, and that that was her name. But aside from Lucy's written appeals first to the assessor's office, and then to the board of registrars, nothing was done. Although the controversy made the headlines in the Boston and New York papers, the *Journal* didn't enter into it, nor did Lucy take her case to the courts. She apparently felt that school suffrage wasn't worth the fuss—when Massachusetts extended municipal suffrage to women, then she might fight. Moreover, she was probably aware that she had little hope of winning her case should she take it to court. Public opinion remained strongly against a wife's using any name other than her husband's, and even though Lucy was admired for her suffrage work, her use of her maiden name was regarded as unfortunate. As the *Boston Post* editorialized: "We yield to no one in our respect for the lady who has labored with so much devotion . . . to break down the barriers which she has believed kept her sex from its full rights and privileges. . . . But . . . we hope there will be no change in the present custom by which the wife takes the name of her husband."

⌇⌇

Library of Congress, Washington, D.C.
Feb. 22. 1877

Dearest Lucy

I left New York night before last, at 9 PM and took sleeping car for Washington. At 7:30 AM I emerged, and having made my toilette, went to Platz' restaurant and breakfasted on six huge fried oysters which looked on the dish like six rolls, so long and large. While I was dressing in the sleeping car, I had a singular experience. I was shaving in front of a mirror facing it when to my surprise I saw in the glass close behind me, an old gentleman with profuse, bushy, grey hair. "What old fellow is that standing with his back to me, so close behind me?" I asked myself, and turned round when lo! he had disappeared. Nobody was there, but there was a long mirror, and I saw at once that I had seen, for the first time in my life the back of my own head and figure. It was a very queer sensation. . . .

At 9 AM I went to the White House and found that President Grant did not receive callers till after 10 and was advised not to come till 12. Then I called at the Patent Office and succeeded in explaining to the Commissioner my right to a patent hitherto denied me on my glucose invention. Called on Spofford at the Library & was very cordially rec^d by him—looked in on the "High Commission" engaged in hearing Senator Kelly orate on the Oregon Case. . . . Went back to the White House & found to my chagrin that Grant had given orders to admit no callers until Friday at 10 AM. However, with some difficulty I sent in my letters from Mrs Howe & Mr Ames, and in return received an invitation to call to-day at 11 AM.

Went again to the patent office and called on Mr Dwight, the librarian of the State Department to get some information relative to a Mr. Ramon S Williams, Assistant US Consul at Havana, who has taken passage on the Tybee and whose character and probable object I wanted, if possible, to ascertain. Back to the Capital & read "Han-

nah," a novel by the authoress of John Halifax till Spofford was ready
to go home to dinner at 6 PM. . . . We had a very pleasant little
family dinner party. I refused ale and wine, but drank infusion of
hops & malt followed by some preserved grape juice of a vinous flavor
mixed with water. At 8 PM Charlie [Spofford] entered the parlor
clad in a gorgeous tunic with tights and slippers and an elaborate
turban of many colored silk with an ostrich feather. He had a jatapan
or some other dangerous looking weapon at his side & was evidently
an Albanian Chieftain of Turkish proclivities. He announced sternly
that he was engaged to attend some kind of a masquerade in behalf
of the Women's Christian Association, in aid of the poor of Washington. Then Mr & Mrs Spofford made themselves grand & beautiful to
go to a reception given by Prof Henry of the Smithsonian—& I went
over to the Capitol & listened in the intervals of slumber, to the
interminable legal harangue of Judge Hoadley addressed to the unhappy High Commission. At 10 PM Hoadley dried up his torrent of
eloquence, the Commission adjourned till this AM & I went off to
bed and slept the sleep of the just.

This morning (Thursday) I visited the Patent office & completed
my business there, after which I called on the President. . . . General Grant received me cordially, asked a number of questions, and
wrote a cordial endorsement on the back of Ames' letter to him—so
that I shall go accredited by him. This was all I wanted & more than
I expected. It was done voluntarily & without any further solicitation
than the request contained in the letters. I then called on Gen O E
Babcock who gave me a very good letter to Baez and several practical
suggestions in reference to my plans. . . . In haste for mail—God
bless you wife & child

Ever yours affy
Henry B Blackwell

Puerta Plata Sunday AM
March 11 1877

Dearest Luciken

I wrote to you from Turks Island four or five days ago, and again
to Alice from Cape Hayti. We spent two days at the Cape. On the

second morning Captⁿ Hall & I went ashore after breakfast &, securing the services of a black boy as pilot went back into a ravine of the
huge mountain that towers above the town & ascended it till a small
stream in which the women were washing clothes, came tumbling
down the rocky gorge. Ascending this by clambering up the rocks,
we were forbidden by a voluble colored woman from the top of a
high bank above our heads to go any higher. There we bathed in a
rocky basin which formed a natural bath tub into which the water
poured from above & out of which it flowed down the steep rocks
into a larger basin below. The ravine was densely shaded by over-
hanging trees & vines. The air was deliciously cool & calm & the
silence was only broken by the fluttering & cries of some large bright
plumaged birds. I soaped myself all over from head to foot & then
plunged into the basin & had a most delicious bath, in the midst of
which I was somewhat disconcerted by being stormed at in mongrel
French by the unseen woman up on the bank, who evidently regarded us as invaders of her native land, taking an unwarrantable
liberty. However Capt Hall got out his pistol & laid it ready for use
on the rock beside our clothes in case of a Haitian invasion & we
plunged & splashed & scrubbed ourselves to our heart's content.
Then we strolled liesurely under the cool shade of ruined roofless
walls of concrete down into the market to buy oranges. The woman
asked us ten cents for four but Capt Hall undertook a negociation
which resulted in her giving us *ten* for ten cents—& doubtless she
got much more than their market value at that. . . .

Next day (yesterday) at noon we reached Puerto Plata & an-
chored off the green island on which stands the ruined fort which you
see in the picture in our parlor. The great mountain Isabella de Tores
towered above us and the little town (much improved since I was last
here) lay in a semicricle in front. . . . Prof Gabb came aboard &
greeted us. . . . Gabb is helping to build an extraordinary elevated
wire railroad designed by means of stationary engines to switch
freight & passengers over the mountains 3000 feet high from San-
tiago, 50 miles, suspended to the wire. The project seems perfectly
chimerical, but similar roads are said to exist in India. We walked
over the town & called at a beautiful cottage in the environs which
proved to be the residence of Prof Gabb. It overlooked the sea which
rolled in great breakers just below the house. Here we were hospit-

ably entertained with great goblets of cocoanut milk, poured from the green nuts whose ends were chopped off with a machete and then poured out—each nut giving about a pint of the pleasant slightly flavored water. We were much struck by the more intelligent friendly & polite manners of the people, in marked contrast with the semi-barbarous, brutal Haytians. . . .

I am struck with the self reliance & activity of the women here, but it is due in part to the laziness & shiftlessness of the men. I think I shall write an editorial entitled "Living on Women"—for this the men do very largely. In the market this morning only the meat was sold by the men—all the produce being brought in & sold by the women. I find that the Cubans settled here are not liked by the Dominicans & have not prospered. The "Gonzalez" party seem to have felt a spite towards them & many have left, frightened away by the "revolutions," tho I do not hear that any of them were killed. I fear this letter will prove very tedious to you, but I have little to write about, as the voyage is tedious. We learned yesterday with great satisfaction *via* St Thomas that Hayes was fairly inaugurated on the 4th inst. The first words I saw here, chalked up in the American Club house were "Hurrah for Hayes."

I am very well, but grow fearfully brown & my nose is fairly copper colored & the skin peeled by the sun. Love to my cub. I think of you and the cold March winds & hope that they will not cause a return of your rheumatism. . . . Once more—good bye. God bless you darling.

Ever affy yours
Henry B Blackwell

Office—Apr. 2 1877

Dearest

I have just come in, & found your most welcome letter. It is too bad that all the delay in arriving must take just so much longer time, before you can come home. First I will say, we are all well, all very busy, and the weather rainy, foggy, and disagreeable, now for several days. Family matters are much the same as when you left. . . .

The Suffrage Amendment passed the Senate, and comes today

into the House, where municipal suffrage was lost last Friday 83 to 127. The Senate agreed not to discuss it and pushed it to a third reading, and then a Mr. Sleeper moved to reconsider but it could not be done, and passed by a large vote. The support in the House on Municipal Suffrage was not feeble exactly, but it was not earnest, while the opposition a la Cenwell [?] "blew"! I shall send you papers to tell you the political and other news. . . . Chamberlain and Hampton are both in Washington holding forth their claims, while in N. Orleans Packard shows fight. Fred Douglass is appointed Marshall of D.C. with growls by many. There is not much stir in business. Now I shall have to stop here, to go to the State House, but I shall send this on that you may be sure to hear. . . .

May the Great Shepherd help ever and forever darling.

We shall be very glad to have you back, and all know the truth that it takes absence sometimes to make us know how much we love those who belong to us.

They would all send love, if they had a chance. Alice means to write.

Ever truly and affectionately your
Wife

Boston, Apr. 12 1877

My dear Mrs. Campbell

I suppose you are now snug and happy with your son, and his family. I hope you are resting, and that you will be well rested before the hard work for Colorado begins—

I wish I could rest too. I am so tired today, body and soul, it seems as though I should never feel fresh again. I have been trying to get advertisements for the Woman's Journal, to eke out its expenses. Yesterday I walked miles to picture stores, crockery stores, grocery stores, book stores, to soap stores, to "special sales" going up flight after flight of stairs, only to find the men out, or not ready to advertise, and for all my day's toil, I did not get a cent. And when I came home at night to find the house cold, the fire nearly out in the furnace, and none on the hearth, &c &c. it seemed as though the tired of a whole life came into my essence. I dont often complain, or feel like complaining. But I do wish there was some way of carrying on the Woman's Journal without such a hard constant tug—and if only the housekeeping would go on without so much looking after! . . .

    With kind regards to your son and his family and much love to you

I am L. Stone

Central—Colorado—Sept. 21 1877

Dear Alice

    I have been reading over your letters this morning and putting them against my cheek, for love of the fingers that lay along on the paper, as they traced the words. I wish I *knew* how your examination passed off though I feel *sure* you had no trouble. You ought to be congratulated, and Mr. Black too, on your success with the Anabasis and Homer. Is my little girl really a member of Boston University? And ready to go on four years more? I shall expect to hear in the next letter, as it was left to you, and to Dr. Emily to decide.

    Papa and I are having a week of meetings, which are only a few miles apart so we escape the long stage rides, that were a dreadful fatigue. We had to rise so early, that we had no appetite for breakfast, and then perhaps only reached the place where we were to speak, so late that there was barely time for supper. The last week I was so ill with diarrhea, that the discomfort of travel was aggravated [?] greatly. Papa has not climbed a single peak yet. But he longs to, and this morning when we stood on a path that looks up & down miles of bare rocky sides of mountains, with the poor little bare, low houses of miners, and others, stuck in the rocks, he said, "I would rather live here earning 2 or 3 thousand a year, than to live in Boston earning nothing." But I agree with a woman who rode with us, in the southern part of the state. She said "I'd rather be hung than live here." Papa likes variety and change, and that is why he *thinks* he could stay here. The air is cool, and the sky clear, and wonderfully blue. There are finer views too, than I ever saw elsewhere. But give me Pope's Hill.

    At the last place where we stopped to lecture before our return to Denver, there was no privy, no chamber vessell, no wash bowl, but a nasty table, at which we ate with miners, who put their knives into the butter, and who declared, that if women voted, they (foreigners) would leave the country. It seemed *so comfortable* to get back to the neat, snug, beautiful home of Dr. Avery at Denver, in Monday last. We are now West of Denver. Still among mines, and most wonderful mountains. But with comfortable quarters. Our noses are peeling, and we are tanned and brown. But both of us are well. We have to abstain from Water, which is full of alkali. I long for a good full drink. . . . This PM I speak at Black Hawk, where I failed to keep the appointment on account of illness, and tonight we both go to Nevada 2 miles from here.

> With much love
> Mamma

Sebago Lake [Maine] Apr. 30. 1878

Dearest Wife of Mine

If I could only spend the 23rd Anniversary of our wedding-day with you tomorrow, I would gladly assign ten per cent of my (prospective) profits in the beet-sugar business for the privilege. But it seems impossible to do so without injury to others as well as myself. So sentiment must yield to duty. Believe me, dear Lucy, I am *glad* and *only glad* of our having united our lives on the first of May 1855. If I were only as sure that you had been the gainer, as I, I should be still more happy. I know I have tried you in a thousand ways,—but most of all by not being able to show you the sincere good will I have had. If it had been necessary I would have *died* for you at any time, but it is far harder to live so as not to wound and grieve the heart that loves one. Neither you nor my Mother can fail to have found in me much to forgive, but I never can forgive myself. But one thing is true, I have never failed in my love for either. The beet-sugar matter will, I think, succeed. Everything is favorable except the shortage of time for getting the seed into the ground. We have as President of the Company, the best merchant in Portland, S. Hunt, the sugar refiner. We have got the best sugar-house in Maine for the 6 winter months, for about interest and taxes. This will insure good refined sugar and a good per centage. We have only four persons in interest, all efficient and needed. All now depends on making contracts for 600 acres of beets.

Give my love to my own dear little Cub. She ought to creep into your bed to-morrow and give you a hug. I will kiss you both 100 times in spirit tomorrow. God bless you, darling dee.

Ever yours
H. B. Blackwell

Boston Aug. 21, 1878

Rev. Dr. Warren
Dear Sir:

I know you will not regard as impertinent if I make a suggestion in regard to the Latin and Greek books used at the Boston University.

I am sure you will agree with me that any reading which will make a modest girl blush, or an impure boy giggle is not good for either of them. But this is inevitable from the books now in use. Oberlin College has expurgated editions of these classics, so they are fit to be used by students of both sexes, in each others presence. This was done as much in the interest of the boys as of the girls. It is a thousand pities that there should be a spot on the soul of either. I write therefore to ask if you will not communicate with Pres. James H. Fairchild of Oberlin, with a view to securing the cleaner editions for the pupils of Boston University.

Very respectfully
Lucy Stone

Portland, Oct 26 1878

Dearest Luciken

Excuse the epistolary neglect of a man who begins work every morning at 1 30 AM & has actually been unable till today to take time to shave or brush his teeth. We have now got things in splendid working order and are running through our 500 tons of beets at the rate of 60 tons per day. 20000 pounds of sugar already in the wagons. Next tuesday we shall make standard granulated sugar and have invited Governor Connor of Maine, Messrs Ames, Stuart, Palmer, and Sturdevant (the last four are all our stockholders) to come on tuesday morning to see the process. If I thought it would be any use, I would urge you & Alice to come too.

I think with regret of the load of the Journal so suddenly thrown on your shoulders. Bear it for one week longer & I will be back with unabated zeal and interest to take hold of your & my work on it & on the annual meeting. . . . Hoping soon to see you & that atrocious young woman who was formerly my Cub, I remain

> Yours affy & forever
> Henry B. Blackwell

Portland, Me. Oct. 28, 1878

[Telegram to Mrs. Lucy Stone, Boston, Mass.]

Beet sugar manufacture a success. Slavery in Cuba is doomed.

> Henry B. Blackwell

Boston, Mar. 4 1879

Dear Mrs. Robinson

I want to say to you, with entire kindness, but decidedly, that I must decline all, and any participation in the suffrage history which Mrs. Stanton and Susan Anthony are preparing.

I wrote this, at the very beginning, in answer to Mrs. Stanton's request that I would furnish facts of myself and of my work—and I wrote her the reasons why I should not.

I must therefore beg you not to mention the subject to me again. I am more than content to be left entirely out of any history those ladies may publish, of the suffrage work. Though I understand how natural it is that they should prefer to write their statement of their connexion with Geo. Francis Train, Mrs. Woodhull, Laura D. Fair, and the Mormons, and that they should be glad to get you, and other women, who had only regret for their action in combining with those persons, to appear with them in the history.

Very truly yours
Lucy Stone

Boston, Apr. 30 1879

Harry dear

I hope you get the line I left for you at the office. I was sorry not to see you to hear how you had succeeded in raising money, and also to beg you to read something that will help free your mind from the care of business, so that you can sleep. Be sure and do this Harry for your own sake and for ours.

You will get this on the 24th anniversary of our wedding day! How long a time we have jogged on pulling together! Well, the last part has been much the best to me. May it grow better and better for both of us till the end!

I have a card from Nette this morning saying she will be here today. So I suppose she will be around till after the May meetings. . . . This is all the news. It is still raining but everything looks fresh and green.

With much love
I am your *wife*.
L. S.

Portland, July 8 1879

Dearest Lucikin

With a real heart-ache I have engaged staterooms by telegraph on Batavia for next Saturday at 3 PM for myself & Alice. I never intended to go to Europe without you, & somehow I feel mean & grieved to leave you all alone in Boston with your (our) heavy load of cares, rheumatism & hot weather. "Old and lame and blind" will sound through my ears all the time I am gone, & tho you are not very old & may not be at all lame & certainly have much better eyes than my own—yet I shall worry about you till I return. I wish you *could* let old Bush take the WJ. & go along with your cub & your husband to see the places & people over the water! . . .

I shall try to get matters to a close here today & tomorrow, so as to return home tomorrow afternoon. Meanwhile I remain, in great haste, present or absent, alive or dead—now & ever—

Ever your own
Henry B. Blackwell

On Board "Gallia," 250 miles
from New York. Sep. 1, 1879

Dearest Lucikin

Here I am on the eve of my return to America and to you! We hope to reach the dock in New York by to-morrow afternoon, and my impulse is to rush back to Boston by the next train. But as one part of our machinery probably reached New York last week, and another part is due there, to-day, I suppose I must stay in New York long enough to see that it is not detained there by any informality at the Custom-house. . . .

I left Alice well. . . . My trip to Bristol with Anna was one of the strangest and most interesting of my life. It was very sad to wander as we did for three days like ghosts, among the scenes of our infancy knowing and known by nobody. We looked up, in some cases, the grand-children of people we remembered. Our memories were 50 years old. For Anna, like myself, had never gone back to Bristol after we left it in 1832. . . .

Ever your own
HBB

Boston, Nov. 26, 1879

My dear Harry

Tomorrow we shall eat our turkey without you. It is too bad. But also we shall not have Charley Spofford as he has gone to Washington, but some of the university girls will be out. . . . I have crowed too soon about my registration. The registrar has sent me a note to say it is "annulled" unless I write Blackwell after my name, which I shall never do.

I hope the sales of sugar and the sugar works are at their best, dear Harrykin. I feel sympathy with your hard work, and anxious care. But I do surely believe it will all come out right, and you will have established a new industry. Love to Sam.

L.S.

At home Friday
Dec. 12, 1879

Dearly Beloved

I have your letter telling me of your arrival and the spilled part of sugar, &c &c. I sympathize with it all Harry dear, and that is the only way I can help you, but of *it* you have abundance.

I suppose you have seen that not a woman was elected to the school committee of Boston. It is hardly possible to tell how it happened. The women put Lucretia Hale's name on *their* tickets in addition to the two names the Republicans gave them. Many Republicans were mad about that. And then there were so many tickets! But everywhere women were treated with regal courtesy, and this is quoted far and wide, and is worth a great deal. Alice went with Mrs. Neal early according to programme, and *voted for us all*. She is proud of her vote, and vexed about mine. I have not yet quite decided what is best for me to do about it. I rather think trial by newspaper is best. . . . Have you any underclothes to change? Some were washed here. I can send them if you need. Love to Sam and much to you.

I n the early spring of 1880 Lucy was finally forced to take a vacation. As she confessed to her good friend Mrs. Campbell: "The care of the different societies, and of the Journal, and of the house, so were upon even my strong health that when a hard cold came upon me, I could not throw it off, and *the accumulated tired* of years, left me a prey to pneumonia." She went first to New York for treatment by Dr. Emily Blackwell, and then south to Delaware, where Alice joined her. Henry was having his troubles with the beet sugar business, but managed to find time for a few activities in behalf of suffrage.

∽

Wednesday Mar. 4, 1880

Dearest Harry

I have today had your card, which went to East Orange, & today Emily says I must not go out at all for a few days. Yesterday I raised bloody chunks, and told E., but she said nothing. This morning I raised the same, and showed her one lump, and she says it is an attack of bronchitis. She has had a warm fire put in my sleeping room and I stay upstairs most of the time. Emily says it would have been better if I had come earlier. But I feel better today than I did yester day, when I had no appetite. She says I ought not to go back at present. I write you all this so you will know all. I inhale fumes of tar every little while, and hope to be well again soon. Emily has looked down my throat and listened to my breathing &c. I think of you many times a day dearest Harrykin and wish I could lighten your load, or put hope into your work. But how true it is, we have each to bear our burden. . . .

> With many kisses and much love
> Ever yours
> L. S.

Take good care of yourself. Dont overwork. It does not pay. Ellen has been showing me old family photographs, one of Aunt Lucy Issacs, and all interesting as family pictures taken years ago.

Monday Morning Boston 9 AM
March 15 1880

Dearest Luciken

. . . I have decided to stay & go to Mr Cook's party tonight, & do the best I can to advocate Woman Suffrage in your stead. I enclose two letters which will interest you, & mail a Harper's Weekly & Victoria Review just arrived. Miss Eva Channing writes an account of a debate in the "Landtag of Leipzig," where all but one were opposed to the recent innovation of admitting women as students to the U. of Leipzig, & the subject of future admissions was referred to the cultur-ministerium, who is opposed to admitting women. So, for the present, future applicants will be barred out, tho the ten who are now in will be allowed to finish their term. . . .

Every glimpse I get at the *filthy* crowd of cheap fare passengers on the st. [steamship] lines thence to Boston, warns me that republican institutions and extended Suffrage *are* on *trial* in this country & not yet an unqualified success. We need *something new* as an element in government. Woman suffrage would be so radical a change as to offer some hope of improvement. . . . If you find yourself ever so little worse telegraph me to Portland & I will come right on. I want you to lose your cough. . . .

Ever affectionately yours
H.B.B.

Portland, March 17th 1880

Dearest little Wife of mine

Your letter enclosing that of Lea Pusey, and your postal of 16th giving me the welcome news of your "steadily getting stronger" are rec[d]. . . . The Joseph Cook Conversation went off very well indeed. It was a funny affair. At 7 30 I found Mr & Mrs Cook and about a dozen people in the parlor & hall. At 8 [15] some sixty were closely packed into seats; ⅔ women. Around the edges about 20 men. Mr Higginson's despatch was read saying that illness in his family prevented his attendance. Mrs Howe, & Miss Eastman spoke well for suffrage—then Prof Gulliver spoke pretty well, against it—tho—in favor of co-education at Harvard Yale & even Andover. Mr Olcott & Ole Bull both spoke briefly in favor & Mr Seelye of Haverhill against. Mr Sewall & I spoke in favor. One or two spoke whose names I don't recall & then Mr Coffin (Carlton of the Boston Journal) spoke very heartily in favor. Miss Eastman, Mr Coffin & myself made the best speeches. Alice's Prof Bowne was called on, but said that "Mr Blackwell had so perfectly expressed his mind that he had nothing to add". At last Mr Cook said, in conclusion, that he was in favor of women's voting on the Temperance question & if they did as well on that as he hoped & believed, then he should be in favor of a constitutional amendment covering the whole ground. We adjourned at 11 PM & I took the 11 ^{15} train home & left for Portland next morning (tuesday). . . .

　　With love to all in New York.

　　I remain ever your own husband

HBB

Boston April 6 1880

Dear Lucy

　　I never made a queerer mistake than when, yesterday, I sent you all the enclosures which I designed to accompany my letter and left out my letter itself, or a large part of it. So I send it along today. . . . . I have nothing to add to my suggestions of yesterday. I think you have over-exerted yourself all your life—& must now turn over a new leaf. In two respects you have especially sinned of late against your health. By missing your regular noonday meals when in the city, & by breaking up the good & settled habit of your life, which has been to go to bed & to sleep at 9 ^{30} PM. By sitting up after others have gone to bed, you have curtailed your sleep, which is of all things the hardest to bear.

　　I think the extreme difficulty you find in writing is a reason why you should try my suggestion of *dictating* to an amanuensis (Alice, or myself, or someone else) what you would like to say on any subject. I know you think you could not do so. But you could, & if you would try it two or three times you would find that what would take you a solid hour to write, you could *speak* & have written by another hand

than your own in five minutes. But I must stop to go to the train—
& remain with love to the Kubbe—

Ever yours affy H B Blackwell

P.S. The weather here yesterday & today is bright & lovely. If we
were only sure it would last! Lavinia Goodell is dead. I have written
the best "In Memoriam" I could for the next week's Journal.

April 6, 1880
Dr. Heald's [Wilmington, Del.]

Dearly Beloved:

Your letter written from the office of the Woman's Journal Sunday at 11 reached me here Monday at 2 PM. It was almost like
seeing you, the time of writing and the time of receiving were so
near. . . . I wish I could help you darling, but the determination you
express to *get the beets* if it can be done, is the way to get them.
. . . I had a lovely walk yesterday along the Brandywine, which is
near here. All the woodland birds were at large, the fever bush in
full flower, the magnolias also. Alice gets frequent communication
from the girls at college, and goes on with her lessons with praise-
worthy persistence, while her care of me is a miracle of thoughtful-
ness. She *is* a good child. She enjoys herself, takes a hand at anything
that is going, croquet, logomachy, and walks off for long walks but
not in the evening. Give love to Sam. A young lady from Swarthmore, Miss Price, a niece of Dr. Heald came here yesterday, tired
out. She says I was at her father's just after she was born, when the
question of her name came up. She says I told her mother "Whatever
you call her dont make a ninny of her." They called her Lucy, & she
is not a ninny, but a nice bright girl. I wish she had been here before
for Alice's sake. . . .

L.S.

Wilmington Friday Apr 9, 1880

Best Beloved Darling Dee

. . . I feel well, eat with a good appetite, and sleep all night.
The hoarseness does not leave as fast as I hoped it would, but it only

needs time, and warm weather, and the last is sure to come, and so is the other too if I live. It seems to me much better that we should have the summer *together at home* where I long to get. Alice is well and bright; is at this moment studying Roman law. She develops a wonderful care of details, and general practical qualities which comfort me in regard to her future. . . .

I saw a "Massachusetts Suffrage Society" was formed to promote school suffrage. I suppose that must have been done by Abby May's Committee who has school suffrage in charge. It may be a good thing. But I think women would easily come to school suffrage without such a society—still everything helps.

It is discouraging how every state except Wisconsin has just come short of taking an advance step for women. The New York law is almost worse than none. N.J. and Iowa lost all they asked for, and I have not heard from Ohio where they were earnestly trying for school suffrage. Massachusetts crowned herself with added shame. Dear Lavinia Goodell! I am so sorry for her death! I had a letter from her while in N.Y. explaining why she did not write for the Journal. She said she was "flat on her back suffering from sciatica and rheumatism." I wrote her a comforting letter, and asked her to explain to me, or to let me know the exact action Wisconsin had taken. But I never heard from her & saw she went home to Janesville to die.

I wish there was some one to write articles, short ones, and a succession of them, for the newspapers on beet sugar and beets. Could not Mr. Hunt do that? Too much devolves on you else your ready, clear writing is better than that of anyone else. . . .

What a grand event the Channing centenneal makes! It will do good inducing many people to study for the first time the meaning of the works & life of Channing. The address of Wm. H. Channing yesterday and his "four corner stones" was characteristic. Change of place does not change the man. It would be well to find if he can speak at our May meeting.

If I knew you would be at home, on Sunday, I should send this there. But I have sent a card to Portland to tell you we are well . . . so if you go to Boston or stay at Portland you will know we are thriving. . . .

Ever truly
L.S.

Portland Monday Apl 12 /80
11 PM. Office just going home to bed.

Dearest Wife of Mine

The Beet Sugar business is likely to *die out* here for want of
Beets. Only 250 acres contracts & in four weeks there will be nothing
more to be done for a year to get more. Unless N Hampshire &
Canada help us out we shall be left without enough Beets to run a
month.

Sic transit gloria Beet Sugar Industry!

I neither worry nor grieve. I am doing all I can & it is beyond
my help. It is too late to raise price & there is no money in the Beets
at a higher price. Farmers have made up their minds that Beets wont
pay & the 250 who got $100 per acre cannot overcome the 750 who
got less or nothing.

I will write more fully when I have time. I enclose a short, cordial letter from Anna who seems ill & forlorn herself. Love to the
Cub. I am glad you are more comfortably situated.

Yours in haste *ever*

H B Blackwell

Schenectady, N.Y. Wednesday
April 21 1880

Dearest little wife of mine

I reached here day before yesterday, Monday night at midnight—& have been very busy getting acquainted & making arrangements for the meeting this afternoon. I find here a superb valley of
land capable of raising all the Sugar Beets needed, if the farmers once
get started in that direction. . . .

This valley with canal & railroads running its whole length would
be the very place for a factory of all I have ever seen. But for a man
of 55 whose heart is with his wife & child far away there is little
temptation to undertake it. All I can do is to pave the way for mean
& mercenary men to follow & make fortunes from the path I have
opened. They will never so much as thank me. This was my poor
father's fate. It must be mine.

No matter—the sun shines, the winds blow—the birds sing—&
next Saturday week I hope to be with you & Alice somewhere. . . .
Do not hurry home on my account. We will spend our silver wedding
day together at Wilmington, if it seem best. Only you must let me
know in time, so I shall start from Portland in season to be with you.

Ever affy yours
Henry B. Blackwell

L ucy returned home at the end of April, and was soon back
on the familiar treadmill of newspaper, home, and suffrage
work. In August, however, a bad sore throat forced her to go
to Gardner, Massachusetts, for a vacation of several weeks,
and the next spring she confessed to her friend Margaret Campbell
that she was suffering from a sense of faintness that made her feel as
if she were dissolving. Around the same time, she also admitted that
she did not think the American could continue much longer, because
"it is too much for Harry and me, to lift it bodily, as we have to." Yet
when certain members of the American sought a rapprochement with
the National, Lucy resisted the idea. "There was a deal of talk," she
wrote Margaret Campbell, "but none that made it seem to me any
more desirable than it ever was to unite with those who advocate
buying and selling votes, and going for any party that will go for
them." She was referring to what she considered to be the latest
outrage perpetrated by Miss Anthony—her public support of a New
York woman who had bribed voters in order to defeat a candidate for
the state legislature.

For his part, Henry was still preoccupied with beet sugar—"this
strange half crazy infatuation which has dragged me away from home
and happiness & comfort & peace of mind." When the business failed
in Maine for lack of enough beets, he reorganized the company and
moved it to Schenectady, New York, where it also failed. By the next
year his enthusiasm had shifted from beets to sorghum as a source of
sugar, and the grounds around their home were planted with this
grain.

But even at the height of his obsession with beet sugar, reform work wasn't entirely forgotten. In September of 1880 he made his customary appearance at the Republican state convention at Worcester to lobby for a prosuffrage resolution, and in the fall of 1882 he and Lucy traveled to Nebraska to take part in a suffrage-amendment campaign. Although they extended their stay from ten days, as originally planned, to more than a month, and spoke in twenty-five counties, the amendment was voted down. This new defeat brought a change in strategy: From then on Lucy and Henry decided that the American should concentrate on lobbying state legislatures rather than conducting mass campaigns among the general populace, who were usually less enlightened than their legislators.

Having graduated from Boston University the year before, Alice carried on the work of the *Journal* during her parents' absence in Nebraska, and when they returned, she was installed as one of the paper's three joint editors. In July of 1883 she was again left in charge of the paper when Henry, Lucy, and Antoinette Brown Blackwell journeyed to Ohio to speak at the Oberlin Jubilee. Years before, Lucy had not been allowed to read her graduation essay on the platform, because the college officials were opposed to public speaking for women. Yet now she was there as an honored guest, urging the college to support suffrage as it had education for women.

Boston, Sep. 16, 1880

Harry Dearest

I am very grateful to you for the constant effort, the patient faith and courage with which you do, single handed, year after year, try to secure political recognition for women. It is a shame you have no seconding. But among the pleasantest things we shall have to remember when we sit, an old couple, by our snug hearthstone, will be this very part you have taken in the interest of political justice for women. Distasteful and hard as it now seems, then, the end accomplished, it will look very different.

I mean to write to Mr. Chadbourne. The arrogance and falsehood of his speech ought to be rebuked. He says the people of the

United States are once more called upon to decide who shall control the affairs of this nation, for the next four years. Further on he says still worse and then when you try to get a bit of recognition not he or any man of the Convention seconds you! Well, shame on them all. But it is a long road that has no turning.

Ever yours
Lucy Stone

[Worcester, Mass.] Sept 17 1880

Dearest Luciken

Your letter of 16th has just reached me & is very welcome. Believe me, dearest, the approval & sympathy you offer me compensate me a thousandfold for all the annoyances of being voted down in a good cause.

It is a question about which I have some doubt, whether it is really *best* to push the matter quite so far as I did in Worcester. To urge a resolution on the Committee was well. To offer it in the Convention & have it referred to the Committee was, I think, well. But to attempt, without cooperation & backing, to add it to the platform as an amendment is to incur certain defeat, & the absence of support and backing prevents our having the prestige of a real struggle. To get up alone, *simply* to be so easily knocked down by a five minutes speech of Col Codman, is in a certain sense to belittle the cause itself. There were Dawes & Beard, & Claflin & [George Bailey] Loring & Frank P Goulding & twenty other Suffragists present, but not a word of support & perhaps not a vote of support either! I saw Higginson's name among the list of delegates, but did not see him in the Convention. He was probably there.

Mr Faxon, who is vain & noisy, does one a little discredit by offering wild resolutions & inane speeches for Prohibition. But I was indebted to him for my substitute ticket to represent Nantucket. However no harm was done, perhaps good.

I shall be home tomorrow night some time. . . . Dont worry or work very much on the paper. I can get it up on Sundays, if you will put the *manuscripts* all in one place for me.

Yrs ever
H B Blackwell

Wisner Neb.
Sunday PM
Sept 24/82

Dear Alicekin

I would give $100 if you could have gone with Mamma & me
over this wonderful wild new country with its chaotic, mixed population from every state in the Union & every nationality in Europe.
The people are a perpetual joke. They are just like grown up children—indeed they are mostly about your age. We dont see a grey-
haired man or woman in a whole day! Young men & women with
hosts of children. Everything is jolly. The graveyards have no graves
in them. The sun *shines all day every day*, & the rolling prairies &
valley plains fairly *shine*. At night the air turns suddenly cold, as tho
the world had thrown off its bed-clothes. The air is so dry that it
seems impossible to catch cold. The sky is softer in its blue & in its
clouds than with us—fleecy, gauzy clouds. One never tires of the
rolling prairies with their beautiful curved outlines—gay with sun-
flowers & rich with great cornfields & sorghum patches. The yellow
plains & hills are dotted with great herds of cattle & sheep. Every
farm has its own grove of silver poplars, or cottonwood trees in long
rows planted along the roads. You see for miles & miles the valley-
plains studded with immense hay ricks. The weeds grow by the road-
side twice as high as your head—& the dust rises as you drive along
as fine as flour. Not a stone nor a grain of gravel in a hundred miles.
People living in shanties mostly—some in good frame houses—some
in dug-outs. The wind blows fresh & soft, & almost every house has
its wind-mill to pump water to the stock.

Between ourselves—there is no more hope of carrying woman
suffrage in Nebraska than of the millennium coming next year. Both
parties have avoided it. The republicans refused to endorse it day
before yesterday in their state convention. I had not been in Omaha
48 hours before I saw how the matter stood, but as we dont want to
discourage the workers, we keep our opinions to ourselves & talk and
work as if we expected to win. But the prospect is not nearly so good
as it was in Kansas in 1869. I am confirmed in my opinion that we
shall have to get what we can from the State legislatures· *by statute*
without going *down* to the masses—to be beat.

Dont publish my predictions as to Nebraska. I count the days till we can return to relieve you from your cares. God bless you Kubbe— We hope to be home about Oct 5 or 6.

HBB

Mama's throat is relieved by this dry air. She is *unusually* well.

Wisner Nebraska
Sunday Sept 24 1882

My dear child

Our last letter from you was dated Sept 12th. So you see it is very long since we have heard, and of course we are anxious to hear. I sent you a list of the places at which we should be there—on Friday Sept 15th. . . .

In my last I asked you to get Mr. Bush if you found yourself overburdened. I should not be in the least anxious if you had not been tired before we left. As it is, I wish I knew how you are. We are well, Papa is as good as new and as full of food as he can hold. He improvised a ride 16 miles across the country to this place, where we had no meetings appointed, for the sake of the ride, across lots, to enable us to see the country as we do not see it on the cars He is out now to post bills that give the notice of our meeting into every house. We have the M.E. [Methodist Episcopal] Church, and on this short notice less than half a day, we dont expect a good audience. But we came across the country, which was beautiful. But the dust poured in on us, and when we got here, we were black with dust. I *never saw such dust*. It is everywhere, and there is no rain, so it flies on the least provocation. We have good audiences, but in this country the foreign population is 9/10 of the whole, and there is not a ghost of a chance to carry the amendment and that too, on account of the Germans, Bohemians, & Irish, and Scandinavians who will all vote against it. We would not have staid if we had known how it was. But all the same we do our best. We tell the truth, scatter leaflets, and collect the names of friends for the use of the Nebraska society—and leave the good seed to grow.

I came along in the cars yesterday with a young woman who told me she was 31 years old, had had 9 children—5 were dead. She lived in a dugout and said she had had "an awful hard time." But a good husband who did all he could to help her—but she could not get help, and was killed with work. That is the story so many women tell. Lots of them live in hotels with their children, because they cannot get help, and they have a hard time. I shall be glad when we set our faces homeward. . . .

Mamma

Boston, Nov. 7, 1882

My dear little Kubbe
    Soul of my Soul.

    Today is the eventful day for Nebraska and for women. I am anxious to know, but I dread to hear the result.

    As usual, I carried Papa down to vote. My political superiors were standing around quietly. Some smoking, some talking. One fellow said he was waiting to get five dollars for his vote. A ticket was passed to Papa who took it with a polite bow. It was a Butler ticket. People came and went—male people. Our Irish fellow citizens lingered around the polls. At last I asked for a ticket, which was promptly handed to me. I said, "Is it not rather hard that I, who live in this ward, own property, pay taxes, and am an orderly citizen cannot vote?" "But you can vote on School." "Yes," I said, "but why should I not vote this ticket." "Did you ever ask for it?" said he. "Oh, yes many times." "But it has never been brought to the polls?" "No, the Democrats put it in their platform this year." "Only promises, I suppose," said he. Then Papa came and we left.

Mamma

Chardon, Ohio
June 24 1883

Dear Alicekin
    It is Sunday noon. We are staying at the comfortable, one story home of Mr. and Mrs. Farr. They and the grandmother and two

young lady boarders are all at church, and your mother and I have a delightful hour of quiet, which is rare during the interminable "visiting round" which is unavoidable in this lecture routine. We had been looking forward to hearing from you on our arrival here, but hope that "no news is good news." We have not had a line from you since we left home a week ago to-day. It is probably our own fault for not letting you know our whereabouts in time. I am glad you did not come with us so far, for you would have found it *dull*. We have a kind reception and good meetings, but the "hanging round" meanwhile is tedious. I have been lucky in getting George's "Poverty and Progress," which I peg away at from time to time. It is a somewhat dry book, but contains much instructive suggestion. Your Mother's throat is better and she does not seem to suffer from the exertion of speaking. Your Aunt Nette is *one too many*, and we all have to curtail our speeches. But to-night Nette has the Congregational Church and is to preach, while Lucy and I are to do the same to the "Disciples" or "Campbellites," who are a numerous body in the West.

It is my impression (entre nous) that I shall be the worst-bored man at Oberlin who ever visited it at a Commencement. One day I could stand; yea two;—but a whole week of contact with people who believe in hell and also mention the devil will, I fear, be too much of these good things for a person of impaired spiritual digestion like myself. I shall try to get up a scrimmage if I can; if not, I shall quietly prepare an essay to disprove the existence of a Deity, *so as to keep my balance even*. Good bye—wretched cub. Keep a sharp eye out for a nice young man—take things easy—let Miss Wilde help you all you can & believe me the

Old Harry

T he year 1884 brought another presidential campaign, and with it a bitter controversy between Lucy and one of her oldest friends: Thomas Wentworth Higginson, the minister who had married the Stone-Blackwells, who had helped to found the American Woman Suffrage Association, and who for fifteen years had served as an associate editor of the *Journal*. Soured by the tarnished political record of the Republican candidate, James G.

Blaine, Higginson and a number of other Republicans gave their support to the Democratic nominee, Grover Cleveland. But when it was revealed that Cleveland had fathered an illegitimate child while a young bachelor, Lucy and other suffragists turned against him. To them he was a despoiler of innocent female virtue, and therefore morally unfit to serve as President. As Lucy wrote in *The Woman's Journal:* "Women must be opposed at all cost, to that which is the destruction of the home. They know with an unerring instinct that the purity and safety of the home means purity and safety to the State and Nation." Higginson countered with the argument that public virtue was more important than private, and even suggested that both sexes bore equal responsibility for lapses of this kind. The controversy between Lucy and Higginson over Cleveland filled the pages of the *Journal* until election time. Henry kept silent during most of it, waiting until the day before the election to acknowledge his continued support of the Republican party. But the damage was done: After the election Higginson resigned from the *Journal*.

Undaunted by his defection, Lucy continued to crusade against all who threatened "the purity and safety of the home." She wrote a state legislator urging stronger penalties in rape cases, and worked to get the "age of consent" raised in Massachusetts. Yet suffrage remained her primary concern. She took an active part in the fight for municipal suffrage in Boston, and in the fall of 1885 she and Henry embarked on a lecture tour of Indiana, Michigan, and Minnesota. That year, too, Lucy met Susan B. Anthony on a personal basis for the first time in a number of years, when she came to Boston to collect her share of a bequest made to both of them by Eliza Eddy, the daughter of Lucy's old abolitionist friend, Francis Jackson. However, the meeting scarcely improved relations between them. Although Lucy had invited Miss Anthony to spend the day with her, the latter was determined to make the visit as brief as possible. After receiving her part of the legacy, Miss Anthony immediately departed with over two thousand dollars in stocks, bonds, and securities sewn into a pocket of her petticoat.

In the spring of 1886 Henry went to Washington to urge Congress to establish equal suffrage in the territories. Since women had been enfranchised in three territories (Wyoming in 1869, Utah in 1870, and Washington in 1883), he could point to the specific good results of suffrage in those places. Otherwise, the general argument he, Lucy, and most other suffragists advanced in favor of woman suffrage was undergoing a significant change. Whereas previously they had claimed the vote because all human beings, male and female, were equal, now they were beginning to claim it because all human beings, native and foreign-born, white and black, weren't equal, and the inferior class shouldn't be allowed to rule over their superiors.

From the mid-1880s onward, the huge influx of non-English-speaking immigrants into the cities of the North aroused deep-seated fears on the part of the older, predominantly Anglo-Saxon segment of the population. Coming from native stock themselves, most suffragists shared these fears and used them in their arguments for the vote. They cited statistics showing that there were more native-born women than foreign-born men and women, and urged woman's enfranchisement as a means of combating the "foreign menace."

A similar rationale for woman suffrage was used in the South, where Southerners feared the black vote. Henry had been one of the first to utilize statistics showing that there were more white women than black men and women combined, and as the century wore on and Reconstruction was followed by a Southern backlash, his argument was given wide currency. In their fear of the black vote Southern suffragists found a common ground with Northern suffragists, who feared the immigrant vote. Eventually the discovery of this common ground would transform what had begun as a Northern offshoot of the abolitionist crusade into a national movement uniting Northerners and Southerners. The beginnings of this transformation were already apparent. Thus in Mobile, Alabama, Henry urged woman suffrage on an educational qualification "as the only cure for the evils of ignorant voting," while in Boston, Lucy argued "that the votes of women are needed to add to those of the better class. . . . to save this dear old city from going to the bad!"

⚬⚬⚬

Boston, Nov. 28 1884

My dear Mrs. Hussey

Your letter with the check for $25. reached me safely, for which accept my thanks. . . . I wish very much that there *could* be a conference of suffragists. We need to plan and consider what course to pursue, or how to take advantage of what we have gained. Mr. Higginson has sent us a short note saying that he should resign his connection with the Woman's Journal at the close of this year. He gave no reason, and the note was very brief. This was followed very soon by another, asking not to re elect him a vice president of the American suffrage ass. & he gave no reason. I am told that he is to write for Harpers Bazar hereafter. He has always been paid $600 a year— $50 each month. This he has never failed to get when the Journal was so poor that H.B.B. & I gave all our time for nine years without a cent of compensation. We shall save the $600, but we shall miss his good articles, (and the bad ones too), and some subscribers who say they only took the Journal for his articles. But the cause grows and flourishes, and it will continue to do so no matter who falls out. We had *excellent* meetings at Chicago and there were so many bright young western women, able, and good that it did my heart good. They will carry the cause on, when the old ones worn out, fall by the way. . . .

Yours truly always
Lucy Stone

I want to thank you for your offer to make good the six subscribers who stopped their Journal on account of the ground we took about Cleveland. Some have stopped for the side *we* took and some for the side T.W.H. took, but not many of either. We had ever so many letters and articles on both sides, bitter, and personal. We quietly put them in the waste basket. T.W.H. will never know the service we rendered him in that way. So many were *mad* with him. Rev. Mr. Gilbert at Chicago told us that Judge Thacher had a friend whose own niece was seduced and ruined by Cleveland. Mr. Ball says he is a gross sensualist "preying wherever he can find prey." Think of it, a male prostitute in the White House, & no woman a voter!!

Boston, Dec. 18, 1884

Dear Col. Higginson

As the time draws near when we shall not see every week the well-known initials, I trust we shall all remember on how many of our respective articles we have all agreed, and on how few we have differed in this long pull for an unpopular reform, and "something must be pardoned to the spirit of liberty."

No difference that has occurred makes the least difference in my feeling toward you. No one will give you more cordial good wishes that I shall always, nor more sincerely wish success to you and to all yours, as I do now.

Lucy Stone

Boston, Feb 11 1885

Dear Mr. [James Freeman] Clarke

The suffrage "hearing" in the green room is to come at 10 o'clock on Tuesday next. The remonstrants are to have theirs, the next day, Wednesday at the same hour and place. The committee *say* we may have an hour to reply to remonstrants. They said that also last year, and then they only gave us five minutes.

We should be glad to have you both days. I mean at our hearing, and at that of the remonstrants. *They* would feel *your* reply, more than they would anything that could come from any of us.

Can you not make a special service for your congregation and speak to them of the importance of municipal suffrage for woman *for the sake of the public welfare*, now when the need of reform is so evident. It is easy to see how the power is going into the hands of the least valuable class, and that the votes of women are needed to add to those of the better class.

There are 14,000 majority of native born American women over the foreign born who can not read and write. They pay taxes in millions of dollars. Their large property and personal interest necessarily puts them on the side of good order and decency [?]. What a thousand pities it is not to use this power which is right at hand to save this dear old city from going to the bad!

If people only saw it, they would act upon it. Do speak to your people about it.—The poll tax should be a dollar. The opposition of the priests would keep away the class of women who might endanger us, & for the time, we should be safe.

Yours truly
Lucy Stone

Mobile, Ala. Apl 5, 1885

Dearest Lucikin & Kub

It is Sunday evening. I have had a very delightful day, & made some pleasant friends. Arriving here about 4 AM this morning, I went to bed & slept until 8 AM—then breakfasted & took a steamboat at 9 AM for *Point Clear*—a beautiful point 18 miles below the city on Mobile Bay where it opens out into the Gulf of Mexico. . . . There were only about a dozen passengers, but they were leading business men of Mobile & their families—a fine young lawyer named Chamberlain & the proprietor of the hotel on the point, &c. I soon became acquainted with them all & was welcomed very hospitably. After going over the large hotel buildings with (literally) ¼ mile of piazzas, & accommodations for 700 guests, I was invited to ride with the owners of the property & Mr Chamberlain. . . . By talking with these people together, & then with one at a time, I became quite well acquainted. . . . Mr Chamberlain pleased me most. He is a native of Mobile, graduated at Columbia College Law School in New York, practiced law two years in Denver, suffered so much from rheumatism (tho he looked the picture of health) that he has returned & is practicing law here. . . . Mr Chamberlain is a democrat about as independent as I am a republican, & much to my surprize extended his hearty approval of my suggestion of the need of woman suffrage on an *educational* qualification as the only cure for the evils of ignorant voting. Like everybody I meet, he speaks of their present with profound dissatisfaction, & of the political future with anxiety. He says he fully believes in the abstract idea of human equality & right of participation in government, but says that they are in a terrible dilemma from the sudden influx of sheer barbarism & ignorance which they have to contend with. He frankly admits that the South is solid largely from force & fraud in many localities, & that this is *wrong*—but evidently feels it to be inevitable to prevent absolute chaos & ruin.

I fully believe that in the present state of Southern opinion, if the subject of Woman Suffrage on an *educational* qualification were properly presented in the Legislatures & the press it would get a considerable sympathy & attention. But it is perfectly clear that a demand for woman suffrage on the general basis accorded to men

would not be listened to for a moment. For to add the still greater
ignorance of the poor white & black *women* to that of the *men*, while
the men's votes are coerced on the ground of their utter incompe-
tency would seem to them simple *insanity*. But men here are far
more liberal than I imagined. They freely admit that in the North the
Republicans are "the better element" & do not relish their Northern
democratic associates very well. . . .

On my return to Mobile this afternoon, I got on board an extraordinary open horse-car propelled pell-mell at a gallop by a pair of
unhappy little mules, 2½ miles into the suburbs, & then walked back
along the "shell road" making a most Websterian speech on the subject of an imaginary new "peoples' party" with "woman suffrage on an
educational qualification" as its cornerstone. What think you of trying
to enlist the Nationals & SBA. with the American W.S.A. on the
basis of a *modified* demand for W.S. on an educational basis—instead
of on the "same terms as men"? It seems to me that inasmuch as
suffrage means governing *others* as well as helping govern
ourselves,—society has a right to prescribe such reasonable limita-
tions (not insurmountable in their character) as will afford some evidence of acquired fitness for the intelligent fulfillment of the duty. I
do believe that a journey through the South, as things now stand,
would impress you & Alice with the *need* of limiting the demand in
some way. It is difficult in the North to overcome the scepticism
which the abuses of suffrage generate. But in the South I think it will
be for our lifetimes *hopeless* to do so. The ignorant *men* who now
vote will not consent to any curtailment which shuts them out, but
they might consent to let in the educated women & then the educated men & women together as voters might be able to bring about
a restriction if necessary.

Tell Alice that Mr Chamberlain apparently agrees with her in his
estimate of the editor of the *Register*, whom he considers an unscru-
pulous partisan, unfair in his spirit & methods. I enclose a magnolia
leaf. The tree is very imposing with its dense clusters of these shining
leaves—four in number with the flower-bud in the center.

Ever yours
H.B.B.

Warsaw Indiana Oct. 27 85

Dear little Alicekin

This is Friday morning. You are up at the printing office probably, and busy with the proofs. . . . We found a lot of women here,
who had never heard a suffrage speech. They had written to ask, that
there might be a meeting here. One bright woman brought her 4
months old boy, and said, she dedicated him that day to the suffrage
cause, and as she nursed him from her own breast, he will probably
drink in all his mothers spirit.

I am not at the meeting this morning which is to organize only,
and I stay to write instead. We are both well, and papa speaks with
his easy grace and his good logic convinces. But between times he is
trying to organize a sorghum co. to work in Des Moines where a
disused glucose factory, is all ready for sorghum. He is planning to
engage Mrs. Campbell to engage farmers to raise sorghum, and at
every point where we stop long enough he writes letters. . . .

Everybody has sent their love to you. Mrs. Campbell, Mrs. Ripley, whom you know, and others whom you do not know. They praise
your editorials and rejoice that my daughter is on the suffrage side.
Mrs. Ripley got up a little surprise party just before I left (Papa had
gone to Des Moines for sorghum). She invited the friends, Prof.
Clarke to sing, and presented me with a lovely basket of flowers, a
knot of long streaming ribbons red, white, and blue with my name
painted on the white in graceful spray, on the red was "Minnesota,"
on the blue was "woman suffrage." It came with a speech from Mrs.
Ripley & Mrs. Duniway—and then Miss Isaacs of Walla Walla presented me a lovely bronze lamp or candle stick with a bronze bay leaf
at the side. She too made a neat speech, to all which I responded as
well as I could, and then, after a song I hurried to the cars where
Mrs. Ripley gave me a tearful good by. . . . We wished for you,
when we saw the strange new sights along the Mississippi at St. Paul
and at Minnehaha at the great flour mills &c. . . . this country is all
flat, it is still green, and the autumn colors are bright. We found
leaflets here, but not Journals. They are to be hunted for. . . . With
much love to all little & big at Dorchester, and at No. 5.

I am always Mamma

[Boston] Jan. 10, 1886

Dear Nette

I was glad to get a sight of your old familiar hand. . . . As to meeting Mrs. Stanton it is out of the question with me. She sent a letter to Mr. Shattuck of this city, which he read to a little group, of which I was one, in which she said I was "the biggest liar and hypocrite she had ever seen." After that, you will see that I cannot with any self respect meet her with a pretence of good fellowship. For yourself, of course, such a letter about me need make no difference. Mrs. Stanton is as bright and as witty as ever, and Susan just as egotistical. When Susan came here to get her share of the Eddy fund, I invited her to come and spend the day with us. I gave her a time table, and told her I would meet her at any train, if she would let me know. Instead, she sent me a hateful note, that made me feel the last plank between us had broken. I am too busy with the work that remains, to take time to mend broken cisterns.

We were glad of the letter of Grace lately received, and to see that she still goes on with her painting. Agnes too gives us family glimpses. Alice is taking a little outing in Providence with Mrs. Elizabeth B. Chace, and with some of her old schoolmates. . . .

> With love to all, and always
> with warm remembrance
> Every affy
> L.S.

Boston, Mar. 2, 1886

Dr. Gleason
Dear Sir

I sent to the State House for the bill you had in hand for the punishment of rape. I find it is not at all the bill that I thought it was. I find the words *"any* term of years" a door for the smallest punishment, which in view of increasing atrocities perpretrated upon girls and women seems to me utterly wrong. There *ought* to be a punishment that will deter. But there is need of a statute to raise the "age of consent" from ten, where it now is, so that a minor girl may have the same protection for her person that she does for her property. She cannot dispose of her property till she is of age. She should not be permitted to dispose of her honor any earlier than she is permitted to dispose of her property. Every one must see that this is so. We, i.e. many women who are mothers talked it over, and decided that it was best to get the age of consent raised without having any public mention made of it, in the quietest way possible. I do not know the proper committee to attend to this.

Will you kindly let me know whether anything has been done about this, and if not, how it may still be done, and who is the chairman of the proper committee?

The question should be of common interest to men and women.

Respectfully
Lucy Stone

Washington DC March 20/86

Dearest Luciken

I have been so busy & preoccupied that I neglected to write you of my goings on & last night sent a brief despatch to say that all is well. When Miss Shaw & I reached NY on Thursday morning we had just time to take the 8 AM train from foot of Courtlandt St. & reached Washington at 2^{30}. I sent Miss Shaw to the Riggs House & myself went to the Capitol where Mr Spofford soon introduced me to the delegate from Wyoming Judge Carey, a very straight forward, manly fellow, who promised to come to the hearing & testify to the good results of WS in Wyoming Ty. Mr Voorhees the delegate from Washington Ty was cordial but did not approve of forcing Woman Suffrage on any Territories. He thought the people of the Terys & their legislatures had too little control of their local affairs now, & that no interference was desirable. So I was glad, altho he is a strong friend of Woman Suffrage that another engagement prevented his attendance. I called on Mr Caine the delegate from Utah who said he should come to the hearing, but did not think it best to take any part in it. He says there were 42000 voters in Utah; that 12000 are cut off because, now or at some previous time, they have been living in plural marriage—30000 are left—½ men, ½ women—4/5 of the men who now vote—men like himself who have never married more than one wife—are Mormons. Therefore the Mormon supremacy will not be affected by the disenfranchisement of women. But the Mormons stand by woman suffrage, and desire it retained. I returned to the Riggs House after lunching with Mr Spofford. . . . & after tea called on Gov Long & Rep Tom Reed of Maine. Both greeted me very cordially & Long promised to come to the hearing & speak for us. I sent a note next morning to Senator Hoar by Mr Spofford.

At 10 AM Miss Shaw & I were at the Com Room where we found about 25 ladies and half a dozen gentlemen awaiting the advent of the Com. Mr Hill came first then other members till about 10^{45} nine of the 15 had gathered. . . . Gov Long introduced me as the Cor Sec [corresponding secretary] of the As^n &c & I made a brief statement of our position &c & introduced Miss Shaw who made a bright, earnest telling speech of half an hour. Mrs Mary Hunt of Hyde Park had meanwhile come in & the room was packed full the hall & entry being also full. I then spoke for half an hour dwelling on the experience of Wyoming & Wash, tracing the growth of suffrage &c. Then Mrs Hunt spoke *remarkably well* for 15 minutes. Then Gov Long was called on, but introduced Mr Carey the delegate from Wyoming who gave a brief, manly endorsement & made them all laugh by his funny reply to an enquiry about domestic discord. He had seen none. In his own case his wife had voted for him several times, and once, he believed, she had voted against him; but he was happy to say that his mother-in-law had voted for him repeatedly. The men of Wyoming liked to have their women have independent opinions & be free to express them. The schools of Wyoming are unusually good & are almost wholly controlled by the women.

Gov Long made a very earnest closing speech of 5 minutes. He said the claim was just and the power of the Com & of Congress unquestionable. At the close I handed leaflets to the members present. . . . I hope to see you at home tuesday morning. Love to my hard worked faithful Cub. I hope to relieve her from part of her care next week.

Yours affy
Henry B Blackwell

By February of 1887, Lucy was so ill that she was forced to leave Boston for the milder climate of Thomasville, Georgia, where George Blackwell; his wife Emma Lawrence, Lucy's niece; and their two children were spending the winter. In Massachusetts, Henry was still trying to find a practical substitute for cane sugar; now he was working on a plan to extract sugar from molasses at a very low cost. He had also gone back into real estate, and was busy building houses and either selling or renting them. Yet this activity didn't prevent him from taking part in a woman suffrage amendment campaign in Rhode Island in the spring. The campaign contributed to his growing awareness of the extent to which the connection between prohibition and woman suffrage damaged the latter cause.

With both parents away, Alice was carrying the full load of the *Journal*. In January of 1887 she had introduced a new feature, the Woman's Column. This collection of suffrage items sent out free to newspapers all over the country was very successful, but made for extra work. Moreover, Alice had to deal with unpleasantness on the part of Rachel Foster, a wealthy young protegée of Miss Anthony, who was writing for the *Journal*. But that summer it was her turn for a vacation: While she traveled in Europe with one of her Blackwell aunts, her parents took charge of the paper. In the fall of 1887 Henry had his own run-in with Miss Anthony herself when he went to Kansas for the annual state suffrage convention.

∽

[February] 20 1887

Harry darling

If anything happens [to] me that we never meet, again [you] will find my will, and respect its conditions. I shall be sure you will help Alice in the business part of her property, and do your best for her. I should be glad to live to see you both through, but as I am the oldest this is little likely.

For the abundant and unselfish work you have done for women Harry dear you know how thoroughly I appreciate it and how grateful

I am for it. Few men would have done it, leaving business, friends, pleasure for it. But in all the long hereafter the world will be better for it. Was it not worth doing for so great a result? I wish I could have made it more agreable, or less hard, but it could not be easy because it was all upstream against wind and tide.

I feel very tender of you dear and wish there were rest and liesure for you to do the things you like best and in any event and for always my heart is warm to *you*, dear darling Harry.

Boston, March 5 1887

Dearest Lucikin

Your first letter from Thomasville lies here at the office addressed to Susie V. Doubtless we shall get one from you at the house tonight.

I am pretty busy, with preparations for the RI campaign. I had arranged with RI friends to furnish $500 & they to raise $2000 & get another $500 from Susan A or other outside sources. But Mr Wm I Bowditch with his usual blundering magnificence—proposed to give them $1000 & it was voted—Mr Chace having come up to attend the Com meeting & state the emergency. This is conditional on their raising $2000 besides.

Miss Pond is to go down for a month. Miss Shaw is engaged to go to Kansas instead of to come here in April. I have agreed to speak 4 times a week. 30000 leaflets each of seven kinds are to be mailed in one envelope to 30000 voters. Mrs Livermore is to speak for them 4 or five times. Mrs Ellen Foster is also engaged &c &c. . . .

In great haste, with love to all, ever your own

Henry B Blackwell

Thomasville March 5, 1887

Dearest Harrykin

Your telegram telling of the passage of the RI amendment by such a handsome vote came just after breakfast. It would be a joy if it *could* be carried by the voters. I am sorry to have so much of the work of the campaign there devolve on you. The R. Islanders will take the brunt of the planning it, but you will have to go down for speaking. No speech will be so effective as yours. Especially that part of it that shows the feminine qualities. I do wish RI would adopt the amendment! I saw the Maine Senate *has* passed its amendment. The Record adds coolly, "but it will be killed in the house."

The weather here today is a little warmer than it has been. The thermometer at 60. I have a fire in my room and every morning I have one. . . .

Ever affy.
L.S.

Boston, March 15 1887

Dearest Luciken

Dont be distressed about me. I will take care of myself. I spoke last night at Ashton; tonight I am to speak with Mrs Bowles at Tiverton. We are all well. I am a little alarmed at your report of cases of malarial fever. If they continue I advise you & George & Emma to "get up & git" to *Marietta*, which I imagine is much cooler & probably healthier being among the hills.

I feel ashamed to write you such short letters but they are better than none. I fear there is *very little* hope of carrying RI. If we can get even a decent minority I shall feel relieved. More & more I see that it is *premature* to go to the voters. We must stick to the Legislatures, here in the East especially. But we are getting a good hearing & shall do much to break the crust of conservatism & liberalize the little hide-bound State.

In haste
Ever affy yrs
Henry B. Blackwell

This morning was a snow storm. All day yesterday it was *bleak* & pinching. It is now clearing off finely & pleasantly warm. You must not come back here I think before May 15. So make your plans to journey gradually Northwards with Geo & Emma.

Thomasville, Tuesday Mar. 15, 1887

Dearly Beloved People at Home

Whoever first gets my letters may open them, no matter to whom they are addressed. If there is anything private to anyone I will enclose it with a "taboo" sure it will be respected. The Woman's Journal came yesterday, also a letter from Alice. I was relieved to see that you had not followed the wish of Col T.W.H. to have his article double leaded. It would have been very silly, and if done at all, it should have been said "by request." But the fact that he *asked* to have it made conspicuous in that way, shows how keenly he felt the compliment of the remonstrants, as on their side, where he does not *wish* to be reckoned, and where spite of all his suffrage crochets, he does not belong.

I had seen the result in Maine and N.Y. before the Journal came, and also the scanty note in the Herald saying we are defeated in Massachusetts. H.B.B. makes a hopeful showing of the figures as usual, and this at least is true, that we are one year nearer to victory than we ever were. As for Rhode Island if all the speakers would try in a simple way to show what can be done by votes, and that voting is the power by which we get schools & school houses, streets, sidewalks, water supply, hospitals asylums and good laws, good drainage, &c It does seem to me in that little state everyone could be reached and, shall I say convinced? Certainly it will make a difference. But we shall see. The Lord reigns at all events.

It is cold here today and it was cold yesterday, frost last night— Thermometer at 44 this morning. Polly comes and builds me a roaring pine fire, which blazes up in a minute. When the room is a little warmed I get up, and dress. Anna rings the bell, as her special prerequisite, and I come out to breakfast, about which I have not had a thought. I was never so waited on, or so free from work or care. Until yesterday it has been pleasant to be without fires, after the early morning. But yesterday and today, fires are kept all the time. Yesterday 2 ladies called on me, and announced they were from the Berkshires, which I found later meant from Becket. They were here, one with a consumptive husband, and one with a consumptive father. This is their 3^d winter here, and their invalids are failing. I have had several calls, and have returned one, & must return the others.

Emma goes with me. The last night callers brought a great bunch of roses, 3 varieties, and at the moment the air is sweet with them.

Good bye

Boston, March 25 1887

Dearest Lucikin

. . . We are keeping up the best fight we can in RI but I have not the slightest hope of success & fear for the result of defeat on Mrs Chace's health, as she cannot help being disappointed deeply. Mrs Ex Gov Wallace is in RI for 10 days & speaks *remarkably* well. . . .

Alice was at West Newton last night at Mrs Tolman's. I was invited but had to go to RI instead. Mrs Howe was there & Col Higginson. About 125 were in the parlor. Mrs Howe spoke first & spoke well. Then Col Higginson eulogized the Remonstrants: said they were noble broad-minded, public benefactors who had read all our arguments & were not convinced & intimated that their objections had not been answered. He said that *now* it could no longer be said as formerly that *all* literary & eminent women were with us. Thought the suffragists were lacking in candor & courtesy & took exception to the remark of a Rabbi quoted by Mrs Howe who recently said at the 19th Century Club in New York that opponents of W.S. were influenced by ignorance, selfishness, & cowardice. Alice was called on to reply & made a 6 minute speech. She said that it might not be true, but *either* ignorance, selfishness, *or* prejudice might fairly be attributed, that no *new* objections had been made & no strong arguments advanced against us by the half dozen active remonstrants—that we had no reason to expect their conversion & that too much attempt at candor & courtesy had sometimes resulted in making them think that they had converted *us* to *their* views. That we should have to do as we did with the supporters of slavery, fight them, outnumber them, & carry our reform over their opposition. That if better arguments were considered needful those who felt thus were the persons to supply them. She thinks she did pretty well tho as usual not quite satisfied with her performance. I wish I could have been there to make a rejoinder. Judge Pitman had attempted one before Alice spoke.

We are all well. . . .

> Yours affy
> Henry B Blackwell

P.S. March 25/87 Yesterday the bill to give women who register a right to vote on the license question *passed* the House by 98 to 78. . . . it will probably be killed in the Senate. But it is the first time WS has ever had a majority in the House of Reps of Mass.

> HBB

> Thomasville—Thursday
> Mar 31/87

Dear Darling Alicekin

This is Thursday, and I think how the short eds. and the long eds. gnaw at you, and however tired they hold you with relentless grip! But it is a great immortal work, and well worth the weariness and fatigue. Nevertheless I do not want the sole daughter of my heart to be drawn to death in it, nor the man whose name I do not take hurried to death by it. I am glad you find Edith a comfort and help. . . . Who edits the column in the Providence journal. It would be good to put in the story the Wyoming woman told me. I will enclose it. Of course the remonstrants will send their articles. But it is not worth while to tear your soul about. The Lord reigns and the remonstrants work is part of "the all things that work" to establish the truth. . . . Tell Papa when he comes home that I think of him *all the time* toiling away at RI.

> With love to all
> L.S.

> [Thomasville Ga. 1887]

[The beginning of this letter is missing.]

. . . I went to visit a colored school the other day. It is taught by two Yankee women. Excellent women, but so unfit for the place! One of them did not change the expression of her face once during the whole time I was there. She stood up before the school and her face said: "Do you believe in G-a-w-d? If you do not believe in G-a-w-d you will go to h-e-l-l!" It was a most melancholy showing! She told them nothing about their lessons, but asked the dry questions, and had the answers without a word. She asked me to question, and as the lesson in Geography was about Oregon and the Columbia and the Yellowstone, I asked if they had ever heard of the geysers and of the Yellowstone Park. They knew nothing of these. I told with glee of the geysers in the most graphic way, and of the Park, and of the cascades. The whole school lighted up with interest, eager and all alive, showing how far removed they were from the dull, stupid set they appeared to be before the ghastly solemn face of their too pious teachers! At last I was asked to address the school, and I told them the things to do them good, stir their pride, their hopes, their ambitions to be as good as the best, and their wide-open eyes told how well they understood.

It seemed a thousand pities to have them just dragged along without aspiration or inspiration. At last they were dismissed in a manner just as formal and cold by the touch of a bell repeated 5 or 6 times. Each time for a maneuvre to get ready to go. I felt as though I could not forgive the teachers for the dreadful way they neglected the chance to lift up a race in pitiful need of help.

L. S.

Boston, Apr. 7. 1887.

Dearest Lucikin

Last night Edith and I got home at 8:30 PM from Woonsocket, RI, where we had been offering the "Approved" ballots all day at the polls. Not a single Woonsocket woman came out to help us, tho' appealed to do so. The W.C.T.U. tho' nominally friendly did not appear. Mrs Davis of Worcester, Mass., and Edith and I were the only workers there. The opponents had a young Brown University student hard at work against us. He was in close alliance with the principal liquor dealers of Woonsocket, and had such active aid and co-operation from the Democrats that I really think money must have been used to secure their aid. Well, we are beaten, as I feared, 5392 to 15398—only 26 per cent of the votes were cast for Woman Suffrage; 74 per cent against it. But if you had seen the voters you would not have been surprised. The wonder is how the Prohibition Amendment was carried last year. It was simply a miracle, and will soon be repealed, I think. The Democrats have carried their entire State ticket, and RI has ceased (for the present) to be a Republican State.

If placing four leaflets and a copy of "The Amendment" in the hands of every voter in Rhode Island by mail, and about 100 public meetings large and small (mostly small), and active discussion in the papers during the past month—have any educational or converting influence, much good seed has been sown. But a large proportion of the voters will have to die and be born again before they can be converted, and the mass of the population (factory operators of Irish and French Canadian extraction) are as incapable of being reached by reason as Choctaw Indians. I have no hope that Rhode Island will become woman suffrage during Mrs E B Chace's life-time, or that of most of us.

Now I am going to give my undivided attention to renting or selling my two houses. Your letter has just come to hand naming May 1. as the time of your return. But to do so will be very unwise. There is, as yet, no sign of Spring. The air is harsh and bleak. Snow-drifts are everywhere. It is as bad as February. . . .

H B Blackwell

[Thomasville] Apr. 12 1887

Dear Little Alicekin

Your letter congratulating Emma, and telling of Rachel Foster came yesterday. I only sent a card this AM because I wanted to write more at length. I am surprised about Rachel Foster. I thought her a straight forward person. But there does seem to be something not quite honest, frank, and straight in the whole of them. It is really the dividing characteristic between the two societies. But do not let it trouble you dear. If she furnishes a good column, only so much good is done, and if you furnish a great many more good columns, so much more good is done, and the great public does not know of the mean trick behind Miss Foster. Nevertheless I am disappointed in her, and sorry to be so.

You need have no fear of our being "gobbled" up. We can at any time make a statement of the facts which divided us, to leading members of the state societies, and it would be proof of the need of the separation that was made in 1869. But on entirely other grounds and for other reasons I have been thinking that there might be a union possible. This is what I have been thinking. Miss Anthony intends to have a great celebration of the 40th anniversary of the movement, [and] if after conferring with our auxiliary societies, it was thought best to do so, we might propose to make it a Jubilee Anniversary and union of the two national societies under the name of "the United Suffrage Societies", with an American Branch and a National Branch which should each be responsible for the management of its work, but all *meeting* upon occasion, and working together as friendly societies, and in this way, escaping for the most part, any indiscretions which the National Branch might run into. I mean escape responsibility for their false moves, or for their indiscreet ones.

They are now doing very good work as an association, and APPARENTLY there is no reason why we should not unite. Besides it would take away the feeling of grievance &c &c &c, and would on the whole perhaps be best. I have about come to the conclusion that this will be the best for the cause.

You will be glad of any real help any of them give to the cause, even the worst of them, if you put the cause FIRST OF ALL. If I were starving or freezing, you would be glad if your worst enemy brought me food or warmth. But this is the cause, not of any one woman, but of all women, and of the whole race. Its success and prosperity have always been more to me, than any personal feeling, and any damage to IT far more than any personal ill will, or misunderstanding of myself, so I could always rejoice in good work no matter who did it. Try to look at it in this way dear, and let Rachel Foster's little trick go out of sight in the hope of the good to the cause in Penn. I am glad you wrote me about it, and I hope you will always tell me when anything hurts or troubles you. What are mothers for if they cant take the children up when they need comfort?

How could the RI campaign cost $4.000? I know Ellen Foster charges a great deal, and the columns cost too. Well, may be it could not be less. Did Susan B. give anything? Isn't it too bad that the Brown students were so *poor* in money and in spirit as to be tempted to do just for hire what they will always despise themselves for doing!

. . . It was a pity not to have put Kansas with its great fact, at the head of the column on the 4th page last week with the RI defeat lower down. The voting in Kansas was on the 5th. The Journal came out on the 9th, and the first voting by women in a great state could have been made much of—should have had a large heading. We never know how to blow our horn or to make the most of our successes. But then you all had too much to do, and so the chance to make much of the Kansas voting was lost. It is too bad. . . . I suppose Papa is home from Montclair, and I shall soon hear the result. Some of the people who come to our houses should take them. Emma gives up her school today. It is very hot. Thermometer at 82. . . .

L. S.

Boston, Apr. 30. 1887

Dearest Lucikin

. . . Why do you not go over to Tallahassee and get a hearing for Woman Suffrage before the Florida Legislature now in session there? Their bill for liquor license, woman suffrage gives you the needed opening, and you could at same time urge full municipal and county suffrage on an educational qualification. That last clause will gild the pill because it will exclude the illiterate women, and they feel swamped by the prevailing illiteracy Suffrage for women on an educational qualification like what we have in Massachusetts, would command respectful consideration.

We are busy with preparations for Festival May 23 at Hotel Vendome and for Annual Meeting 24 & 25. Bazaar circulars going off next week.

Yours affy
H.B.B.

Thomasville, May 1, 1887

Dearest Harrykin,

This is Sunday, May 1, the anniversary of our wedding-day 32 years ago—more than half your life time! ! And on Wednesday will be your 62nd birthday! How time flies! But all the same best wishes to you for "many happy returns" of these anniversaries, and for our usefulness till the end.

We had another meeting here yesterday. It was larger than the one before. Everyone believed women ought to vote, but they were afraid. They said it was here as it was at the North 40 years ago; that they could not do anything; that the legislature would not hear anything about it, &c &c. But I could see that they all wished they could vote. I had written a form of petition for Municipal Suffrage. This I offered. The first woman who put her name to it was Mrs. Armstrong who was left a widow by the War when she was only 22 years old. Stripped of slaves and an abundance, she has ever since been earning her living by teaching music, and who said she should "as soon ask an ourang outang to vote as to ask a negro." . . .

It was thought best not to try to form a society, but to have a class instead, and meet every Saturday and read suffrage literature, and to study the laws of Georgia, and get more information on the subject. So there is hope of a root here. Mrs. Burbank gave me $20 to use for the Cause as I please. Her sister, Miss De Sano, who did all that was done to get this last meeting up, is to be the good protecting mother of it all. There will be one more meeting that I can attend. I am very glad to have helped to set the ball in motion here. . . .

L.S.

[Dorchester] Sunday Aug 7. 1887

Dearest Alicekin

It is one of the loveliest days that ever dawned upon the earth. After a solid month of steaming & stewing with the thermometer ranging from 80 to 90 day & night & a foggy, muggy, sticky air, we have thermometer 65 in shade, sky like a crystal & a glorious breeze murmuring in the trees. Everything is washed clean by yesterday's rain & the grass as green as in May. I have just finished an experiment in apple jelly which I trust will turn out well. . . .

On Thursday next (Aug 11) Lucy & I are going to Newport RI to a Woman Suffrage Convention specially designed to enlist the friends in that state in the Bazaar next Dec. We go down one morning; back the next. Mrs Howe will preside, Mr Foulke will come up from Narragansett Pier, Mrs Livermore & your mother & me & Miss Pond make up the speakers. Mrs Chace has written that she will pay all the debts of the last campaign, so that way money raised by the RI Ex Com by Bazaar or otherwise may go for future work in organizing the State. . . . The annual meeting of the American WSA in Phil[a] will probably be about the middle of October. . . . Stay away until your money gives out, for I do not find myself any busier when I make up the paper alone, & if it is not so good as when you are here people do not notice very much & things go along well enough. I *hope* you will cut loose from the Blackwells & live your own life & make your own way. . . .

Miss Anthony is making great announcements of her intended celebration of the 40th anniversary of the Seneca Falls Convention &c—to last a *week* in March next at Washington D.C. I suppose Mrs Stanton will be brought back on occasion & a great blow will be made of what really was *not* a very special landmark. Very little notice was taken of it at the time. It was the Convention of 1850 at Worcester which started Mrs Mill in the Westminster Review. . . . Goodbye sweet Kub. . . . Make all the acquaintances you can & flirt like the dickens whenever you come across a young male citizen.

Yours affy
Henry B. Blackwell

7.30 PM Newton, Kas. Oct 12 1887

Dearest Luciken

Now that I have been knocking around this uninteresting little Western prairie town all day I realize more than ever before that I *am* a *crank* & my sister Anna's own brother! But I feel better since I have met the party (circus) on the arrival of the train this evening. Here are SBA. & Miss Rachel Foster, Mrs Johns & good Mrs Slocumb of Emporia, Mr & Mrs Stuart &c. Mrs Slocumb tells me that she has come down on purpose to *help prevent* effort for the submission of a Const[l] Amend[t] "which would kill everything" she says. The editor of the paper here Mr Prentiss, & his wife feel the same way. Mrs Prentiss was formerly Engrossing Clerk of the Legislature & has been much among the people & she says she *knows* that we should be badly beaten on a popular vote. I see by the Leavenworth *Times* that in their recent Emporia Convention—the plan of asking the Legislature for Presidential Suffrage was received with much favor. So I hope we may get the policy shaped in that direction. Prof Carruth is expected here tomorrow morning & as he is one of the Secretaries of the Society he expects to be here.

A curious thing occurred to me today which shows that what we met with in RI would meet an Amendment here. One of the active ladies here—Mrs Edwards—gave me the name of a lawyer who was supposed to be in favor of Woman Suffrage. I wanted to post myself on the Kansas Constitution & election laws, so I introduced myself as having been told that he favored Woman Suffrage. He said he was *not*—that he had been so until this Prohibition business came up but *the women were too fanatical on the Temperance question for him*. It is evident from Gov Robinson's letter that *he* is soured for the same reason. These men represent many thousands who accept Prohibition because it is an established fact & popular but who will fight woman suffrage because it could *clinch* the policy they secretly deprecate.

Several of the ladies this evening expressed a strong wish that my *wife* was with me & *I wish it too*. This glorious Kansas air is like a glass of iced lemonade. It is clear, crisp, dry, bracing, and without any of our Eastern *sting*. The sun shines here as nowhere else except in Colorado, which this part of Kansas much resembles in climate. . . . I think with real grief of your load of cares & of poor Alice's slender shoulders put under the heavy old W. *Journal*. . . .

Of all the rushing, roaring, boysterous rough-&-tumble ways of doing things—this Kansas people surpasses any I ever met. I see by the papers that Wilcox has got ten women's votes counted in a village election in N York. Strange to say Kansas resembles N York in one respect—the Suffrage clause names the male citizens who shall vote and the citizens who for immaturity, mental unsoundness or criminality may *not* vote, but does not enumerate female persons in either category. With a Supreme Court supposed to be favor of Woman Suffrage I think it *possible* we might get a construction that would give the Legislature the power to enfranchise the women. I shall try to see Chief Justice Horton about it.

Affy HBB

Newton [Kan.] Friday Oct. 14/87

Dear Lucy

I am well & the Convention is a good one well prepared & carefully managed in the interest of the "Nationals." Mrs Johns is a bright, smart, energetic woman with much tact & grace of manner but thoroughly a partisan of Susan B Anthony. I wish we could have you with us. It would settle the question for the American in the minds of very many. Susan is representing the "Woman's Tribune" for all she is worth—representing it as to be a weekly *organ* of the Kansas Society & the Nationals at $1. a year. "You see, Mr Blackwell, we propose to *cut under* the Woman's Journal", she remarked from the platform. The Ex Com. dont trust the sub-committees by themselves, but "meet with them" before their reports are made to the Convention. The Committee on revision of Constitution last evening voted unanimously (without any prompting from me) to make the Kansas As^n Auxiliary to *both* American & National Societies. But when it got out Mrs Johns set to work vigorously to change that & a meeting "with the Ex Comm" was called for 8 30 AM this morning, with what result remains to be seen.

Prof Carruth & Mrs Slocumb of Emporia are on that Com. I have not yet made a plea for the Woman's Journal, but shall try to do so when a good oppy offers & shall invite new subscribers for *first* year at $1 ^{50}.

We shall get through tomorrow & I shall take first train East if my money turns out—if not, I shall have to draw for some on the Bank.

Good bye
In haste
H B Blackwell

Topeka Kansas Oct 16 1887

Dearest Wife & Cub

The object of my mission is *attained*. The Kansas WSA has voted almost unanimously *not* to ask for a Constitutional Amendment, and has resolved that it will memorialize & petition the next legislature to give female citizens a right to vote for electors of President and Vice-

President on the same terms as men. In the Com on Revision of Constitution there was a lively contest over making the State Association independent or auxiliary to both As^{ns}. Our friends, headed by Prof Carruth and seconded by Mrs Slocum of Emporia, secured a report omitting the clause auxiliary to the Nat^l Association, & submitted the new constitution in that form, to the intense disapproval of SBA and her party. The Com agreed that there should be no discussion by the Com in the Convention, but when it was moved to restore the clause making the Society auxiliary to the National Prof Carruth moved to amend the amendment by adding "and the American." Then Mrs Wait, contrary to her agreement, made an earnest speech in favor of the Nationals, Mr Carruth's amendment was lost, and the clause was restored. I took no part & evinced no feeling. Then resolutions were adopted for Pres Suffrage & a full delegation of nine were appointed to attend the annual meeting of the Am WSA at Phil another to send Mrs Johns to Washington in March another urging work for the Bazaar & another (not to be published) asking the two associations, Nat^l & American, to unite and combine their forces. With the exception of the controversy in committee all was harmonious. . . . To you & myself the feeling expressed was just as cordial as to SBA. I was treated with the highest respect & consideration & invited to take part on the same footing as delegates, or as SBA & Miss Rachel Foster. Prof Carruth gave notice that he should renew his motion to be auxiliary to both or independent next year "because nothing is settled until it is settled aright."

Mrs Slocum of Emporia came to me with tears in her eyes & whispered "Tell dear Lucy Stone that I did all I could for her." . . . Annie Shaw is cutting a bigger figure out here than SBA herself. She is greatly admired & could have entirely spiked Susan's guns if she had chosen. But as she is working in the auspices of Kansas WSA she did not make any expression. It was the ablest and most capable body of women I ever saw convened & Mrs Johns is the right woman for Pres. I stopped today at Topeka & saw Judge Horton about claiming full suff. for women under the present State Constitution.

Affy

H B Blackwell

The Kansas resolution asking the National and the American to unite was indicative of a fairly widespread sentiment within the rank and file of the suffrage movement, especially on the part of the younger generation of workers. The differences between the two organizations had never been that great, and in the years since the original split in 1869, they had, if anything, moved closer together. Under Miss Anthony's leadership, the National had become increasingly conservative; it now focused exclusively on suffrage and no longer championed controversial side issues such as divorce. However, the split itself and the early years of rivalry had engendered so much personal bitterness between the leaders that efforts at union had hitherto been doomed to failure. Lucy had steadfastly resisted such moves in 1880 and again in 1884, but in the intervening years her own declining health may have made her more amenable to union. With her approval, the American passed a resolution at its annual convention in November of 1887, calling on her to speak with Susan B. Anthony about a merger of the two organizations.

The meeting took place on December 21 in the office of *The Woman's Journal*, with Alice and Rachel Foster also present. Lucy and Susan agreed that the new organization would be called the National American Woman Suffrage Association, that it would work for the passage of a Sixteenth Amendment, and also for state and municipal suffrage, and that it would be organized on a delegate basis like the American. But certain friction points remained: Lucy felt that neither she nor Mrs. Stanton nor Miss Anthony should serve as president of the new organization, while Miss Anthony disagreed, and what was even more galling, made no secret of her preference for *The Woman's Tribune* as the united association's organ.

At the end of March a gala celebration of the fortieth anniversary of the Seneca Falls convention was held in Washington, D.C. Lucy was among the honored guests at this international gathering of women organized by Susan B. Anthony. In their opening speeches Miss Anthony, Frances Willard, and Julia Ward Howe each credited Lucy with having converted them to the cause of suffrage. Yet when Mrs. Stanton later traced the development of the woman's movement, she didn't mention Lucy at all. The omission must have rankled, and, as Lucy later explained in a letter to Frances Willard, there were other aspects of the Washington meeting which disturbed her and gave her second thoughts about the desirability of union.

Nevertheless, the wheels having once been set in motion, the movement toward a merger proceeded slowly but inexorably. The following January the National voted by a large majority for a union based on recommendations made by committees of both associations, and the merger was scheduled to take place at the beginning of the next year.

In August of 1888 Lucy celebrated her seventieth birthday. She was now spending only one day a week at the *Journal*'s offices, but that fall and winter she managed to travel with Henry to Iowa, Illinois, and Rhode Island for suffrage meetings. She did not, however, accompany him on the western campaign he undertook in the summer of 1889. Stout and rheumatic, she didn't feel she could endure the rigors of the trip, nor did she want Henry to go without her. Henry himself felt rather "lone and lorn" about going, but according to Alice, he had been "hankering" after the trip for some time, and when business connected with his Kansas land came up, the temptation was simply too great. So he set off, leaving a doleful Lucy behind. As Alice humorously recalled her mother's behavior during her father's absence: "At night Mamma will say in a rather melancholy tone, 'Good night Papa, wherever you are,' and I shall say, 'Amen.'"

In the West the territories of North and South Dakota, Montana, and Washington were about to become states. All four were holding their constitutional conventions that summer, and by attending three of them (North Dakota, Montana, and Washington) Henry hoped to get woman suffrage incorporated into the new state constitutions, or failing that, to secure clauses empowering the legislatures to extend the vote to women. After being enfranchised in 1883, the women of Washington Territory had lost the vote in 1887 when the state supreme court abrogated the legislature's act, and the outlook for regaining suffrage was hardly promising. In all three territories the connection between woman suffrage and prohibition was a major stumbling block, as Henry discovered soon after his arrival.

◦✦◦

[Boston] March 17, 1888

My dear Mrs. Campbell

Your good long letter with the check for $18. is here. . . . I wish you were here that we might talk over the matter of union. I have an utter abhorrence of so many of those who are in that society that it seems as tho' it would be impossible to work with them. And to accept Miss Anthony as president seems to be so unjust to the American, or so like giving her a vindication of her past, and saying that the American had had no occasion for its existence that is, it will *seem* like that, & they and theirs will trumpet it as a surrender—and a vindication. I *did* think when I proposed a union that Miss Anthony would see the propriety of an agreement with me that we would neither of us, (or Mrs. Stanton) take the presidency. But her old grasping spirit is just as fully alive as ever. I would rather the American would die altogether than to seem to condone Susan's past, and put ourselves in the erring [?] historically. . . . You see I write more about the union than about the state of things in Iowa because just now the question presses. . . .

Affy.
L.S.

[Dorchester] Sunday Aug. 12—1888

My dear child

We have a dark gray day. Thermometer at 69. Tomorrow is to be my 70th birthday, and I have made the most beautiful bouquets for my mother royal purple and gold in the dining room from the Monk's Hood and marygolds pink, white and green in the parlor, and red and green in the library. (The sweet peas sit at your plate). I trust my mother sees, and knows how glad I am to have been born, and at a time when there was so much that needed help, at which I could "lend a hand." Dear old mother! She had a hard life, and was sorry she had another girl, to share and bear the hard life of a woman. But I am wholly glad that I came, and she is too, if she sees. And whether she does or not, it is right. Mary Grew has sent me a lovely letter congratulating me, also Margaret Burleigh with a painted card, on which, or *in* which is a unique calendar. Whittier I believe had written me before you went. It seems all a wonder, and not possible that I am really three score and ten! It seems a little while ago, that I skipped with the lamb, and ran down hill, bounding like a cork, my flesh so light, that I scarcely knew I had it. Now, at a slower pace, I still go on with down right good will to help on, as long as I may.

We are glad to hear the details of your daily doings. How far do you go for milk? How far is it to the P.O.? Dont take *great* loads of drift wood. Better go oftener. We are glad you enjoy it so much, this camp life. . . . There is nothing new about union—only Mrs. Hazard writes that "Mrs. Stanton & Miss Anthony will never cease to be what they have always been, and personally I do not care to come into any closer personal relation with them." . . . The Western Women are waking up and working wonderfully. They all take space in their state or county Fair, and put in suffrage literature. We write you every day, or all but one day, I think. Papa is quite well again. Let us know if you sleep better. Papa has ordered a rail for the piazza steps to ease my climb. He also quite wants a set of new china and a carpet but the new house, and the taxes will take all I guess.

Aff.

Mamma

Dorchester Aug 23 1888

My dear Miss Willard

In reply to yours about the American Woman Suffrage Association joining the National Council, I can only say that I hesitate very much to do it or to try to have it done. I cannot forget that at Washington without having the delegates consulted the whole Council had the shame of having asked such a male prostitute as Grover Cleveland if he would recieve them, and that they went from a "social purity" meeting to be recieved by him. I also remember that the Mormon women, and not the Gentile from Utah had a hearing at Washington, and that the same Mormon woman's name stands secured in the Committee for the Council—and that too while the Mormon hierarchy is in direct opposition to the U.S. Government a menace, and a peril to it. Everywhere sewing the seeds, the evil seeds that disrupt the home, and degrade women. How can we welcome them without giving them all the moral support that goes with us? I do not care that you should trouble to answer this. I only state it that you may see how it looks to me. I know others to whom it looks the same, in both cases.

Until the Washington Meeting I never had a doubt that the coming of women every where, would tend to make cleaner, purer and better. Now I see that under the same temptation they do just as men do, they are hale fellows with Grover Cleveland and they have only a welcome to the members of a power that despises the home, and would supplant it with a harem. I shall not say any of this to the public, but you can see why I am not going to join the Council. And I am glad to say that in spite of drawbacks, I am sure the Washington Meeting did *a great deal of good.* Now this letter is not a grist [?] but it is wrung out by pain.

I am sorry to send this very unsatisfactory letter. But I am very sincerely yours

Lucy Stone

[Dorchester] Saturday June 29, 1889

Dear Harry

. . . We got your note from St. Louis this AM at breakfast and were very glad to get a peep of you. . . . Hoyt has written a most discouraging letter about Wyoming. But I guess it is only his nerves. It can hardly be possible that when women have voted 20 years they are to give it all up now. . . . Miss Wilde has sent a large lot of leaflets to Montana, I suppose by your direction. . . . I believe this is all the news only we are all well. You must be very careful. Hear what the people there have to say, and do not be in haste to suggest. Get "the lay of land" first, and dont try to play off one person or party against another. Make the claim for *justice* all the time. . . .

Always with much love from all of us
L.S.

Bismarck Dak. July 3 1889

Dearest Luciken

I left St Paul day before yesterday at 4 P.M. with the thermometer at 95 in the shade and the air languid and dusty. We glided along through the sandy ridges covered with oak thickets and flat prairies until night came on. I tried the Pullman 2^d class sleeper, made like the others but without cushions or bedding. It was cool & comfortable, but crowded with children & families, and the board seat grew harder and harder. So when a halfgrown boy in the opposite seat began to spit in perilous proximity to my feet, I abandoned my economies & went into the regular sleeper.

During the night a shower came up; in the morning it was cool & breezy—we were already past Fargo and in the vast rolling prairies of Dakota a scense of sublime solitude—often with stretches of uninhabited country for 50 miles away till lost in the horizon. We passed through Jamestown about 7 AM. and at 11 AM reached here—a bright clean handsome little village of about 3000 people. I spent my afternoon very busily in visiting Ex Govs Ordway & Pierce—Mr Jewell, the editor of the Bismarck Daily Tribune, & the four pronounced suffrage ladies of the city. . . . These ladies are all absorbed in arranging for the festivities of July 4th. I also called on a number of the delegates to the Convention. I found Ex Gov Ordway's statement correct—every man I have seen is opposed to putting woman suffrage or prohibition into the body of the State Constitution, but willing to submit both separately to the voters. They are also of the opinion that both will be voted *down*. My suggestion to refer WS to the action of future Legislatures meets with favor. . . . I shall try to get by postal card a meeting of say 100 ladies in some parlor as soon as July 4th is over and the Convention organized, to work up public sentiment. I am promised a hearing for Woman Suffrage in the body of the new Constitution, in Committee of the Whole. I shall do my best & ask for objections & questions. I enclose items from Bismarck Daily Tribune of today. Please find also a list of the members of the Constitutional Convention, 75 in number. They are mostly nobodies—all the leading men have kept out of the Convention in hopes of becoming candidates for State & Federal offices. The President will probably be Mr Johnson of Winnepeg—a leader among the Scandinavians, whose wife is, I think, strongly on our side.

One thing is certain that if I had not come the only thing would have been a *separate* submission to the voters. There is no organized woman suffrage sentiment—no women ready to work. The struggles for the past 2 years have created considerable hostility & the failures to carry WS have discouraged the suffragists. The defeat of Prohib in Mass & Pa has been a terrible set back to WS as well as prohibition—the same persons generally being active in both causes. I am more than ever glad I came, for my visit *may* do good & *cannot* do harm. . . .

The wind howls like winter; the sun shines brilliantly; the air is like a dry, bracing, autumn day in Worcester Co Mass—no chance to catch cold in such an invigorating dry atmosphere. The little rose bushes are everywhere in bloom, not over 6 inches high—dwarfed I suppose by the drought. Good bye Love to Kub

Yours

H B Blackwell

Bismarck No Dak

July 8th 1889

Monday evening

Dear Lucy

I have made my speech for Woman Suffrage to the Const^l Convⁿ. It was a good speech & well delivered, but it did not rouse any marked enthusiasm, nor did anyone present move to give me a vote of thanks. There were only three or four ladies present, & two of those were the wives of men who are opposed to woman suffrage. . . .

I think it will be utterly *impossible* to get woman suffrage into the body of the Constitution here. The opponents would be willing to submit WS as a separate question,—feeling, as they do, quite *sure* it will be voted down. They will oppose, many of them, the empowering the Legislature to act, but that is all we can hope to carry, & if we do carry that, it will be a great and fruitful victory. . . . I may get up a public meeting here, but the trouble is that all who would be friendly are more friendly to Prohibition & to link the two questions together would be fatal, for prohibition is being bitterly fought & many prohibitionists are strongly anti-suffrage. I am disappointed very much at the *average* mental attitude here. I dont believe more than 15 out of the 75 delegates are squarely for woman suffrage and not more than one in five of the men of the town. So expect nothing & we shall not be disappointed. I have done my best, and we *may* save the right to have the Legislature act hereafter.

Yours affy
H B Blackwell

Bismarck No Dak July 9 1889

Dearest Luciken

The prospect brightens! The "Farmers' Alliance" has a majority of the Constitutional Convention, & has elected its candidate, F B. Fancher, president. The Farmers' Alliance is friendly to Woman Suffrage, & so is Fancher. He has just told me that he has made up a committee on elective franchise in our interest, & in canvassing I find an evident determination to give the Legislature the power to extend suffrage to women. . . . I have been invited this afternoon by a committee of ladies of Bismarck to address a public meeting on Woman Suffrage on Thursday evening in the Presbyterian Church—the pastor, Rev Mr Anderson (an opponent of suffrage) to preside and music by the choir. All the other ministers (mostly opposed) have been invited to attend, & I think I may succeed in arousing an interest in this hitherto conservative community, which may react favorably on the convention.

On Friday morning I shall leave here (D. V. [Deo Volente]) for Montana. Today I begin to feel like myself again after ten days of diarrhea, stomach-ache, langour, and dry mouth. Care in diet and avoidance of ice water will soon set me right again. As things look tonight, I really *hope* I may have saved No. Dakota. For the Farmers' Alliance & the Temperance people will both want the women's vote so much, that it will be easy to carry the Legislature within two or three years at latest, if only the Legislature is empowered to extend suffrage to women.

If I find Montana a promising field I may be detained there a week or ten days. But the enclosed letter from Mrs McCoy rec^d today shows that I ought to get to Washington soon. Do not be afraid that I shall divide or antagonize or compromise any available ground.

I shall respect the wishes of Mrs McCoy. But if possible antagonism to the new State Constitution must be made unnecessary or the Suffragists will become odious to the general public. We shall see.

Yours ever   Henry B Blackwell

Bismarck Dak July 10/89

Dearest Luciken

I leave here for Helena Montana tomorrow (friday) AM. I am sorry to leave, for I am gradually securing votes, until today we are reasonably sure of *30*. Now *38 is a majority* & another week would get them. But if I am to return to Boston by Aug 1st, I *must* go on, & so I leave the matter in the hands of my friends. . . . Here there is no question of compromise—it is simply one of life & death. Woman suffrage is *unpopular* here. With the best newspaper notices & the effort of several public spirited ladies we got barely 200 people into the church to hear & these mostly ladies & children. If Dakota is saved it will be *wholly* due to my coming & I think I could surely save it by remaining two or three weeks longer. But I have written urging Miss Cora E Smith, a bright talented young No Dakota lady, a graduate of the State University at Grand Forks to come down & follow up my work here. If she comes, all will be well. . . .

Yours affy
HBB.

Helena Montana July 14, 1889
Sunday morning

Dearest Luciken

As I wrote you by postal card last night I arrived here safely yest^y aft^n—after a very interesting ride of 30 hours from Bismarck through the extraordinary "Badlands" which are 10000 . . . cliffs and eggheads surrounded by narrow flat vallies themselves seamed by ravines so as to make an extricable labyrinth of clay, sand, rocks, & pebbles—with petrified stumps & trunks of trees and occasional small patches of verdure on the low flats—then through the desolate weird cliffs which hem in the dry bare Yellowstone Valley with its clear beautiful river. At Livingston we had a fine view of distant snowclad mountains & envied the tourists who there got off for a week's trip in the Yellowstone National Park.

Here I find myself in the queerest city you ever saw, built along the gulches & on the sides of mountains—a huge miner's camp developed into a bustling active city of 15000 inhabitants swarming with miners, prospectors & politicians. I at once proceeded to deliver my letters & in doing so learned that our friends the McAdows of Minden Montana were keeping house here. Their mine has proved a bonanza—& after taking out $160000 more than they have spent in developing it, they have just sold it for the snug little sum of half a million dollars cash & are coming East to find them a home. Meanwhile Mr McAdow is a member of the Constitutional Convention & on the com of 5 on Suffrage. He is a very superior man in mind, manners & appearance but is unfortunately crippled in his legs by partial paralysis & has to sit in a chair—but is in perfect possession of all his faculties. He is a Democrat & will be a great help to us. I find that it is as impossible, either here or in N Dakota, to get woman suffrage into the *body* of the Constitution as to do so in NH. or Mass. To submit it to a vote of the "people"—(or males) would be certain & ignominious defeat. It would be Colorado over again, without any campaign. *There has never been a woman suffrage meeting held in Montana.* The subject has never been discussed. There is nothing but the general unsettledness and openhearted liberality of a new country to aid it—the people are ignorant, poor, & preoccupied, but enterprizing & bold & well meaning. The politicians are timid and now aspiring to State & National offices. The *only hope here,* as in No Dakota, is a clause *empowering the Legislature.* If we get that, we shall have here a woman suffrage state within five years; else not in 20. With McAdow's aid among the Democrats & Carter's aid among the Republicans there is good hope of success. The McAdows have brought me to their house & I am entertained with true Western hospitality.

Yours affy
H B Blackwell

[Helena, Montana] Monday morning July 15/89

Dear Lucy

Yesterday being Sunday, I was only able to see three or four gentlemen to whom I had letters of introduction & who were not out of the city—most of the members having been off on an excursion to Butte, Falls City, & Boulder. . . . The President of the Convention, Mr Clarke, is away, but will be back *today*. He has been drunk while away. I shall work like a beaver here for a day or two & then go to Tacoma. . . . There is not nearly as much woman suffrage sentiment here as in Mass. Mrs. McAdow says she is the only woman she knows in the Territory who is active for WS. Every man I meet is either opposed or indifferent. And yet, if we had come here, three years ago or two years ago when Mrs McAdow wrote to us to come, we could have carried WS *without difficulty*. So different are the social & political conditions in a Territory. Now all is changed. The people are being *driven* into statehood by the politicians, who are crazy for the State & National offices & who are afraid of *anything* that may endanger the ratification of their new constitution by the voters. This statement is true both of No Dakota and Montana, but more of Montana which is immense in size but sparse in population (about 200000 all told)—& not likely to grow very fast, being almost wholly mining & incapable of agriculture without irrigation. Yet its mines are a source of such great & unknown wealth that it may grow faster than would otherwise seem possible.

I rode out on the "Motor", a steam street car, to the Hot Springs 3 miles North around Mount Helena. Here some enterprizing lunatic is building a hotel with a swimming bath 300 feet long by 120 feet wide occupying an immense dome-roofed structure with dressing rooms &c all around it—the basin varying from 3 feet to 18 feet in depth—the water brought in by pipes from the mountain over an immense artificial pile of huge rocks 25 feet high in an artificial cascade. Here I drank water from the Spring as hot as I could swallow and waded about in dust six inches deep & sat on a tower & looked out over a beautiful but dry panorama of mountains, & valleys, bare and desolate as Palestine or Arabia Petrea, except where refreshed by irrigation. I walked back over the mountain, or rather on and around it, following a water ditch which supplies Helena with water—looking off over the vallies of the Prickly Pear, 7 mile, 10 mile, and Missouri to the huge piles of Rocky Mountains beyond which bound the view on the North.

If we get the Suffrage referred to the Legislature, we can, with the aid of Mr & Mrs McAdow, and the friends I shall make here, carry Woman Suffrage within 3 years. If we fail, WS will be postponed for a generation. Do you wonder that I fairly gnash my teeth to think that with two National Societies, we have allowed things thus to *drift* until the golden opportunity is so nearly lost?

Now it is perfectly certain that unless things are *totally different* in Washington Ty from No Dakota & Montana—women can only be enfranchised, if at all, by the State Legislature. To oppose statehood will be like a man trying to dam Niagara—futile. The politicians of both parties are just wild for the offices in State & Nation. If they will compromise by agreeing that "All persons who are or have been constitutionally & legally enfranchised in the Terry shall be voters in the State" & add the Legislature is empowered hereafter at its discretion to extend suffrage to "all citizens of mature age & sound mind not convicted of crime without regard to sex"—then it will be all right. I think I can make our friends see it but shall not antagonize them. . . .

I am now very well—have regained my appetite & got rid of my diarrhea. The McAdows have given me a turndown bed in an alcove of the parlor & I am really extremely comfortable & as nearly at home as I can be, away from *you* & Alice. I like the people here, and the dry air would cure Alices or Howards catarrh, for here one *cannot* catch cold. I sopped my head dripping wet with water on the mountain yesterday & in five minutes it was perfectly dry. I walk in the sun with the air 100 in the shade without apparent perspiration. Everybody looks brown & hardy—no pale faces. All is dry, dusty, glaring, parched & jolly. Good bye darling dee. This is written in the morning before breakfast.

Yours affy
HBB

Helena, Montana July 16th 1889

Dearest Lucikin

Your 2 letters and two postal cards reached me today, with news from home dated 11th, which is *very welcome*. I am working hard here, under great obstacles, but not quite without hope, tho the chances are *against* us. We have 22 men who have promised to vote for the empowering of the Legislature, but the Democratic party is, as a whole, against us, with half a dozen exceptions. The Republicans, as a rule, are with us I think, with perhaps eight or ten exceptions. The committee on Suffrage voted *against* the empowering clause 4 to 1. Mr McAdow the sole affirmative. But he will move an amendment & fight it out in the Convention, with all the backing of both parties that we can secure. Tomorrow morning I shall have placed on all the members' desks printed copies of the letters I bring. Gen Warren will move that I be invited to address the Convention on Woman Suffrage. Martin McGuinis, an influential Democratic opponent, will second the motion. I shall probably have a chance to do my best for the cause, & then go on. . . .

This is a queer place—as different from Bismarck as possible. The people generous, extravagant, reckless, enterprizing, and impulsive. But great fortunes suddenly made, and the gambling spirit which mining generates are not conducive to reflection or repose of character.

The women here care nothing & know nothing about the suffrage question. The Remonstrants could easily get up here a remonstrance that would floor me completely. Do not say much about my effort— the less the better. We must tell the story after the battle is won or lost as the case may be. God bless our home & one ewe-lamb! I enclose a pleasant letter rec^d yesterday from Mrs Johns.

Yours affectionately
H B Blackwell

Dorchester July 18, 1889

Darling Dear

We think of you dear every day and all day, and hope you are well. You must say in every letter how you are. If you are well enough, you should by all means stay as long as is necessary to secure all that can be secured. It is a great thing you have in hand. Not in our life time there be such a chance to help secure equal rights. The Eddy money cant be put to better use than to pay your expenses, and you should make yourself comfortable. I cant bear to think of your coming past the Yellowstone Park without seeing it. Today is Thursday—and Alice is at the printing office and she is taking it easy—i.e., she is not feeling overburdened.

Bessie Issacs has sent a report of their meeting. But the papers out there are singularly barren of any news on the great questions. They take and report everything else. Our appeal signed by Mrs. Howe, Livermore, and me will be in today's Journal, and I am to have slips to send to the leading papers. It might be quoted and help to the end we so much wish. There is no special news here. The days are full of work, and we have no time to be blue. . . . I can send you money. If I were young I would go and even now add something in the way of service in this for which I care so much. It seems awful to think that we may lose this great opportunity to put great principles square & sure into these new states. Stay if you can dear and do your best. . . . We are both well, and today we have it cool and sunshine.

> With much love darling
> Yours always   L. S.

> Olympia, Wash.,
> July 22 1889

Dear Luciken

Here I am at Olympia, where I have been since Saturday afternoon. I find the Convention, as I feared, elected by the politicians of both parties to *keep out the women.* The feeling against woman suffrage in the Convention is so strong that men like Judge Dennison of Vancouver . . . when they come here to represent the women's rights, are shunned and avoided by members of the Convention as though it was dangerous to be seen conferring with them. It is an organized conspiracy of all the baser elements of society with the managers of both parties. Judge Turner, who first decided the law to be unconstitutional which enfranchised women, is the recognized republican leader of the Convention, which here, as in the other Territories, consists of one house of 75 men. Under these circumstances my position is one of great delicacy as representing Eastern public men who advocate women suffrage and the Am. WSA. . . .

Another thing that has hurt us terribly is the political independence of the women. Three years ago the Republicans nominated for Congressional Delegate, one Bradshaw—a totally unfit man who for years had lived with an Indian squaw and had a family of halfbreed children—a man without character or capacity. The Democrats nominated a fair candidate, Mr Voorhees, son of "the tall sycamore of the Wabash." The women helped elect Voorhees. That soured the Republican managers. Then along came the WCTU & arrayed the women for local option. That soured the Democratic managers & set the Republican ones more strongly against the women. And so for their very virtues—independence, discrimination of character, love of Temperance and good morals—the women are politically slaughtered.

Another element in the situation is the sudden increase of population due to the completion of the Northern Pacific RR. This has brought in a floating population—often rough, ignorant and depraved—also a great body of conservative Eastern people who bring with them the narrow ideas of Eastern Society. With this great addition of "Do as you damn please" and "Do as our fathers did," the women are in imminent danger of being excluded by a Constitutional prohibition of the word "male." I dont believe a separate amendment *just now*, under all the circumstances would get one vote in seven; *certainly not a* majority. Of course our only hope is in *temporizing* with this hostile Convention. A clause authorizing the Legislature to confer suffrage is the only possible immediate salvation.

If ever there was a proof of the suicidal folly of arraying women against men by seeking politically to *coerce* a large male majority—it is here.

Think of urging Prohibition for instance in Helena where every other house is a saloon, a licensed gambling house, or a house of prostitution—when stores, mines, & all forms of work know no Sunday. Mr & Mrs McAdow tried to stop their mine works on Sunday. The miners protested & on Sunday went off for a general drunk and did not get back to work till the following Thursday—So the Sunday had to be abandoned as *demoralizing*!

Things are not quite so bad in Washington, but the temper is such that the mere word "prohibition" makes men mad. Yet the WCTU. are all the time plying the politicians with "Are you in favor of this?" "Will you vote for that" without the slightest regard to expediency or common sense. No matter. We will do what we can!

Yours ever   HBB

Olympia, Wash., July 29 1889

Dearest Luciken:

. . . Every day's effort confirms me in the opinion, or rather in the knowledge, that W.S. in this Territory is doomed to *extinction*. I do not think we could get over six or eight votes for putting WS into the State Constitution. I doubt if we can get 20 for the clause authorizing the Legislature to extend Suffrage. All we can get (& it will be given to *kill* it) is a *separate submission* of WS. either this year or next. . . .

It looks as if we *might* carry our point in No. Dakota. If we do, we shall be well repaid for the labor & expense of my coming out here. For if we do, North Dakota will be a woman suffrage State within 3 years, unless I am greatly mistaken. I shall have the consolation of feeling that I have done all I could, & that we have not lost Wash^n & Montana by neglect. And I am forever cured of the dream of a prohibition alliance. Miss Willard & her third party associates are the most dangerous enemies of our cause, because just so far as they educate the women, they array them *against the men* as a means of *coercing* the habits of the other sex. And men will not submit to this coercion. I never before realized the necessity of respecting personal *liberty*, even when that liberty takes injurious forms. The Kansas & Wyoming successes are now our *sole hope*, & to maintain them the women must stand by the Rep. party, which, as Douglass says, is "the ship; all else the sea."

Yours affy
HBB

Olympia, Wash., July 31 1889

Dearest Luciken

The Oregonian of this date gives us bad news from Montana, tho it is really better than I expected—viz. a defeat by a tie vote 33 to

33. I enclose the cutting. It is *possible* that had I remained there, the missing vote might have been had, but to spread myself over three Conventions sitting at [the] same time hundreds of miles apart is not easy. I shall write asking Mrs [Mc]Adow to send the Womans Journal full particulars. Here I am fighting against odds—both the party conventions & leaders having dropped woman suffrage in order to conciliate the whiskey interest & the very general opposition which the men have manifested since the Judges have overthrown the women's right of suffrage. It is a most discouraging & perplexing condition of things. In the case of men there would be bloodshed, insurrection, & civil war. But the women are not fighters & seem simply cowed and discouraged. Not a dime has been subscribed, not twenty ladies of Olympia have come out to the meetings.

Mrs McCoy came up on today's boat & returns tomorrow morning. She called with Miss Hindman this evening. Says she has collected in all about $700. for the campaign in advance of the election of delegates to the Constitutional Convention, and is out of pocket on its expenses. She wanted to know what help if any we in the East could give financially in case a separate amendment is submitted. I said that I did not believe the East would raise any such large sums as it had formerly done—that much would depend upon the action of the people here—that when the Convention had acted and adjourned & the situation was defined—the suffragists of the Territory ought to hold a meeting & take action. The more they did for themselves the more help they would get from abroad, but that the main force of speakers & *money* would have to be raised by themselves. I am chafing under the slow & tedious lobbying which I have to do single-handed and alone. . . . I dont know whether I shall stay here till the vote is taken, or how long that will be. If I leave all will collapse. If I stay we *may* succeed. In haste. Yours ever

Henry B. Blackwell

Olympia, Wash., Aug. 1ˢᵗ 1889

Dearest Luciken

We have saved one of the new States to Liberty! Thanks to Cora E. Smith, our excellent young "lobbyist," & our good friends in the Convention, the State Legislature has been empowered to extend

Suffrage to women. I need not say that this result is directly due to my visit, & I feel repaid for the time & labor we have expended. Rev. Dr Thompson has come from Vancouver. He is the chaplain of the Convention & a most vigorous & successful politician. With his wide acquaintance & earnest interest, I shall for the first time hope for success here.

I shall leave here on Saturday morning for Seattle. Shall go to Tacoma Sunday, to Portland Monday—& to Boise City on Tuesday. If we can only get the Legislature empowered to extend suffrage to women in *this* State—the submission of Woman Suffrage as a separate Amendment will be harmless. In that case I shall counsel that the Suffragists of the State issue a manifesto declining to make a campaign and advising suffragists *not to vote* on the question. This will deprive the defeat of any significance & the future fight will be made in the Legislature.

Thank God for North Dakota! She will be a woman State within four years.

We are still enveloped here in a haze of smoke. The nights are cool, with a genuine sea breeze blowing up the Sound. The sun has much power during the day but no languor or stickiness. This is the most wonderful country for fruit of every kind, especially plums, prunes, grapes, berries &c. We have ripe peaches, pears, green corn, & blackberries. Currants & raspberries & cherries are past.

Yours ever
H B Blackwell

Dorchester Sunday Aug. 4, 1889

Darling Harrykin

We were rejoiced yesterday to see . . . that N. Dakota *has put in the clause* empowering the legislature to extend suffrage. Now dear you will feel paid for going. And it is worth all the cost and trouble. I am almost as glad for *you* as I am for the cause of equal rights— after all your effort to get this is a great deal.

But is it not strange that women do not or cannot see how they stand in their own light when they push prohibition?

I send this at a venture not at all sure you will get it. Today the sun shines. Yesterday all day it poured. . . . We are all well and shall be glad when you can come home to your good room, clean clothes & comfort.

> With much love
> L.S.

H enry did, indeed, have cause for satisfaction with the results of his western trip. Besides empowering the legislature to extend full suffrage to women, subject to ratification by "a majority of the electors of the State voting at a general election," the constitution of North Dakota gave women school suffrage. Montana also granted its women school suffrage (which they had already possessed under the territorial government), and gave taxpaying women a vote on all questions of taxation. In Washington the campaign went much as Henry had feared: Despite his eloquent appeals to the entire convention and to its suffrage committee, the convention voted against a clause empowering the legislature to extend suffrage. Instead the question was submitted as a separate amendment to be voted on at the same time as the constitution, and then, as Henry had predicted, it was defeated. In 1890, however, the first state legislature extended school suffrage to women.

The new year also witnessed the formal unification of the American and the National. The first annual meeting of the united suffrage association was scheduled for February of 1890 in Washington, D.C., but when the time came, Lucy was ill with a "hard cough," and so Alice and Henry had to leave for the convention without her.

[Dorchester] Sunday Feb. 16, 1890

Dearly Beloved

It is 10.30 o'clock. I hope you are safely at the Riggs, your faces washed, and you all ready for breakfast having had a good trip and the racking cough of H.B.B. no worse. Mine seems the same. I had one spell of hard coughing, for which I took a cup of hot water, and was thankful to be where it could be got. . . . The Herald and Globe have each about a third of a column acct. of Susan's birthday. It is very good, and about right for us to use. . . .

I think that [at] *our* meeting tomorrow at 10 o'clock it should be said that I had proposed for the sake of good feeling all round neither Stanton, Anthony or I should be president, that Miss Anthony had declined and that Rachel Foster, &c. Now you will have to do of course what seems best at the time and I have great sympathy with you in the humiliation which will be poured upon our side—only for the cause, we would not bear it. I shall add a line before this goes to say how my throat is. Hope you both have warm rooms.

[Dorchester] Dining Room Monday Feb. 17 1890

Dear People

Yours en route came while I was at breakfast, and was gladly welcomed. Hope the warm climate will be good for you papa.

My cold is no worse except that I have spasmodic fits of coughing when it seems as if I should choke to death. I had 2 yesterday and one in the night. I did not get up till Ethel and her girls had gone, but I ate my breakfast with relish, and am not sick. . . . You are now at the last meeting of the American Association and I hope it will go right, and still more do I wish that the first meeting of the two to elect may be right. . . . The papers here this morning have further reports of Susan's birthday, and her red velvet gown, and the letters from various persons sent as special despatches. . . . I do not see *sure* that I *can* go in for my Thursday speech, but I shall if I can, or if I can hope not to cough and strangle on the platform. . . . It is cold today, and there is no news.

Aff.

L.S.

Pope's Hill
Feb. 18, 1890

Dearly Beloved

I sent you a scrap of a note this morning to catch the mail, I having kept in bed till Ethel and her one friend (she had only one last night) were off to school. Now at noon, I only write to say that I think of you and sympathize. Probably you are now listening to Mr. Foulke who I hope will clear the air after Mrs. Stanton.

The papers give very full accounts of Susan's banquet, the dress, the trails &c. I shall make an acct. of it if you do not send me.

Mrs. Stanton is made president and Susan vice, so that as Mrs. S. is to go away, Susan may preside. You as secretary and Chair Ex. Com., me complimentary. But in any case it means work if we stick. . .

I fear you may have had a tough time with the enemy. Keep fires in your rooms and *be particular. Now mind* to take my cashmere skirt out of the trunk, shake it out and hang it up, else it will be all in creases and not fit to wear if I come, and I shall if I can.

Love to all of you
L. S.

Lucy failed to make her scheduled appearance at the Washington meeting, although she did attend the next two annual conventions of the united association. Despite poor health, she continued to contribute to *The Woman's Journal,* but didn't accompany Henry on another western trip in the summer of 1890. This time, however, Henry went to only one state, and this time, too, he didn't have to lobby "single-handed and alone." The summer before, South Dakota had been unwilling to jeopardize it chances for statehood by incorporating woman suffrage into its constitution, but it did instruct its first state legislature to submit the question to the voters in November of 1890, and the campaign brought Susan B. Anthony and a number of other suffragists from elsewhere to the state.

❦

Washington, Monday 12 M. August 18th, 1890

Dear Lucy

I could not find Senator Pettigrew of South Dakota on Saturday, nor could I get a decisive answer from Speaker Reed to my request for a letter endorsing W.S. amendment until he should confer with the Dakota representatives. So I accepted Mr Spofford's invitation to go out to Rockville Md., 16 miles north of Washington to spend Sunday. . . .

Today I have had a long talk with Pettigrew who doubts the wisdom of putting a W.S. plank into the platform either for the sake of suffrage itself or for the Rep party—he thinks that the Republicans who are opposed to WS would *vote against* Suffrage at the polls all the same, & that individual independents and democrats who are personally in favor would be more likely to vote *against it* if it was made a republican party issue. Several of the German (Russian) Counties have instructed the delegates to the Rep State Convention to *oppose* the W.S. Amendment, & the Republicans fear they will lose the legislature if the Russians & Scandinavians go over to the Democrats. All I can hope from Pettigrew is that he will not *oppose* our getting the W.S. plank. Yet he is a sincere suffragist & gave $100. at the Feby meeting to the W.S. Campaign fund. . . .

4 PM. Well I have seen Speaker Reed again and he *declines* to give me a letter. He says he has so large a load to carry in the *direct line* of his duty that he does not think it best to go out of his natural course to volunteer an expression of opinion on a question which South Dakota must settle for herself.

Mr Spofford did a brave and kind thing for me this afternoon. He introduced the subject to the Mississippi delegation & got them to go with him & me in a body into a committee-room, where I read them the last part of my editorial slip—"Educated Woman Suffrage in Mississippi" with the facts and figures. It was well *received*—several members expressed themselves in its favor, two opposed, but all were interested. They advised me to send it to the Convention at Jackson and took copies of it which they promised to show to their friends & to talk it up. I wish you would write to Mr Spofford thanking him for his efficient help.

Yrs   H. B Blackwell

Let me know from day to day how you are, and whether your heart-trouble returns & how much.

Ever yours   *HBB*

Sioux Falls, South Dak., Aug 23, 1890

Dearest Luciken

Alice's cheerful letter of the 19th following yours of 18th both have been like rays of sunshine in a cloudy day. . . . Cloudy indeed so far as the prospect of Republican endorsement or success at the polls go. . . . In one respect things here are much like Rhode Island in the Amendment Campaign. Prohibition has been put into the Constitution by an organized effort, & now a great many, who voted for it without really expecting it to carry, would be glad to get it out again. We shall meet the full force of this ebb tide against prohibition—and the prohibitionists themselves will oppose W.S. for fear it may lead to a revolt against both & put the State into the hands of the Democrats who are opposed to both. I am trying to get a moderate plank *patting the women on the back* & paving the way for Republican help in the future when the exigency is less alarming than now. If I can get *anything*, I shall be happily disappointed. . . .

Like Alice I have had a touch of diarrhea, but have got over it without medicine. I shall take good care of myself. Thermometer at 40 night before last & today a dashing pouring rain.

Affy yours
H B Blackwell

Mitchell, South Dak., Aug 24 1890

Dearest Luciken

On leaving the sleeping car at Mitchell this morning at 7 AM, I met Mrs Carrie May Chapman just arrived from Iowa. There are now here, of outsiders, Miss Anthony, Miss Shaw, Miss Hindman, Mrs Chapman, Olympia Brown, myself. Miss Shaw preached this morning at the ME [Methodist Episcopal] Church an excellent sermon. In spite of rain the church was full. Miss Brown, I am told, preached in the Baptist Church. This evening Miss Shaw is to preach in the Congregational Church & Father O'Hane to speak for WS at the Court House. I have got all my leaflets folded & prepared for distribution at the Convention *"The Elective Franchise."* I have quite a family here unexpectedly on my hands. Last night a coarse, rough Swedish woman with four small children and a baby 6 months old came into the Station at Canton trying to work her way to her husband at Seattle WT. She seemed *lost* and almost in despair. I came away, feeling guilty at leaving the wretched little crowd in such distress. Today at 3 PM she came along & I have promised to help her out to get a ticket through to Seattle—she has $15 & I add $20 & she is to send it back to me if ever she is able, which is extremely doubtful. It seemed to me positively *inhuman* to see a woman so burdened & destitute in a strange land.

Tomorrow at 9 AM our convention will begin with a private council of war at Mrs Robinson's house—public meetings in the afternoon and evening & on Tuesday afternoon & evening. I would gladly return home at once, but fear I shall have to give the campaign 30 days of stumping. If the Republicans give us any kind of a plank I think I shall do more good to go on the stump for *them,* with the privilege of talking *my* suffrage speech, with Rep campaign at beginning & close.

I enclose a telegram from Mississippi, which shows that my dose is beginning to take effect. It will be a most *admirable* thing to get even property proxy woman suffrage in Mississippi. For it will forever break down the *sex* line—it will lead thousands & tens of thousands of men to put property in their wives' name. It will make voting women a privileged class, & women will become proxy voters in large numbers. It will stimulate *negro* women to get property so as to become voters like white folks. Of course *we* dont ask for anything less than Woman Suffrage on an educational qualification. Yet this may prove a still better beginning because it will make suffrage as *honorable* [?].

> Yours affy
> H B Blackwell

PS Please follow up the Mississippi propaganda *at once* mailing to *each* member of the Constitutional Convention at Jackson a copy of The Elective Franchise leaflets in an envelope. The Wyoming and Kansas testimony will probably have *great weight* with them.

Mitchell So Dak., Aug 26, 1890

Dearest Luciken

We had excellent meetings yesterday afternoon and evening— the evening audience about 700 including a good many Republican delegates. Mrs [Clara Bewick] Colby not appearing, I had most of the evening to myself and made a good speech well received. I enclose the resolutions, the programme, and the report of this morning's Republican. . . .

Miss Anthony is only *tolerably* well liked here. Miss *Shaw* is the favorite and next to her Mrs Howell and Mrs Johns. Olympia Brown is here and Matilda Hindman who has made herself very unpopular among her fellow-workers by her growlings and pessimism and sensitiveness to imagined slights. But she is doing good work in her own way in the field.

Dear Lucy: I think of you every day & wish you could be here without fatigue or exposure to meet these fresh sympathetic, young western audiences which are an inspiration.

Ever yours affectionately
Henry B Blackwell

P.S. Love to Alice. I am glad she has gone to Wiauno. SBA made a very pleasant reference to you last evening.

9 AM Mitchell So Dakota Aug 27, 1890

Dear Luciken

Yesterday was a busy day. Mine ended at 2 AM this morning. We have made the best fight we could before the Platform Committee and have failed. The platform will contain *nothing* on Equal Suffrage. It is a question how far it will endorse prohibition. But the ladies have been twice heard and Annie Shaw has covered herself with glory. She addressed the convention by invitation during a wait in the proceedings last evening & brought down the house in an admirable twenty minutes speech. If a vote of the Convention could have been had then & there, Miss Shaw could have carried almost everything. But the manipulation of the managers has been too shrewd to be overcome. There is a bitter & determined opposition to WS. by the worst element of the party & the representatives of the foreign voters. The Boston Remonstrants have flooded the various headquarters with their anonymous Remonstrance & had [a person] in a canvass helmet at the door to the Convention distributing it to every delegate. . . . We dont expect that any fight will be made on the floor or that if made, it could succeed. The settled sentiment of the Convention (even of a majority of the Suffragists in it) is against naming it in the platform. We have made a great many friends among the delegates who will help us hereafter in the canvass. But we shall have to fight our fight again, here as hitherto outside of party lines.

I will write a fuller report of the Convention if possible this afternoon. I am well. Love to Alice whose pleasant letter from Wyauno reached me yesterday & believe me dearest darling dee

Yours affy
Henry B Blackwell

PS Tomorrow I shall start on my tour of meetings.

St Lawrence So Dak
Aug 30/90

Dearest Luciken

. . . I had a small meeting last night—not over 50 present, in consequence of insufficient notice & also, I fear, in a want of earnest interest on the part of the men. . . .

I am very sorry to hear of the return of your rheumatism. I do believe that this climate would help you. It is a succession of brilliant sunshiny days with an elastic, dry, bracing air and a little refreshing breeze. The nights are glorious, cool, dry, delicious air equal to that of Martha's Vineyard but without its moisture. Now that the intense heat is over the climate is simply *perfect*. Why not come out & join me & let us see this campaign *through*. Leave the housekeeping for Bridget, or Mary, or both, to carry on. Let Alice & Mrs Adkinson run the paper.

It seems to you a formidable thing to leave home & comfort, but really there is no hardship in riding on the Pullman cars. You have almost all the way a dining car attached. You can reach any point on the railroad in So. Dakota as comfortably as in Mass. My list of appointments will show you where & when you can join me & I will take the best care in the world of you and we will return together. I do believe that this dry air will be the very change you need.

Yours affy
H B Blackwell

Dorchester Sept. 1 [1890]

Darling Harrykin

This is Labor day. Mr. Killian and the girl have gone for a spree. Lizzie and I are alone. . . .

Yours telling us of the final refusal of the Republicans came this AM. We had seen the fact in the despatches. How blind they are not to see what a power on their side, such honor [?] as addressed them would be! Well, there is now no hope for S. Dakota this year. But we have woman suffrage in the Constitution of Mississippi! That is a good fact if the voters adopt it. The Remonstrants will no doubt try to prevent it. Shame to them.

Alice really needs more holiday than she will get if you stay through Sept. She is nerve-worn, and looks pale and tired. She is at the Vineyard now, but she meant to come up Wed. to get the paper off—so she will have only 4 days there—so I hope you wont stay the whole month, all the more as we cannot carry S. Dakota no matter how many stay. Besides, here are the houses to rent and sell and this month is the best month for either selling or renting. . . . The days are cool but pleasant and each day brings more than we can do. Mrs. Duniway writes that the Washington women mean to fight for their political rights. We are all very well—my heart better all the time, but the rheumatics are not better. . . . I wrote you at Huron.

With much love
L.S.

Blunt, South Dakota Sept 2, 1890

Dearest Luciken

While waiting in this clean and comfortable hotel a long, rainy day, after a failure to get out a meeting last night, in this dried-up, dying town, I take advantage of my enforced liesure to add to the few hasty lines which I wrote you this morning. Judging from my own observation & experience I dont believe we shall get one third of the votes next November & indeed shall be *surprised* if we get one *fifth* of them.

The great majority of the men do not believe in Woman Suffrage, & do not take the trouble to go to the meetings or to give the matter any serious thought. They are very busy trying to earn a living under hard conditions. This country has been *boomed* in the most reckless way. Thousands of families have come here with little or no means, hoping by a successful crop to live while "proving up" their pre-emptions or homesteads or tree claims. In most cases they have been met by a series of short crops, often by repeated absolute failures—they have become discouraged, have borrowed what they could get from loan companies on farm mortgages without any intention of paying either principal or interest & have used the money to get away. We are now in the midst of the collapse of that boom. Houses are empty, thousands of claims are deserted and the towns are slowly dying out. The men who have stock—horses, cattle & sheep—& who cut hay & have succeeded in getting some wheat—are doing *well*. The Eastern half of the State is *growing*, but west of Huron lands and even houses are almost unsaleable. To get a people so situated to give money, time, or thought to woman suffrage is a hopeless undertaking. . . .

Miss Anthony is doing her very best. But our woman speakers all make the mistake of seeming to censure men and of using sarcasm instead of a little harmless, good-natured taffy [flattery]. Especially they speak sharply of *foreigners* & every time they do, the opponents use the fact to solidify the foreign voters. If only our women would *not* follow Mrs Stanton's foolish counsel & would use *womanly conciliation* we should be much more successful. As it is I fear we rouse more *opponents* than we make *converts*. But I dont say this to anyone but you. I speak well of everything & everybody & *work to win*.

Ever affy yours
Henry B Blackwell

Hosmer So Dak. Sept 11. 1890

Dearest Luciken

Here I am in McPherson County, a locality settled largely by foreigners; two thirds of the inhabitants being German, Russian, and Scandinavians. A majority of them do not speak English. Many have only been in this country a year. Yet, under existing state laws, the *men* are all voters, and, as might be expected, are a unit against the Suffrage Amendment. There seems something extremely wrong in allowing persons wholly unacquainted with our institutions and controlled by European prejudices to vote against the social and political rights of American women. To avoid antagonizing these old world prejudices, both the Republican and Independent parties have declined to put a woman suffrage plank into their platforms while the Democratic party has made a higher bid for the vote by adopting an anti-woman suffrage platform. The foreign vote of So. Dakota is estimated at 30000 out of 75000. This will be a very important factor in the fall election. If the result depended upon the American population, the Amendment would undoubtedly carry next November. As in Rhode Island and in the other states of the Northwest, Woman Suffrage is complicated with Prohibition, to the disadvantage of the former. Constitutional prohibition was carried a year ago by a small majority but very many localities are opposed to it. Here in McPherson, for instance, liquor is openly retailed in defiance of the law, and the county officers do nothing to stop it. They dare not do so. These Republican officials believe that enforcement would result in a wholesale transfer of the foreign voters to the Democratic party and would prevent any possibility of their own re election. So, here and in similar localities, prohibition does not prohibit and free rum prevails. Of course woman suffrage is opposed with added bitterness as likely to aid enforcement of Prohibition. . . . I am well & *am making* good speeches to very small and uncultivated audiences.

H.B.B.

[Dorchester] Sunday Sept 14/90

This is Alice's birthday 33 years!!! How astonishing it is! And I am very grateful for her good intellect, her good conscience, and for HER. I have given her a birthday present of $5. to do as she pleases with.

The Montclair taxes bill has come $309.68 cts. The property is assessed at $9.800. We shall no doubt get higher and higher valuation and more taxes on it. But it is good property.

With Much love   L.S.

I do not write about Dakota matters much. Of course Susan will be glad to keep you, and you are doing good. The papers give you much praise. They say your speeches do not leave a sting behind as do those of some others. Tis a pity the women cant learn! Mrs. Howell praises your work in an article to the Journal and she told of the Swede woman. Dont feel under any obligation to stay.

Leola, South Dakota Sept 16 1890

Dearest Luciken

I spoke here last night to an audience of about 100 in this little dried-up county seat of McPherson Co.—a very intelligent enterprizing American community struggling to live in a county now overwhelmingly German & Russian. 1½ years ago a frightful prairie fire swept away the entire town except the court-house burning several people to death & destroying all their houses furniture & livestock. How on earth they ever rebuilt the place is one of the mysteries— but they did so in the hope of a railroad which was being graded. The failure of crops & consequent want of business has put an end to the railroad building & one half of the American population of this county will leave this fall because they have nothing to live upon & no seed, food, or fuel. There never was so distressed a community as the inhabitants of So Dak. I did not take a collection last night because I was told that it would be cruel to ask for money, as people are situated. The Russians will remain because they have to & because they can live on almost nothing. They burn cow-dung for fuel—live in houses of sod without ventilation, dress in sheep-skins and eat anything that will support life. They are a hard lot—stupid violent and ignorant. Dr Gamble who lives here tried to stop diptheria which swept off entire families of children, but the Russians drove him away and threatened to mob him. What business is it of ours, they said. If God wants to kill the children let him. It is none of our affair. So they refused medicines and disinfectants & let the children die. Think of such men being voters.

H B Blackwell

Huron, S Dakota Sept 22 1890

Dearest Lucikin

This is Monday morning, and in another week I shall have finished my round of meetings. . . . Yesterday (Sunday) Mr Fink drove across the prairie with me to this city where I met Mr & Mrs Wardall, Mr & Mrs Devoe, Mrs Pickler, Mr Bailey & other friends. The state of affairs was a little peculiar. Several of the ministers, instigated it is said by leading members of their congregations opposed to woman suffrage, had refused the use of their churches for my Sunday evening meeting & declined to give notice of it on the ground that politics were not proper for Sunday evening. So we secured the Opera House & I called on all the ministers—who were polite, but all united in a union-Bible meeting except the Episcopal & Catholic ministers, who are both friends of W Suffrage. The Episcopal Rector, Rev Mr Potter, kindly agreed to conduct the exercises and introduce me which he did. I spoke to a deeply interested audience of 250— one fourth voters, and we had an excellent meeting. . . .

Do not think me indifferent to returning home when I say that I wish I could spend next month in this State. Altho the battle seems *hopeless* against the indifference & opposition—with three parties struggling for success all ignoring us, & with the Capital fight between Huron and Pierre complicating the issues,—yet, so long as the result is undecided, it seems a pity not to keep up the fight. I see that Mississippi has gone back on woman suffrage. Perhaps it is best. Force and Fraud are too rampant down there to affiliate with more civilized methods. The Kentucky Const^l Conv^n ought now to be tried. The figures for Kentucky should be copied from my magazine article manuscript & reprinted in the W.J. & W.C. [Woman's Column]

Copies of it should be sent to every member of the Ky Const^l Conv^n. How I wish you could be here with me to enjoy every day this heavenly climate—so fresh, dry, elastic and balmy atmosphere. With ever so much love believe me

Ever yours
Henry B Blackwell

I am *well* and am counting the days till my return to "home sweet home."

HBB

As feared, the woman suffrage amendment in South Dakota was defeated, 45,862 to 22,072. An amendment extending the suffrage to male Indians received more affirmative votes, and in a letter to a friend several weeks later, Lucy couldn't resist commenting, "Is it not a shame that the men of S. Dakota gave more votes for the enfranchisement of Indians who are now after their scalps than they did for women!" Still, she remained hopeful of eventual victory; her optimism was apparent in letters she wrote to Susan B. Anthony and to another suffragist and good personal friend, Judith W. Smith of East Boston, in 1891 and 1892 respectively.

∽

Dorchester, Sept. 6, 1891

Dear Miss Anthony

I came through Rochester last Friday night and was sorry not to stop, but I was miserable. The lime water of the West always makes me ill, and I had no courage to add even a straw to the situation.

I am sure we have no reason to fear a lack of representation and opportunity at Chicago. We saw Senator Palmer, Mr. Bonney, Mrs. Potter Palmer, Mrs. Henrotin, Mrs. Flower, and others and we found only the earnest good will to our cause and to its proper representation. Mr. Bonney's idea of a Committee on several broad sub-

jects, one of which will be suffrage, will give us a larger hearing than
we could have on our single question alone. I mean larger under the
circumstances. The whole question of suffrage (not merely as applied
to woman) will come up, and it will give the best possible opportunity
to put in and show the claim of woman. . . . The outlook at Chicago
is certainly very good for our cause. It will be lifted on a whole age
by this effort *in a new situation*. The women themselves will learn so
much!

I happened to be in Chicago at the time of the five-days business
meeting of the Women's Department. So many distinguished women
were there from all over the Union, and so many of them were fine-
looking, noble women. And the best of them were suffragists. I
stopped at the Palmer House. Here were headquarters for the
women. They came to me from everywhere to say they were suffragists. Especially the Southern women to whom the question is a fresh
gospel. It did my heart good to meet them, and to see and feel their
warm enthusiasm. And they are still young, able to fight when we
are gone. Mrs. Potter Palmer is herself a host on our side. She is so
beautiful and so gracious. So tactful, so rich and so clearly a suffragist
that she will win for our cause by her very personality. Everything
seems to be helping now. How good it is after those long years of
endeavor!

We got home last night. At our meeting at the Winnebago
County Fair in Ills., the great audience almost unanimously (apparently *wholly* so) voted their approval of Woman Suffrage. It was a
sight worth seeing when the great crowd rose up on our side, and
the President of the Fair wore the yellow ribbon as did the Mayor of
the City.

> Yours in good hope of the victory
> not so far off as it was once,
> Lucy Stone

Boston, July 22, 1892

Dear Mrs. Smith:

. . . It was a good idea of yours to take the leaflets. They are
the best little missionaries we have. I am having some more of Mr.
Bowditch's pamphlet "Woman Suffrage a Right," printed and bound

in flexible covers, and then I mean to put one in all our State town libraries and in all the college libraries. The money to pay for it comes from a legacy left by Wm. Hamilton of Indiana.

The work for the Cause is going on wonderfully, not all wisely, I think, but it goes at a rapid rate. Women have gone in pledged to work for each one of the political parties on this side the ocean. While in England, in the elections that are just over, women from Lady Henry Somerset down have an active part. When they come in on the edges in that way, they will crowd in wholly being invited to do so.

We are all very anxious about the labor question at Homestead,—the Carnegie Iron Works. The troops are still there, and the strikers do not yield, though yesterday was the last day on which they were to be allowed to do so. When I saw what "furies" the women made of themselves at the time of the Pinkerton slaughter it seems to me we must claim that women who are to vote must have been 21 years in the country first. In that time they may, free from old world ideas, have learned some self-control. I presume you have the papers and see that is going on.

I have never been so miserable with rheumatism. More pain, keen like a hard digging of a knife into my joints. It is three Mondays since I have been at the office. But I remember that Emerson says— "Dont talk about your ails, not even if sciatica tears you." That is his meaning, not the words.

Yours affectionately
Lucy Stone

In the spring of 1893 Lucy and Henry were once again separated on the anniversary of their wedding day. Her letter for that occasion showed that nearly forty years of happily married life hadn't succeeded in completely eradicating her distrust of men. Henry had gone to Louisville, Kentucky, for the convention of the National League of Republican Clubs, and when he returned to Boston, Lucy and Alice had already left for Chicago, where they were to speak at a special congress on suffrage, held as part of the World's Fair.

It was to be Lucy's last public appearance. Later, another suffragist, Lillie Devereux Blake, remembered her at the Fair as "a small figure somewhat bent, touchingly slow & feeble of motion," who had to be assisted to her seat. Lucy had planned to return to Chicago later in the summer for more suffrage programs, but when the time came, she was too ill to go and so Henry went in her stead. She was now suffering from a stomach disorder that made it almost impossible to eat, and hopeful that a change of scene would do her good, she went to her sister's home in Gardner, Massachusetts.

⌘

[Dorchester] May 1, 1893

Dear Harry

This is our 38th wedding day. After this *always,* I shall like to have my rents, interest, &c put in my bank. It is the *right* way. I shall be just as willing as heretofore to help you out upon occasion. But all my property will be simpler in the final settlement if it appears according to the facts.

I have never liked the having it put in your bank but as I have said, you did so much for women that I had allowed it. But now we will let it go into my bank.

Yours always affectionately
Lucy Stone

Glascow Junction Ky May 12, 1893

Dear Lucy

The Convention adjourned yesterday (thursday) afternoon too late for the train making Eastward connections. So I joined a number of Kansas delegates & with Mr Dow of Portland, a delegate from Maine, we made up a party of six to visit the Mammoth Cave. . . .

We had a very queer & amusing experience on the cars. Our party of six got into an empty smoking car & Mr Greene of Lecompton, chairman of the delegation, read aloud a very pleasant description of the Cave written by a Mr Prentis of Kansas entitled "Southern Letters." Then we got to talking politics & that stirred up a colored man named Smith, who proved to be an agent of the Congo Emigra-tion Co. He criticized Mr Clarkson's address and expressed his dis-approval of Mr Blaine for his opposition to the Federal Elections Bill. He announced his hatred of the Democratic party and his disgust with the Republican party—& assured us that the Reps were now so completely subjugated in the South, that we might count on the *Solid South* as a permanent fact in our future politics. Just then came in another Mr Smith of Salt Lake City a Rep delegate from Utah—& we got to discussing the Mormon question and then the institution of polygamy. He announced himself as the son of a polygamous father who had had two wives & finally told us that he had been twice married himself & was the father of 16 children, 13 still living. He seemed a thoroughly sincere & very intelligent man & argued for the institution as both natural & beneficial to both sexes. Our party ques-tioned, argued, and listened, until the trains divided and our Mor-mon acquaintance left us.

Now as to the Convention. I worked for our resolution on the cars and at the Galt House, which was headquarters & where I stopped. I found a majority of the men I talked with more or less friendly to the resolution, securing among others the support of Rev Dr Morrison of Balto. a very conservative Old School Presbyterian minister & an intensely Southern man in his views on questions con-cerning the negro &c.—a son-in-law of Rev Dr Breckenridge of Lex-ington Ky. who was so eminent 30 years ago. Thanks to Major Gould I was placed on the Com on Resolutions & there fought a battle which culminated at 3 AM in the adoption of a compromise resolution prepared by Mr Bundy of Bucyrus [Kansas] presenting the WS ques-tion to the "favorable consideration" of the Republican Leagues of the United States. A majority of the Com on Resolutions were in favor of WS., but were doubtful of their right to express views in advance of the platform of the party, claiming that the work of formulating a platform belonged solely to the National Convention. That the work of the National League of Rep Clubs was by its constitution purely educational & executive—its province being to organize locally for practical work.

We met at 5 PM in the parlor of the Ills delegation. About 25 States were represented. The Resolution which I had in the morning read in Convention & had referred to the Com. on Resolutions, I read again & moved for adoption. A com of 7 was appointed, of which I was not one, with instructions to prepare a platform. We then adjourned to 10.30 PM when we again met. By invitation Mrs. [Ellen] Foster made an admirable little address to the Com:—She made so favorable an impression that the Com while still unwilling to put in an affirmative declaration as inconsistent with the constitution of the League accepted the compromise, which I opposed, but voted for as a separate measure, good as far as it went. It was brought up & adopted just before adjournment at 3 AM after a long & tedious contest over many other questions. . . .

Next morning I conferred with Mrs Foster as to the propriety of renewing the fight in Convention for my resolution, but we decided that it would be unwise. The chances of success in face of a hostile com. would be very slight while the *moral effect* of the adoption of our resolution would be lost by the wrangle. Results showed our wisdom. Even our platform resolution met with a motion to lay on the table. But we carried it by 375 to 130 with great applause & enthusiasm. The Kansas, Colorado, Utah, Mass & RI delegations voted solid in its favor, and the warmest good feeling was manifested. It was universally regarded as a great victory for W.S., putting the endorsement of the National League behind it. Mr Clarkson made a capital allusion to WS in his address, avowing himself a believer in it. This passage was heartily & repeatedly *cheered*—receiving more applause than anything else in his address.

The large Southern delegations account almost wholly for the negative vote. Ky of course was there in force, and the Southern men felt that it would make them still more odious—& add to the almost hopeless burthen which they are trying to carry. The Southern Rep delegates on the Com on Resolutions were all *white* men & very desirous to have a resolution recommending *separate* primaries of whites & blacks as indispensable for winning *white* cooperation. They want a *white* Republican party in order to give the negroes a chance to come in as a balance of power. I am quite well. The weather is *lovely*. Home Monday morning.

Yours affectionately
Henry B Blackwell

3 Park St Boston May 15/93

Dearest Luciken

When I reached the office this (Monday) morning at 9 AM. I was quite surprised to learn that you & Alice had left on Saturday for Chicago. I had it in my mind that you were not to leave Boston until tomorrow (Tuesday). I am sorry I was not here to help you off, but hope that poor Alice will not be broken down by having had all the preparations devolve upon her. Had I known that you were to go so soon, I should not have felt at liberty to go from Louisville to the Mammoth Cave, which occupied an additional 48 hours. I went down with a jolly party of Kansas delegates & one from Maine. . . . We took the little branch RR from Glascow Junction to Mammoth Cave on Friday at 9^{30}. At 11 AM we went to the cave with a guide and emerged at 6 PM—having walked, so they said, 15 miles (7½ miles & return). We took what is called "the long route." This Alice could do perfectly well, but you could not. I think however that you could take the *short route* perfectly well by taking time, & returning if necessary before going to the end of it. I do most urgently advise you & Alice to return by way of the Mammoth Cave. The *Monon Line* of railroad runs cars from Chicago to Glascow Junction direct & without change or fatigue. At Glascow Junction you can stop overnight and get a good sleep & rest. Mr & Mrs Wentz are very kind and Mrs Wentz, the landlady is in love with you from your picture & biography by Alice and asks me to say that she will *do everything for your comfort & go with you to the cave if you like*. . . .

My trip to Louisville *paid*. It brought the question of W.S. before the country & before the Republicans. I made many friends for the cause. The resolution we got will do as much good as the stronger one I tried to get, because the Nat^l League is not formed to formulate a platform, but is *educational* and for *organization*. We carried it by a two-thirds vote & over. It has gone all over the country that the Rep Nat Conv^n has endorsed woman suffrage & that is the main point. I will not bore you with particulars but in justice to Mrs J Ellen Foster I will say that her presence was a great help to us. She spoke finely for woman suffrage at the mass meeting in Louisville Wednesday evening. She made a very impressive address before the Resolutions Committee in support of my resolution & made a *very fine* impression. Thank her for her good work if you see her. Nothing could have been better. Mrs Johns wrote that she could not come & it was *better so*. I have here today a letter from Mr Johns (Mrs Johns husband) from St Louis rejoicing over the passage of the W.S. resolution. I got none of the home letters to me from you & Alice except the card from Alice telling of the fine *Reception*. But all agree that everything went off well & was a great success. . . .

Yours affectionately
H B Blackwell

Wednesday Boston, May 17 1893

Dearest Luciken

I find in this morning's Globe a very pleasant and graphic account of the meeting in Chicago at which you discussed the Bloomer costume. It is far more interesting and appropriate for our paper than the longwinded generalities of Mr Bonney, which Alice has sent on to be published, & which will crowd it out. Tell Alice that the WJ. is *dying of long articles*! If I had my way I would religiously exclude or cut them down to one column or less! We are all well. It is cold & rainy here still. I sat last night by a fire in the library, & enjoyed the hot water bag which Beth had put into my bed. . . .

I am very anxious that you should avoid exposure to colds & draughts. You must *wear your cap* & keep *wraps* with you. In case you find the slightest danger of pneumonia, remember the two grain doses of calomel.

I am glad to hear from Alice that so far you are well & not bored. I feel decidedly the better for my Western trip, & if I can avoid eating too much, I hope to retain the good effects of it. . . . The little cow continues so wild & restless that Michael dares not put her out of the barn for fear she will break loose & run away. She wont eat grass or meal; only hay & seems never to have been milked before. I dont see what old Bleiler means by sending us such an one. Last time he gave us a goat; this time it is a deer. Love to Alice. Tell her to take things easy & dont forget the Mammoth cave.

Ever affectionately
Henry B Blackwell

Tell Alice that her last paper was very interesting. Her report of the festival was *excellent*. But darn old *Bonney* all the same!

HBB

Boston, May 19 1893

Dearest Luciken

I enclose a letter from Howard [Blackwell] received today. The Boston Herald today has a little allusion to you which I enclose, as also a similar kind of item from the Transcript. Your quaint sayings seem to be appreciated. . . .

I wish that you & Alice would call Laura Johns & Mrs Carrie Lane Chapman into a *Council of War*. If I understand aright Colorado votes *first* on the WS Const^l Amd^t. It is *very important* to carry Colorado & if that be impossible (of which I am not at all sure) then it is very important to get the largest possible vote. Now the Kansas summer is inconsistent with work. It is too sultry & debilitating. But the Colorado summer tho hot is *not* debilitating. I suggest that Mrs Johns & Mrs Chapman confer with Mrs Louise Tyler of Denver & work up Colorado *first of all*. Not merely by meetings, but by a quiet move on the newspaper press and the Labor Unions & Knights of Labor. If we can get 1. The Republican machine of Colorado 2^d the Labor Organizations & 3^d The newspapers—and push the *Enrolment* which can use the same books as Kansas (I have 500 printed)—we can get a *committee of men at each voting precinct* of Colorado and that will carry the State. Dont try to enlist the W.C.T.U. Let the Temperance question quietly alone. *You four people* can plan it all out at Chicago. The Colorado & Kansas delegations at Louisville voted *solid* for WS.

[Dorchester] Sunday 10 30 AM May 21 1893

Dearest Luciken

We feel very uneasy at hearing of the accident at the Woman's Congress yesterday. The names of persons seriously injured are given & no one I know is among them. But this & the fact that you seem not to have got any of my letters leads me to telegraph today to know if you are safe. The trouble is I dont know to whom to telegraph. Mrs

McCulloch is not at her office on Sundays. Mrs Carrie Lane Chapman may no longer be at the Palmer House. If you & Alice are hurt you cannot answer. I am puzzled just what to do. . . .

The black cat seems to have lost his appetite & spirits since you left. He goes round disconsolately looking for you & then quietly disappears. We offer him food regularly. Do not be in a hurry to return. I can get along & keep myself occupied. . . .

In haste for morning mail
Yours affy
H B Blackwell

Chicago Sunday May 21 1893

Dearest Harry

The congresses are all over, but I have to speak for Mrs Governor Eagle in the Womans building on the Fairgrounds next Wednesday the 24 and tomorrow Mrs Potter Palmer gives a reception at her house which we are both to attend. After that we go to the Unity Home near the Fair . . . till Saturday, when we expect to start home, reaching there on Sunday next at 6.05 o'clock.

Today I spoke for Jenkin Lloyd Jones' Sunday School and staid and heard John W Chadwick preach. After that I went to dine by invitation with a nice member of the Chicago Woman's Club. Alice went to hear Anna Shaw preach. We have been conferring with Mrs Carrie Lane Chapman about Colorado, with a Colorado woman, who says they need $300 a month for six months. They mean to make a still hunt. They have no money, only one small society &c. Laura M. Johns, and her husband are here. We have had two meetings of conference about Kansas here in one of the parlors with a general agreement that we are to raise money and speakers for Kansas. Colorado seems to me to be a hopeless case, but we are to confer once more with the Colorado woman. Mrs. Duniway is here.

I got your telegram, and now think we have all your letters. We are glad to get them. Nette is in the Woman's dormitory, glad the girls get on so well without house. You will please let Beth have money. She was to ask you for it. It is for a dress, and you will keep the acct. We are both well. It is bed time.

Good night

Pittsburg Pa Sunday aft 3 PM
Aug. 13 1893

Dearest L.

This is your birthday. I telegraphed you last evening from Chicago to show you that the fact was not forgotten. "Increasing happiness with revolving years." I am thus far on way home. . . . I expect to be in Boston *Tuesday morning*. Do not return home if you find the change of air & food good for you. I will get off next week's WJ and then run up to Gardner to spend Saturday & Sunday with you there if you like. . . .

Ever affy yours
Henry Blackwell

Gardner Aug. 15/93

Darling Harrykin

I sent you a line this morning on a postal card to the office. With this go some business letters, as you will see.

About myself, I am far enough from well. I continue to throw up the dark matter which you and Emily saw, and all that passes my bowels is as black as ink & to get a movement I have to use a syringe. I have no appetite at all. I would rather not eat than to eat. This morning I had the small end of a just done potatoe (baked) half a cup of mutton broth with rice, and half a cup of tea. I ate no supper last night, and for dinner yesterday I had bread about as large as two fingers. But I *can* eat it. The milk soured so on my stomach I had to leave it off. I take the dandelion and pepsin which Emily recommended, and I have at this moment got a letter from her advising me to continue them and to take some pills which she sends the prescription for. I have been thoroughly bathed, and the pores well opened. Last night I took a liver powder which Clara Barlow has found useful to herself, and in consequence I have had today 2 movements of my bowels—billious enough, which must be a relief. I had to leave off the rides. They were too much for me. But I sit out a great deal, and lie down a good deal, and take once a day a little walk in the garden.

I hate to write you all this, but you will want to know just how

I am. In these large airy rooms and with other healthy conditions, I hope to be better. But I think my working days are over. I have had several pleasant birthday letters, and I am not worrying about anything. Be careful of yourself for Alice's sake. She will need you. I am sorry to send you this sickish letter. Alice sends me a daily line, and she seems well.

Ever affy
L.S.

EPILOGUE

～

And if from beyond the grave, it be indeed permitted
to influence and inspire—dear Lucy—you shall always
find an *open* heart & an expectant longing.
Henry Blackwell to Lucy Stone, September 8, 1857

By September it was clear that Lucy was dying. The dandelion and pepsin remedies prescribed by Emily Blackwell
were of no use in stemming the tide of her illness, because
she had cancer. She returned to the Dorchester house,
where Henry and Alice were at her side almost constantly. As they
sat together, Lucy's mind often wandered back to her childhood on
the farm at Coy's Hill, but the present and planning for the future
occupied her as well. She continued to dictate short editorials for the
Journal, and to correspond with other suffragists. One of her last letters was to a Denver suffragist, urging her to do all she could to help
Mrs. Carrie Lane Chapman, who had gone to Colorado for the
amendment campaign.

Many old friends came to see Lucy, and a visit from Julia Ward
Howe provided one of the lighter moments of her last illness. When
Mrs. Howe brought the news that Lucy's old rival Mrs. Stanton was
also dying (actually, Mrs. Stanton was to survive Lucy by almost a
decade), Lucy speculated that the cause of death would probably be
apoplexy, and remarked how odd it would be if the first person she
met on the other side was Mrs. Stanton.

Looking back on her own long, full life, she appeared to have
few regrets. At one point when she and Alice were talking of an old
friend whose husband had turned out to be very unsatisfactory, Lucy
took the opportunity to reaffirm her faith in the institution of marriage. "But I do believe that a woman's truest place is in a home,"
she told Alice, "with a husband and with children, and with large
freedom, pecuniary freedom, personal freedom, and the right to
vote." However, her ideas had changed somewhat since the early

days of her marriage when Henry had protested: "If you are not willing that your husband should *support you*—at least do not think it
will ever be necessary to support him." For now Lucy told Alice that
she didn't think the wife should take part in the breadwinning: "She
bears the children and her hands are full."

By the end of September, weekly reports on Lucy's health began
to appear in *The Woman's Journal*, in answer to inquiries from concerned readers. On October 14 the *Journal* noted that Lucy was only
able to speak a few words at a time, but that her mind was clear, and
when told that the Democratic State Convention in New York had
adopted a suffrage plank, "a flash of joy passed over her face." Four
days later, on October 18, 1893, at 10:45 P.M. Lucy Stone passed
away. Her last intelligible words, whispered to Alice before she
lapsed into unconsciousness, were "Make the world better."

Newspapers throughout the country paid ample tribute to Lucy
Stone as "one of the noblest women of the century"; and when funeral services were held at the Church of Disciples in Boston, more
than eleven hundred people came to pay their respects, filing sol-
emnly past the coffin where Lucy lay, dressed as for a reception in
black silk "with lace at her throat and wrists," a gold pin, and her
best cap.

The final disposition of Lucy's embalmed remains didn't take
place until more than two months later. She had left instructions for
her body to be cremated, and since the nearest crematory was in
New York State, Henry and Alice decided to wait until the one under
construction at the Forest Hills Cemetery in the Boston area was
ready. Henry confessed to "a profound reluctance to have Lucy's
body thus disposed of," but in death as in life he honored her wishes.
To reassure himself as much as anyone else, he wrote a detailed account of the proceedings in a letter to his three sisters in England.
He described how he, Alice, and William Lloyd Garrison's youngest
son traveled by carriage and then on foot through a wintry landscape
to the cemetery; how the furnace was heated; and how as the coffin
moved toward the oven, he "saw for the last time the dear form and
face lying in the same peaceful attitude as when the coffin lid was
closed in the church 2½ months before." The next day he and Alice
returned by sleigh in a blinding snowstorm to collect Lucy's ashes,
which Henry had placed in two urns.

Henry and Alice were overcome with grief at their loss, but of the two, Alice was the first to recover. She clearly cherished her mother's memory throughout the rest of her life, but in a certain sense, Lucy's death had a liberating effect on her. She had once told her cousin, Emma Blackwell, "that her father was like an angel in the house, and her mother like the shelter of a great rock under which you felt a sense of safety and strong protection." In Emma Blackwell's words, the comparisons "fairly characterized the difference between the two—the sparkle and brilliance of the one and the quiet steadfast strength of the other." Besides safety and protection, Alice's simile for her mother hints at a degree of oppressiveness; and in fact, she was not to feel free to be her own person until her mother was gone. Two years after Lucy's death, Emily Blackwell wrote to Elizabeth: "Alice is wonderfully developing her individuality in her independent position. She will always be good and conscientious, but she shows a sort of self-will and positive determination in everyday life which is quite new, and shows what an unconscious subordination her mother's strong will impressed upon her."

One way in which Alice expressed her newly found individuality was by falling in love. In the summer of 1893 when she was almost thirty-six, she had met an attractive Armenian theologian, Johannes Chatschumian, at the camp in Canada where she had vacationed earlier. The two had become good friends and spent many hours together translating Armenian poetry into English, but it wasn't until after her mother's death that Alice acknowledged her love for Chatschumian. Unfortunately, the romance ended tragically with his death a few years later, and so Alice remained single and devoted her life to the cause.

Henry didn't weather Lucy's death as well as his daughter. Alice recalled how he sat alone in the dark in Lucy's room night after night, in the hopes that her spirit would come to him; and failing to receive any sign from her, he was inconsolable in his grief. A little less than a year after Lucy's death, Emily Blackwell wrote to Elizabeth:

Poor Harry is almost morbid in his regret for Lucy. It takes the form of self reproach for shortcomings and neglects. He loses sight of the fact that with all her good qualities, she was in many respects difficult and trying and quietly domi-

neering, and that all their married life was full of trial, which
was largely due to her peculiarities. He was one of the best
husbands possible, and certainly modified his whole course
. . . to adapt his life to hers, and yet now he dwells upon
every dissonance that ever occurred as though he alone
were to blame.

Besides blaming himself for "shortcomings and neglects" during
their married life, Henry reproached himself for having persuaded
Lucy to marry him in the first place. "I have often wondered," he
wrote in his Reminiscences, "whether it was best for her and for the
cause to have thus complicated her mission with domestic cares &
duties which she was too simple and faithful to neglect for any public
vocation. Lucy was constitutionally *intense* and concentrated. She
could not carry two trains of thought at the same time so well as
many."

Yet while Henry dwelt obsessively on the mistakes he felt he
had made, others tended to concur with Emily's judgment that he
had been one of the best husbands possible. In 1894 the temperance
leader, Frances Willard, hailed Henry "as one of the noblest lights of
the new chivalry"; and a year later, at his seventieth-birthday celebration, Professor Ellen Hays of Wellesley College said of him: "He
seems to me more perhaps than any man I know, to represent in his
character and life the elements of the ideal man whom we women
love and reverence and admire."

Henry brushed aside such praise, saying that if he hadn't promised Lucy to work for woman's rights, she would never have married
him, and "Therefore, am I not under an honorable obligation to devote every energy of mind and body to make that promise good—
knowing as I do that all I can do in a life-time will not be as much as
she did in the first three years after I knew her." He considered
himself a failure on two counts: moral and financial. He didn't believe
he had done enough to make the world a better place, nor had he
realized his youthful dream of becoming a millionaire. In a letter to
Elizabeth which was, in effect, a summing up of the family's fortunes,
he rated himself beneath his brother Sam, who now had a secure
position and comfortable living, and also below his brother George,
who had become a wealthy man through real estate.

Actually, Henry's financial situation was such that it was difficult for him to keep *The Woman's Journal* afloat. But he rejected a suggestion that he switch from a weekly to monthly paper, because he didn't think Lucy would have approved of the change. As he had said to Alice immediately after her death, "We must try to keep Mamma's flag flying."

Besides keeping the suffrage flag flying, Henry lent his voice and pen to a variety of other causes. He supported Henry George's single tax; called for reciprocity and freer trade; denounced imperialism and "the growing control of legislation by industrial monopolies"; and protested the Russian pogroms, the Armenian massacre of 1895, and the deportation of political refugees. He also found time to indulge his old passion for "change and variety." He made a second trip to Europe with his daughter, went on a Caribbean junket with George and Emma Blackwell, and accompanied by Alice and Antoinette Brown Blackwell, traveled to Portland, Oregon, for the first national suffrage convention held on the West Coast. Old age and grief for his dead wife hadn't completely robbed him of his boyish exuberance and zest for living. According to Emma Blackwell, he was especially proud of his feat of climbing a glacier while in Oregon, "for he distinctly did not wish to be thought of as old or referred to 'as our venerable friend'—or anything else venerable."

In 1909 Henry and Alice traveled to Seattle for the annual convention of the national suffrage association. Over a forty-year period, Henry hadn't missed any of these national conventions, and it seemed likely that he would continue to attend them for at least a few more years. His health was good, and his morale, excellent. But toward the end of the summer, he accepted a friend's last-minute invitation to go to his summer home on the coast to discuss tariff reform, and while there caught a bad cold. Admitting that he had been "going at full speed" up until the time of his illness, Henry acknowledged that if he recovered, he would probably have to slow down a bit.

He did not live to do so. On September 7, 1909, Alice wrote to Elizabeth's adopted daughter, Kitty, "Papa passed away peacefully soon after noon today, after lying unconscious for some hours." Early in their marriage, Henry had written Lucy that when they both died, he wanted to be buried in the same grave, and now, although the idea of cremation was repugnant to him, he left instructions for his body to be cremated, and his ashes mingled with his wife's in one urn.

His daughter Alice survived him by forty-one years. After his death she assumed the editorship of *The Woman's Journal,* which continued to be published until 1917 when it was merged with two other suffrage papers to become *The Woman Citizen.* Following her retirement from the *Journal* and the ratification of the Nineteenth Amendment, Alice helped to organize the League of Women Voters in Massachusetts. She also supported other more radical causes. Together with William Dudley Foulke and George Kennan, she was instrumental in forming the Friends of Russian Freedom, and became a close friend and partisan of Catherine Breshkovsky, "the little grandmother of the Russian Revolution." The twenties found her a professed socialist radical, rallying to the cause of Sacco and Vanzetti. Day after day she appeared at protest meetings in Boston, a small white-haired woman carrying books and her lunch in a brown paper bag. In 1930 she paid final tribute to her mother with the completion of her biography, a book over which she had labored lovingly, off and on, for several decades. At her death in 1950 at the age of ninety-three, her body was cremated like her parents', and her ashes deposited at the Forest Hills Cemetery in Boston.

Alice had lived long enough to see that the enfranchisement of women did not bring about the millennium envisioned by her parents. But to acknowledge the failure of woman suffrage as an instrument of radical change is not to deny the significance of the movement as a whole, or of the lives of those associated with it. Through their participation in the suffrage movement American women began to forge a new definition of the relations between the sexes, and thus paved the way for the modern women's-liberation movement.

Lucy Stone and Henry Blackwell helped to further this drive toward equality by such specific actions as their protest against the unjust marriage laws of their time, and by Lucy's retention of her maiden name. But perhaps their most significant contribution to feminism was their life together: In a partnership of nearly forty years' duration, they provided a model of what today is known as an "emancipated marriage."

NOTES

ONE

Courtship, 1853–1855

HBB–LS, 6/13/53

my old enemy the "skunk cabbage."
The roots and stems of skunk cabbage—so called because of its rank odor—were used medicinally as an antispasmodic, expectorant, and stimulant with a slightly narcotic effect.

her book. The Laws of Life in Reference to the Physical Education of Girls, published in 1852. In this book, the outgrowth of a series of lectures given in New York, Dr. Elizabeth Blackwell advanced a number of ideas considered quite revolutionary at the time; she argued that young girls needed exercise, fresh air, and proper hygiene, and also that they should receive sex education, beginning at an early age.

Mr. & Mrs. Weld & Miss Sarah Grimke. Theodore Dwight Weld (1803–1895), a noted abolitionist leader. His wife, the former Angelina Grimké (1805–1879), and her older sister Sarah (1792–1873) were also abolitionists and the first American women to speak in public before mixed audiences. In 1839, shortly after Weld and Angelina Grimké married, the trio had retired to a farm in Belleville, New Jersey.

twenty or thirty . . . children. For several years the Welds had been operating a boarding school in their home.

Theodore's "Thousand Witnesses." American Slavery As It Is: The Testimony of a Thousand Witnesses, compiled largely from reports in Southern newspapers by Weld with the help of his wife and sister-in-law, and published by the American Anti-Slavery Society in 1839. As indicated, Harriet Beecher Stowe relied heavily on Weld's book when she wrote *Uncle Tom's Cabin.*

the associative life. This term had a peculiar nineteenth-century meaning, referring to groups of individuals living "in association" in utopian communities such as Brook Farm.

the "Raritan Bay Union." Communal settlement at Perth Amboy, New Jersey, which had recently been established by Marcus Spring (1810–1874), a New York merchant and philanthropist.

the Tribune. Founded in 1841, *The New York Tribune* espoused a variety of reforms, including woman's rights.

LS–HBB, 6/21/53

those sickly regions. "Sickly country" meant any area with extensive wetlands where mosquitoes bred, and malaria was rampant. The Wabash Valley, where Henry was going, fell into this category.

HBB–LS, 7/2/53

nobody about but Mother my two brothers & my books. Henry's oldest sister, Anna, was living in Paris; Elizabeth, Emily, and Marian were in New York; Ellen had yet to return from the East; and Henry's younger brother, Howard, was living in England and working for a cousin in the iron trade.

Anne Hutchinson. (1591–1643) Religious leader, who was banished from the Massachusetts Bay Colony for her heretical beliefs. She was regarded as a heroine by nineteenth-century feminists.

Bancroft. George Bancroft (1800–1891), diplomat, cabinet officer, and historian, who wrote a carefully researched ten-volume *History of the United States* (1834–76).

The American Antislavery Society. Founded in 1833, the American Anti-Slavery Society called for immediate and unconditional emancipation of all slaves.

Southern men. Many of Henry's customers in the hardware business were Southerners from across the border in Kentucky, and he had also become friendly with a number of sons of slaveowners during the year he studied at Kemper College in St. Louis. By his own account, his sympathy with their point of view had led to a temporary abandonment of his abolitionist beliefs.

drudge, as Mrs. Weld. Here Henry voiced a much sharper criticism of the Welds' life-style than he had in his previous letter. But what he said was true: Angelina Grimké Weld, once a star orator of the antislavery movement, had been reduced to little more than a household drudge. A firm believer in manual labor, Weld decided that he would work on the outside while the women took charge of the household—a task for which neither of the sisters, who had grown up with servants, was prepared. Angelina herself was aware of the irony of her situation; to a friend she wrote, "Indeed, I think our enemies would rejoice could they look in on us from day to day and see us in our domestic life, instead of lecturing to promiscuous audiences."

laws of the old Medes & Persians. Proverbially unalterable.

Mrs Ernst. Sarah Otis Ernst, Cincinnati antislavery leader.

Judge Matthews. Stanley Matthews (1824–1889), judge in the court of common pleas in Cincinnati, and later an associate justice of the U.S. Supreme Court.

a free soil man. The Free Soil party was opposed to the extension of slavery into territories newly acquired by the United States.

Mrs. Stanton. Elizabeth Cady Stanton (1815–1902), New York feminist leader, who was one of the prime movers behind the convention at Seneca Falls.

Mansfield's "Rights of Woman." Legal Rights, Liabilities and Duties of Women, written in 1845 by Edward D. Mansfield (1801–1880), author and editor for many years of the *Cincinnati Daily Gazette.*

I shall pay the postage. Up until 1847 the recipient of a letter paid the postage; in that year, however, the first adhesive postage stamps for the prepayment of postage went on sale in New York

the "anti-Bible Convention." Convention held at Hartford, Connecticut, in June of 1853 to discuss the "origin, authority, and influence of the scriptures." An angry crowd, consisting mostly of theological students from nearby Trinity College, mobbed Garrison when he attacked the clergy for failing to take a stand against slavery, and denied the inspiration of the Bible.

LS–HBB, 7/27/53

Wendell Phillips. (1811–1884) Wealthy, Harvard-educated abolitionist, who was one of the great orators of his time.

first National Woman's Rights Convention. Held at Worcester, Massachusetts, in October of 1850.

"Earth waits long . . . room." Lines from one of Lucy's favorite poems, written by Anne Whitney (1821–1915), who many years later sculpted a bust of Lucy that was exhibited at the Chicago World's Fair.

the wise-acres of our Constitutional Convention. Convention held in Boston in the summer of 1853 for the purpose of revising the Massachusetts state constitution. Lucy Stone was among the signers of a petition urging "the extension to women of all civil rights," and spoke in its behalf at the hearings, but the conven-

tion decided it was "inexpedient to act on the petition."

HBB–LS, 8/24/53

little yellow treasure. Pale lemon was a common color for envelopes during this period.

your two glorious meetings. A woman's rights convention and a temperance convention held to protest the exclusion of women from a World's Temperance Convention held in New York the previous May.

Judge McLean. John McLean (1785–1861), U.S. Supreme Court associate justice nominated by the Ohio legislative caucus as a presidential candidate in the election of 1836.

fugitive law. Law requiring the return of runaway slaves to their owners. Originally enacted in 1793, the fugitive-slave law was strengthened as part of the Compromise of 1850. All fugitive-slave cases were placed under the jurisdiction of the federal government; special U.S. commissioners were authorized to issue warrants for the arrest of fugitives after a summary hearing; and citizens who interfered with the arrest of fugitives or otherwise aided them were subject to fines of as much as $1,000.

Judge Mansfield. Sir James Mansfield (1733–1821), English judge, who in 1772 ruled that the slave Somerset had to be freed, because "free soil makes free men." This historic opinion meant that slavery could not legally exist in England.

a friendly controversy. In a lecture delivered in Boston in January of 1853, Wendell Phillips criticized Horace Mann and other abolitionist congressmen for voting and holding office in the U.S. government while the Constitution approved of slavery. Mann defended himself in an open letter to Phillips, and an increasingly heated exchange between the two was published in *The Liberator* from February to June—much to the dismay of the friends of both.

an intimate friend, a bookseller of this City. Ainsworth Rand Spofford (1825–1908). Later to become librarian-in-chief of the Library of Congress, Spofford was working as a bookseller and publisher in Cincinnati. In 1852 he had married Sarah Putnam Partridge.

Count Albert of Rudolstadt . . . Consuelo. The hero and heroine of two novels by the French writer George Sand (1804–1876): *Consuelo* (1842–43) and *La Comtesse de Rudolstadt* (1843–44).

"Spring guns." Guns which could be discharged by a person's coming into contact with them, and which were used as a guard against trespassers and poachers.

Theodore Parker. (1810–1860) Unitarian minister and Transcendentalist who contributed to *The Dial,* and was involved in the antislavery and prison reform movements.

unsuitably married like Mrs Stanton. Elizabeth Cady Stanton was left in charge of the household and the rearing of their seven children while her husband, Henry, was frequently away from home pursuing his work as a lawyer, politician, and journalist. More-over, he had little sympathy with woman's rights: He left town at the time of the Seneca Falls convention to avoid witnessing the "farce" he was certain would occur when his wife presented a resolution in favor of woman suffrage; and was known to complain about the amount of time she spent in agitation.

in difficult circumstances like Mrs Weld formerly. Mrs. Weld's situation improved somewhat with the move to the Raritan Bay Union, but she was not to return to public life until the 1860s, and was never to realize the brilliant promise of her first years as a public speaker.

HBB–LS, 9/9/53

Mr Greeley. Horace Greeley (1811–1872), reformist editor of *The New York Tribune,* who sympathized with the woman's rights movement, but did not agree with all of its demands.

rowdies included. Since the woman's rights and other conventions were open to anyone who purchased a ticket at the door, they attracted many hecklers as well as serious listeners. The "mob element" made its presence felt at the antislavery and temperance conventions which preceded the woman's rights convention, and by the time of the latter, it had become particularly conspicuous: "Gentlemen and ladies who attempted to speak were interrupted by shouts, hisses, stamping, cheers, rude remarks, and all manner of noisy demonstrations."

Mrs. Mott. Lucretia Coffin Mott (1793–1880), Quaker minister, abolitionist leader, and feminist, who, with a sympathetic husband and six children, was an important role model for the younger women in the antislavery and woman's rights movements.

calomel treatment. White, tasteless powder containing chloride of mercury that was given as a purgative. Doctors of the period administered such large doses of calomel that if the illness didn't kill the patient, the treatment often did.

the Emancipator. Weekly antislavery paper published in New York by the clergyman and editor Joshua Leavitt (1794–1873), and considered less radical than Garrison's *Liberator.*

Geo. Thompson. (1804–1878) Prominent English abolitionist. The meeting at which Henry heard Thompson speak in New York in the 1830s was disrupted by a mob that was both anti-English and antiabolitionist.

Political anti-slavery men. This group believed that slavery must be prohibited by law, and that such laws could only be obtained through political pressure. They formed a political party, the Liberty party, which ran an exslaveholder, James G. Birney (1792–1857), as a presidential candidate in the elections of 1840 and 1844, and combined with the Free Soil party in 1848.

loco-foco. The Loco-Focos were a radical urban-based wing of the Democratic party, who wanted to abolish monopolies and special privileges, and advocated hard money, direct taxes, and elections by direct popular vote.

The name came from a new self-lighting friction match known as a loco-foco. At a meeting in New York when party regulars tried to oust the dissident faction by turning off the gas lights, the latter lit candles with these matches, and proceeded to carry on the meeting.

lawyer Joliffe. John Jolliffe (1804–1868), Cincinnati lawyer and abolitionist who frequently aided fugitive slaves.

LS–HBB, 9/24/53

Mr. Channing. William Henry Channing (1810–1884), nephew of the famous Unitarian minister, William Ellery Channing (1780–1842), and an important figure in his own right. A Unitarian minister and author like his uncle, Channing was active in both the antislavery and woman's rights movements.

LS–HBB, 11/11/53

Mrs. Guild. Neighbor of the Blackwells with whom Lucy had stayed when she passed through Cincinnati in 1850.

Alcott. Bronson Alcott (1799–1888), educational reformer, Transcendalist, and the father of Louisa May Alcott. At this point in his career, Alcott was traveling around the country holding "conversations" or discussions on various subjects, which in his case, were not so much conversations as they were monologues, occasionally interrupted by assenting noises from the audience.

"Harper." *Harper's New Monthly*

Magazine (later *Harper's*), first published in New York in 1850.

Putnam. *Putnam's Monthly Magazine*, published in New York from 1853 to 1857.

LS–HBB, 12/30/53

Charles. Charles Burleigh (1810–1878), Connecticut abolitionist and personal friend of Lucy's, known for his brilliant oratory and eccentric appearance; as a matter of principle, he let his hair and beard grow very long.

Nette. Antoinette Brown (Blackwell) (1825–1921), Lucy's close friend from Oberlin and the first woman to be ordained as a Protestant minister.

come by telegraph. At the time Lucy made this suggestion, the telegraph was still a relatively new invention, the first successful message having been transmitted in 1844.

LS–HBB, 1/54

war against Mexico or Cuba. The United States was at war with Mexico from 1846 to 1848. As for Cuba, the seizure of a U.S. merchant vessel by Havana authorities in February of 1854 produced a call for war among expansionists in Congress. The call angered abolitionists, who saw in it an attempt to acquire more slave territory.

a ship to China. The United States had been trading with China since 1784.

HBB–LS, 1/22/54

little black picture. In his *Reminiscences*, Henry described how during one of Lucy's stays in Cincinnati, they had gone "to the rooms of a colored daguerreotype artist named Ball," and he "secured two excellent likenesses of her in a small gold locket."

HBB–LS, 2/12/54

Waverly. Historical novel (1814) by Sir Walter Scott.

Passion Flowers. Volume of poetry by Julia Ward Howe (1819–1910), who later wrote "The Battle Hymn of the Republic." *Passion Flowers* was published anonymously, because Mrs. Howe's husband didn't approve of her writing.

Daisy Burns. A tale by Julia Kavanagh (1814–1877).

the Congressional debates, the Nebraska conspiracy. Congress was engaged in a heated debate over a bill for the organization of the Nebraska Territory, introduced by Stephen A. Douglas (1813–1861). The bill provided for the division of the region into two separate territories, and allowed for their admission to the Union, with or without slavery, thus, in effect, repealing the Missouri Compromise of 1820, which had prohibited slavery north of the 36°30′ line between Missouri and the Rocky Mountains. Abolitionists condemned the bill as a slaveowners' plot.

the Mitchell treachery. An Irishman seeking the overthrow of British rule in Ireland, John Mitchell (1815–1875) was exiled to Australia, escaped, and went to New York, where he generated controversy with his defense of slavery in America.

the Turkish war. The Crimean War (1854–1856), in which Russia was pitted against Turkey, Great Britain, and France.

lots in Toledo. Interested in investing some of her savings in real estate, Lucy had initially consulted Lucretia Mott's husband, James (1788–1868), a Philadelphia businessman, whose brother lived in Toledo.

law of property as regards married people. Under the laws in many states a married woman had no right to money or property acquired before or after her marriage. Her very clothing could be sold by her husband, or seized by his creditors in payment of his debts. In 1845 Maine became the first state to give married women control over their property, and then in 1848, after a twelve-year campaign, New York passed a Married Woman's Property Act, giving wives the right to hold property in their own name.

Blackstone. Sir William Blackstone (1723–1880), English jurist whose *Commentaries on the Laws of England* (1771–72) had a great influence on both English and American lawyers.

LS–HBB, 3/17/54

Nebraska bill will be defeated. As of March 17, the Nebraska Bill had passed the Senate (37 to 14), but Lucy hoped it would be defeated in the House by a coalition of Whigs, Free Soilers, and antislavery Democrats. As it turned out, however, the bill passed the House 113 to 100 on May 22.

Stephens of Georgia. Alexander Hamilton Stephens (1812–1883), a Democratic congressman who generally favored moderation, but held firm on the question of slavery. When the South finally seceded, Stephens was elected vice-president of the Confederacy.

Dr. Beecher. Henry Ward Beecher (1813–1887), New York clergyman and one of the most influential public figures of his day.

Rev. Mr. R. Storrs. Richard Salter Storrs (1787–1873), Massachusetts Congregational minister, and champion of antislavery.

delivery of fugitive at Milwaukee. On March 9, 1854, Joshua Glover, a fugitive slave from Missouri, then working at a sawmill outside of Racine, was arrested and jailed in Milwaukee. When word of his arrest reached Racine, a group of abolitionists led by the newspaper editor Sherman Booth secured his forcible rescue.

LS–HBB, 4/23/54

Mrs. Bloomer. Amelia Jenks Bloomer (1818–1894), editor of the feminist and temperance paper, *The Lily*, and popularizer of the costume named after her.

H. C. Wrights book. *Marriage and Parentage; or The Reproductive Element in Man as a Means to His Elevation and Happiness* (1854) by the abolitionist, Henry Clarke Wright (1797–1870). The second half of the book consists of correspondence between an imaginary couple, Nina and Earnest, on such aspects of marriage as "Variety in Love, or Polygamy," "Harmony of Development," and

"The Reproductive Element." As these letters are on a rather abstract level, it is difficult to imagine a real couple writing them.

LS–HBB, 4/26/54

Sarah Pellet. Oberlin classmate of Lucy Stone and Antoinette Brown, and early woman's rights activist.

HBB–LS, 5/2/54

Mrs Abby Foster. Abby Kelley Foster (1810–1887), Massachusetts schoolteacher, who became one of the most outstanding of the early women antislavery lecturers. Throughout the 1840s she lectured in different parts of the country, exercising a strong influence on Lucy Stone and other women.

HBB–LS, 5/12/54

the Ladies Anti-Slavery Society. Beginning in the 1830s, women in Philadelphia, Boston, and other towns and villages had responded to an appeal by the American Anti-Slavery Society to the "ladies of the land" by founding female antislavery societies. These societies performed an important fund-raising function, distributed tracts and periodicals, ran schools for the local black population, and petitioned Congress for the abolition of slavery.
Redmond. Charles Lenox Redmond (1810–1873), black abolitionist and follower of Garrison.

HBB–LS, 6/18/54

Mr Ryland. James W. Ryland, one of Henry's partners in the hardware business.

HBB–LS, 9/1/54

Edmund Quincy. (1807–1877) Boston abolitionist and one of the editors of the *National Anti-Slavery Standard.*
covenant with death & agreement with Hell platform. Garrisonian abolitionists denounced the U.S. Constitution as a "covenant with death and agreement with hell," because of its acceptance of slavery.
A Hunker [?] *Whig lawyer.* The Hunkers were actually a faction within the Democratic party, representing the more conservative element. The name was a corruption of the Dutch "hunkerer," which meant a self-seeking individual who "hunkered" or hungered for office.
the Disunionists. Another name given to Garrisonian abolitionists because they believed the Union should be dissolved over the question of slavery.
Emigrants Aid Societies. Societies started in New England to promote the settlement of antislavery groups in Kansas with the goal of making it a free state. Between 1854 and 1857 the societies brought in some two thousand settlers, and founded Lawrence, and other "free state" communities.

LS–HBB, 9/3/54

Jacques. 1834 novel by George Sand.

LS–HBB, 10/8/54

ult. Abbreviation of *ultimo*, meaning in or of the month preceding the current one.

rescue at Syracuse. In 1851 an attempt was made to kidnap Jerry McHenry, an escaped slave who had been living in Syracuse for several years. However, abolitionists succeeded in rescuing McHenry from the officers of the law.

LS–HBB, 10/10/54

sang like Jenny Lind. Although she possessed a beautiful speaking voice, Lucy had no ear for music, and thus was hardly in the same league as "the Swedish Nightingale," whom Henry had heard when she came to Cincinnati in 1851.

LS–HBB, 10/22/54

Mr. Higginson. Thomas Wentworth Higginson (1823–1911), Massachusetts Unitarian minister, abolitionist, and feminist, who wrote essays on reforms and edited the poems of Emily Dickinson.

like Ajax. During the Trojan War, Odysseus and Ajax, son of Telamon, quarreled over which of them should receive the dead Achilles' arms. The arms were to be awarded to the most valiant Greek, and when they went to Odysseus, Ajax went mad and during the night slaughtered the herds that were to provide food for the Greeks. The next morning when he saw what he had done, he committed suicide.

LS–HBB, 10/26/54

inst. Instant, an archaic usage, meaning the present or current month.

HBB–LS, 12/22/54

Dr Hunt. Harriot K. Hunt (1805–1875), Boston woman's rights advocate and physician, who was the first woman to practice medicine with considerable success, despite the fact that she did not hold a medical degree. She began her practice in 1835, was refused admission to Harvard Medical School in 1847 and again in 1850, and in 1853 was finally awarded an honorary M.D. from the Female Medical College at Philadelphia.

in the hands of our firm. Lucy had lent Henry's firm $5,000, which represented all of the proceeds from the western lecture tour he had arranged for her.

HBB–LS, 1/3/55

Jan. 3. [1855]. Although the original of this letter is dated 1854, it is clear from internal references (e.g., to their forthcoming marriage) that it was actually written in 1855; Henry made a common mistake in forgetting to change the date after the beginning of the New Year.

HBB–LS, 3/18/55

Senator Chase. Salmon P. Chase (1803–1873), antislavery leader from Ohio who served in the U.S. Senate from 1849 to 1855.

Sumner, Seward. Charles Sumner (1811–1874) and William H. Seward (1801–1872) were abolitionist senators from Massachusetts and New York respectively.

Henry Wilson. (1812–1875) Abolitionist congressman from Massachusetts.

Dr. Baileys . . . the Know Nothings. Gamaliel Bailey (1807–1859), editor of the *National Era,* an organ of political abolitionism. The Know-Nothing party, officially known as the American party, was rooted in the anti-Catholic and anti-immigrant movement of the 1840s. The national party came into existence after the election of 1852, and by 1854, had gained considerable support among disaffected Whigs and Democrats. Its platform called for the exclusion of Catholics and foreigners from public office, and a twenty-one-year residency requirement for immigrants seeking citizenship. The name Know-Nothing stemmed from the password "I don't know," that was used by members of the party's secret lodges.

LS–HBB, 3/29/55

Sam J. May. The Reverend Samuel Joseph May (1797–1871), Unitarian minister and the agent of the Massachusetts Anti-Slavery Society who originally hired Lucy as a lecturer.

HBB–LS, 4/2/55

Elizabeth's objections. In her letter of February 22 Elizabeth had written Henry, "You haven't the vulgar vanity to wish to make a fuss about your marriage, and do not take the human nature out of it, by crushing it with platforms and principles." She objected to the idea of a public protest, calling it foolish and in bad taste to drag "one's private, personal affairs into public notice," and added that "Lucy, and you, too, have protested enough, in all conscience, both by public and private parlance, to define your position." But she did advise on the wording of the protest in case they chose to make it anyway.

LS–HBB, 4/8/55

The slave girl went free. On April 6, 1855, a fugitive female slave, hidden on a Southern steamship, escaped when the ship docked in New York.

HBB–LS, 4/13/55

the most hopeful State. Massachusetts had passed its own Married Woman's Property Act in 1854.

TWO

A Model Couple, 1855–1864

HBB–LS, Summer/55

[*summer, 1855*]. The original of this letter is undated, though it was later identified as having been written in March of 1856. However, internal references elsewhere in the letter to a

proposed visit to Katahdin, a
mountain in Maine, on the third
of September, show that it could
not have been written at that
time, but was instead written
toward the end of the summer
of 1855 when Lucy had gone
east for the woman's rights convention.

your Appleton investment. Lucy had
invested in land in Appleton, in
the eastern part of Wisconsin.

Lucy Stone Blackwell. The name
Lucy used during the first year
of her married life.

HBB–LS, 9/12/55

not getting yourself vaccinated. The
technique of vaccination against
smallpox was brought over from
England to the United States in
the early nineteenth century.

"free lovers." Henry was obviously
joking when he made this suggestion, for while both he and
Lucy believed that spiritual affinity should be the basis for
union between man and woman,
neither would have dreamed of
insisting, as did the free-lovers
of their day, that such a union
could take place outside of marriage.

HBB–LS, 9/17/55

Mrs. Nichols' "Mary Lyndon." Mary
S. Gove Nichols (1818–1884)
and her husband, Dr. Thomas
Nichols (1815–1901), were New
England reformers who es-
poused free love—in addition
to vegetarianism, mesmerism,
spiritualism, and water cure
or hydrotherapy—and tried
through writings to convert

others to their views. *Mary Lyndon* (1855) was Mrs. Nichols's
autobiographical novel.

Charles Lane. (1801–1870) Radical
English educator, who together
with Bronson Alcott, organized
the utopian community of Fruit-
lands at Harvard, Massachusetts.

Dr Edgeworth Lazarus. Physician-
writer-reformer, known for his
doctrine of "natural optimism,"
in which he held that man could
not achieve happiness unless society gave him the freedom to
express his desires and passions.

my sister Anna. Anna Blackwell
spent the summer and fall of
1845 at the utopian community
of Brook Farm, and within the
next few years came under the
influence of Albert Brisbane
(1809–1890), the chief American
advocate of the free-love ideas of
the French socialist, Charles
Fourier (1772–1837).

Nichols is coming to Cincinnati. Nichols and his wife did, in fact,
move to Cincinnati in 1855. A
year later they established the
Memnonia Institute, or "School
of Life," in Yellow Springs,
Ohio, near Antioch College.
The college's president, Horace
Mann, attacked them for their
"licentious doctrines," although
the Nicholses now demanded a
strict chastity of the members of
their community. In 1857, after
being converted to Catholicism,
they took to preaching at con-
vents and finally in 1861 fled to
England.

"Womans Rights" disguise. Henry's
words were prophetic: The
woman's rights movement did
become associated with free
love in the 1870s through Mrs.
Stanton's and Susan B. An-

thony's connection with the notorious Victoria Woodhull.

Francis Jackson's. (1789–1861) Wealthy Boston businessman and abolitionist, at whose home Lucy often stayed when she was in the Boston area.

HBB–LS, 10/13/55

Mary Wolstoncraft's "Rights of Women." A Vindication of the Rights of Women, written in 1792 by the English feminist, Mary Wollstonecraft (1759–1797). The book became the bible of nineteenth-century American feminists.

Ruth. 1853 novel about a fallen woman by the English writer Elizabeth Cleghorn Gaskell (1810–1865).

many of our best woman-novelists' books. Sentimental novels by such "scribbling women" as Mrs. E.D.E.N. Southworth, Augusta Jane Evans, Maria Cummins and others so dominated the best-seller lists in the 1850s that the decade was dubbed the Feminine Fifties.

Modern Times. Free-love community started on Long Island in the 1850s by the reformer, anarchist, and inventor Josiah Warren (1798–1874).

LS–HBB, 1/24/56

Godey's Ladies book. Founded in 1830, *Godey's Lady's Book* was the most important of the early woman's magazines.

LS–HBB, 1/25/56

calico balls. Dancing was an important means of socializing on the frontier, where the dances were less formal than in the East (usually they included versions of the Virginia reel and the square dance), and where the women wore dresses of plain-woven printed cotton—hence the name "calico ball."

Mr. Pierpont. John Pierpont (1785–1866), Unitarian clergyman, poet, and reformer, who was a well-known lecturer. His wife had died in 1855, and he remarried in 1857.

LS–HBB, 1/30/56

Jan. 30 [1856]. The original of this letter has no yearly date. The date of 1861 was added later, and the letter used as evidence in Elinor Rice Hays's biography of Lucy Stone that she had returned to lecturing just before the Civil War. However, internal references (to Mr. Ostrom, a new partner in the hardware business) show that the letter had to be written in January of 1856.

quite in Louisville style. Lucy had given some of her most successful lectures in Louisville, Kentucky, during the tour Henry arranged for her in the fall of 1853.

Mr. Ostrom. New partner that Henry was helping to break into the hardware business.

John G. Saxe. (1816–1887) One of the most often quoted and widely read American poets of his day.

Bryant's poems. William Cullen Bryant (1794–1878), poet and New York newspaper editor; his "To a Waterfowl" was one of Lucy's favorite poems.

LS–HBB, 2/3/56

doughface style. Doughface was the name given to Northerners who sided with the South and slavery.

HBB–LS, 4/3/56

Sholes. Charles Clark Sholes (1816–1861), Wisconsin senator, who, in the minority report mentioned, maintained that woman suffrage in his state was "only a question of time, and as sure to triumph as God is just."
Hale's speech. John P. Hale (1827–1873), abolitionist congressman from New Hampshire.

HBB–LS, 4/12/56

C. M. Clay. Cassius Marcellus Clay (1810–1903), flamboyant Kentuckian, who published an antislavery paper and ran for governor on an abolitionist platform. Clay had a strong backing for the vice-presidency in 1860, but instead Lincoln gave him a diplomatic post in Russia.
Colonization. The idea of colonization as a solution to the problem of slavery dated back to 1776 when Thomas Jefferson put forward a plan for sending blacks back to Africa. The American Colonization Society was founded in 1817, and between that time and 1860 twelve thousand blacks were colonized first in Sierra Leone, and later in what became the independent republic of Liberia. However, since the Society lacked the money to purchase very many slaves, most who went were free blacks.

HBB–LS, 4/29/56

George . . . La Crosse. George Blackwell had moved to La Crosse, Wisconsin, where he owned a mill site, and together with other western capitalists, laid out the town of La Crescent.

HBB–LS, 5/18/56

the Kansas matter. By May of 1856 the struggle between the free-soil and proslavery forces for the control of Kansas had erupted into a small scale civil war, giving rise to the term, "Bleeding Kansas." On May 24—less than a week after Henry wrote this letter—the Ohio abolitionist John Brown and his sons massacred a proslavery family near Pottawatomie, Kansas, setting off a new wave of violence and destruction.
"Sharpe's rifle" & "Colt revolver." Sharps rifles were popularly known as Beecher's Bibles after Henry Ward Beecher, whose Brooklyn congregation sent boxes loaded with rifles but marked "Bibles" to free-soil groups in Kansas. Invented in 1836, Samuel Colt's six-shot revolver had first been used on a large scale by the United States Army in the war against Mexico.

LS–HBB, 1/4/57

Lalla Rookh. (1817) Popular work by the English lyricist Thomas Moore (1799–1852), who was widely read in America after his visit in 1804, despite the fact that a few guardians of the public morality censured him for his "voluptuous performances" that "overturn the ramparts of female innocence."

the life of Horace Greeley. James Parton's *The Life of Horace Greeley, Editor of the New York Tribune,* published in 1855.

Aurora Leigh. (1857) Novel in verse by the English poet Elizabeth Barrett Browning (1806–1861).

Miss Griffith. Mattie Griffith, Louisville native whose poetry was published in the local papers. Her *Autobiography of a Female Slave* appeared in 1857; in 1860 she moved to Boston and continued to write poems and tales that were published in the papers of that city.

Prentice. George D. Prentice (1802–1870), editor of the *Courier Journal,* who had called on Lucy when she lectured in Louisville in the fall of 1853.

LS–SBA, 7/20/57

Mrs. Elizabeth Chace. Elizabeth Buffum Chace (1806–1899), antislavery organizer, whose home in Valley Falls, Rhode Island, was a station on the Underground Railroad; and early feminist, who was among the signers of the call to the Worcester Woman's Rights Convention.

Arnold Buffum. (1782–1859) Quaker farmer and hat manufacturer, who in 1832 helped to found the New England Anti-Slavery Society and served as its first president.

his wife, from Mr. Jackson's. Eliza Eddy (1816–1881) was the daughter of the Boston abolitionist Francis Jackson. Her husband's action in taking away her children would later prompt

her to leave a sizable bequest to Lucy Stone and Susan B. Anthony to further the cause of woman's rights.

Mr. Crosby. Howard Crosby (1826–1891), New York clergyman, college professor, and reformer, active in the temperance movement.

HBB–LS, 3/3/58

help with you. They now had a young Irish girl as a nurse and helper.

Mr Tilton. Theodore Tilton (1835–1907), New York reformer and editor of *The Independent.*

the Atlantic Monthly. Under the editorship of James Russell Lowell, this magazine had been established in Boston in 1857.

HBB–LS, 3/12/58

Seward's speech. In a speech on the Kansas question delivered in the Senate on March 3, Senator William H. Seward said that the question of slavery in the territories involved "a dynastical struggle of two antagonistical systems, the labor of slaves and the labor of free men, for mastery in the Federal union." Moreover, in his view, slave labor in the territories was "opposed to the natural, social, and moral developments" of the country.

a permanent breach in the party. Douglas Democrats took the lead from the Illinois Senator Stephen A. Douglas in invoking the principle of "popular sovereignty"—let the settlers decide—as a solution to the problem of slavery in the new

territories of Kansas and Nebraska. Douglas assumed that
because of their geography,
both territories would remain
free. Thus when the Lecompton
constitution, recommending the
admission of Kansas as a slave
state, was submitted to Congress for approval, Douglas condemned it as a violation of the
principle of popular sovereignty.
The split between the Northern
Democrats, who took Douglas's
position, and the Southerners,
who supported the proslavery
Lecompton constitution did, in
fact, lead to the breakup of the
Democratic party.

No new boils. Before proper sanita-
tion of the water supply, boils
were a common affliction.

HBB–LS, 3/25/58

Abby Hutchinson. Abigail Jemima
Hutchinson (1829–1892), a member of the Hutchinson Family
Singers, a popular group whose
repertoire included songs in
behalf of antislavery, temperance, and woman's rights. After
her marriage in 1849 to an up-
and-coming New York stockbroker, she had abandoned her
singing career for several years,
but was now attempting to resume it. She and her husband
were the Stone-Blackwells'
neighbors in Orange, New Jersey.

LS—HBB, 4/4/58

Mrs. Johnson. Mrs. Rowland Johnson, a neighbor in Orange.
her daguerreotype. Lucy had gone to
a daguerreotypist and had a pic-

ture of herself and the baby
made. She hid it in Henry's
suitcase when he went West,
but he was so preoccupied that
he failed to unpack properly,
and thus didn't find the picture
until some weeks later. Recall-
ing the incident many years
afterward, Henry reproached
himself for his thoughtlessness.

anti-Lecompton triumph grand! On
April 1, 1858, the Crittenden-
Montgomery Amendment, providing for the resubmission of
the Lecompton constitution to
popular vote, passed the House,
120-112.

HBB–LS, 5/1/58

Irving's Life of Washington. Five-
volume biography of George
Washington by the well-known
American author, Washington
Irving (1783–1859).

LS–HBB, 5/9/58

the Convention. Annual woman's
rights convention held in New
York; according to the *History of
Woman Suffrage*, Lucy did attend this convention.

LS—HBB, 9/14/60

Eddy. One of Bowman's children.
Aunt Hetty. Mehitable Haskell, an
old abolitionist friend of Lucy's,
who lived in West Gloucester,
Massachusetts.

HBB—LS, 7/23/61

*Yesterday . . . a terrible day in New
York.* Henry's letter was written

two days after the disastrous rout of the Union forces in the Battle of Bull Run.

LS–HBB, 6/14/64

at the Highlands. The Atlantic Highlands on the New Jersey shore.

"Mill". The English philosopher, John Stuart Mill (1806–1873). His book *Utilitarianism* was published in 1863.

Mr. Frothingham. Octavius Brooks Frothingham (1822–1895), Unitarian and independent minister and author, whose weekly sermons, delivered in New York, were published in the newspapers and in pamphlet form, and widely discussed.

Sylvias Lovers. 1863 novel by Elizabeth Cleghorn Gaskell.

LS–HBB, 6/21/64

a homoepathic Dr. Instead of bleeding their patients half to death, or feeding them large quantities of calomel, homeopathic doctors flooded them with water containing minute doses of the appropriate herbal remedy. Originating in Germany in the theories of Samuel Hahnemann, the treatment had become popular in English-speaking countries.

the Stanton custom house affair. Through his political connections Elizabeth Cady Stanton's husband, Henry, had received a New York custom house appointment at the beginning of the war. He was now accused of taking bribes, though actually his son Daniel was the guilty party. The incident contributed

to Mrs. Stanton's disenchantment with the Republican party, which was to intensify after the war.

"Ten acres enough." *Ten Acres Enough: A Practical Experience Showing How a Very Small Farm May Be Made to Keep a Very Large Family* (1864), by Edmund Morris (1804–1874).

LS–SBA, 7/12/64

Pillsbury. The Garrisonian abolitionist, Parker Pillsbury (1809–1898), with whom Lucy had sometimes lectured when she first started as an agent of the Massachusetts Anti-Slavery Society.

the Cleveland platform. At a convention held in Cleveland on May 31, 1864, a group of Radical Republicans and abolitionists, dissatisfied with Lincoln, nominated John C. Frémont (1813–1890) for the presidency.

John Cochran. The vice-presidential choice, John Cochrane (1813–1898) was a New York politician and former Democrat who had favored conciliation with the South before the war.

the New Nation. Newspaper established in New York City to promote the Frémont candidacy.

Montgomery Blair. (1813–1883) Missouri lawyer and politician, who before the war had advocated colonization as a means of solving the slavery problem. Blair served as postmaster general in Lincoln's cabinet, but the Radical Republicans considered him too conservative and in 1864 passed a resolution calling for his dismissal, which Lincoln eventually acted on.

Mr. Chase is out. Secretary of the treasury under Lincoln and himself a presidential aspirant, Salmon P. Chase resigned from the cabinet in June of 1864, but the following December Lincoln appointed him Chief Justice of the Supreme Court.

LS–HBB, 7/22/64

Lake Hopatcong. Lake in northern New Jersey.
business proposition, to me. Possibly a suggestion that she return to lecturing.
Greeley & Sanders correspondence. Mr. Lincoln's reply. George N. Sanders and three other commissioners of the Confederate government had approached Horace Greeley regarding an informal peace conference. With Lincoln's approval, Greeley arranged to meet the commissioners at Niagara Falls on July 20. They submitted a peace proposition, and Lincoln replied with a statement of his terms, which included the restoration of the Union and an end to slavery After considerable correspondence between the two parties, it was decided to refer the matter back to the two governments for consideration.

LS–HBB, 7/31/64

Elizabeth's half the farm. Henry's sisters, Elizabeth and Emily, also had a country place in West Bloomfield (Montclair).

LS–HBB, 8/9/64

Martha's Vineyard. Lucy, Henry, and Alice first visited Martha's Vineyard at this time in the company of Henry's friend Ainsworth Spofford, whose father was a Congregationalist minister in the island town of Chilmark. They went to the island by sailboat and boarded at the Gay Head Lighthouse. Martha's Vineyard pleased them so much that they returned the next summer, and by 1868 the island had become a regular summering place for them as well as for other members of the Blackwell family.
Clara. Lucy's niece, Clara Barlow.

LS–HBB, 9/4/64

the Convention at Chicago. At their national convention held in Chicago on August 29 the Democrats had adopted a platform calling for an immediate end to the war, and a restoration of peace "on the basis of the Federal Union of the States."
dear old Mr. Walcutt. Robert Walcutt (1797–1884), a Boston abolitionist and Unitarian minister.
Martha C. Wright. (1806–1875) New York abolitionist and feminist, who was Lucretia Mott's sister.
Henry. Lucy's brother-in-law, Henry Lawrence, who had married her sister Sarah in 1845.
more goods than the laws of N.Y. allow a widow. In response to appeals by Mrs. Stanton and other feminists, the New York legislature had passed a liberalized married woman's property law in 1860. However, two years later the legislature amended the 1860 act, withdrawing many of the property rights it had granted. Among other provisions, the 1862 act took away

from a widow the control of property left at her husband's death.

LS–HBB, 9/20/64

"Very Hard Cash." . . . "Love Me Little, Love Me Long." Published in 1864 and 1859 respectively, both novels were by the English author Charles Reade (1814–1884), who wrote propagandist works in support of various causes.

McClellan's letter. In his letter of acceptance of the Democratic nomination for the presidency, General George B. McClellan (1826–1885), former commander of the Army of the Potomac, hedged on the question of when the war should be ended; while the Democratic platform called for an "immediate" end to the hostilities, McClellan said the war should be ended "so soon as it is clear or probable." His position angered the Copperheads, who had opposed the war from the very beginning.

LS–HBB, 10/10/64

no winter school, for small bipeds. Excluded from the regular winter school term, very young children and older girls generally received instruction during the summer session, which varied in duration from two to as much as six months (April to October).

LS–HBB, 12/4/64

Parker's Life. Life and Correspondence of Theodore Parker (1864) by John Weiss.

Rev. Andrew. Possibly William Watson Andrews (1810–1897), a well-known evangelist of the Catholic Apostolic Church.

Emmerson. Ralph Waldo Emerson (1803–1882), the influential New England philosopher, essayist, and poet.

LS–HBB, 12/17/64

Frank Donaldson . . . Gen. Sherwood. Frank Donaldson was a Cincinnati abolitionist friend of Henry's; George Sherwood, an acquaintance at whose home in Evanston Lucy and Henry had boarded during the year they spent in the Chicago area.

Sherman has got to the coast. Union forces under General William T. Sherman had begun the invasion of Georgia the preceding May; Atlanta fell on September 1, and on November 14 Sherman began his march to the sea. He reached Savannah on December 10, and succeeded in taking that city on December 22.

the Canadian authorities have released the raiders. Confederate agents were using Canada as a base from which to launch raids against the Union. The most serious of these raids took place on October 19, 1864, when Confederate agents swooped down on the town of St. Albans, Vermont. Although thirteen men were arrested in connection with this raid, the Canadian judge decided he had no jurisdiction over the case, and so released the raiders.

LS–HBB, 12/22/64

Alice's ambrotype. A picture made by placing a glass negative against a dark background, and named for its inventor, James Ambro(se) Cutting.

Florence. Florence Blackwell, Sam and Nette's first child.

rejoicing in the great victories. Sher-

man's capture of Savannah; also the Union victory under General John M. Schofield in the Battle of Nashville, December 15–16.

THREE
Gray-Haired Champions, 1866–1893

LS–AKF, 1/24/67

Edward M. Davis. (1811–1887) Abolitionist son-in-law of Lucretia Mott from Philadelphia.

Robert Purvis. (1810–1898) Wealthy black abolitionist from Philadelphia.

Oliver Johnson. (1809–1889) New York abolitionist and editor of a succession of reform newspapers including the *National Anti-Slavery Standard* and *The Independent.*

Tayler Lewis. (1802–1877) New York abolitionist and professor of oriental languages and biblical literature at Union College.

The "World." The New York World, a Democratic paper.

the Hovey fund. Bequest of $50,000 made by the Boston abolitionist Charles Hovey to Wendell Phillips and his associates for use in the antislavery and woman's rights movements.

The Greeks, abroad are remembered. In 1866 when Greeks on the island of Crete rebelled against Turkish rule, a meeting of sympathy attended by Wendell Phillips and other prominent reformers was held at the Music Hall in Boston, and funds were collected to aid the cause.

HBB–ECS&SBA, 4/21/67

D. R. Anthony. Susan B. Anthony's brother, Daniel Read Anthony (1824–1904).

Mrs. Gage. Frances Dana Gage (1808–1884), Ohio abolitionist and feminist, who as "Aunt Fanny" wrote popular stories for children.

Anna Dickinson. (1842–1932) Lyceum lecturer and Civil War orator, who, with her short curly hair and eloquent speeches, became known as the Joan of Arc of the Union.

Ben Wade and Carl Schurz. Wade (1800–1878) was a Radical Republican congressman from Ohio; Schurz (1829–1906), a German-born journalist and reformer, who at this point in his career was based in the Midwest.

Mrs. Mills article on the Enfranchisement of Women. Article written in 1851 by the English feminist Harriet Taylor Mill (1807–1858), the wife of John Stuart Mill, and published in *The Westminster Review.*

Robinson. Charles Robinson (1818–1894), first governor of the state of Kansas and a relation of Lucy's by marriage; her brother

Bowman had successively married two of Robinson's sisters.

LS–HBB, 10/11/67

the autograph of Clarke. Sidney Clarke (1831–1909), Republican congressman from Kansas, who was among the signers of the appeal to the voters of Kansas, but who refused to speak out on woman suffrage while campaigning for reelection in Kansas. George Francis Train referred to him in these lines from a jingle: "While your Rosses, Pomeroys, and your Clarkes / Stood on the fence, or basely fled."

the Jackson fund. Bequest of $5,000 made by the Boston abolitionist Francis Jackson to Lucy, Susan B. Anthony, and Wendell Phillips for the purpose of furthering the cause of woman's rights.

LS–HBB, 10/13/67

Frances. Frances Alofsen, daughter of friends of Marian Blackwell.

LS–HBB, 4/68

Olympia. Olympia Brown (1835–1926), Universalist minister and feminist from Massachusetts who had participated in the Kansas campaign.

Mrs. Spooner. Zilpha Spooner, Massachusetts antislavery leader.

LS–ACF, 3/24/69

Mrs. Field. Anna Cromwell Field (1823–1912), New York abolitionist, feminist, and member of the American Equal Rights Association.

Geo. W. Julian. (1817–1899) Radical Republican congressman from Indiana.

Quaker help for the Indian. A number of Quakers had recently been appointed Indian agents.

LS–SJM, 4/9/69

the "Advocate." The Woman's Advocate, suffrage paper published for a year (1869–1870) in New York from the offices of the *National Anti-Slavery Standard*.

Geo. F. Hoar. (1827–1904) Republican senator from Massachusetts.

LS–JFC, 10/6/69

James Freeman Clarke. (1810–1888) Unitarian minister, reformer, and religious writer associated with the Transcendentalists.

LS–ABB, 10/31/69

Mrs. Livermore. Mary A. Livermore (1820–1905), former New England schoolteacher, who worked for the Sanitary Commission in Chicago during the Civil War, became converted to woman suffrage, and in 1869 began to edit a suffrage paper, *The Agitator*.

HBB–LS, 11/1/69

Jackson Davis & wife. Andrew Jackson Davis, the "Poughkeepsie seer and clairvoyant" (1826–1910) and his wife, Mary Fenn Davis (1824–1886). Both were spiritualists who lent their support to other causes: Mary Davis lectured and wrote articles on temperance and woman's rights, and together with her husband, was active in the New Jersey Woman Suffrage Association.

the Gages. John and Portia Gage. John Gage (1846–1927); a New Jersey fruit-grower, real estate broker, and reformer, was the brother-in-law of Frances Dana Gage, the well-known author and feminist; he and his wife helped to form the New Jersey Woman Suffrage Association.

Fielder Israel & John Cameron. Delaware suffragists.

Mary Grew. (1813–1896) Philadelphia abolitionist and feminist.

Geo. Wm. Curtis. (1824–1892) Author, orator, and abolitionist, who in 1863 had become the editor of *Harper's Weekly*.

Whipple. Charles K. Whipple, (1808–1900), Boston abolitionist, and one of the signers of the call to the First National Woman's Rights Convention at Worcester.

Jas Hutchinson Jr. (1826–1911) Vermont state senator involved in the abolitionist and temperance movements.

the Hartford Convention. Woman suffrage convention held in Hartford on October 28 and 29 for the purpose of forming a Connecticut suffrage society.

John Neal. (1793–1876) Author, editor, and reformer, this "downeast Yankee" from Portland, Maine, made his first woman's rights speech in 1832 and continued to speak in behalf of the cause for the next forty years.

LS–HBB, 11/27/70

meeting here yesterday. A local suffrage association meeting, which took place after the American's convention on November 22 and 23. Henry had attended the regular convention, but was apparently too ill to stay for this meeting.

Bradwell. Judge James B. Bradwell (1828–1907), Chicago woman's rights advocate who in 1868 secured passage of a bill making women eligible for school offices, and assisted his wife, Myra (Colby), in establishing *Chicago Legal News*. He was considered friendly to Miss Anthony since at the first convention of the American at Cleveland, he moved that she be invited to take a seat on the platform.

Judge Waite and his wife. Judge C. B. Waite and his wife, Catherine Van Valkenburg Waite (1829–1913), author, lawyer, and Illinois suffragist.

LS–RDSJ, 3/19/71

Mrs. Janney. Rebecca Smith Janney (1814–1886), Ohio suffragist.

Mrs. Hooker. Isabella Beecher Hooker (1822–1907), Connecticut suffragist and sister of Henry Ward Beecher.

Paulina Davis and Josephine Griffing. Paulina Wright Davis (1813–1876), Rhode Island feminist, former editor of the *Una*, one of the earliest woman's rights publications, and a member of the National. Josephine Griffing (1814–1872), antislavery and woman's rights activist who ran a settlement program for the freedmen in Washington, D.C. after the war, and lobbied for the creation of the Freedman's Bureau. She was corresponding secretary of the National.

names to a Declaration. Declaration

to be presented to Congress, expressing the desire of American women for "the rights and privileges of citizenship," and claiming these rights and privileges under the Fourteenth and Fifteenth amendments. In her article Mrs. Livermore urged women to send in their signatures to this declaration, though she did not agree that women should claim the right to vote under the Fourteenth and Fifteenth amendments.

death of Mrs. Tilden. Mrs. D. R. Tilden, Ohio suffragist.

LS–JKW, 11/7/71

Friend Wildman. John K. Wildman (1833–1905), Quaker suffragist from Philadelphia.
Mrs. Cole . . . Mrs. Churchill. Miriam H. Cole, Ohio suffragist. Hannah Tracy Cutler (1815–1896), classmate of Lucy's at Oberlin, Ohio woman's rights leader and physician. Margaret V. Longley, Ohio suffragist. Margaret West Norton Campbell (1827–1908), agent for the Massachusetts Woman Suffrage Association, and later president of the Iowa Woman Suffrage Association. Elizabeth K. Churchill (1821–1881), suffragist from Providence, Rhode Island.
Mr. Furness. The Reverend William H. Furness (1802–1896), a Unitarian minister in Philadelphia, and former abolitionist.

HBB–LS, 3/20/72

breakfast at Second Avenue. At Emily Blackwell's New York residence.

Mr Spofford. Paul N. Spofford (1822?–1912), of the mercantile and investment house of Spofford, Tileston, and Company, which operated a steamship line between the United States and Santo Domingo.
Col. Fabens. Joseph W. Fabens (1821–1875), Boston-born adventurer, who had figured in the Texas struggle for independence, and later became interested in Santo Domingo. From 1854 onward he had been involved in various development schemes, and had lobbied to secure some form of American political control over the island.
Mr Barlow. Samuel L. Barlow (1826–1889), New York lawyer specializing in corporate law, who had a substantial investment in real estate in Santo Domingo.
Aaron Powell. (1832–1899) Prominent New York abolitionist and temperance leader, who was one of the editors of the *National Anti-Slavery Standard.*

HBB–LS, 4/1/72

Miss Eastman . . . Emma's aid. Mary F. Eastman, a member of the Massachusetts Woman Suffrage Association; Lucy's niece, Emma Lawrence. An entry in Alice's diary for March 20, 1872, noted: "Emma arrived under convoy of Mamma. . . . She immediately set to work clipping slips for the Journal like a born editor."

LS–HBB, 4/11/72

Ed Eggleston. Edward Eggleston (1837–1902), Methodist preacher and novelist from

Indiana whose most popular work was *The Hoosier School-master*.

Mr. Livermore. Daniel Livermore (1818–1899), Universalist minister from Massachusetts, and husband of Mary Livermore.

Iowa has "gone back" on Woman Suffrage! A woman suffrage amendment to the Iowa state constitution passed the House 58 to 39, but was defeated in the Senate, 24 to 22.

Greeley . . . the Cincinnati Convention. Dissatisfaction with Radical Republican policy in the South and with corruption within the Grant administration gave rise to the Liberal Republican movement. In May of 1872 Liberal Republicans met in Cincinnati, and nominated Horace Greeley as their presidential candidate.

HBB–LS, 6/5/72

Dr Loring. George Bailey Loring (1817–1891), surgeon, farmer, and Massachusetts Republican leader.

R D Hayes. Rutherford B. Hayes (1822–1893), governor of Ohio from 1868 to 1872, and President of the United States from 1877 to 1881.

the Massachusetts resolution. The resolution adopted by the Massachusetts Republican party at its annual convention in 1871 went as follows: "That the Republican party is mindful of its obligations to the loyal women of America for their patriotic devotion to the cause of freedom; that we rejoice in the recent action of state legislatures in recognizing the fitness of women for public trusts, and that in view of the great favor which

the movement has received from many of the Republican party, the subject of suffrage for women is one that deserves a most careful and respectful consideration."

LS–MC, 3/30/74

Mrs. Swisshelm. Jane Swisshelm (1815–1884), Pennsylvania abolitionist, newspaper editor, and sometime feminist, known for her barbed pen.

The women on the school board. In Boston six women had been chosen to serve on the school board for the first time.

the Smith cows. Rather than pay taxes while women were denied the vote, two elderly sisters, Abby (1797–1878) and Julia (1792–1886) Smith of Glastonbury, Connecticut, let their livestock be taken away and sold.

Abby Foster's house. Abby and Stephen Foster also made a tax protest by allowing their home to be sold for $100 in taxes.

Mr. Hudson. Thomson Jay Hudson (1834–1903), lecturer, author, and Michigan newspaper editor.

LS–MC, 6/13/74

Mrs. Hazlett. Mary Adelle Hazlett (1827–?), Michigan suffragist and president of the Northwestern Woman Suffrage Association.

HBB–LS, 6/13/76

Blaine . . . Bristow. James G. Blaine (1830–1893), Maine congressman who served as Speaker of the House from 1869 to 1875; Benjamin H. Bristow (1832–1896), Kentucky lawyer and secretary of the treasury under Grant. Both men belonged to a faction within the party known as the Halfbreeds, which deplored the open stealing of the Grant administration, and favored modest reforms, especially in the area of civil service. Of the two, Blaine had been the stronger contender for the presidency, but his chances were weakened by the publication of letters implicating him in certain shady business dealings, and by his own attack on the opposing faction within the party.

Conkling and Morton. Roscoe Conkling (1829–1888), senator from New York and controller of patronage in the New York Customs House; Oliver Morton (1823–1877), Indiana congressman who had control of internal revenue in his state. Both belonged to a rival faction within the party, known as the Stalwarts, which had remained loyal to Grant despite the corruption of his administration.

HBB–LS, 6/16/76

Mrs. Spencer. Sara Andrews Spencer (1837–1909), Washington, D.C. suffragist and officer of the National.

Lizzie Boynton Harbert. (1845–1925) Illinois suffrage leader and member of the National.

LS–MC, 7/19/76

a cute thing . . . on the 4ᵗʰ July. Miss Anthony and Mrs. Stanton had requested permission to present a woman's protest and bill of rights after the reading of the Declaration of Independence at the Centennial Celebration at Philadelphia on the Fourth of July. Although their formal written requests were refused, they went ahead anyway. After the Declaration of Independence was read, Susan and four other members of the National advanced to the platform and presented their Declaration of Rights for Women to the astonished officials. They then went to another platform set up for musicians in front of Independence Hall, and from there Susan read the declaration to a large crowd.

John Hutchinson. (1821–1908) Brother of Abby Hutchinson and member of the Hutchinson Family Singers.

LS–HBB, 8/22/76

Maria Mitchell. (1818–1889) Astronomer who discovered a comet in 1847, and in 1865 became the first woman professor of astronomy at Vassar College. Miss Mitchell had heard Lucy Stone lecture on woman's rights when she was a young woman, and in 1873 helped organize the Association for the Advancement of Women, a group of moderate professional women who met at annual congresses to discuss their work and the problems of their sex.

LS–CCH, 11/29/76

Mrs. Hussey. Cornelia Collins Hussey (1827–1902), New Jersey suffragist and philanthropist.

those photographs. Photographs of women law professors at the University of Bologna.

The Congress. The annual Congress of Women held by the Association for the Advancement of Women.

Contagious Diseases Acts. Laws requiring prostitutes to be licensed and submit to periodic physical examinations. Their purpose was to control the spread of venereal disease, but they were opposed by women reformers on the grounds that they made vice legal.

Miss Willard . . . coming on grandly. Frances Willard (1839–1898), corresponding secretary of the Woman's Christian Temperance Union, founded in 1874, and soon to become its president. Of all the nineteenth-century woman's organizations, the WCTU was by far the most popular, drawing a membership of more than two hundred thousand women from all classes and from all parts of the country. Part of the reason for its success lay in the scope of its activities: Besides campaigning for temperance, the WCTU pushed for kindergartens, prison reform, child labor laws, and woman suffrage.

HBB–LS, 2/22/77

Spofford at the Library. Henry's good friend Ainsworth Spofford was now chief librarian of the Library of Congress.

Senator Kelly. James Kerr Kelly (1819–1903), U.S. senator from Oregon.

the Oregon case. Oregon was the fourth state (Florida, Louisiana, and South Carolina were the other three), in which the electoral votes cast for the Democratic candidate, Samuel J. Tilden, were disputed. The case was eventually resolved in favor of the Republican candidate, Rutherford B. Hayes, when it was found that the Democratic governor, in violation of the state law, had disqualified a Republican elector and certified a Democrat in his stead.

Mr Ames. Oliver Ames (1807–1877), Massachusetts shovel manufacturer, promoter of the Union Pacific Railroad, and one of the directors of the Samana Bay Company.

the authoress. Mrs. Dinah Maria (Mulock) Craik (1826–1887).

Prof Henry. Joseph Henry (1797–1878), scientist who served first as secretary and then director of the Smithsonian.

Judge Hoadey. George Hoadly (1826–1902), Cincinnati lawyer and judge.

Baez. The president of the Dominican Republic.

HBB–LS, 3/11/77

Prof Gabb. William More Gabb (1839–1878), paleontologist from Philadelphia, who had earlier made a geological and topographic survey of the island, and had returned to develop a mining claim.

"Living on Women." This editorial was, in fact, written, and appeared in the *Journal* of April 7, 1877.

LS–HBB, 4/2/77

Chamberlain and Hampton. Daniel H. Chamberlain (1835–1907), a

New Englander (he was born in Lucy's hometown of West Brookfield) and Radical Republican governor of South Carolina, and Wade Hampton, a Democrat and former Confederate general, were the two contenders for the governorship in 1876. By this time South Carolina was one of the few remaining states where the Radical Republicans were still in control, and white South Carolinians were determined to oust them from power. Thousands enlisted in companies, known as Redshirts, and on election day the Redshirts kept blacks from the polls, and stuffed ballot boxes in Hampton's favor. His victory was contested by Chamberlain, and both men took the case to Washington, where it was decided in Hampton's favor.

Packard shows fight. Both Stephen B. Packard, a Republican, and Francis Tillou Nicholls, a former Confederate general and a Democrat, claimed to have been duly elected governor of Louisiana. The election was ultimately decided in favor of Nicholls, whose victory marked the end of Radical Reconstruction in Louisiana.

LS–ASB, 9/21/77

the Anabasis. Greek prose history by Xenophon dealing with the retreat of the Ten Thousand from Persia c. 399 B.C.

Dr. Avery. Alida Avery (1833–?), former resident physician at Vassar College, who left her post to practice medicine in Denver, and there became president of the state suffrage association.

LS–FW, 8/21/78

Dr. Warren. William Fairfield Warren (1833–1929), Methodist Episcopal minister, educator, and first president of Boston University (1873–1903).

LS–HHR, 3/4/79

Mrs. Robinson. Harriet Hanson Robinson (1825–1911), former Lowell mill girl, Massachusetts suffragist, and wife of the prominent antislavery journalist, William Robinson.

Laura D. Fair. Young woman charged with the murder of the wealthy San Francisco attorney, Alexander D. Crittenden. In the summer of 1871, Susan B. Anthony and Mrs. Stanton had visited her in prison while on a speaking tour of the West. Their action aroused newspaper criticism, and Susan's defense of Laura Fair on the lecture platform created such an uproar that she and Mrs. Stanton were forced to cancel all further speaking engagements in California.

the Mormons. While Lucy and many other easterners condemned the Mormons for their practice of plural marriage, Mrs. Stanton and Miss Anthony welcomed Mormon women into the National after their enfranchisement in 1870.

HBB–LS, 7/8/79

"Old and lame and blind." According to Alice, Lucy took old age and the approach of death "beautifully," though occasionally upon

waking up stiff-jointed in the morning, she would groan a little, and murmur, "Old and lame, and blind, and stiff!"

old Bush. Reverend Solon Wanton Bush (1819–1898), occasional editor of the *Journal* during absences of Lucy and Henry.

LS–HBB, 11/26/79

Charley Spofford. Ainsworth Spofford's son had been living with the Stone-Blackwells while studying in Boston.

Love to Sam. Samuel Blackwell had joined Henry in the beet sugar business, and was now spending most of his time in Portland, Maine.

LS–HBB, 12/12/79

Lucretia Hale. Lucretia Peabody Hale (1820–1900), author of popular children's stories, and sister of Edward Everett Hale (1822–1909), the well-known author and Unitarian clergyman.

LS–HBB, 3/4/80

Aunt Lucy Issacs. The youngest and prettiest of Henry's father's sisters, who married late in life.

HBB–LS, 3/15/80

Mr Cook's party. Flavius Josephus Cook (1838–1901), preacher and lecturer whose Monday Lectures in Boston's Tremont Temple were considered one of the cultural highlights of the city for almost twenty years. In 1880 Mr. Cook organized a series of "conversations," or discussions

on topics of interest, which were held in the parlor of his home. The last of these, which Henry attended, concerned woman suffrage.

Miss Eva Channing. (1859?–1930) Granddaughter of William Ellery Channing, and a member of the Massachusetts Woman Suffrage Association.

HBB–LS, 3/17/80

Lea Pusey. Delaware suffragist and member of the American.

Prof Gulliver. Reverend John P. Gulliver (1819–1894), professor at Andover Theological Seminary.

Ole Bull. (1810–1880) Distinguished Swedish violinist who supported various reforms.

Mr Seelye. Julius Hawley Seelye (1824–1895), clergyman, college president, and congressman from Massachusetts.

Mr Sewall. Samuel E. Sewall (1799–1880), Boston lawyer and woman's rights advocate who petitioned the Massachusetts legislature in behalf of woman suffrage and wrote a pamphlet on the laws relating to married women.

Mr Coffin. Charles Carleton Coffin (1823–1896), journalist and author of a number of books on American history.

Alice's Prof Bowne. Borden Parker Bowne (1847–1910), philosopher and author, who served as the head of the philosophy department at Boston University from 1876 on.

HBB–LS, 4/6/80

Lavinia Goodell. (1839–1880) Contributor to *The Woman's Jour-*

nal, and the first woman to practice law in Wisconsin. Miss Goodell was admitted in the First Judicial Circuit Court in 1874, and afterward practiced in Janesville.

LS–HBB, 4/6/80

logomachy. Game in which words are formed from letters printed on cards.

LS–HBB, 4/9/80

Abby May. Abigail Williams May (1829–1888), leader in Boston reform circles for over three decades; in 1880 she helped to form the Massachusetts School Suffrage Association, and served as its president for the next eight years.

every state except Wisconsin. According to laws enacted in Wisconsin in the 1870s, married women could hold and convey real estate, make contracts and transact business in their own names, possess their separate earnings, and sue or be sued in their own names.

The New York Law. New York women won school suffrage in February of 1880, but as the bill providing for this right contained the words "school meeting," antisuffragists argued that women could only vote where such meetings were held, and not at elections in the large cities.

the Channing centenneal. Celebration held in honor of the hundredth anniversary of the birthday of William Ellery Channing.

LS–HBB, 9/16/80

Mr. Chadbourne. Paul Ansel Chadbourne (1823–1883), Massachusetts state senator and college president.

HBB–LS, 9/17/80

a resolution. Henry's resolution endorsed the right of women to vote in school elections, granted them in 1879. Although the convention was only asked to endorse an already existing right and one granted by a Republican legislature, it refused to do so.

Col Codman. Charles Russell Codman (1829–1918), Boston lawyer and former congressman.

Dawes . . . & Claflin. Henry Laurens Dawes (1816–1903), lawyer and U.S. senator from Massachusetts; and William Claflin (1818–1905), merchant, former governor of Massachusetts (1869–71), and congressman.

Mr Faxon. Henry H. Faxon (1823–1905), prohibitionist and member of the Massachusetts Woman Suffrage Association.

LS–ASB, 11/7/82

a Butler ticket. Benjamin Franklin Butler (1818–1893), Civil War general and Republican congressman from Massachusetts who supported woman suffrage. After several unsuccessful bids for the governorship of Massachusetts, he was finally elected in 1882. Because of Butler's prosuffrage stance Lucy and Henry endorsed him in this election. However, their position brought them into conflict with Higginson, who claimed that Butler was little more than a demagogue, and who used the *Journal*'s pages to attack him.

HBB–ASB, 6/24/83

"*Poverty & Progress.*" In this best seller for the year 1879, the reformer Henry George (1839–1897) argued that poverty accompanied progress because of the system of private land ownership. George didn't want to do away with this system, but he did believe that since land took its value from the people who lived on it, this unearned rent should come back to the public in a "single tax" on property values. Although Henry was a former land speculator and continued to derive much of his income from real estate, he was in favor of George's "single-tax" plan, and spoke in its behalf on a number of occasions later on.

"*Disciples*" or "*Campbellites.*" Followers of Alexander Campbell (1788–1866), who advocated a return to the simplicity of early Christianity. The group was at first joined to the Baptists, but later broke away to become the Disciples of Christ.

Miss Wilde. Catherine Wilde, assistant editor of *The Woman's Journal*.

LS–CCH, 11/28/84

excellent meetings at Chicago. The American had held its annual convention in Chicago that year.

Rev. Mr. Gilbert. James Eleazer Gilbert (1839–1909), former city

editor of the *Buffalo Courier*, clergyman, temperance worker, and organizer of the American Society of Religious Education.

Mr. Ball. Possibly George Harvey Ball (1819–1907), educator and pastor for many years of a Baptist church in Buffalo, New York.

LS–JFC, 2/11/85

The remonstrants. Group of Boston women opposed to suffrage. In the early 1880s a Boston Committee of Remonstrance was organized to campaign against municipal suffrage. Its representatives made regular appearances at legislative hearings on municipal suffrage, and within a few years' time, had extended their activities into other states, working against the suffragists in Oregon, Rhode Island, Vermont, Kansas, and the Dakotas by sending out telegrams and distributing antisuffrage literature. Beginning in 1887, they hired "male counsel" to represent them at legislative hearings.

HBB–LS, 4/5/85

Mobile, Ala. Henry made this trip to the South for both business and pleasure; in another letter he mentioned going to a meeting of sugar planters "to talk sorghum to them."

an imaginary new "peoples' party." Having failed to make any real headway with either the Republicans or the Democrats, Lucy and Henry toyed periodically with the idea of creating a political party of their own. In 1876 Henry suggested in the *Journal* that what was needed was a new party "organized on a woman suffrage basis with men and women as members," and in 1877 he and Lucy helped to organize a party to endorse the prohibitionists who supported woman suffrage. But by the next year, their enthusiasm for this approach had waned, and they turned again to the Republicans for backing.

LS–ASB, 10/27/85

Mrs. Ripley. Martha George Rogers Ripley (1843–1912), physician and suffragist, who was president of the Minnesota Woman Suffrage Association.

Prof. Clarke. James G. Clark (1830–1897), former antislavery singer, and member of the American.

Mrs. Duniway. Abigail Jane Scott Duniway (1834–1915), Oregon pioneer and suffrage leader.

Miss Isaacs. Elizabeth J. Isaacs (?–1916), suffragist from Washington territory.

LS–ABB, 1/10/86

Mr. Shattuck. George Cheyne Shattuck (1813–1893), Boston physician and educator.

Grace . . . Agnes. Two of Nette's daughters.

LS–DAG, 3/2/86

Dr. Gleason. Daniel Angell Gleason (1836–1908), Massachusetts public official.

raise the "age of consent." In other states besides Massachusetts the age of consent in sexual relations was ten, but in Delaware it was as low as seven. Kansas led the way by establishing eighteen as the age of consent in 1887, and other states eventually followed suit. In Massachusetts the age of consent was raised from ten to thirteen in 1886; to fourteen in 1888; and to sixteen in 1893.

HBB–LS, 3/20/86

Miss Shaw. Anna Shaw (1847–1919), English-born minister, lecturer, and suffragist, who grew up on the Michigan frontier.

Judge Carey. Joseph Maull Carey (1845–1924), justice of the supreme court of Wyoming, U.S. senator, and later governor of the state.

Gov Long. John Davis Long (1838–1915), governor of Massachusetts (1880–83), and later secretary of the navy under McKinley and Roosevelt.

Mrs Mary Hunt. Mary Hannah Hanchett Hunt (1830–1906), leader of the campaign for temperance education in the schools. Born in South Canaan, Connecticut, Mrs. Hunt made her home in the Boston suburb of Hyde Park.

LS–HBB, 2/20/87

my will. Lucy made two wills. In the first, dated April 20, 1866, she left Henry sixteen acres in Montclair and all of her "house furniture"; and Alice, the twenty-acre farm in Montclair plus the use of all notes held on the sales of her Wisconsin and

Iowa lands, and all of her government bonds. In her second and final will, dated July 31, 1884, Henry received the Dorchester house and $2,000 in stocks—provided that he returned to her estate $6,000 in stocks he was holding—while Alice was given "for her sole and separate use free from the control of any husband she may have" the Montclair property and $4,000 in stocks. Henry was well aware of the conditions of this will, because under Massachusetts law at the time, the husband's written consent was required when the wife didn't leave the bulk of her property to him.

HBB–LS, 3/5/87

Susie V. Susie Vogel, business manager of *The Woman's Journal*.
Mr Wm I Bowditch. (1819–1909) Former abolitionist and member of the Massachusetts Woman Suffrage Association.
Mr Chace. Samuel Chace, husband of the Rhode Island antislavery and suffrage leader, Elizabeth Buffum Chace.
Miss Pond. Cora Scott Pond (Pope) (1856–?), Wisconsin-born suffragist then working as an organizer for the Massachusetts Woman Suffrage Association.
Mrs Ellen Foster. Judith Ellen Horton Foster (1840–1910), "the Iowa Lawyer" who was one of the first women admitted to the bar in that state and probably the first to practice law there. Mrs. Foster served as the legal adviser to the WCTU, and was also active in the suffrage movement.

HBB–LS, 3/15/87

Mrs Bowles. Ada Chastina Bowles (1836–1928), Universalist minister from Massachusetts and lecturer for the WCTU and the American.

LS–HBB, 3/15/87

Col T.W.H. Although he had left the *Journal* in 1884, Higginson's work continued to appear in the paper in the form of lengthy excerpts republished from the columns he wrote for *Harper's Bazaar*.

HBB–LS, 3/25/87

Judge Pitman. Robert C. Pitman (1825–1890), senator, judge, and one of the vice-presidents of the Massachusetts Woman Suffrage Association.

LS–ASB, 3/31/87

Edith. Edith Blackwell, one of Sam and Nette's daughters.

HBB–LS, 4/7/87

74 per cent against it. The vote in Rhode Island marked the worst defeat woman suffrage had yet suffered in a state campaign.
Choctaw Indians. This tribe inhabited southern Mississippi; in Southern regional slang, "Choctaw" had come to mean something that was unintelligible.

LS–ASB, 4/12/87

congratulating Emma. Emma Blackwell had just become pregnant.

mean trick . . . Miss Foster. Alice's original letter describing this mean trick is missing, but in a letter dated April 14, she related how two or three of the Pennsylvania papers had written her saying that they no longer wanted the *Woman's Column*, as they were going to be supplied with a column from Philadelphia—i.e. from Rachel Foster.

Kansas with its great fact. In 1887 Kansas became the first state to grant women municipal suffrage.

HBB–ASB, 8/7/87

Mr Foulke. William Dudley Foulke (1848–1935), newspaper editor, author, lecturer, and reformer primarily concerned with civil service reform and woman suffrage. Foulke was president of the American from 1885 to 1890.

Mrs Mill . . . the Westminster Review. A report of the Worcester convention had, in fact, inspired Harriet Taylor Mill to write her article, "The Enfranchisement of Women," for *The Westminster Review*. Her article generated agitation for the vote in Great Britain, with the result that municipal suffrage was won in 1869.

HBB–LS, 10/12/87

a crank & *my sister Anna's own brother!* Ever susceptible to quack theories and wild schemes, Henry's sister Anna was at the time squandering a small fortune in an attempt to uncover treasure she believed to

be buried in a village in France.

Mrs Johns. Laura M. Johns (1849–?), Kansas suffragist whose home was in Salina.

Prof Carruth. William H. Carruth (1849–1924), professor at Kansas University and a member of the American.

Wilcox . . . election in N York. A New York lawyer active in the state woman suffrage party, Hamilton Wilcox (1842–1898) had been encouraging women to go to the polls. Thanks to his efforts, ten women voted for village officers in Alfred Centre, New York.

Chief Justice Horton. Albert Howell Horton (1837–1902), lawyer and chief justice of the Kansas supreme court (1877–1895).

HBB–LS, 10/14/87

the "Woman's Tribune." Suffrage paper started in 1883 by Clara Bewick Colby (1846–1916), one of the founders of the Nebraska Woman Suffrage Association, and its president for thirteen years. Mrs. Colby was a strong partisan of Miss Anthony, and so her paper naturally reflected the latter's views.

HBB–LS, 10/16/87

Mrs Wait. Anna C. Wait (1837–1916), editor of a reform paper, the Lincoln, Kansas *Beacon,* and Kansas suffragist.

LS–ASB, 8/12/88

Margaret Burleigh. (1818–1893) Close friend of the Philadelphia feminist Mary Grew with whom she lived for many years, and the sister-in-law of Lucy's abolitionist friend Charles Burleigh.

Whittier. The Quaker poet and reformer, John Greenleaf Whittier (1807–1892).

camp life. Alice was vacationing at a camp on the shores of Lake Memphremagog, in the province of Quebec, that was run by the reformer, Mrs. Isabel Barrows (1845–1913).

Mrs. Hazard. Mrs. Rebecca N. Hazard (1826–?), Missouri suffragist and philanthropist.

LS–FW, 8/23/88

the National Council. At the time of the international conference held in Washington in March of 1888, an International Council of Women was established, with an affiliate, the National Council, of which Frances Willard was president and Susan B. Anthony, vice-president at large.

a "social purity" meeting. The champions of "social purity" condemned rape, prostitution, and sexual overindulgence on the part of husbands, which they claimed made marriage little better than "legalized prostitution." At the meeting referred to, one of the speakers put forward Catherine Beecher's suggestion of "mothergartens," where pregnant wives could find refuge from the sexual importunities of their husbands, while another attacked prostitution as the vehicle through which men transmitted "every hideous disease from thousands of centuries of . . . syphilitic poisons."

Mormon woman's name. Emmeline Blanche Woodward Wells (1828–1921), Utah feminist and leader of Mormon women. Mrs. Wells was a member of the National, and a close friend of Mrs. Stanton and Susan B. Anthony. She spent several months in Washington lobbying unsuccessfully against the threatened disenfranchisement of Mormon women in 1885 and 1886; in 1888 she became a life member of the National Council of Women.

LS–HBB, 6/29/89

Hoyt . . . letter about Wyoming. John W. Hoyt (1831–1912) was the former territorial governor of Wyoming. In 1889 Wyoming was also applying for statehood, and having been the first territory to enfranchise women, it now hoped to be the first state to do so. But since Wyoming looked to be a Republican state, its admission to the Union was opposed by the Democrats. As the congressional debate over admission dragged on, Southern Democrats took the ground that a state didn't have the right to decide on the franchise, and that Wyoming's woman suffrage provision was therefore unconstitutional. For a while it seemed as if Wyoming would have to give up woman suffrage in order to achieve statehood, but the state legislature held firm on the issue, and finally in 1890 Congress voted to admit Wyoming with its woman suffrage provision intact.

HBB–LS, 7/9/89

The "Farmers' Alliance." By the late 1880s new farmers' organizations had taken the place formerly occupied by the Grange. In the South there was the Southern Alliance, and in the Northwest, the National Farmers' Alliance of the Northwest, headquartered in Omaha. Both of these two powerful regional bodies called for public ownership of the railroads, a more plentiful money supply, and easier credit for farmers. Moreover, they were united in their support of woman suffrage—"the bright light whose rays have carried equality, happiness and good cheer to thousands of rural homes."

Mrs McCoy. Zeralda N. McCoy, president of the Olympia, Washington, suffrage club.

HBB–LS, 7/14/89

our friends the McAdows. Perry W. McAdow (1838–1918), and his wife, Clara L. McAdow. In January of 1887, Mrs. McAdow had written to *The Woman's Journal,* asking the eastern suffragists to send an organizer to Montana.

Carter's aid. Thomas Carter (1854–1911), who went on to become Montana's first congressman, and later a U.S. senator.

HBB–LS, 7/15/89

Mr Clarke. William A. Clark (1839–1925), the Butte mining king, who later became a U.S. senator.

Howard. Howard Lane Blackwell, George and Emma's son.

HBB–LS, 7/16/89

Gen. Warren. Charles S. Warren, a mining operator and Republican from Silver Bow County, Montana.

LS–HBB, 7/18/89

The Eddy money. Bequest made by Mrs. Eliza F. Eddy, daughter of the Boston abolitionist, Francis Jackson, to Lucy and Susan Anthony for the purpose of furthering woman's rights.

Our appeal. Appeal to the constitutional conventions of North and South Dakota, Washington, Montana, and Idaho to incorporate woman suffrage into their state constitutions.

HBB–LS, 7/22/89

Judge Dennison. Benjamin Franklin Dennison (1820–1896), Washington lawyer, judge, and territorial legislator.

Judge Turner. George Turner (1850–1932), associate justice of the Washington territorial supreme court.

Mr Voorhees. Charles S. Voorhees (1853–1909), territorial delegate to the U.S. Congress from Washington.

"the tall sycamore of the Wabash." Daniel Wolsey Voorhees (1827–1897), Indiana senator with a reputation as a stump speaker and orator.

completion of the Northern Pacific RR. The Northern Pacific's route from Lake Superior to Portland, Oregon, was completed in 1883.

HBB–LS, 7/31/89

Miss Hindman. Matilda Hindman, suffragist from Pennsylvania.

LS–HBB & ASB, 2/16/90

Susan's birthday. On February 15, 1890, two hundred people gathered at the Riggs House in Washington, D.C., to celebrate the seventieth birthday of Susan B. Anthony. Lucy was among the many who sent letters, poems, or telegrams of congratulation.

LS–HBB & ASB, 2/17/90

Ethel. Ethel Blackwell, Sam and Nette's daughter, was staying at the Stone-Blackwell home in Dorchester while studying at the Massachusetts Institute of Technology.

HBB–LS, 8/18/90

Speaker Pettigrew. Richard Franklin Pettigrew (1848–1926), Republican senator from South Dakota.

Speaker Reed. Thomas B. Reed (1839–1902), Maine congressman, who served as Speaker of the House from 1889 to 1891 and again from 1895 to 1899, and was known as Czar Reed, because of his vigorous exercise of power.

HBB–LS, 8/24/90

Mrs Carrie May Chapman. Carrie Clinton Lane Chapman Catt (1859–1947), Iowa suffragist, and later president of the National American Woman Suffrage Association. Although she married her second husband, George W. Catt, in 1890, Mrs. Catt was still calling herself Mrs. Chapman at this time, since in a prenuptial contract, it had been agreed that she would continue to use the name of Chapman, by which she had become known as a suffrage leader. In her decision to keep her former name, she was influenced by Lucy Stone, but shortly after the latter's death in 1893, she began to use the surname of Catt.

HBB–LS, 8/26/90

Mrs Howell. Mary Seymour Howell (1850–1913), suffragist from New York State and lecturer for the WCTU.

Wiauno. Locale on the Massachusetts coast. Alice and Lucy Anthony, Susan's niece, went for the weekend to the home of a Mrs. Dietrich there to plan the next National-American convention.

HBB–LS, 8/30/90

Mrs Adkinson. Florence B. Adkinson (1847–1925?), a neighbor of the Stone-Blackwells and for many years an editor of the *Journal*.

LS–HBB, 9/1/90

Lizzie. A young servant woman from Cape Breton Island in Canada who was so devoted to Lucy that during her last illness she refused to leave even though she was about to be married, and her fiancé became so impatient with the delay that he broke off their engagement.

HBB–LS, 9/11/90

Independent party. Third party formed by the Farmers' Alliance and the Knights of Labor.

HBB–LS, 9/22/90

Mr & Mrs Wardall, Mr & Mrs Devoe, Mrs Pickler. Dakota suffragists. Elizabeth M. Wardall was the local superintendent of press for the campaign; Emma Smith Devoe (1858–1927), one of the "most effective" local workers; and Alice M. A. Pickler (1848–1932), another important local worker, who was also active in the WCTU.

LS–SBA, 9/6/91

representation and opportunity at Chicago. Preparations were under way for the World's Columbian Exposition to be held in Chicago in 1893.

Senator Palmer. John McAuley Palmer (1817–1900), former governor of Illinois, who was elected to the Senate in 1891.

Mr. Bonney. Charles Carroll Bonney (1831–1903), Chicago lawyer and reformer who advocated the establishment of a permanent international court of justice. It was his idea to hold auxiliary congresses in conjunction with the regular programs of the Columbian Exposition.

Mrs. Potter Palmer. Bertha Honoré Palmer (1849–1918), Chicago socialite who was mildly in favor of woman suffrage. Mrs. Palmer was chairman of the Board of Lady Managers of the Columbian Exposition, and in this ca-

pacity she was to be chiefly responsible for making the Woman's Building at the fair a huge success. She arranged for exhibits from forty-seven countries, showing both the advances made by women, and the handicaps under which they still suffered.

Mrs. Henrotin. Ellen Martin Henrotin (1847–1922), woman's club leader, labor and social reformer, and joint author of *The Social Status of European and American Women* (1887).

Mrs. Flower. Lucy Louisa Coues Flower (1837–1921), Chicago philanthropist and member of the Chicago school board.

the yellow ribbon. In 1887 Kansas suffragists chose the yellow ribbon as their state suffrage badge in honor of the state flower, the sunflower. It was later adopted by the National-American as a suffrage badge in recognition of the state's progressive stance on woman's rights.

LS–JS, 7/22/92

Wm. Hamilton of Indiana. (1811–1891) Missionary to the Ioway and Sac Indians.

Lady Henry Somerset. Isabella Caroline Somerset (1851–1921), British suffragist and temperance leader.

the labor question at Homestead. The Homestead strike began on July 1, 1892, when the president of Carnegie Steel, Henry Clay Frick, tried to cut wages. The "Pinkerton slaughter" referred to by Lucy took place on July 6 when the strikers fired on two barges of Pinkerton detectives, sent in to protect company property, killing seven. Lucy's condemnation of the Homestead strike was typical of her attitude toward organized labor and strikes in general. In 1877, at the time of a general railroad strike, she wrote in *The Woman's Journal*, "This insurrection must be suppressed, if it costs a hundred thousand lives and the destruction of every railroad in the country," and now she protested "the wasteful and bloody way of strike at Homestead."

HBB–LS, 5/12/93

Mr Clarkson's address. James C. Clarkson (1842–1918), New York politician who served as president of the Republican League (1891–92).

the Federal Elections Bill. Under the Force Act, or Federal Elections Bill, federal elections were to be supervised by the national government as a means of protecting black voters from state measures designed to keep them from voting. The bill passed the House in July of 1890, despite the opposition of James G. Blaine, but was finally defeated in the Senate.

the Mormon question. Intense disapproval of the Mormon practice of plural marriage had led Congress in 1869 to pass the Cullom Bill, outlawing polygamy in states and territories of the United States, and later, in 1887, another act strengthening the provisions of the original bill, and depriving Mormon women of the vote. Not until 1896 when the Mormon Church abandoned the doctrine of plural marriage was Utah admitted as a state and suffrage returned to Mormon women.

Breckenridge . . . so eminent 30 years ago. John Breckenridge (1797–1841), a Presbyterian clergyman and aggressive defender of the Protestant faith. One of the few challengers of orthodoxy that Breckenridge refused to take on was William Lloyd Garrison, because in his opinion the latter was "too debased and degraded in community for me, occupying the station that I do to hold a controversy with you."

HBB–LS, 5/15/93

your picture & biography by Alice. Portrait and biographical sketch of Lucy, originally published in *The Woman's Journal;* Alice's full-length biography of her mother did not appear until 1930.

HBB–LS, 5/17/93

Beth. Beth Haggar, a teen-age girl whom Lucy and Henry had taken in (though they never legally adopted her) when her dying mother, a German immigrant who had once worked for the Stone-Blackwells, appealed to them for help.

HBB–LS, 5/19/93

Mrs Louise Tyler. Colorado suffragist, who helped to organize the City League of Denver, the Young Woman's League, and other prosuffrage leagues in other parts of the city.

HBB–LS, 5/21/93

accident . . . yesterday. When the floor to the entrance of Washington Hall at the Exposition collapsed, seventy-five women fell twenty-five feet. No one was killed but eight women were seriously injured. Lucy Stone was not one of them.

Mrs McCulloch. Catherine Gougar Waugh McCulloch (1862–1942), Illinois suffragist and lawyer.

LS–HBB, 5/21/93

Jenkin Lloyd Jones. (1843–1918) Unitarian minister of All Souls Church in Chicago, who advocated the establishment of a universal religion and edited a religious weekly called *Unity*.

John W. Chadwick. (1840–1904) Unitarian clergyman and author, who was well known as a preacher and lecturer.

a still hunt. Quiet or secret pursuit of an object.

LS–HBB, 8/15/93

Alice . . . a daily line. Alice was vacationing at the camp on the shores of Lake Memphremagog in Canada.

INDEX